Paradigms of Research for the 21st Century

Counterpoints

Studies in Criticality

Shirley R. Steinberg
Series Editor

Vol. 558

Paradigms of Research for the 21st Century

Perspectives and Examples from Practice, Second Edition

Edited by Antonina Lukenchuk

PETER LANG
New York - Berlin - Bruxelles - Chennai - Lausanne - Oxford

Library of Congress Cataloging-in-Publication Data

Names: Lukenchuk, Antonina, editor.
Title: Paradigms of research for the 21st century : perspectives and examples from practice / edited by Antonina Lukenchuk.
Description: Second edition. | New York : Peter Lang, [2025] | Series: Counterpoints, 1058-1634 ; vol. 558 | Includes bibliographical references.
Identifiers: LCCN 2024042384 (print) | LCCN 2024042385 (ebook) | ISBN 9783034351270 (paperback) | ISBN 9783034351300 (hardback) | ISBN 9783034351287 (pdf) | ISBN 9783034351294 (epub)
Subjects: LCSH: Education—Research—Methodology. | Education—Research—Philosophy.
Classification: LCC LB1028 .P244 2025 (print) | LCC LB1028 (ebook) | DDC 370.72—dc23/eng/20241009
LC record available at https://lccn.loc.gov/2024042384
LC ebook record available at https://lccn.loc.gov/2024042385
DOI 10.3726/b22356

Bibliographic information published by the Deutsche Nationalbibliothek. The German National Library lists this publication in the German National Bibliography; detailed bibliographic data is available on the Internet at http://dnb.d-nb.de.

Cover design by Peter Lang Group AG

ISSN 1058-1634 (print)
ISBN 9783034351300 (hardback)
ISBN 9783034351270 (paperback)
ISBN 9783034351287 (ebook)
ISBN 9783034351294 (epub)
DOI 10.3726/b22356

Published by Peter Lang Publishing Inc., New York, USA
info@peterlang.com - www.peterlang.com

This publication has been peer reviewed.

To all lovers of wisdom

Contents

List of Figures

List of Tables

Preface

What is research and who is a researcher? Why engage in research and what is its value? How do we come to know what we know? What can we *really* know? *Paradigms of Research for the 21st Century* opens the door for wondering about these and many other important questions pertaining to the nature and process of educational research. Conceived as a journey into the familiar and the uncharted territories of knowledge, this book offers an insightful and detailed account of Western and non-Western worldviews and perspectives on reality, knowledge, and values, many of which have been instrumental to the development of different research traditions and methods in North America.

This book demonstrates how essential components of educational inquiry such as ideas, theories, philosophies, ideologies, epistemologies, value statements, methodologies, and methods can be applied to conducting and implementing robust research projects. The aforementioned essential components form a *paradigm*—a system of inquiry, a model, and a way of knowing. Empirical-analytic, pragmatic, interpretive, critical, poststructuralist, and transcendental paradigms are delineated as alternatives to a more orthodox division of conceptualizing research as quantitative or qualitative. The discussions on the nature of science and scientific method shed light on a number of misconceptions of these notions in educational research. Resulting from these discussions is an exposure of misconceived and misrepresented links between positivism and quantitative research.

Venturing on a paradigm journey are the dedicated contributors to this edition who share their tales of learning to theorize and practice educational research. Their hope is that graduate students, professional researchers, and scholars will benefit from this project and it might be of interest to all lovers of wisdom.

Welcome to a paradigm journey!

A Preneopragmatic, Postmodern Ditty About Existential Phenomenon

Walking in the classroom
I was feelin' fine.
Asked about some questions
What's a Paradigm?
Naturally my fears grew
I felt so abused.
Looked around for confidence
You all seemed so confused.

"Hey folks have some handouts."
"Take 'em, have a ball"
Rorty, Kant, and Hegel
Dewey and Foucault.
Habermas, Adorno, take Nietzsche
For some sparks.
What's a Timbred Research?
Giroux, Freire, and Marx

We climbed out from an Existential mineshaft.
There is no deny'n,
the class became Gemeinschaft.
Feyerabend tells us
"You can bend the rules.
Research call for
using all the tools"
Look beyond the task when
Conceptualizing Framework
The threads of solid research exist
On many spools

Now we've all survived it
ESR610
A world of information
Shall we do it all again?
Adapting Methodology will help us in our showing.
Hermeneutics finds a way,
Cartesian ways of knowing.
To make our journey forward,
we must use the past
To Bacon, Locke, and all the rest
Thanks I've had a blast
The courtesy of Kerry Muldowney, colleague and
former student of Paradigms of Research

Acknowledgments

I would like to express my warm gratitude to all contributors to this book—my colleagues and friends without whose assistance this manuscript would be an impossible undertaking. I am especially indebted to Baudelaire Ulysse and Eileen Kolich for sharing their talent and knowledge in our collaborative work.

To my former and current doctoral students—thank you for sustaining my sense of curiosity and inspiring me to pursue this project. I am grateful to Kerry Muldowney for supporting my first steps in teaching paradigms and sharing his big heart, wit, humor, and the gift of poetry and music with me.

I wish to acknowledge the support from the staff at Peter Lang Publishing: managing director Alison Jefferson, series editor Shirley Steinberg, editorial assistants, production managers, and all unnamed persons who have contributed to the production, marketing, and publication of this edition.

Introduction

ANTONINA LUKENCHUK

The Beginning—the Wondering

This book has been writing itself for a number of years, at least since the time I started teaching a graduate course in paradigms of research at a Midwestern private university. However, I can probably trace the deeper roots of this project to as far back as my childhood memories. Faded and almost forgotten, they nonetheless elicit recollections imbued with enchanting images. I enjoyed a highly imaginative childhood. My less-than-exciting external surroundings led me to search for wonder in the realm of the transcendent. This imaginary land of myths, folk songs, and stories became my safeguard and a lovely haven in the midst of the crude and dreary reality of the outside world. Entrance into adulthood brought with it the experiences that demystified a great deal of my childhood's imaginings, but the wonderings about the world and what lies beyond its horizon has persisted.

My first encounter with the word *philosophy* during my undergraduate studies has turned into an affectionate and lasting affair, and throughout the years of academic training, philosophical inquiry has been sustaining my sense of curiosity and the purpose of my educational pursuits. I feel intuitively drawn to the word *philosophy* because it speaks to me in a female voice in the language of my origin. The affectionate words *phileo* (Greek for love) and *sophia* (Greek for wisdom) that comprise philosophy are, in fact, of a female gender. I am a lover of wisdom, that is, a woman who loves and seeks wisdom. I become a philosopher by default the moment I wonder who I am by nature or what the meaning of this project is. There is hardly a person in this world who is not a philosopher *by nature* (the drive to know is evidently intrinsic to a human being). The questions that Paul Gauguin (1848–1903) assigns to his painting are endemic to humankind: *Where do we come from? What are we? Where are we going?* These questions impel people to fly to the moon, to delve into the depths of the oceans, to penetrate the nuclear layers of energy and the human body, and to create ambitious social projects. What would our lives be like if it were not for some courageous individuals who dared to pursue unimaginable projects?

Education makes an inquiry attainable and, until fairly recently in Western modern history, education has been inseparable from philosophical pursuits. Seekers of wisdom in ancient Western and non-Western world cultural traditions have been philosophers, scientists, *and* educators—catalysts of intellectual, moral, and political transformations in their respective societies. The modern age of scientific and technological advancements in the West provided an impetus for a sharp division of sciences into "natural" and "human" and the ensuing methodological debates surrounding these sciences. Educational inquiry was forced to find its place within the new division of sciences and to develop methods best suited for its needs and purposes.

Since the nineteenth century in the West, education has been defined as a human, social, or behavioral science, depending on the object of its inquiry and its juxtaposition to natural sciences. The twentieth-century revolutionary theories of relativity and quantum mechanics overturned the Newtonian explanation of the universe as the only true scientific paradigm, and the discovery of DNA radically changed the understanding of living things (Grof, 1985). These revolutionary events also represented the strongest challenge to the positivistic assumption of science. Twentieth-century philosophy had to engage with a scientific world and rethink its role in providing the all-encompassing metaphysical systems of explanation of the universe and the predicament of a human being within it. Subsequently, the new conception of science was to be developed to account for the paradigm shifts in twentieth-century physics, biology, chemistry, and other natural sciences.

Contemporary science is no longer expected to produce certain knowledge, and scientific method is employed by natural sciences to generate alternative paradigms of knowledge, some of which can be accepted as the best explanations available, and in the long run, they can be discarded and replaced by new paradigms. The present-day philosophy of human and social sciences is concerned with the study of both the human realm and the natural realm, which until very recently were regarded as distinct and different and, therefore, required different methods of investigation. Moreover, natural science is viewed by today's scientists as an effectively human practice in which a researcher is actively engaged (Polkinghorne, 2004). Contemporary scientific, philosophical, and educational inquiries focus on a variety of issues pertaining to individual areas of study that can only incrementally contribute to the whole of the understanding of various phenomena. To keep up with the aforementioned changes in the conception of science, educational researchers need to reconsider the obsolete methodological debates still raving on the pages of some academic publications (e.g., Howe, 2009).

This book was conceived out of love of wisdom and the desire to provoke imaginative thinking about educational inquiry. Gaston Bachelard (1884–1962) once said that when imagination works, everything works. We first imagine things before we know them. Bachelard's (2004) poetic turn led him to reconsider his epistemology as a project of a scientific mind, thus, giving primacy to imagination in the process of inquiry. Scientific knowledge "emerges only after we use some imagination, both in formulating questions and in framing hypotheses to answer them" (Audi, 2003, p. 260). Bachelard's name is important to consider in context of this book because he was an originator of the theory of epistemological breaks (1938/2002) in the philosophy of science that was developed many years prior to the similar theory of paradigm shifts put forth by Thomas Kuhn (1962/2000).

This book intends to bring to light obscure, forgotten, or unknown facts pertaining to educational research that can be instrumental to its conceptual rigor and accuracy. Like any pursuit, this work represents an open-ended inquiry that is subject to critics' scrutiny and questioning, which we would welcome. This book is an invitation to readers to join the *paradigm journey* undertaken by a few dedicated persons with the purpose of gathering their patches of wisdom that are scattered around the world and sharing their love messages with others.

Why This Book and What Is It About?

Paradigms of Research for the 21st Century contributes significantly to the field of educational research in the following ways: it is (1) filling in considerable gaps in the existing educational research publications, which lack philosophical foundations; (2) expanding on the definition of *paradigm* and its alternatives for educational research grounded in various philosophical traditions since most current definitions of paradigm are insufficient; (3) amplifying the importance of vital links between epistemological and methodological assumptions; (4) exposing and clarifying misconceived links between positivism and quantitative methods of analysis; (5) elucidating a new conception of science and its impact on educational research, information that is rarely, if ever, mentioned in current research sources; and (6) advocating epistemological and methodological pluralism be on equal footing in all educational inquiries.

For the past 20 years, I have been teaching a number of doctoral-level courses, including research methodology, primarily interpretive and critical, as well as theoretical courses that focus on epistemology and various ways of knowing, teaching, learning, and doing research within educational settings. These courses are designed to acquaint students with a broad range of philosophical, ideological, and theoretical perspectives on educational research as the tools to conceptualize research and scholarly projects such as dissertations.

The recurring discussions that I have with my colleagues who teach research courses and serve on dissertation committees reveal how ill-prepared some of our doctoral candidates are to conduct dissertation research projects, even after taking a number of research courses. The lack of students' knowledge and skills is especially apparent when they are faced with making appropriate choices regarding research methodologies and conceptual tools that adequately fit their research purposes. Our doctoral candidates often face the proverbial chicken or the egg conundrum and which comes first. In other words, should they first consider a paradigm and then a toolbox of methods, or vice versa? Students must be equipped to answer other related questions. What are the relationships between theoretical frameworks and specific methods of investigation? To what extent can a research project be successful in terms of properly made epistemological and methodological choices?

Most educational researchers agree that "methods of analysis do not emerge out of thin air. They are informed by, and extend out of, particular theoretical sensibilities" (Holstein & Gubrium, 2012, p. 5). All research is anchored to basic beliefs about the nature of the world, knowledge, and values. How each researcher "conceptualizes the best way to apprehend the social world is clearly dependent upon what she or he believes about the nature of existence. What constitutes data? What constitutes a pattern in data? What does the pattern mean?" (Pascale, 2011, p. 5). Theoretical models, frameworks, philosophies, ideologies, beliefs, or perspectives, the terms that can be housed under the umbrella definition of *paradigm*, provide a road map for successful research or scholarly projects. The definition of *paradigm* generates interesting discussions and debates among contemporary educational researchers (Anfara & Mertz, 2006; Creswell, 2003; Lather, 2004; Polkinghorne, 1983). The notion of paradigm permeates this book and renders its content relevant to the educational research process.

While the consensus on the importance of the role of paradigms in educational research is widely acknowledged, most research methods texts provide fairly limited space to philosophical discussions pertaining to educational inquiry. There are only a handful of current editions that offer in-depth accounts of the theoretical foundations of research (Anfara & Mertz, 2006; Cohen et al., 2008; Jackson & Mazzei, 2012; Merriam & Simpson, 2000;

Olsen, 2010; Pascale, 2011; St. Pierre & Pillow, 2000; Yu, 2006). Moreover, most of these sources focus exclusively on either theoretical frameworks of qualitative research (e.g., Anfara & Mertz) or particular areas of study such as, for instance, feminist poststructuralist theory (e.g., St. Pierre & Pillow). By comparison, *Paradigms of Research for the 21st Century* provides a more comprehensive and detailed historical and philosophical analysis of educational inquiries pertaining to all types of research: qualitative, quantitative, or mixed methods. This book abounds in philosophical terminology, which is rarely given proper attention in research methods textbooks (e.g., McMillan, 2008).

Despite an unequivocal repudiation of positivism in the mid-twentieth century, some contemporary researchers continue to misrepresent quantitative methods of analysis as positivistic (e.g., Hesse-Biber & Leavy, 2011; Pascale, 2011). The agreement has been reached by the philosophers of science that *all* of our knowledge is conditional and constructed within the contingent conceptual systems relative to time and place (Nelson, 2012). Given the contingency of truth/knowledge, what can educators count on as effective and critical methods of investigation? Paradigms of educational research represent a rich bricolage of methodological possibilities, and this book considers and discusses six of these.

The word *paradigm* is derived from the two Greek words *para* (beside) and *deigma* (example). The etymology of paradigm clearly presumes a relational construct, a pairing of sorts. Modern dictionary definitions elaborate on paradigm as follows: model, conjugation, giving all the inflections of a word, example, archetype, beau ideal, chart, criterion, ensample, exemplar, ideal, mirror, model, original, pattern, prototype, sample, standard (Kipfer, 2010). Kuhn's definition of paradigm is most frequently cited as "constellations of law, theory, application and instrumentation . . . ; models from which spring particular coherent traditions of scientific research" (Runes, 1983, p. 240).

Our conception of paradigm integrates its major existing definitions and the etymology of the word, all of which lead us to designate the following threefold meaning to paradigm: (1) a system of educational inquiry, (2) a model, and (3) a way of knowing. Chapter 3 elaborates on the justifications for this definition of paradigm. Figure 1 portrays a paradigm pyramid built on its multiple definitions.

Educational researchers tend to differentiate primarily between quantitative and qualitative research. While such distinction is valid in terms of data and methods of their analysis, paradigms as theoretical frameworks of research require more expanded philosophical renditions and more diverse

PARADIGM
Par-a-digm
archetype
example
pattern
sample
model
chart
ideal
theory
system
original
standard
exemplar
framework
worldview
belief system
way of knowing

Figure I.1: Paradigm Pyramid

differentiations. The construct of paradigm encompasses a number of conceptual tools (referred to in this book as "conceptual repertoire"), epistemological assumptions, and corresponding methods of analysis. Creswell (2003), for instance, distinguishes between the four "alternative knowledge claim positions": postpositivism, constructivism, advocacy/participatory, and pragmatism (p. 6). Lather (2004) proposes four paradigms in a slightly different configuration: prediction (positivist), understanding (interpretive), emancipatory (critical), and deconstruction (poststructuralist) (p. 207).

The analysis of various philosophical traditions of inquiry in Western and non-Western cultural traditions allows us to delineate six paradigms of educational research: empirical-analytic, pragmatic, interpretive, critical, poststructuralist, and transcendental. These six paradigmatic constellations do not exhaust all possibilities; however, they encompass major existing positions on knowledge, reality, and value statements in the philosophy of science. An important message intersecting the content of this book and being advocated by its contributors is that of an epistemological and methodological pluralism that recognizes and validates all Existing paradigms on equal ground.

Organization of the Book and What Is New in This Edition

The book consists of two conceptually related parts foreshadowing the interconnectedness of theory *and* practice. The constructs of theory and practice are often conceived as separate entities. The word *theory*—via Late Latin from Greek, *theoria* (contemplation or speculation)—means a "system of ideas intended to explain something," a "set of principles on which the practice of an activity is based," or an "idea used to account for a situation or justify a course of action" (Stevenson & Lindberg, 2010, p. 1799). Polkinghorne (2004) renders practice as an "engaged action or activity," a "tradition, tacit knowledge, worldview, paradigm, ideology, framework, or presupposition" (pp. 6–7). More than two centuries ago, Immanuel Kant (1724–1804) emphasized that experience without a theory is blind, and theory without experience is mere intellectual play. Present-day philosophers of science consider the quest for knowledge as an activity in which a researcher is actively engaged, thus affirming the *reciprocity of theory-practice relationships.* Accordingly, Part I chapters of this book represent a theory component of this synergetic duo, and chapters 4 through 14 of Part II of this book exhibit its practice piece. Hence, paradigms and examples from practice should be understood as relational and mutually dependent constructs, whereby one informs the other and in turn is being informed and enriched by the other's experience. Examples from practice represent research and scholarly projects based on doctoral dissertations completed within various educational programs at three institutions of higher learning in the Midwest.

Part I. Chapter 1 takes readers on a fascinating philosophical journey across continents and traditions. It weaves the tales of ancient, modern, and postmodern worlds into a tapestry of beliefs that have been instrumental to the development of educational inquiry in North America. Chapter 2 amplifies the discussions on epistemology and philosophy of science and their relevance to educational research. It foregrounds the importance of methodological debates in natural and human sciences that have provided an impetus for radical changes in the conception of science and paradigm shifts in educational inquiry. New to this chapter is a number of additional sections that focus on the most recent developments within the context of digital technologies and artificial intelligence. Finally, Chapter 3 integrates the content of the preceding chapters in terms of relevant links among philosophical, epistemological, and methodological assumptions. Chapter 3 also provides a brief analysis of the Part II excerpts from the dissertation research exemplifying various theoretical perspectives and portrays a pluralistic paradigmatic image by means of graphical and textual representations.

Part II. The contributors to the scholarly work presented in Part II are persons of diverse socioeconomic, racial, ethnic, gender, and immigrant backgrounds, lifestyles, and political persuasions. What binds them together is a sheer love of and dedication to intellectual pursuits resulting in positive change in their immediate or global communities. Part II features six new chapters based on the content of recent dissertations defended with distinction and/or awarded with the title of the best dissertation of the year of graduation in a specific institution.

Research begins in wonder and thus bears an imprint of thousands of years of the human history recorded in tales, dialogues, teachings, myths, legends, and stories. Storytelling is the most primordial form of research and it continues to cast its spell on storytellers and their followers. The ancient art of storytelling gave rise to narrative research, which, since the 1960s, has been gaining considerable popularity among educational researchers (Goodall, 2008; Holstein & Gubrium, 2012; Riessman, 2008). As its critical component, counter-narrative allows for investigations of various critical issues in contemporary American education.

Thus, Part II opens with powerful research conducted by Thera Tilmon (Chapter 4) that focuses on the stories of elementary school teachers navigating the normative discourses of whiteness while advocating for African American students who may lack support and encouragement from their teachers. Thera calls on professional educators to commit their utmost support for connecting with and supporting Black students.

Matthew Woolsey (Chapter 5) presents an ethnographic investigation of first-generation Asian Indian immigrants who have attained senior-level leadership positions in U.S. higher education. Matthew explores the evolution of the field of leadership since the Industrial Revolution onward and its global perspectives. His purpose is to offer a “lantern” that sheds light on the unchartered territory of insight into the sociocultural contexts that enable Asian Indians to gain extraordinary heights in higher education leadership.

Joanne Yonan (Chapter 6) ventures on a complex case study of high school teachers dedicated to build classroom inclusion for LGBTQ+ students of color. Joanne asserts that these students represent the most bullied group of students in American high schools. Joanne calls on educational professionals to make schools welcoming places particularly for this group of students and to integrate the practices that can offset the oppression that LGBTQ+ students of color often experience.

Case studies provide ample opportunities for researchers to explore, in depth, classrooms and other settings as real-world contexts, or “natural” phenomena that bind time and space, individuals and environments, thus ensuring a comprehensive understanding of specific issues (Creswell, 2003). Thus, Amy Kendryna (Chapter 7) presents a compelling case study that explores adverse childhood experiences (ACEs) among elementary school students within the school district where she has been serving as school principal for several decades. Amy asserts that ACEs are potentially traumatic events that can have negative lasting effects on the health and well-being of children and in their later lives as adults. Amy's research has resulted in the development of the social-ecological model that can serve as a road map for all educators concerned with the students' academic performance and, more importantly, their well-being.

A grounded theory study by Regina Schurman (Chapter 8) demonstrates how the classical Glaserian approach can be applied to generate a model of sustainable professional employment for clinical exercise physiologists. Regina's research is firmly positioned within the pragmatic paradigm that enables her to recast Peirce's (1839–1914) method of rigorous scientific inquiry and his proverbial flash of insight. The pragmatist view allows the features of grounded theory to become clearer and more understandable in terms of generating substantive theory.

Cheryl Jean DeRoo (Chapter 9) invites readers on a passionate case-study journey to explore civically engaged curriculum within the elementary school district where she has been serving as school principal for several decades. The purpose of Cheryl's research is to investigate ways in which teachers can develop and implement civically engaged curriculum, which, in turn, can motivate students to understand the importance of civic responsibility and engagement in civic learning. Cheryl calls upon educational professionals to develop agency in order to advocate for action-oriented civic education.

Eirini Adamopoulou (Chapter 10) presents an empirical-analytic study of Greek parents' perceptions and experiences regarding their children's learning and social-emotional difficulties in elementary schools. Eirini employs the Test of Psychosocial Adaptation and the Parent Survey to identify Greek parents' perceptions of the causes and responsibility for solving their children's problems, the level and type of parental perceived burden due to their children's challenges, and their actions to support their children's learning and social-emotional difficulties, including their use of available community services.

Irene Garcia-Benavides (Chapter 11) ventures on a comprehensive case study to investigate barriers that prevent speech-language pathologists from providing appropriate services to deaf and hard of hearing children ages two to five. Irene is a dedicated professional and scholar whose research provides a compelling critique of a medical model of hearing loss. Based on her research findings, Irene passionately advocates for a sociocultural model and encourages her colleagues to develop culturally and linguistically informed practices from which both deaf and hard of hearing children and their parents can benefit.

Chapter 12, written by Baudelaire K. Ulysse, presents a sophisticated discourse analysis of the politics and economics of neoliberalism in local and global perspectives. Baudelaire poses the two following questions: In what way does neoliberalism embody imperialism and breed hegemony, exploitation, inequity, and inequality? Why does neoliberalism pervade education, and what effect does it have on the orientation of education? As an educator, Baudelaire has a deep conviction that it is his vocation to be involved in the political process and, more important, to shun political neutrality on issues that concern society and the human condition.

Toya Michelle Webb (Chapter 13) offers yet another unique example of a narrative study—the "narratives of grit" by African American women aspiring for community college senior leadership positions. Toya turns to the tradition of storytelling and counter-storytelling to portray the lives of nine extraordinary women paving their way to professional accomplishments while overcoming overt or hidden microaggressions, stereotypes, and racism. Reflecting on her own path to a senior leadership position, as well as the findings of the study, Toya appeals to educational professionals and the institutions that they represent to challenge their preconceived assumptions of African American women within the context of institutional practices.

Chapter 14 closes the circle of a constellation of examples from practice by dedicated educational professionals and scholars. Authored by Sharon Duncan, this chapter presents a generational phenomenological story of disability closes the circle of the storytelling tradition represented in this part of the book. Compelling, moving, and empowering, this study uncovers the meaning of the lived experiences of four individuals with intellectual disabilities and their families over three generations. Through the stories of resistance and resilience, the voices of the individuals with intellectual disabilities and their families reach out to the world beyond illusory or self-imposed fences, and gain prominence and power.

Finally, the postscript reflects on the experience of walking through the paradigm journey and offers a parting message to all lovers of wisdom.

References

Anfara, V. A., Jr., & Mertz, N. T. (Eds.). (2006). *Theoretical frameworks of qualitative research*. SAGE Publications.

Audi, R. (2003). *Epistemology: A contemporary introduction to the theory of knowledge* (2nd ed.). Routledge.

Bachelard, G. (1938/2002). *The formation of the scientific mind: A contribution to a psychoanalysis of objective knowledge* (M. McAllester Jones, Trans.). linamen.

Bachelard, G. (2004). *The poetics of reverie: Childhood, language, and the cosmos* (D. Russell, Trans.). Beacon.

Cohen, L., Manion, L., & Morrison, K. (2008). *Research methods in education* (6th ed.). Routledge.

Creswell, J. W. (2003). *Research designs: Qualitative, quantitative, and mixed methods approaches* (2nd ed.). SAGE Publications.

Goodall, H. L. (2008). *Writing qualitative inquiry: Self, stories, and academic life*. Left Coast Press.

Grof, S. (1985). *Beyond the brain: Birth, death, and transcendence in psychotherapy*. SUNY Press.

Hesse-Biber, S. N., & Leavy, P. (2011). *The practice of qualitative research* (2nd ed.). SAGE Publications.

Holstein, J. A., & Gubrium, J. F. (Eds.). (2012). *Varieties of narrative analysis*. SAGE Publications.

Howe, K. R. (2009). Epistemology, methodology, and education sciences: Positivist dogmas, rhetoric, and the education science question. *Educational Researcher, 38*(6), 428–440.

Jackson, A. Y., & Mazzei, L. (2012). *Thinking with theory in qualitative research: Viewing data across multiple perspectives*. Routledge.

Kipfer, B. A (Ed.). (2010). *Roget's international thesaurus* (11th ed.). Collins Reference.

Kuhn, T. (1962/2000). The structure of scientific revolutions. In S. Rosen (Ed.), *The philosopher's handbook* (pp. 503–519). Random House.

Lather, P. (2004). Critical inquiry in qualitative research: Feminist and poststructural perspectives: Science "after truth." In K. deMarrais & S. D. Lapan (Eds.), *Foundations for research: Methods of inquiry in education and the social sciences* (pp. 203–215). Lawrence Erlbaum.

McMillan, J. H. (2008). *Educational research: Fundamentals for the consumer* (5th ed.). Pearson.

Merriam, S. B., & Simpson, E. L. (2000). *A guide to research for educators and trainers of adults*. Krieger.

Nelson, G. (2012). Fighting for the humanities. *Academe, 98*(1), 16–21.

Olsen, W. (2010). *Realist methodology*. SAGE Publications.

Pascale, C.-M. (2011). *Cartographies of knowledge: Exploring qualitative epistemologies*. SAGE Publications.

Polkinghorne, D. E. (1983). *Methodology for the human sciences: Systems of inquiry*. SUNY Press.

Polkinghorne, D. E. (2004). *Practice and the human sciences: The case for a judgment-based practice of care*. SUNY Press.

Riessman, C. K. (2008). *Narrative methods for the human sciences*. SAGE Publications.

Runes, D. D. (Ed.). (1983). *Dictionary of philosophy*. Littlefield, Adams.

Stevenson, A., & Lindberg, C. A. (Eds.). (2010). *New Oxford American dictionary* (3rd ed.). Oxford University Press.

St. Pierre, E. A., & Pillow, W. S. (Eds.). (2000). *Working the ruins: Feminist poststructural theory and methods in education*. Routledge.

Yu, C. H. (2006). *Philosophical foundations of quantitative research methodology*. University Press of America.

Part I Paradigms of Research: Multiple Ways of Knowing

Chapter 1 Presaging Educational Inquiry: Historical Development of Philosophical Ideas, Traditions, and Perspectives

Baudelaire K. Ulysse and Antonina Lukenchuk

Inquiry and the Pursuit of Wisdom

> Philosophy is a battle against the bewitchment of our intelligence through the means of language.
>
> —Ludwig Wittgenstein, *The Oxford Dictionary of Quotations*, 2001, p. 824

Inquiry has been a vital and constant element in the pursuit of knowledge. Education makes the pursuit or attainment of knowledge, whether directly or indirectly, one of its main objectives. Therefore, education must embrace inquiry as a perpetual ally to succeed in this pursuit. Hence, the term *educational research* ought to represent inquiries that are focused, albeit not exclusively, on pursuing knowledge and that are aimed at understanding knowledge of all types. The pursuit as well as the attainment of knowledge that is presumed in inquiry does not involve the teleological conjecture, as such conjecture varies from researcher to researcher and from project to project; rather, such pursuit aims to grasp the essence of, the process leading to, as well as the reliability of knowledge.

These aspects of knowledge—essence, process, and reliability—underscore the questions that have driven intellectual activities since the beginning of time. Moser (2006) discusses these aspects of knowledge respectively in terms of "defining features," "sources," and "justification" (p. 273). The essence of knowledge—that which comprises knowledge of any type—evokes the "what" question and is presumed to exist, unbeknownst to us or not, until that knowledge is accessed, uncovered, or discovered. Further, Moser breaks down the essence of knowledge into distinct kinds, which he labels "explicit" and "tacit":

> Explicit knowledge is self-conscious in that the knower is aware of the relevant state of knowledge, whereas tacit knowledge is implicit, hidden from self-consciousness. Much of our knowledge is tacit: it is genuine but we are unaware of the relevant states of knowledge, even if we can achieve awareness upon suitable reflection. (p. 273)

Moser's perceptive remarks seem to establish an equation that accounts for the link or the missing link between the known and the unknown, and evidently the nexus of the knower, the known, and the unknown. In addition, Moser (2006) asserts:

> Philosophers have identified various species of knowledge: for example, propositional knowledge (that something is so), non-propositional knowledge of something (i.e., knowledge by acquaintance, or by direct awareness), empirical (a posteriori) propositional knowledge, non-empirical (a priori) propositional knowledge, and knowledge on how to do something. (p. 273)

While the plethora of epistemic species might seem overwhelming, they, however, exude and underscore the cognitive diversity and relativity, which drives the vehicle of inquiry pertaining to the attainment of wisdom. This effectively led philosophers to surmise whether "extent of our a priori knowledge [was] relative to the extent of our a posteriori knowledge" (Moser, 2006, p. 273). Evidently, contemporary scholars and educators embrace inquiry as an effective method in the pursuit of knowledge. But the effective use of inquiry, particularly in educational research, requires a refined grasp of the history of inquiry as well as its historic contribution to the pursuit of knowledge. The Greek origin of the word *philosophy* means love of wisdom (Foley & Mohan, 2003; Ozmon & Craver, 2008). However abstract, this meaning is suggestive of a relentless and unrestrained pursuit of wisdom. This pursuit is neither characterized by aimless and desultory meandering in epistemological terrains, nor contained by ideological commitments; rather, it embodies a judicious and vigorous investigation of complex and open-ended questions regarding both the immaterial and the material realms.

Knowledge, in its variegated forms and sources, may exist independently of human existence, but the pursuit of knowledge by intelligent beings has largely been a human enterprise. There might be other intelligent beings that exist and inhabit places lying beyond earth's orbital threshold, but insofar as our general knowledge of the material world is concerned, one cannot assert with even the slightest degree of certainty that there are, in fact, intelligent beings inhabiting other planets or coexisting planet Earth with human beings. A concession must be made regarding the immaterial realm, which becomes largely a matter of speculation and belief as truth that can be deduced from reason (Plato), and/or experienced through faith and reason (Aquinas). While this concession is plausible, its subject lies outside the scope of the current project.

Granted knowledge writ at large is and has been a project of human enterprise, it follows then that the pursuit of knowledge as well as the grasp thereof remains inextricably linked to the human species. Further, knowledge writ at large, widely conceived as the objective of human intellectual enterprise or activity, is neither new nor old—it is evolving. Knowledge as such represents a diversely adorned and intricate tapestry with billions of pieces being potentially scattered across a wide array of intercontinental spaces that have been gathered by lovers of wisdom from distant and disparate lands. This creates a whole that is paradoxically unified and diversified. Each piece of this intricate and gigantic tapestry that is collected is valuable in time and space to the group of peoples living in those spaces, and it embodies answers to puzzling questions germane and relative to their material conditions and metaphysical assumptions. One might raise the question of whether the ultimate goal ought to be to find all these pieces and connect them so the big picture might become visible. Still, another might ask whether the ultimate goal ought to be for people in those respective places to use whatever piece or pieces they have culled from this intricate and beautifully adorned tapestry and direct them toward the creation of additional pieces based on what they already have in order to portray or convey their vision of that tapestry, however relative such vision might be in respect to their distinct perception.

Relevance of Philosophical Inquiries to Research

Let us suppose that this painting referred to hitherto represents a tapestry embedding various forms and sources of knowledge. Assuming this is the case, whether symbolically or actually, the forms and sources would have to be both universal and evolutionary. This is to say then that there are forms of objective knowledge, both material and metaphysical, accessible to intelligent human beings from different places across all continents. Once accessed, these forms of knowledge are extracted, analyzed, interpreted, elaborated on, and applied by intelligent human beings to material conditions relative to these beings while at the same time metamorphosing into new forms and laying foundations for further investigations. Could this then be the way human beings have been interacting with their world? Are human beings always eager to grasp what is immediately available and known while at the same committing themselves to know more about that which has been grasped in order to develop a multidimensional view of it for further inquiry, elaboration, explication, and articulation?

The known always triggers the search for the unknown, creating an unending cycle of epistemological quest, at the core of which lies the assumption that knowledge is not final but evolutionary. Philosophers and scholars alike have conceptualized this epistemological cycle as the pursuit of wisdom, a pursuit that has continued to fascinate philosophers and scholars from all parts of the world. Hence, the pursuit of wisdom epitomizes research. By research is meant the inquisitive process that seeks to uncover and discover new phenomena as well as explain and expand existing ones. Research, being proper, may be qualified in accordance with the objectives or the disciplines, in which case such research could be educational, psychological, neurological, or economic. The process and the impetus of research do not change but are only varied by the methods used (e.g., empirical-analytic, interpretive, or mixed).

The cumulative work gathered within this book is geared toward research in the discipline of education; hence the focus is educational research. As the introductory chapter has stipulated, the objective of this project is to show how research in education is grounded in various enduring philosophical traditions of inquiry. Because educational research is grounded in the philosophical traditions of inquiry, it necessarily follows that properly conducted educational research must factor in the philosophical schools or paradigms that embody this inquiry and its pursuit of wisdom.

Properly situating academic works in these larger philosophical frameworks is the act of a skilled researcher. This postulate is consistent with the premise of this book and with the notion that knowledge of any type is somehow predicated upon previously known facts or proposed theories. Therefore, if an academic work should be considered credible, that work must reflect familiarity with or be interconnected to previous works. For instance, if one conducts research in political science using rationalism as a tool of analysis, that person will demonstrate a more refined knowledge of rationalism by tracing its origin to idealism and realism. By the same token, if another person conducts research in political science using liberalism as a tool of analysis, that person will provide a more rounded treatment of liberalism by tracing liberalism back to John Locke and rationalism. Countless other examples could be provided to illustrate the imperativeness for researchers to show the connection they claim to philosophical traditions that preceded, informed, and shaped contemporary tools, or the theoretical perspectives underpinning the respective researches of these researchers. It is for that reason that the focus of this book is on delineating the most influential philosophical schools in the history of ideas while showing their interlinks to tools and theories researchers currently employ. The understanding of these philosophical schools is vital for the effective use of tools and theories in research projects, but such understanding is best served with an introduction of philosophy writ at large, particularly considering its major components such as metaphysics, epistemology, and axiology.

Branches of Philosophy: Metaphysics, Epistemology, and Axiology

Metaphysics is one of the branches of philosophy. The etymological makeup of the term *metaphysics* is telling and relevant to its meaning and focus. Two Greek words, *meta* and *phusia*, are joined to form the word metaphysics. *Meta* is a preposition, which could mean with, after, or behind. If it is accompanied with the genitive case, it could mean with, among, or against (Trenchard, 1998); if it is accompanied with the accusative case (direct object), then its meaning could be after or behind (Wallace, 2000). The term *metaphysics* does not provide sufficient syntactical context to determine whether the construction is genitive or accusative, but drawing from its emphases and orientations, we may infer that *meta* in metaphysics stands for after or behind.

Whereas the modern science of physics concerns itself primarily with the phenomena of "the natural world, that is, in the realm of things existing in space and time" (Lowe, 2002, p. 2), metaphysics, on the other hand, focuses on as well as investigates "the nature of things existing in space and time, with the nature of space and time themselves, and with the nature of causation" (p. 2). In addition, other abstract subjects such as being (ontology), mathematics, logic, time, space, and related aspects of the universe (cosmology) belong to the domain of metaphysics. Here lies the fine line between physics and metaphysics—the scope of physics is confined to the realm of natural phenomena, while metaphysics subsumes the realm of natural phenomena and assumes the existence of another realm beyond the natural one. In addition, metaphysics goes even deeper by investigating the nature/essence of those entities existing within both realms.

The philosophical concept, epistemology, is formed by two Greek words—*episteme* (knowledge/justified or proven knowledge) and *logos* (explanation/study). Epistemology has been conceptually posited as a branch of philosophy whose primary objective lies in "the study of the nature of knowledge and justification [thereof]" (Moser, 2006, p. 273). This study is both reflective and analytic, revolving around the questions of whether humans truly know, the nature of what humans really know, and the certainty of what humans claim to know. The emphases and orientations of epistemology make it a "theory of knowledge" (Moser et al., 1998). Philosophical reflection on the conditions of knowledge and sources of knowledge goes back at least to the ancient Greek philosophers Plato (c. 427–347 BC) and Aristotle (384–322 BC). Plato's *Theaetetus* and Aristotle's *Analytics*, more than any other writings, set the stage for epistemology "by delimiting the concept and the structure of human knowledge" (Moser et al., 1998, p. 4). Congruently, justification of knowledge, aimed at a high degree of certitude, has dominated the discourse on epistemology.

This need for the justification of knowledge has yielded two different schools of thought—foundationalism and non-foundationalism (Grayling, 1996). The former school maintains that knowledge can be justified in terms of finite claims or grounds. In other words, knowledge can be objective. Philosophers such as Rene Descartes (1596–1650), John Locke (1632–1704), and David Hume (1711–1776) shared that view. Those philosophers did not necessarily agree on the ground on which knowledge may be justified. For instance, Descartes posited that reason was the main purveyor of knowledge, while Locke and Hume posited experience as the source from which knowledge emanates. Locke, in particular, believed the human brain/mind is a blank slate until knowledge is wrought on it by experience, experience through the senses that forms the basis for the thesis of empirical knowledge. Similarly, Hume stressed the senses, particularly feeling or human emotion, as the purveyor of knowledge. Like Descartes, Kant (1711–1804) maintained knowledge can be sufficiently justified and stressed reason as an adequate tool by which objective knowledge may be accessed and interpreted. Both Descartes and Kant rejected the thesis of skepticism that challenges the claims of knowledge and suggested "proposed justification [for knowledge] might be insufficient" (Grayling, 1996, p. 47). The latter school, non-foundationalism, stems from skepticism and remains largely skeptical about the justification, the certainty, and the objectivity of knowledge. Foundationalism and non-foundationalism ultimately revolve around the question of whether knowledge can be objective or subjective.

The concept of axiology and its investigative orientations derive from the Greek etymology of the cognate. The Greek *axios* means value and its combination with logos (study/explanation/reason) forms this branch of philosophy, which investigates "the nature of value and what kinds of things have value" (Lemos, 2006, p. 949). Other scholars, like Scruton (1996), refer to this branch of philosophy as ethics and aesthetics. But there are many others who, like Lemos, view axiology as encompassing ethics, aesthetics, and other practical aspects that fit perfectly under this branch of philosophy.

Ancient and Classical Philosophical Traditions

Thus far, this chapter has focused largely on delineating philosophical concepts, ideas, and thoughts that are particularly common in Western philosophy. It is often assumed that ancient Greeks were the first to develop speculative thought, yet a second-century Christian, Clement of Alexandria, claimed that the Greeks borrowed their ideas from the barbarians (in ancient times barbarians represented communities or tribes not belonging to the great civilizations of Greece and Rome). Whichever the truth might be, it is historically important to recognize the contributions of ancient Greeks to the subsequent development of Western philosophy, architecture, science, literature, and arts. No history of ancient thought "can avoid the mountain mass of Plato" (Kenny, 1997, p. 22). English mathematician and philosopher A. N. Whitehead (1861–1947) once said that the European philosophical tradition, generally speaking, consists of a series of footnotes to Plato. Plato was responsible for immortalizing his teacher Socrates (469–399 BC) in the dialogues that gave rise to Idealism. Aristotle of Stageira, a student of Plato and tutor of Alexander the Great, ushered in Realism and the development of natural sciences.

While Western civilizations have significantly contributed to the conceptualization as well as the systemization of the project of contemporary philosophy, philosophizing activities are not exclusive to the West. The philosophic temperament is "found throughout the world and may be assumed to have been present throughout the hundred thousand years of human being" (Kenny, 1997, p. 4). Furthermore, the questions that drive Western philosophy are not unique to Western societies either. By philosophizing activities, we mean the unflinching intellectual drive and quest by human beings that seeks to comprehend as well as explicate existence, and pertains to time and space, and includes the material and the immaterial world. The following sections feature Hinduism and Buddhism as ancient philosophical traditions in order to illustrate the claim that philosophy is not a project unique to Western societies. As such, the ensuing discussions should be construed as a continuity of the project of philosophy that engages metaphysical and physical questions, and more important, reflect the same intense human fascination with the pursuit of wisdom, as is evident in Western philosophical traditions.

Hindu Philosophical Inquiry, Jñāna, *and* Moksha

The Hindu worldview assumes that all beings are caught in a cycle of painful existence where they are bound to experience multiple lifetimes. But this worldview also maintains that the duration of a person's experience in the cycle of existence is contingent upon his or her karma; to the degree that this person's karma has a quality lesser than the requisite to be liberated from the cycle, he or she may consider three different paths toward exiting—knowledge, devotion, and karma. Karma resurfaces, but it presupposes deeds of better quality.

The path of knowledge is of particular interest to the thesis of the pursuit of wisdom for the following reasons. The path of knowledge posits knowledge as a way out of the painful cycle of existence. Johnson (2009) suggests *jñāna* exudes the sense of gnosis as in "realization of ultimate reality" (p. 157). Further, he accurately identifies this path in Hinduism as "the quest for liberating knowledge, identified as the realization of the relationship between [B]rahman [*ultimate reality*] and atman [*human soul*], which informs much of the teaching of the Upanishads, and which subsequently becomes the characteristic means to liberation" (p. 157). While Johnson's view is accurate, the interpretive meaning he suggested is too narrow, limiting *jñāna* to spiritual enlightenment and excluding knowledge (episteme), the object of inquiry. In fact, Chethimattam (1971) offers a compelling case in favor of a more comprehensive view of *jñāna*, which encompasses but is not limited to knowledge (Greek equivalent gnosis) as a spiritual enlightenment. Chethimattam's interpretive meaning is, in our opinion, more accurate, considering *jñāna* is linked to the Vedas.

In fact, this postulation of knowledge as a way out of the cycle of existence presumes that something is lacking epistemologically, hence ignorance entrenches the human soul deeper into the cycle of ignorance (Chethimattam, 1971). Thus, knowledge becomes a requisite toward liberation. Particularly, it states that the acquisition of knowledge is potent enough to erase one's past that may include burdensome bad karma, at which point that person will be liberated from the cycle more quickly. Worth noting is that the knowledge a person is required to acquire is not a random or arbitrary kind of knowledge. Its object [*from the syntactical formulation: I know the Vedas*] is the Vedas; in other words, the Vedas are the content of this knowledge.

In Hinduism, the pursuit of wisdom is stressed, albeit confined, to the Vedas. Even then, the elevation of the Vedas in the Hindu pursuit of wisdom amplifies the thesis of inquiry that is espoused in the present work. The thesis maintains that the known and the unknown exist in an unending cycle of philosophical or scientific inquiry that continuously captures as well as captivates the interest of the human mind, even galvanizing the mind toward greater dimensions of epistemological depth and breadth. The Vedas are the most sacred and ancient texts in the Hindu worldview and were the primary texts in the earliest forms of Hinduism (Van Voorst, 2011). Fittingly, Veda in Sanskrit means "wisdom" or "vision," which underscores the notion of the pursuit of wisdom. The Hindu Vedas themselves are ritualistic and vastly metaphysical, embodying cosmological and ontological speculations, and as such are deeply philosophical, reflecting a profound interest in wisdom of all sorts.

While the Vedas remain vital to the current forms of Hinduism, the notion of knowledge as a pathway toward liberation represents a paradigm shift that was wrought by a series of new philosophical writings referred to as the *Upanishads.* The Upanishads infused the then-oldest forms of Hinduism, Vedism—whose relevance was threatened by the emergence of the vibrant and philosophically elaborate system of Buddhism—with new ideas as well as new deities. But, the *Upanishads* did not necessarily overhaul the Vedas. Instead, they deconstructed the Vedas, particularly the highly ritualistic and elitist elements thereof, while presenting more systematized and philosophical interpretations and elaborations of the Vedas (Chethimattam, 1971; Hiriyanna, 1975). Even with the turn of the philosophical tide, which is evident in the *Upanishads*, the search for enlightenment by the human mind through the grasp of wisdom has remained constant.

No other Hindu book best illustrates this claim than the *Bhagavad Gita.* Composed of 18 chapters and nestled in the epic war between the Pandavas and Kouravas, the *Bhagavad Gita* is replete with references to the infiniteness of wisdom and is infused with repeated calls for the human soul to yearn and search that infinite wisdom. Paradoxically, the call to seek such wisdom should by no means be construed as an indication that such wisdom might be grasped or attained. That wisdom is there but is not there, making it quite elusive. However elusive, it dwells in the Ultimate Reality. In other words, the Ultimate Reality is wisdom, but wisdom is embedded in the Vedas. So, grasping wisdom as such necessitates the seeker or the philosopher to search and to intellectually grapple with the Vedas. Once the seeker or the philosopher has attained a relatively perfect understanding or knowledge of the Vedas, he or she becomes liberated from *samsara* (cycle of reincarnation). That attainment in and of itself is, according to Hinduism, the consummate enlightenment, or realized relationship between the Brahman and that seeker. Worth noting is that this attained knowledge, albeit metaphysical, did not bypass inquiry.

Buddhist Philosophical Inquiry, **Prajna,** *and* **Nirvana**

Emerging from the Hindu background, Siddhartha Gautama (586–466 BC) also stressed the pursuit of wisdom. As an Indian prince, Gautama grew up steeped in the Hindu system; like his contemporary Indian compatriots, he thought of himself as being caught in this cycle of painful existence. The difference between Gautama and many Indians of his generation was that Gautama had grown disenchanted as well as disillusioned about the viability of then existing Hindu ways for a person to escape the cycle of existence. Such disenchantment and disillusion later infused Gautama with indifference so intense that Gautama decided to abandon his domestic life, as he knew it then, so he could proceed to the third and fourth stages of life (respectively, forest dwelling and asceticism). His abandonment represented an act of non-attachment to what was as well as a striving toward reaching what had not yet been grasped.

That which Gautama pursued both sacrificially and passionately was wisdom, or *jñāna*. His quest, which was successful by his later claim, came to embody paradoxically the essence of what he had tried to vanquish—suffering. This is epitomized in his acknowledgment that suffering exists because of things we desire to grasp. Suffering he did experience, even as he strove to overcome suffering, for he nearly died from his extreme ascetic regimen of dieting and meditating, which illustrated his postulation that suffering, in fact, originates in the human heart. When he finally reached his goal, the attainment of a deep level of consciousness—nirvana or enlightenment—which supposedly brought him closest to ultimate reality or transported him deepest into realms of reality, he gasped in gratification and exulted subliminally as he shared his newly obtained wisdom with his followers:

> As long, O monks, as my knowledge and insight were not quite clear regarding each of Four Noble Truths, I was uncertain whether I had attained to the full insight of what wisdom that [is] unsurpassed in the heavens or on earth. But as soon as my knowledge and insight were quite clear regarding each of these Four Noble Truths, then I became certain that attained to the full insight of that wisdom that is unsurpassed in the heavens or on earth. Now this knowledge and this insight have arisen within me. The emancipation of my heart is immovable. This is my last existence. Now there will be no rebirth for me! (as cited in Van Voorst, 2011, p. 82)

Gautama's achievement has been conceived as *enlightenment* in and of itself—knowledge surpassing the bounds of earth and heavens. For his achievement to be properly understood, Gautama's inquiry must be placed within the Hindu cultural and religious background as discussed earlier. The discourse excerpted above introduces the Four Noble Truths that represent one of the major teachings of the Dharma. It was part of the Buddha's first sermon wherein he outlined this Buddhist Dharma that contains two major teachings—the three characteristics of existence (suffering, non-existent self, and impermanence) and the Four Noble Truths (knowledge of suffering, origin of suffering, cessation of suffering, and knowledge of the path) (Prebish & Keown, 2010; Van Voorst, 2011).

The knowledge of the path contains eight teachings or principles referred to as the *noble eightfold path*, of which the first two are *right view* and *right resolve/thought*. Right view and resolve/thought are particularly noted because they embody *prajna* (Prebish & Keown, 2010). Literally, *prajna* means wisdom. Thus, *prajna* can be said to embody intellectual activities, or to be manifest in intellectual activities (Murti, 2010). In other words, knowledge and *prajna*, as conceptualized in the Buddhist Madhyamika system, are coupled, if not inextricably linked, to create a type of dialectic. That dialectic is knowledge and thus philosophy itself.

The examples of Hinduism and Buddhism, as ancient ways of knowing, illustrate the close link between knowledge and philosophical inquiry (research). Evidently, fascination with wisdom and the quest to grasp wisdom are imprinted on the human psyche regardless of their geographical or geopolitical status. Philosophizing activities within Hinduism and Buddhism embody such fascination and quest.

Modern Western Philosophy

Western classical systems of Plato's idealism and Aristotle's realism gave rise to the corresponding traditions of rationalism and empiricism. Stemming from metaphysics, idealism embodies a philosophical approach that separates the mind from the material world (Blackburn, 1996). In this philosophical tradition, "facts about mental life form the familiar class, and the ones about the physical world need some kind of certification from them" (Blackburn, p. 68). The idealist perspective has either informed or conceived various epistemological paradigms. In particular, the questions rationalism and empiricism have raised inevitably fall within the philosophical purview of idealism and realism.

Two philosophers tower over the emergence of rationalism and empiricism respectively—Descartes and Locke. Descartes and Locke were not necessary on the opposite side of the epistemological debate, but their respective ideas were different enough to yield polemical themes. For instance, Descartes postulated knowledge as "clear and distinct ideas," accessible through reason. To arrive at his conclusion, Descartes used the method of doubt. "He rejected as completely false any thought that could be doubted for any reason" (Bishop, 2011, p. 284). Descartes' principle, *cogito ergo sum*, became the basis of his ironic unwavering faith in reason (Bennett, 2001). Using the model inherent in his first principle, Descartes was able to infer "other perfectly clear and distinct ideas, including the existence of God, and the certainty of his own mathematical propositions" (Bishop, p. 285). Overall, Descartes' methodology for the certainty of scientific knowledge became the basis of modern *rationalism*, which maintains reason as the primary and "unique path to knowledge" (Garber, 2006, p. 771).

Like Descartes, Locke ushered in a new science of knowledge, and they both went on to etch lasting imprints on the Enlightenment Movement and, ultimately, on the history of intellectual ideas. Locke viewed knowledge as a product of experience. He argued that no ideas were innate to the mind and that all ideas came to the mind through sensuous experiences and "its own inner workings" (Bishop, 2011, p. 282). Finally, if we must have knowledge or acquire the certainty of knowledge, such knowledge must come "directly or indirectly through sensory experiences" (Moser & Nat, 1995, p. 22).

Philosophical schools of empiricism and rationalism have exerted a significant amount of influence on the history and development of ideas in the West and beyond its borders. These schools seldom agree with each other internally. Notwithstanding their lack of internal agreement, these schools share the profound preoccupation with understanding of both the material and the immaterial world. By the end of the nineteenth century, radical empiricism gave rise to logical positivism that embodies a philosophical approach that jettisons metaphysical claims. Otherwise known as the Vienna Circle, positivists were influenced by the empiricism of Hume and also by the *Tractatus Logico-Philosophicus* of Wittgenstein (1889–1951). The rejection of metaphysical claims by logical positivists was grounded almost entirely in their unequivocal commitment to empirical knowledge and to scientific method as the only tool that could access this knowledge. Any thought, knowledge, or tool outside the realm of empiricism and scientific method was deemed meaningless (Blackburn, 1996, p. 69).

Positivism

Positivism is often identified with several traditions that share common threads in the philosophical, linguistic, and sociological movements of the end of the nineteenth and the beginning of the twentieth centuries: logical atomism, logical empiricism, logical positivism, and logical (or linguistic) analysis. Auguste Comte (1798–1857) appropriated logical positivism as the ground for the development of the science of sociology. Comte was convinced that human phenomena could and should be studied with the methods employed by natural sciences. He attempted to create a positive science of human beings as opposed to theological and metaphysical speculations. Comte claimed to discover an "evolutionary law of three stages" (Runes, 1983, p. 259) that all societies pass through: theological, metaphysical, and positive, the latter being associated with the advent of sociology as the highest positive science in the hierarchy of sciences. Such positive science was meant to result in the discovery of the laws and regulations of human behavior calculated by mathematical formulas. A "perfect" society based on these laws of behavior would subsequently ensue. John Stuart Mill (1806–1873) adhered to a similar positivistic view, yet unlike Comte, he did not claim that the science of sociology could be based on absolutely certain knowledge.

R. Avenarius (1843–1896) and E. Mach (1838–1916) created a more rigid version of positivism. Avenarius' *empiriocriticism* asserts that pure experience should be the ground for certain knowledge, and Mach defends the view that knowledge should be limited to sensations. These ideas found their ultimate expression in the works of the scientists and philosophers who banded together in the 1920s to form the Vienna Circle group, which included Rudolf Carnap, Otto Neurath, Herbert Feigl, Felix Kaufmann, and Kurt Gödel, under the leadership of Moritrz Schlick (1882–1936). Their purpose was to eliminate the so-called metaphysical and speculative errors. Fascinated by the progress of modern science, and especially by the theories of relativity and quantum mechanics, they elevated science to an insurmountable pedestal.

The Vienna Circle members were influenced by a number of prominent philosophers of the time: A. J. Ayer (1910–1989), G. E. Moore (1873–1958), B. Russell (1872–1970), G. Ryle (1900–1976), and especially L. Wittgenstein. Worth noting is the fact that Wittgenstein never associated himself directly with logical positivists and later made considerable revisions to his early philosophical works, particularly with regard to language, as will be discussed. One major preoccupation of logical positivists was with the language, the meaning of words, and how language statements reflect relations between words and the world. Logical positivists understood the link between language and the world as being directly related to sense data (Polkinghorne, 1983). *What you see is what you get!* This is a figurative expression that stands for the central principle of verification posited by logical positivism. The principle of verification, also known as *verificationism*, asserts that "no proposition can be accepted as meaningful unless it can be verified on formal grounds (through logic and mathematics) or verified on empirical or sense-data grounds" (Ozmon & Craver, 2008, p. 259). The only true and therefore meaningful propositions are either analytic (logical and mathematical) or synthetic (empirically verifiable), whereas claims such as "God is love," "This teacher is passionate about her job," or "The third-graders do not like taking tests" are considered nonsensical (Robinson & Groves, 2001).

Logical positivists encountered a series of problems associated with verificationism and other principles. Their disregard of the fact that there are unverifiable propositions in the language as well as some fundamental assumptions of science that cannot be verifiable led to a rapid decline and eventual refutation of positivism in the 1950s. Positivistic reliance on empirical sense data undermines the attempt to obtain an irrefutable knowledge precisely because these data depend on subjective perceptions. Despite its questionable reputation, positivism left an imprint on educational philosophy and research. In the 1950s, "Hardie and O'Connor criticized educational theories as vague and unscientific and hence as mere expressions of opinion" and recommended that educational research "become more scientific" (Kneller, 1984, p. 139). Positivism exerted considerable influence on behaviorism, cognitive science, and systems analysis.

Few professional philosophers can identify themselves with logical positivism today. Whereas positivism has been discarded as a scientific paradigm, it is often mistaken for "scientific" research in education. Yu (2006) points to the misconceived links between positivism and contemporary quantitative research, which might be due to the historical facts about the prominent founders of statistical methods such as Karl Pearson (1857–1936) and Ronald A. Fisher (1890–1962). The primetime of their careers coincided with the dominant position of positivism and fierce debates between evolutionary biologists and Mendel's (1822–1884) geneticists. While C. Darwin's (1809–1882) theory held that evolution is a result of accumulated small changes in traits over considerable periods of time, Mendel's theory of genetics contended that evolution is a discontinuous process and is driven by the mutation of genes. By the beginning of the twentieth century, both theories were blended into the so-called biometrics. Pearson initially adhered to Darwin's evolutionary biology, while Fisher came to support a blended view of a Mendelian-Darwinian-biometrician synthesis (Yu, 2006).

Arguably, statistics is not a subject-free methodology derived from timeless mathematical axioms: "biological themes and philosophical presumptions drove Karl Pearson and R. A. Fisher to develop their statistical schools" (Yu, 2006, p. 20). Different philosophies underlie the various schools of quantitative methods. It is certainly impossible to divorce the names of Fisher and Pearson from their association with positivism, yet it is equally inappropriate to regard the methods they developed and that were eventually accepted (with modifications) by quantitative researchers as positivistic. Yu presents compelling arguments in support of this thesis, which will be further elaborated in Chapters 2 and 3.

By the second half of the twentieth century, positivism had been largely rejected by the Anglo-American and Continental philosophers of science. Frederick Suppe, Willard Quine, Stephen Toulmin, and Michael Polanyi are among the most outspoken critics of positivist view on science (Polkinghorne, 1983). Positivism has "failed in its attempts to reconstruct science into a logically unified system of theoretical statements grounded in the certainty of sense experience" (Polkinghorne, p. 93). A number of anti-positivist movements (e.g., Gestalt psychology, linguistic philosophy, structuralism, post-structuralism, and Wittgenstein's later work) signaled a paradigm shift in the conception of science. These movements shared a common belief, namely, that it is impossible to obtain absolutely certain knowledge in social and human sciences because human beings cannot stand outside their language systems and cultures. A skeptical response to logical positivism captures this assumption through the *Weltanschauungen* (world outlook) analysis, the thesis of which runs as follows: "One never has access to reality: one can only look through the opaque spectacles of the cognitive apparatus of one's historically given *Weltanschauungen*" (Polkinghorne, p. 103). It was Wittgenstein's later work on language games that played a "catalytic role in the origin of the *Weltanschauungen* analysis [for subsequent philosophers of science]" (Polkinghorne, p. 103).

Wittgenstein's departure from his earlier, positivistic position is expressed in *Philosophical Investigations* (1953/2009). In it, Wittgenstein proposes the language game theory, which questions the possibility that there is a direct relationship between a word and an object (which is a positivistic position). The meanings of words, asserts Wittgenstein, are determined by various contexts, or rules of games (such as in a chess game), in which they are used. Wittgenstein maintains a position of radical pluralism on the possibility of different worldviews represented by many different languages, logics, and subsequently "truths"—all functioning within particular language games. It follows then that what we perceive and see as true depends on our world picture. In other words, human perception is fundamentally interpretive; it is always seeing something *as something*. Wittgenstein illustrates this principle of interpretive "seeing" by a duck-rabbit figure (see Figure 1.1) adopted from American psychologist Joseph Jastrow (1863–1944).

Figure 1.1: Jastrow's Duck-Rabbit Figure

With the decline and repudiation of positivism, philosophers of science abandoned the idea of searching for the foundations (or grounds) of knowledge and appropriated instead probabilistic and provisional "truth" statements conditioned by sociocultural and linguistic contexts. The metaphor of knowledge as an unbreakable foundation is often attributed to Descartes. As a counterpoint to this position, the twentieth-century philosophers of science W. Quine (1908–2000) and R. Rorty (1931–1650) proposed instead a net or spider web as a metaphor of knowledge, entertaining the idea that within the web of knowledge, some of its elements can be "weak" or "worn out" and we can subsequently "repair them while hanging on to the relatively stable parts, which still offer support" (Palmer, 2002, p. 108).

Subsequently, many philosophers of science turned to ideas developed prior to the reign of positivism in the 1920s. One of the richest sources of these ideas was American pragmatism and especially the philosophy of Charles S. Peirce, who claimed that science does not represent a "systematized knowledge but the pursuit itself in which scientists are engaged" (Polkinghorne, 1983, p. 119).

American Pragmatism

The story of pragmatism begins in Cambridge, Massachusetts, in the 1870s, when several young and talented minds (C. S. Peirce, W. James, C. Wright, J. Fiske, and F. E. Abbot) who referred to themselves as members of "Metaphysical Club" would gather to discuss and debate philosophical problems. The most prominent of these thinkers, Charles S. Peirce (1830–1914) and William James (1842–1910), were considered the official founders of pragmatism. John Dewey (1859–1952) developed pragmatism further and made it central to his educational philosophy, which "encourages the process-oriented, problem-solving instruction that is so popular with American teachers" (Gutek, 2004, pp. 71–72).

James popularized pragmatism and applied it a great deal to his work in psychology, known as *functionalism*. James added a value component to the practicality thesis of ideas. From a pragmatic standpoint, one should not be concerned with whether ideas are true or false, but rather with the difference that they can make in our lives. The ideas should have "cash value" (James's famous expression).

Despite his major contributions to pragmatism, Peirce's name remained in obscurity until about the second half of the twentieth century when his collected works were published for the first time. Subsequently, Peirce's genius gained worldwide recognition. In his later career, Peirce became highly dissatisfied with the way James, Dewey, and others used the term *pragmatism*, which made him rename his original philosophy into *pragmaticism* (the word that he himself considered ugly). Peirce insisted that pragmatism is not a philosophy or a theory of truth, but rather a method to assist us in finding solutions to problems. His celebrated definition of pragmatism is expressed in the following passage:

> Our idea of anything *is* our idea of its sensible effects. It appears, then, that the rule for attaining the third grade of cleanness of apprehension is as follows: Consider what effects, that might conceivably have practical bearings, we conceive the object of our conception to have. Then, our conception of these effects is the whole of our conception of the object. (1998, p. 146)

Derived from the Greek word *pragma* (action or deed), pragmatism emphasizes the synergy of relations between theory and practice, knowledge and action. Pragmatism is said to be a distinctly American philosophy and a natural outgrowth of the American spirit and way of life (Sellars, 2010) that reflects the American experience of the early settlers in a new land and their demands for the ideas to solve everyday problems. American pragmatism emerged as a response to long-standing European philosophical influences that seemed too "abstruse and too remote from the immediate concerns of a young, vigorous nation" (Popkin & Stroll, 1993, p. 274) recovering from the devastation of the Civil War. There was a sense among many American philosophers that the European eschatological traditions exhausted themselves and were in need of a revival that would bring the new scientific discoveries to the forefront of philosophical inquiry.

Pragmatists embrace scientific inquiry as a radical departure from positivism. Peirce (1966) contends that although positivism has a "favorable influence upon scientific investigation, its fundamental position is false"

(p. 137). Peirce's essential position on knowledge, in contrast to positivism, was that our knowledge about the world of objects is fallible and that scientific knowledge has limits. Peirce revered science and thought of it as a living and breathing process. Peirce's (1998) consensus theory of truth elaborates on the process of validating true ideas by the community of scientists. It is the "COMMUNITY" [Peirce's emphasis] that has "definite limits, and [is] capable of a definite increase of knowledge" (1998, p. 115). Peirce firmly believed that scientists and philosophers are motivated by pure love of the pursuit of truth. An inquiry begins because of a genuine doubt: "The irritation of doubt causes a struggle to attain a state of belief. I shall term this struggle inquiry ... It is certainly best for us that our beliefs should be such as may truly guide our actions so as to satisfy our desires" (1998, p. 126).

Peirce's method of scientific inquiry translates perfectly into Dewey's problem-solving method. Known as instrumentalism, or experimentalism, Dewey's pragmatic philosophy combines a theory of logic and a principle of ethical analysis and criticism. His expression *warranted assertions* entered the philosophical and educational vocabulary to designate pragmatic truth. In his "Logic: The Theory of Inquiry" (1938), Dewey proposed the notion of intelligence as an essentially evaluative experience. We cannot separate experience as moral, scientific, practical, or theoretical, hence his notion of the reconstruction of human experience. The purpose of inquiry is thus to resolve a doubt or to solve a problem and, while doing so, to exhibit moral practical value of that experience. Dewey's philosophy connects the continuity of experience with the idea of education as growth: "The educative process can be identified with growth when that is understood in terms of active principle, *growing*" (as cited in Johnson & Reed, 2012, p. 111).

Dewey's instrumentalism and experimentalism are linked through the notion of evolutionary philosophy, which influenced a great number of thinkers of that time (Interestingly, Dewey was born in 1859, the year when Darwin's *The Origin of Species* was published). Dewey tested his ideas as the experimental method of education in the University of Chicago Laboratory School, which he directed from 1896 to 1904. It was against the metaphysical theories of reality and knowledge that Dewey defended his "unity of knowledge" system, designating the relation between knowing and doing and the active social conception of human intelligence (Gutek, 2004).

The recent revival of pragmatism finds its expression in the neo-pragmatist critique of normativity in Western analytic philosophy. Particularly, Richard Rorty is critical of the American philosophy as being greatly influenced by the search for objective knowledge and thus attempting to establish a "normal" discourse. As a counterpoint, Rorty proposes an "abnormal" discourse as a criticism of this position (Ozmon & Craver, 2008). Cornel West (b. 1953) advocates *prophetic pragmatism*, which merges the ideas of Emerson, liberation theology, and classical pragmatism (Ozmon & Craver). In Rorty's view, the current neo-pragmatists' agenda has to do with "reconciling the antimetaphysical antiabsolutist trends in twentieth-century English, American, and Continental philosophy" and with envisaging the role of philosophy as helping people and society to "break free from outworn vocabularies and attitudes, rather than to provide 'grounding' for the institutions and customs of the present" (as cited in Popkin & Stroll, 1993, p. 316).

The reconciliatory spirit of pragmatism makes itself manifest in educational inquiry through its attempts to do away with the so-called paradigm wars between quantitative and qualitative purists (see, e.g., Johnson & Onwuegbuzie, 2004). Wedded to this spirit are pragmatism's remarkable contributions to the theory of truth and the method of rigorous scientific inquiry that in turn have become instrumental to an overall nineteenth-century anti-positivist movement launched by European existential-phenomenological and hermeneutic philosophers.

Existential-Phenomenological and Hermeneutic Inquiries

Where do we come from? What are we? Where are we going?

Several philosophical traditions developed in nineteenth-century Europe would make the existential questions central to their inquiry as well as part of a concerted effort to articulate the anti-positivist response to the excesses of rationalism and the disputes over the methods by which to approach the study of human phenomena. In 1858, the German historian Droysen distinguished between the terms *erklären* (explanation) and *verstehen* (understanding), which further marked an important distinction between the methods used in natural sciences based on the explanation of natural phenomena, and the methods employed in human sciences that relied on the understanding of human phenomena (Polkinghorne, 1983). Henceforth, *verstehen* becomes not only a legitimate source of knowledge, but more important, an alternative to a foundationalist epistemology way of knowing that is firmly embedded in historically particular and contingent vocabularies (Westphal, 2006).

Giambattista Vico (1668–1744) is said to be the forerunner of the anti-positivist response. Yet it was the German Romantic movement of the nineteenth century that contributed to the response most significantly. The Romantics were philosophers, poets, writers, and artists who questioned the ultimate authority of human reason and its privileged status as espoused by Enlightenment thinkers. Romantics turned their attention to human emotions and desires, the "perennial features of human existence that haunt those who celebrate the rational" (Oliver, 1997, p. 116). Finding a creative outlet in art and aestheticism, the Romantics launched an era of sensibility as a counter-current to a systematic rationalized approach to life. Their purpose was to achieve harmony between the intellect and passion.

Schelling (1775–1854), Novalis (1772–1801), and Hölderlin (1770–1843) are perhaps the most prominent names associated with German Romanticism. Schelling's identity philosophy represents a complex, dialectic ontological system that integrates subject and object, real and ideal, the *uni*verse and the *multi*plicity of being or self. Schelling resolves the internal struggle between artistic eros and systematic reason in favor of art as a unifying principle and the ground for the ultimate expression and realization of self. F. von Hardenberg (Novalis) reifies the unifying principle through poetry and attempts poetic philosophy—an understanding of the self and its world not in abstractions but by romanticizing them. Romanticizing is understood as a portrayal of the unexpected that interrupts our ordinary life and shows what we are *not*, what we are potentially: *Die Welt muß romantisirt werden* (The world must be romanticized), proclaims Novalis. In his major work, *Hyperion*, Hölderlin advances the All-Unity principle as the ultimate self-knowledge and self-expression through aesthetics. The Romantics inspired other philosophers of the anti-positivist response (e.g., Dilthey, Husserl, Heidegger, Merleau-Ponty, Gadamer, Ricoeur, and Habermas) whose philosophies of life laid foundations for the existential-phenomenological and hermeneutic inquiries.

As a systematic philosophy, existentialism was founded by Søren Kierkegaard (1813–1855) and Friedrich Wilhelm Nietzsche (1844–1900) and further developed by a number of European and American thinkers, psychologists, literary figures, and educators: Sartre, de Beauvoir, Buber, Jaspers, Marcel, Tillich, Rogers, Maslow, Camus, and Greene, to name a few most widely acclaimed. Existential themes of freedom, passionate choice, and an acute sense of responsibility for creating one's own destiny and meaning of life in a seemingly absurd and lonely world; living the values that one espouses; and overcoming the fear of death in the situations that require an ultimate choice and subsequently displaying courage and integrity of one's character run across the spectrum of existentialism in a variety of its representations.

Kierkegaard, the leading figure in Christian existentialism, contends that a true Christian lives a life of constant internal conflict in his or her search for God, and it is not through doctrine, theological studies, or regular church attendance, but instead through the leap of faith that he or she can find God, the God from within. Assuming that God exists and one can find Him, the human being is still in a precarious situation—still absolutely alone and abandoned in a seemingly indifferent and hostile world. Out of this complete isolation and despair comes the cry of one in the wilderness. But instead of God's answer, there is only silence: "the human being's experience of nothingness before God, which is at the same moment the complete fulfillment of human existence" (Gutek, 1997, p. 109).

Along comes Nietzsche who proclaims, "God is dead!"—the expression that does not have much to do with a theological argument but rather with Nietzsche's critique of modernity with its reliance on speculative philosophy and slave Christian morality. Nietzsche's concerns with the expression of truth and falsehood leads him to explore the Greek culture in the light of rational (embodied by Apollo) and irrational (embodied by Dionysus) principles. From the synthesis of these two principles arises "the beauty of an art in which life is contained but not destroyed, and in which the terrible and the irrational exist side by side with the serene" (Kenny, 1997, p. 217). Art and aesthetic, not knowledge, are given ontological priority in Nietzsche's existentialist project. Unless one creates something, it would be better that one had never been born. Existence, therefore, can be justified only artistically: only as an "aesthetic product can the world be justified to all eternity," and only as the "genius in the act of creation merges with the primal architect of the cosmos can he truly know something of the eternal essence of art" (Nietzsche, 2000, pp. 261–262).

Art owes its continuous evolution in the Apollonian-Dionysian duality. Being a moral deity, Apollo persistently attempts to retain his self-control in the midst of the warring spheres of influence [non-Apollonian Titans and extra-Apollonian barbarians], until the "effects of the Dionysiac spirit struck the Apollonian Greeks as Titan and barbaric ... Their whole existence, with its temperate beauty, rested upon a base of suffering and *knowledge* which had been hidden from them until the reinstatement of Dionysos uncovered it once more. And lo and behold! Apollo found it impossible to live without Dionysos" (Nietzsche, 2000, p. 256). Nietzsche ultimately favors the Dionysian principle as an expression of will—the will to power, to be more precise. To put it differently, each and every one of us has the potential to become reborn into *Übermensch* (Superman), which is an unrealized potential within us, as long as we are *willing* to overcome the external limitations of our existence: "The individual, with his limits and moderations, forgot himself in the Dionysiac vortex and became oblivious to the laws of Apollo. Indiscreet extravagance revealed itself as truth, and contradiction, a delight born of pain, spoke out of the bosom of nature" (Nietzsche, p. 257).

Nietzsche's philosophy had a profound influence on twentieth-century thinkers, especially on Sartre and Heidegger. Existentialism as a European phenomenon became especially pronounced during and after WWII when philosophers, writers, and ordinary citizens questioned the rationality of the war machine and the sanity of decisions behind it that resulted in the death of millions of people, many of whom sacrificed their lives in the name of false and destructive ideologies. Jean-Paul Sartre's (1905–1980) existentialism was shaped by the anguish, atrocities, and devastation of war. Sartre was part of the French Resistance during WWII and experienced the confrontation with death directly when he was captured by the Nazis. Sartre explicitly positions himself as an atheistic existentialist. In "Existentialism and Humanism," he defines existentialism through his famous dictum, "existence precedes essence." What does he mean by that?

> Man first of all exists, encounters himself, surges up in the world—and defines himself afterwards ... There is no human nature, because there is no God to have conception of it. Man simply is. Man is nothing else but that which he makes of himself. (as cited in Ozmon & Craver, 2008, p. 249)

Regardless of God's presence or absence in our lives, we are doomed to freedom in our earthly existence with its little pleasures and sorrows, and with the burden of making our own choices and assuming full responsibility for them and for the world that we create. Sartre's lifelong partner and philosopher in her own rite, Simone de Beauvoir (1908–1986), created an original version of existential philosophy and became widely known for her feminist classic, *The Second Sex* (1949/1989). The book details the analysis of patriarchal societies and the predicament of woman as the Other within them:

> Humanity is male and man defines woman not in herself but as relative to him; she is not regarded as an autonomous being. For him she is sex, absolute sex, no less. She is defined and differentiated with reference to man and not he with reference to her. He is the Subject, he is the Absolute—she is the Other. (1989, p. xxii)

Beauvoir's celebrated credo, "one is not born but becomes a woman," reifies the existential condition that renders the choice for emancipation both possible and justified.

The beginnings and development of phenomenology are most commonly attributed to Husserl, Schutz, Heidegger, Sartre, Merleau-Ponty, and Freire. Edmund Husserl (1859–1938), notably the father of phenomenology, studied the structures of human consciousness and developed phenomenology along rationalist lines (transcendental phenomenology). Phenomenology literally means the study of appearances (Gr. < phenomena) that are being structured by our consciousness in specific patterns and come in different shapes as objects, ideas, memories, or images. The phenomenological process of uncovering the structures of consciousness can be compared with an archeologist excavating a prehistoric site. One has to carefully describe the various strata in order to reveal the meaningful structures that are taken for granted in everyday experience, which Husserl calls "lifeworld" (*Lebenswelt*). Lifeworld designates the everyday world of our affairs (family, work, pleasure, etc.). We may think of this world as "objective and independent, yet it is we who sustain it and give it meaning" (Kneller, 1984, p. 30). The task of phenomenological inquiry is, therefore, to describe the phenomena as they appear to our consciousness and to endow them with meaning.

Alfred Schutz (1899–1959) brought Husserl's phenomenology to the social world and made human action central to its inquiry. Maurice Merleau-Ponty (1908–1961) developed phenomenology along the lines of embodied consciousness. As embodied beings we relate to the world primarily through senses. Sense perceptions that originate in our thoughts are rooted in childhood, when we learn how to move and experience things in a "prereflective" manner. We think, act, and feel as we do "because of the omnipresent, prereflective stratum of [our] experience" (Kneller, 1984, p. 43). Our bodily perception of the world is "dehiscence, a splitting open of the body as touching and touched, as seer and seen that allows the body to experience things" (Low, 2000, p. 17).

Martin Buber (1878–1965) contributed immensely to the existential-phenomenological educational theory by advancing the argument of the *I-Thou* dialogue as an authentic and mutually appreciative form of relationships between individuals. *I-Thou* is counter-positioned with an *I-It* mode of objectified and self-interested relationships. Buber advocates the *I-Thou* relation among teachers and students and conceives of it as a communion of divine and human character, whereas "one's faith in God and in one's fellow human beings is witness to one's devotion to a higher end" (Ozmon & Craver, 2008, p. 227).

The tradition of hermeneutics has a long and fascinating history. The term comes from the Greek *hermeneuein*, "to interpret," and is linked to the name of Hermes, the Greek god messenger. Hermes was the son of Zeus and Maia, the daughter of Atlas, and was born out of wedlock. His regular duties included carrying messages to and from Zeus, between the other gods and mortals. Known for his devious character, Hermes was a protector of mischief makers (Couch, 1997). He is often portrayed as wearing winged-shoes or sandals, a round helmet-shaped hat, and carrying a staff entwined with serpents. Worth noting is the fact that Hermes has siblings in other cultural traditions, for instance, Mercury in Roman mythology, Garuda the mythical bird in Hinduism and Buddhism, and Slava the messenger bird of Perun (equivalent of Zeus) in Slavic mythology.

Hermeneutics acquired its revolutionary spirit from the Protestant Reformation of the sixteenth century when, in opposition to the Catholic Church's authority over biblical texts, the Protestants "called for a return to the text itself" (Polkinghorne, 1983, p. 219). With the spread of literacy and the printing press, it became possible for common people to have access to biblical texts. M. Luther's (1483–1546) translation of the Bible into modern German revolutionized and shifted the consciousness of the religious laity in Germany, and eventually throughout Europe, from the confines of church dogmas to the vast and open prairie of hermeneutics wherein they were able to read freely and interpret independently the word of God.

Wilhelm Dilthey (1833–1911) is recognized as the leading figure in hermeneutics, although he credited Friedrich Schleiermacher (1768–1834) with the development of the art. Dilthey attempted to shape hermeneutics as a human science capable of generating knowledge for social and political decisions. Dilthey realized that it would be impossible to gain certain and objective knowledge of the human realm, yet one could strive for approximation of such knowledge in which "there are degrees of truth which move closer to a sure understanding" (Polkinghorne, 1983, p. 223). Significant to the study of hermeneutics are also the philosophies of Martin Heidegger (1889–1976) and Hans-George Gadamer (1900–2002).

Heidegger's *Being and Time* (1927) marks a radical departure from conventional assumptions of knowledge and the ego-subject in Western philosophy. It is not about the way we know the world, but the way we *are*. The question of being, thus, acquires ontological priority over all other questions. Heidegger posits the question of being within the context of *Dasein*—the realm of our existence. Human existence constitutes the openness where being can be revealed. For something to be means for it to be revealed, uncovered, made manifest. We exist in the world because we understand what it means to be. Our authentic existence—being-in-the-world—is possible only when self as ego is eclipsed by the manifestation of our finitude. The modes of being in the world also include being-with-others and being-toward-death. "The being of *Dasein* means ahead-of-itself-being-already-in-(the world) as being-amidst (entities encountered in-the-world). This Being fills in the signification of the term '*care*' [Sorge]" (Heidegger, 1962, p. 237). I *am* care (Sorge), the unity of lived experiences, temporal transcendence, openness to and involvement with worldly affairs, my being "here" (the *Da* of *Dasein*). The more open and authentic I am, the more able I am to care for myself and others.

In his seminal work *Truth and Method* (1960/2004), Gadamer extended and applied the main concepts developed by Heidegger regarding the historical and interactive conditions of human understanding. As a model for his method, Gadamer suggests translation from one language to another. Interpretation is not just reconstruction of meaning, it also involves a fusion of horizons, an interaction between the interpreter and the meaning in the text. Interpretation is a mediated process that has a circular character. The parts of the text constitute a complex whole that is the meaning of the text. The horizon is "something into which we move and that moves with us. Horizons change for a person who is moving. Thus the horizon of the past, out of which all human life lives and which exists in the form of tradition, is always in motion" (Gadamer, 1992, p. 271). The process of movement from the first pre-judgmental notion of the meaning of the whole (in which the parts are understood) to a change in the sense of the meaning of the whole is called the *hermeneutic circle*. Hence, interpretation is never final, and the process of understanding does not result in finite and objective truth. Hermeneutic understanding is conditioned and mediated by language, culture, and context. Hermeneutic method aims at "maintaining the intersubjectivity of mutual understanding in ordinary-language communication and in action according to common norms" (Habermas, 1972, p. 176). More important, the philosophical hermeneutics of Heidegger and Gadamer call into serious question the very possibility of objective historical knowledge.

Existential-phenomenological and hermeneutic (life) philosophies have opened extraordinary venues for researchers to pursue the study of human phenomena as a multi-paradigmatic endeavor. Their emergence and development signaled a radical shift from a positivistic view of scientific knowledge to epistemological and methodological pluralism. The legacy of early hermeneutics and its rebellious spirit was inherited by the twentieth-century thinkers for whom it was not enough to understand the world—they ventured to change it. This iconoclastic spirit of the twentieth century emanating from a desire for change and a new voice might be framed as postmodernism.

Critical and Postmodern Inquiries

The paradigm of postmodernism, which gave rise to various critical projects, particularly critical theory, is set against the postmodern backdrop. These critical projects originated in Western thought, focused on the notion of truth and the certainty thereof, and objected to the view of knowledge as neutral and rational. In addition, reflecting a shift away from modernism, as well as being heavily informed by the works of Karl Marx (1818–1883),

Friedrich Nietzsche (1844–1900), and Sigmund Freud (1856–1939), these critical projects conceived two important schools of thought—Frankfurt School and poststructuralism (Carrette, 2005).

While Michel Foucault and Jacques Derrida were the more prominent figures within poststructuralism, Frankfurt School featured Max Horkheimer, Marcus Adorno, and Habermas as its key thinkers. While these two critical schools had their differences, they nonetheless shared some basic assumptions about knowledge, society, and political institutions:

> Following Marx critical theory is aware that all knowledge is linked to economic and political ideology; following Nietzsche it understands that all knowledge is linked to the "will to power"; and following Freud it understands that all knowledge is linked to things outside our awareness (the unconscious). (Carrette, 2005, p. 28)

Traces of these critical pioneers are evident in almost every critical work that has been undertaken since then, and the fact that the three thinkers highlighted above viewed critical work from various prisms are also signs that critical project is neither monolithic nor homogeneous.

Grounded in the historical materialist tradition, critical theory embodies an unflinching interest in the social, political, spatial, and economic conditions of humans (Rush, 2004). From a Marxist standpoint, historical materialism is a philosophical perspective that is strongly grounded in all things physical and material, and even empirical in many ways (Smart, 1999), while the dialectic method represents a tool of analysis that views "every social system as having within it immanent forces that give rise to contradictions that can only be resolved by a new system" (Rush, 2004, p. 12). Thus, dialectic materialism is critical at its core and vies that agency is imperative for humans to determine and transform their respective material conditions, or the realities of their physical existence, or "sensuous existence" (Rush, p. 20).

Emanating from that background, critical theory "represents a sophisticated effort to continue Marx's transformation of moral philosophy into social and political critique, while rejecting orthodox Marxism as a dogma" (Bohman, 2006, p. 324). Critical theorists may have had varying degrees of perspectives on the unfolding of critical endeavor, but they were unequivocally united on the questions and issues that led to the conception of their critical enterprise:

> The motivation for this enterprise appears similar for each of the theorists—the aim being to lay the foundation for an exploration, in an interdisciplinary

> research context, of questions concerning the conditions which make possible the production and transformation of society, the meaning of culture, and the relation between the individual, society and nature. (Held, 1980, p. 16)

Held (1980) underscores this unity on the questions and concerns of critical theory as the central and melding theme that underlie collaboration and co-existence among the Frankfurt School scholars. Indeed, this unity has contributed to the success of critical theory, legitimizing it as a theoretical analysis that concerns itself with the actuality of life as it unfolds.

Geuss (1981) breaks down the fundamentals of critical theory and posits them as its central theses. The first thesis, according to Geuss, claims that critical theory is "aimed at producing enlightenment in the agents" who subscribe to the framework, in terms of "enabling those agents to determine what their true interests are" (p. 2). A second prong to the first thesis is that critical theory is "inherently emancipatory"; that is to say, it liberates "agents from a kind of coercion which is at least partly self-imposed, from self-frustration of conscious human action" (p. 2). The second thesis maintains that critical theory has a "cognitive content" that makes this theory intrinsically a "form of knowledge" (p. 2).

Flowing logically from the second thesis, the third one maintains that critical theory is dissimilar "epistemologically in essential ways from theories in the natural sciences": while "natural science is objectifying," critical theory is "reflective" (Geuss, 1981, p. 2). Objectifying refers to natural science making human beings the objects of its studies and embracing empirical standards that supposedly make findings about humans objective; but the "reflective" qualification of critical theory underscores its interest in understanding and interpreting the human condition and inspiring actions to improve it (Geuss, 1981). Critical theory seeks to transform human conditions materially while aiming to shift and balance power dynamics between the oppressed and their oppressors, between those in power and their subordinates. As such, critical theory has been established as an effective tool to critique dominant establishments or discourse, and to foster human emancipation (Bohman, 2006; Freire, 1971/1998; McLaren & Farahmandpur, 2005).

In this chapter, we endeavored to trace the historical development of philosophical ideas, traditions, and perspectives while highlighting their prevailing theme of pursuit of wisdom, including their significance to various paradigms of knowledge and to educational research. Thus, the preceding discussions fittingly preface the discussion of epistemology in the next chapter.

References

Bennett, J. (2001). *Learning from six philosophers: Descartes, Spinoza, Leibniz, Locke, Berkeley, Hume* (Vols. 1–2). Oxford University Press.

Bishop, P. (2011). *Adventures in the human spirit* (6th ed.). Prentice Hall.

Blackburn, S. (1996). Metaphysics. In N. Bunnin & E. P. Tsui-James (Eds.), *Blackwell companion to philosophy* (pp. 64–89). Blackwell Publishing.

Bohman, J. (2006). Frankfurt school. In R. Audi (Ed.), *The Cambridge dictionary of philosophy* (2nd ed., pp. 324–325). Cambridge University Press

Carrette, J. (2005). Critical theory and religion. In C. Partridge (Ed.), *Introduction to world religions* (pp. 28–31). Fortress Press.

Chethimattam, J. B. (1971). *Patterns of Indian thought.* Geoffrey Chapman.

Couch, M. (Ed.). (1997). *Greek and Roman mythology.* Todtri.

de Beauvoir, S. (1989). *The second sex.* Vintage Books.

Foley, M., & Mohan, W. J. (2003). *Philosophic inquiry: An introduction.* Xlibris Corporation.

Freire, P. (1971/1998). *Pedagogy of freedom: Ethics, democracy, and civic courage* (P. Clarke, Trans.). Rowman & Littlefield.

Gadamer, H.-G. (1992). The historicity of understanding. In K. Mueller-Vollmer (Ed.), *The hermeneutics reader: Texts of the German tradition from the Enlightenment to the present* (pp. 256–292). Continuum.

Garber, D. (2006). Rationalism. In R. Audi (Ed.), *The Cambridge dictionary of philosophy* (2nd ed., pp. 771–772). Cambridge University Press.

Geuss, R. (1981). *The idea of a critical theory: Habermas and the Frankfurt School.* Cambridge University Press.

Grayling, A. C. (1996). Epistemology. In N. Bunnin & E. P. Tsui-James (Eds.), *The Blackwell companion to philosophy* (pp. 38–63). Blackwell.

Gutek, G. L. (2004). *Philosophical and ideological voices in education.* Pearson.

Habermas, J. (1972). *Knowledge and human interests* (J. J. Shapiro, Trans.). Beacon Press.

Heidegger, M. (1962). *Being and time.* Harper & Row.

Held, D. (1980). *Introduction to critical theory: Horkheimer to Habermas.* Athenaeum Press.

Hiriyanna, M. (1975). *Outlines of Indian philosophy* (10th ed.). Lewis Reprints.

Johnson, R. B., & Onwuegbuzie, A. J. (2004). Mixed methods research: A research paradigm whose time has come. *Educational Researcher, 33*(7), 14–26.

Johnson, T. W., & Reed, R. F. (2012). *Philosophical documents in education* (4th ed.). Pearson.

Johnson, W. J. (2009). *Oxford dictionary of Hinduism.* Oxford University Press.

Kenny, A. (Ed.). (1997). *The Oxford illustrated history of Western philosophy.* Oxford University Press.

Kneller, G. F. (1984). *Movements of thought in modern education.* Macmillan.

Lemos, N. L. (2006). Value theory. In R. Audi (Ed.), *The Cambridge dictionary of philosophy* (2nd ed., pp. 949–950). Cambridge University Press.

Low, D. (2000). *Merleau-Ponty's last vision: A proposal for the completion of "The visible and the invisible."* Northwestern University Press.

Lowe, E. J. (2002). *A survey of metaphysics.* Oxford University Press.

McLaren, P., & Farahmandpur, R. (2005). *Teaching against global capitalism and the new imperialism: A critical pedagogy.* Rowman & Littlefield.

Moser, P. K. (2006). Epistemology. In R. Audi (Ed.), *The Cambridge dictionary of philosophy* (2nd ed., pp. 273–278). Cambridge University Press.

Moser, P. K., Mulder, D. H., & Trout, J. D. (1998). *The theory of knowledge: A thematic introduction.* Oxford University Press.

Moser, P. K., & Nat, A. V. (1995). *Human knowledge: Classical and contemporary approaches* (2nd ed.). Oxford University Press.

Murti, T. R. V. (2010). *The central philosophy of Buddhism: A study of Madhyamika system.* Munshiram Manoharlal.

Nietzsche, F. (2000). The birth of tragedy and the geneology of man. In S. Rosen (Ed.), *The philosopher's handbook: Essential readings from Plato to Kant* (pp. 243–266). Random House.

Oliver, M. (1997). *History of philosophy.* Metro Books.

Ozmon, H. A., Craver, S. M. (2008). *Philosophical foundations of education* (8th ed.). Merrill Prentice Hall.

Palmer, D. (2002). *Does the center hold? An introduction to Western philosophy* (3rd ed.). McGraw-Hill.

Peirce, C. S. (1966). *Selected writings (Values in a universe of chance).* Dover.

Peirce, C. S. (1998). *The essential writings.* Prometheus Books.

Polkinghorne, D. E. (1983). *Methodology for the human sciences: Systems of inquiry.* SUNY Press.

Popkin, R. H., & Stroll, A. (1993). *Philosophy made simple* (2nd ed.). Broadway Books.

Prebish, C. S., & Keown, D. (2010). *Introducing Buddhism* (2nd ed.). Routledge.

Robinson, D., & Groves, J. (2001). *Introducing philosophy.* Totem Books.

Rush, F. (2004). Conceptual foundations of early critical theory. In F. Rush (Ed.), *The Cambridge companion to critical theory* (pp. 6–39). Cambridge Press.

Runes, D. D. (Ed.). (1983). *Dictionary of philosophy.* Littlefield, Adams.

Scruton, R. (1996). *Modern philosophy: An introduction and survey.* Penguin Books.

Sellars, R. W. (2010). *The essentials of logic.* Houghton Mifflin.

Smart, N. (1999). *World philosophies.* Routledge.

Trenchard, W. C. (1998). *Complete vocabulary guide to the Greek New Testament.* Zondervan.

Van Voorst, R. E. (2011). *Anthology of world scriptures* (7th ed.). Wadsworth.

Wallace, D. B. (2000). *The basics of New Testament syntax: An intermediate Greek grammar.* Zondervan.

Westphal, M. (2006). Hermeneutics as epistemology. In J. Greco & E. Sosa (Eds.), *The Blackwell guide to epistemology* (pp. 415–435). Blackwell.

Wittgenstein, L. (1953/2009). *Philosophical investigations* (4th ed., G. E. M. Anscomber, P. M. S. Hacker, & J. Schulte, Trans.). Blackwell.

Yu, C. H. (2006). *Philosophical foundations of quantitative research methodology.* University Press of America.

Chapter 2 Epistemology and Philosophy of Science: Traditions, Perspectives, and Controversies

Antonina Lukenchuk and Baudelaire K. Ulysse

Epistemology and Philosophy of Science: Overview

Epistemological Legacies and Controversies

In Chapter 1, we defined epistemology as a branch of philosophy whose primary objective lies in "the study of the nature of knowledge and justification [thereof]" (Moser, 2006, p. 273). Kenny (2010) suggests that the Greek word for the term epistemology has special significance. According to Anthony, episteme "is often used to indicate a knowledge of a rather grand kind, so that one of its English equivalents is science" (p. 121). That is a valid point, considering the important role science has played in explaining and justifying knowledge; hence, epistemology has been conceptually defined as "the science of knowing" (Pojman, 1999, p. 1). Throughout Chapter 1, we perused the philosophical concept of epistemology and showed how various schools of thought in the history of philosophy have captivated the human mind and contributed to our understanding of knowledge and the pursuit thereof.

In the present chapter, we propose to focus primarily on knowledge—scientific knowledge of all sources. This primary focus immediately thrusts us into terrains that are already charted. This means that our intention is not to reinvent the wheel, but to account for the spokes that hold the wheel together. In other words, we will attempt to identify, review, analyze, and synthesize various theories of knowledge while guiding the reader/researcher to the shore where they could either coast, however comfortably and uncomfortably, or chart a new course. We hope, however, that readers will not settle comfortably, but that they will instead continue to navigate critically the various waves and currents ushered in their direction.

In addressing the theory of knowledge, Moser, Mulder, and Trout (1998) suggest that a theory of knowledge should first and foremost differentiate between "genuine knowledge and merely apparent knowledge, between the real thing and likely counterfeits" (p. 23). This suggestion raises a fundamental question that is rather recurring in the debates on the concept of knowledge. But is the supposed line between genuine knowledge and apparent knowledge real, or is it imaginary? Or, more importantly, could such a supposed line represent an unnecessary dichotomy? The philosophers, both past and present, who spent considerable time investigating knowledge were indeed interested in distinguishing among various types or kinds of knowledge. In the process, they focused on the following questions, among others. How do we know what we know? What counts as knowledge? Whose knowledge is of most worth? What is the scope of knowledge? What are its limits? In what ways might some types of knowledge be considered more credible than others?

Introducing his anthology of classical and contemporary readings on the theory of knowledge, Pojman (1999) highlights three different types of knowledge: *knowledge by acquaintance*, *competence knowledge*, and *propositional knowledge*. Pojman's types of knowledge are general categories that may be labeled differently in other literature, and we do not necessarily view them as exhaustive.

However, Pojman makes a compelling point about the connection between epistemology and propositional knowledge. Thus, he explains what comprises propositional knowledge:

> Person S knows that *p* (where *p* is some statement or proposition). Propositions have truth value; that is, they are true or false. They are the objects of propositional knowledge. When we claim to know that *p* is the case, we are claiming that *p* is true. Here are three examples of propositional knowledge: "I know that the sun will rise tomorrow," "I know that I have a mind," and "I know that Columbus discovered America in 1492." (p. 2)

All three examples of propositional statements provided above can be either verified or falsified. Logically, none of those statements can be both true and false simultaneously. Wherever one of such statements is false, then its opposite must be true; conversely, wherever one of such statements is true, then its opposite must be false. Thus, the verification process may use various methods that test both the "truth" value of knowledge claim and the source of that knowledge.

It should be noted that philosophers' attempts to distinguish among various kinds of knowledge is not new. The Greek language, which has immensely informed philosophical discourses of knowledge, features various Greek equivalents for the English verb "to know." In addition to "episteme," *oida* is also a Greek word for "to know" and it is suggestive of experiential knowledge. *Ginosko* is another Greek equivalent for "to know." Perhaps more important than the Greek words affecting our understanding of knowledge are the notions of knowledge, which have been extensively and judiciously treated in the works of Greek thinkers.

The list of Greek thinkers is without a doubt extremely long, featuring Protagoras, Pythagoras, Socrates, Plato, and Aristotle, along with other distinct groups of Greek thinkers such as the Sophists, the Epicureans, and the Stoics. All of the aforementioned Greek thinkers or groups have, in one way or another, contributed to modern concepts of knowledge or have contributed to projects seeking to answer questions related to the source, the essence, and the certainty of knowledge (Kenny, 2010). But we want to focus on the works of Plato, particularly the *Theaetetus* that casts Socrates and the *Republic* as well as the works of Aristotle in *Nicomachean Ethics* and *Posterior Analytics.*

The importance of Socrates, Plato, and Aristotle in understanding the concept of knowledge cannot be overstated. *Theaetetus*, for instance, focuses on answering the question "what is knowledge?" Most of the domains that are referred to as sources of knowledge—perception, reason, memory, and consciousness (Audi, 2003)—have their origins steeped in the works of Greek thinkers. For instance, according to Kenny (2010), *Theaetetus* proposes knowledge be viewed as geometry, astronomy, shoemaking, and carpentry, and he argues that "to know something is to perceive it with the senses" (p. 123). The notion of knowledge as perception was a position apparently held by Protagoras, but Plato set the stage where Socrates examined that position in considering its soundness (Kenny, 2010). In his evaluation of perception as knowledge, Socrates, as Kenny points out, readily granted that there are "ordinary cases" when this notion of knowledge as perception is not "erroneous," but denied these might be "cases of real knowledge" (p. 124).

Kenny (2010) skillfully breaks down the reasons why Socrates denied the notion of knowledge as perception:

> There are cases of perception without knowledge: we can hear a foreign language spoken, and yet do not the language (163b). There are cases of knowledge without perception: when we shut our eyes and recall something we have seen, we know what it looks like and yes are no longer seeing it (164a). But if knowing = perception, then both these must be cases of simultaneously knowing and not knowing, and surely that is an absurdity? (p. 124)

The dialogue continues between Theaetetus and Socrates, even after Theaetetus' proposition of knowledge as perception has been rejected. Determined to gain Socrates' assent on a definite understanding of knowledge, Theaetetus theorized once more that knowledge should be "thought (*doxa*), and thought is an activity of the soul by itself" (Kenny, 2010, p. 125). Theaetetus' proposition of knowledge as "thought" suggests that the thinking process of the mind is in and of itself "knowledge."

The assumption of this proposition is that when the mind thinks, it is engaging in an activity of questioning and answering different topics while "forming opinions" in the process. That, according to Theaetetus, equals to knowledge. According to Kenny, Socrates rejected that proposition on the basis that "there are false thoughts" (p. 125). Expanding on the notion of knowledge as thought, Theaetetus then added *logos* as a buffer, claiming that knowledge is "true thought, plus *logos*" (Kenny, 2010, p. 125). Theaetetus hoped to further qualify "true thought" with logos. This seems an apparent effort to capitalize on Socrates' slight willingness to grant "knowledge as true thought," as suggested by Kenny (2010). Hence, *logos* is expected to manifest in three different forms—expression, analysis, and description—which, in Socrates' assessment, turned out to be insufficient to support the proposition of knowledge as thought, plus logos (Kenny 2010).

Like Socrates and Plato, Aristotle spent considerable energy unraveling questions pertinent to the sources and the essence as well as the validity of knowledge claims. Aristotle's elaboration on these questions takes place primarily in the *Nicomachean Ethics. Arete*, *techne*, *episteme*, *phronesis*, *ergon*, *poiesis*, and *praxis* are recurring terms in the *Nicomachean Ethics* (Kenny, 2010). The ultimate question for Aristotle is how these seemingly varying terms could work to produce knowledge. Kenny (2010) captures how Aristotle synthesized these notions to conceive a knowledge that is deemed excellent:

> The nature of the *arete* of anything depends on its *ergon*, that is to say its job or characteristic output. The *ergon* of the mind and all its faculties is the production of true or false judgments (*NE* 6.2. 1139a29) That, at least is its *ergon* in the sense of its characteristic activity, its output whether it is working well or ill; its activity, when it is working well and doing its job, and therefore its *ergon* in the strict sense, is truth alone (2. 1139b12). The intellectual *aretai*, then, are excellences that make an intellectual part of the soul come out with truth. There are five states of the mind that have this effect—*techne, episteme, phronesis, sophia, nous*—which we may translate as skill, science, wisdom, understanding, and insight (3. 1139b16–17). (p. 132)

For Aristotle, insofar as knowledge of any subject regarding the world (both material and immaterial) is concerned, the human mind is always at work.

Hence, the mind plays a central role in understanding as well as obtaining knowledge whose object is related to the material and the immaterial world. *Logocentric* principle of knowledge in both Plato's and Aristotle's philosophies necessarily include a value component. Both philosophers sought proper ways to apply reason for the ultimate benefit of human beings—for them to live a fully satisfied life. Plato was convinced that his philosophy "could provide a science of the soul that would cure diseases of thought, judgment, and desire and deliver people from the sufferings of their ordinary lives" (Polkinghorne, 2004, p. 101). Conversely, Aristotle, although primarily agreeing with his mentor on the centrality of the reason-*logos* principle to make good judgments, claimed that living a fulfilling, happy and, therefore, a good life cannot be reduced to the skills of science-*techne* coupled with an ultimate ("true") knowledge-*episteme*. Aristotle believed that people know from experience what happiness and fulfillment are about and he conceived a human being as "fully embodied entity" with both reason and emotions involved in their "decisions about how to live the good life" (Polkinghorne, 2004, p. 109). Therefore, Aristotle's treatment of *phronesis* as "practical wisdom" acquires a more interesting and complex rendition than it does in Plato's philosophy.

Aristotle distinguished between three major tasks in human life and their corresponding activities. First, we need to develop a theory (*theoria*) which requires an application of mathematical and logical reasoning (*episteme*); then follows the task of *techne*, or the "scientific" skills of making artifacts which requires *poiesis*—the knowledge or wherewithal to produce objects; and finally, there is a need for *praxis*, or "acting for the good life of the other or the state," which requires the use of *phronesis* or practical reasoning (Polkinghorne, 2004, p. 112). *Praxis* acquires an important place in Aristotle's philosophy which intentionally connects the benefits that we can reap from proper application of reason to make good decisions which consequently lead to a fulfilled and happy life. Aristotle's principles of *phronesis* and *praxis* influenced the works of such twentieth-century thinkers as Arendt, Collingwood, Habermas, Heidegger, and Lyotard.

In *The Human Condition* (1998), Arendt expresses deep concerns about the decline of genuine political life in contemporary Western democracies and urges us "to think what we are doing," to invigorate a sense of the good and purposeful life through the synergy of *vita activa* (active life) and *vita contemplativa* (contemplative life). Arendt (1998) revitalizes the Aristotelian notion of *bios politikos*—the life "devoted to the matters of the *polis*," the "realm of human affairs," stressing action, or *praxis*, as the activity that will "establish and sustain it" (p. 7). Through acting and speaking, or "good deeds" and "good words," which Arendt associates with full engagement in social and political life, we can reclaim the lost meaning of *bios politikos* and can thus restore the notion of the good life. In the evolutionary process of re-awakening *bios politicos*, Arendt distinguishes between several fundamental human activities—"labor," "work," and "action," of which only "action" epitomizes genuine *praxis* and a fulfilled life. Although labor and work are worthwhile practices, they cannot satisfy our political aspirations, for it is only an action due to its condition of plurality that is "specifically *the* condition of all political life" (Arendt, 1998, p. 7).

The caveat of a logocentric principle in Western philosophy is that the mind must do its work well to arrive at any of its objectives such as skill, science, wisdom, understanding, and insight. Fast forwarding to the eighteenth century, these terms—skill, science, wisdom, understanding, and insight—which were wrought on the history of ideas by Greek philosophers, had continued to dominate the discourse on knowledge. Medieval philosophy is similarly important, but we consider it beyond the scope and objectives of this project; hence we have fast-forwarded to the eighteenth-century era, which might arguably be the stepping-stone or precursor to contemporary philosophy.

As stated earlier, Greek philosophical ideas, as enshrined particularly in the works of Socrates, Plato, and Aristotle, have had an immense influence on modern and contemporary Western ideas; however, the relationship between Greek philosophers and European philosophers during the eighteenth century is seldom consonant. Kenny (2010) illustrates this quite beautifully with his observation on the anticlimactic end of the discourses between Theaetetus and Socrates:

> Perhaps Theaetetus gave up too soon. If he had offered a fourth account [the three accounts he gave were words of expression, analysis, and description] of *logos* as meaning something like "justification," "reason," or evidence, then his definition of knowledge as true belief plus logos would have been found satisfactory by many a philosopher during the subsequent millennia of philosophy. (p. 126)

Indeed, Theaetetus would have found an eager audience among philosophers in the eighteenth century and today, not simply because "logos" is widely viewed as rational method to justify belief or ideas, but also because perception, which was rejected by Socrates, is widely accepted as a source of knowledge by contemporary philosophers. In this regard, Winkler (2006) writes:

> For the most part, eighteenth century philosophers viewed the understanding as one of several "faculties" or powers of the human mind; perception (or one

> of its cognates) was their preferred label for its characteristic or most basic act or operation. In this they followed the example set by Descartes, Malebranche, and Locke. The word perception was also used, however, as a synonym for idea—that is, as a label for the object of an act of understanding. (p. 236)

If Winkler is right about how eighteenth-century philosophers viewed perception, which he is, then the result of whatsoever the human mind attempted to understand would be understood. According to those philosophers, the mind would yield an epistemological product, which would have been "labeled" perception. This is not the only instance where modern or contemporary philosophers have departed from their Greek forefathers such as Socrates, Plato, and Aristotle. The Sophists espoused a view of knowledge which Socrates and Plato loathed. In particular, they emerged and thrived approximately in the same era as Socrates and Plato, although many prominent sophists preceded both Socrates and Plato. Sophists shared a deep skepticism about absolute knowledge and truth. Essentially, they rejected the existence of absolute knowledge and truth which they rendered relative (*cognitive relativism*). Sophists embraced and taught rhetoric as a special skill, and they emphasized "process, skill, and technique" (Johnson, 1998, p. 202). Sophists believed that special skill, rhetoric, could be applied to personal and social matters. Hence, rhetoric, for sophists, was the only skill that mattered and was worth teaching.

Perhaps, more important is the deep skepticism that was embedded in the notion of truth as subjective, as opposed to objective (Johnson, 1998). The philosophical commitment of the Sophists was devoid of absolute truths and ethical standards, which undermined what Socrates, Plato, and Aristotle taught and propagated. Particularly, Socrates contended that having expert knowledge is important and is in fact requisite for anyone to be able to teach genuinely and skillfully (Johnson, 1998, p. 208). Various modern and contemporary philosophers who have also raised reasonable doubt regarding the nature of knowledge have espoused this same philosophical commitment as the sophists.

In addition to reason and perception, many philosophers have proposed memory as a source of knowledge as well. Hartley and Hume placed varying degrees of reliability on memory. Winkler (2006) provides an insightful summary of how Hartley and Hume, along with other eighteenth-century philosophers, conceived memory:

> Memory was generally understood as a power to reproduce earlier ideas or representations. It was often described as a faculty of recalling sensations and the ideas derived from them—one that preserves the combination or order they had when they entered the mind. In Hartley, for example, traces of sensations

> and ideas are recalled "in the same order and proportion, accurately or nearly" (Observations). Like others who offered this standard definition, Hartley did not ask whether memory is a faculty that somehow aspires to accuracy or one that achieves it by definition. (p. 256)

The ability to reproduce and to represent ideas is posited as "a faculty of recalling sensations," but the mind plays a vital role in that it serves as the space housing objects, images, or ideas that might have crossed the mind at earlier stages. Interestingly, Hartley stops short of claiming the reproduction and representations engendered by these so-called "recalling sensations" are accurate. But there are many other philosophers who posit memory as a valid source knowledge capable of producing reliable understanding and knowledge. For instance, Audi (2003) claims: "Our beliefs are countless and varied. A vast proportion of them are stored in memory, though beliefs do not originate there" (p. 330). The caveat with memory is that it supposedly preserves beliefs but does not produce them. Furthermore, Audi goes on to elaborate:

> Metaphorically, [this] epistemological picture portrays both knowledge and justification as grounded in looking and thereby seeing. Perception looks outward, and through it we see the physical world. Memory looks backward, and through it we see the past, or at least some of the past. Introspection looks inward, and through it we see the stream of our own consciousness. Reason looks beyond experience of the world of space and time, and through it we see concepts and their relations. Testimony, our chief social source of knowledge, looks to others and thereby draws on all of these individual sources in those who convey their knowledge to us. (Audi, 2003, p. 332)

In the preceding quote, Audi elaborates on his perspective on memory as a source of knowledge. In addition, Audi briefly describes other sources of knowledge, such as reason, consciousness, and testimony, while showing their connectivity as well as their collective contribution to knowledge, or our grasp and certainty thereof. Also important in Audi's remarks is the notion of belief.

For many philosophers, knowledge is belief justified by reason or other evidence. In their piece "Knowledge: Undefeated Justified True Belief," Lehrer and Paxson (1999) advance the thesis of knowledge as belief. First, they use two different notions—justified true belief and undefeated justified true belief—to support their claim of knowledge as belief. Lehrer and Paxson begin their piece with the following explanation:

> If a man knows that statement is true even though there is no other statement that justifies his belief, then his knowledge is basic. Basic knowledge is completely justified true belief. On the other hand, if a man knows that a statement is true because there is some other statement that justifies his belief, then his knowledge is non-basic. Non-basic knowledge requires something in addition

> to completely justified true belief; for, though, a statement completely justifies a man in his belief, there may be some true statement that defeats his justification. So, we must add the condition that his justification is not defeated. (p. 153)

Hence, "undefeated justified true belief" represents something someone believes to be true and which has been justified by something or someone other than that thing believed to be true or justified by someone other than the claimer. The importance of justifying claims of knowledge and the persistence of the view of knowledge as belief have conceived two different philosophical frameworks—*foundationalism and non-foundationalism*—within which issues of subjectivity, relativeness, objectivity, validity, and truthfulness of knowledge are raised. Kuehn (2006) claims that the seventeenth-century philosophical issues related to knowledge and the certainty thereof are antecedents of the philosophical concerns of the eighteenth century. He elaborates:

> During the Middle Ages, the problem of knowledge and belief has been assimilated into the problem of knowledge versus (religious) faith. The thinkers of the eighteenth century tried to escape the problem connected with this religious dimension. In doing so, they were deeply influenced by developments of the preceding century (the beginning of the modern period). It has been argued that all of their problems had their roots in the seventeenth century. This is an exaggeration, but it is true that for understanding the framework in which the problem of knowledge and belief arose for the eighteenth century, it is necessary to know the broad outlines of the discussion of knowledge in the seventeenth century and especially theories of Rene Descartes and John Locke. (pp. 390–391)

Indeed, the mid-seventeenth century in Europe was marked by major paradigm shifts in the developments of philosophical ideas. Descartes and Locke indubitably represent two foremost and perhaps most influential thinkers of that era, and their ideas have laid the foundation for epistemological foundationalism. Conceptually, foundationalism embodies

> the view that knowledge and epistemic (knowledge-relevant) justification have a two-tier structure: some instances of knowledge and justification are non-inferential, or foundational; and all other instances thereof are inferential, or non-foundational, in that they derive ultimately from foundational knowledge or justification. (Moser, 2006, p. 321)

Thus, foundationalism represents a larger philosophical framework, which is underpinned by the presupposition that human beings can be certain of knowledge and that their knowledge claims can be objective. Both Descartes and Locke embraced scientific knowledge, but they disagreed sharply on the process to obtain such knowledge (method).

For Descartes, "knowledge was essentially independent of sense perception" (Kuehn, 2006, p. 391). The process leading to the grasp as well as the certainty of knowledge involves belief and subjectivity, but does not end at either one (Kuehn, 2006). However, Locke's view of knowledge was grounded in a deep and even unwavering commitment to sense perception, which one could say is empiricism at its purest. Essentially, Locke posited that the mind was an empty slate (tabula rasa) with knowledge of its own but has to rely on the experiences wrought on it by sensuous experiences. Moreover,

> Locke believed that there were basically three kinds of such perceptions, namely, intuition, demonstration, and sensation. Intuitive knowledge is based on immediate agreements and disagreements between ideas. In demonstrative knowledge, we must rely on intermediate ideas when we compare two ideas. It needs arguments and proofs, or demonstrations. Sensitive knowledge reaches "no farther than the Existence of Things" actually present to our Senses. (Kuehn, 2006, p. 393)

While Descartes and Locke obviously disagreed on the process and method to obtain knowledge, they shared the belief that human beings are able to acquire knowledge and be certain of that knowledge once acquired. For Descartes, the certainty of cognitive objectivity can be acquired by deduction (mathematical), and for Locke such certainty can be reached through sense perception. The legacies of Descartes and Locke, particularly they relate to the justification of knowledge, live on in the philosophy of science as well.

Philosophy of Science: Science Challenged and Redefined

Philosophy of science deals with the application of epistemological concerns to a variety of areas of study and it proposes methods that can lead those areas of study to satisfactory results. Due to major scientific and technological advancements in nuclear physics, mathematics, neuroscience, chemistry, and biology, twentieth-century philosophy had to engage more vigorously with a scientific world to rethink its dominant role in liberal arts and sciences. Until about the seventeenth century, in the West, philosophy's domain included both physical and metaphysical concerns and its reign as *philosophia vero omnium mater* (from Latin, "the mother of all arts and sciences") was unquestionable. This started to change rapidly from the industrial revolution onward, and by the end of the twentieth century, philosophy clearly lost its ultimate authority in providing an all-encompassing picture of the world. This task was left to individual disciplines, whereas philosophy acquired a more supportive role in examining language statements and their meaning within these disciplines. Philosophers of science became preoccupied with the methods (and their critique) used by natural sciences and the analysis of a variety of concepts pertaining to scientific theories. It became apparent that a critical reexamination of scientific method was overdue. The very question of what counts as knowledge was subject to an unprecedented scrutiny by the twentieth-century advancements in theoretical physics.

According to Papineau (1996), two sets of concerns dominate the current philosophy of science, creating "two broad areas" (p. 290). The first broad area investigates the question "whether science ever uncovers permanent truths, whether objective decisions between competing theories are possible and whether the results of experiment are clouded by prior theoretical expectations" (p. 290). The last broad category, according to Papineau, focuses on "the metaphysics of science," examining scientific claims about the natural and related phenomena.

Contemporary philosophy of science features various philosophers, but we want to highlight the contributions of Gaston Bachelard (1884–1962) and Thomas Kuhn (1922–1996). Because of the fact that the translations of the works of Continental philosophers from a variety of their respective languages into English can be a matter of time, many of their works often become available to English-speaking audiences later than their original publications. This was the case with French philosopher Gaston Bachelard who in the 1930s developed a theory of "epistemological breaks," which was further elaborated in Thomas Kuhn's theory of paradigm shifts.

The corpus of Gaston Bachelard features work encompassing science, poetry, epistemology, and imagination. To Bachelard, imagination, more than reason, is a unifying force in the human soul. Bachelard's poetics is linked essentially to his epistemology and more general views on the history of arts and sciences. His widely acclaimed notion of ***epistemological obstacle*** (also known as ***epistemological break*** or, interchangeably, ***epistemological rupture***) provides, on the one hand, a sharp criticism of positivism, and on the other, a solid justification for an integrated approach to knowledge and intuition, rational and irrational, and scientific and poetic.

Yet, another fascinating feature of Bachelard's work is the integration of epistemology and psychoanalysis. This integration of epistemology and psychoanalysis ends up functioning as a sort of "therapeutic" effect on "objective" knowledge, whereby utilitarian and mundane irrationalities that impede the progress of objective knowledge are removed. In addition, psychoanalysis helped him understand how "blockages" are formed in some people that prevent them from the formation of the scientific mind. He called these blockages "epistemological obstacles." Even a healthy mind, he thought, still has some "dark areas, traces of the old in our new ways of thinking" (Bachelard, 2002,

p. 20). Eventually, his study of "pre-scientific" texts led him to conclude that "the age of reason" was also marked by "unreason" as he determined how even some among the so-called "educated" people of his era displayed "disturbed" minds about some scientific discoveries such as electricity.

Bachelard posited that the formation of the scientific mind requires three stages of development: the concrete, the concrete-abstract, and the abstract. Having examined the epistemological obstacles to objective thought (2002), he changed his position on the primacy of the scientific mind. The impetus that caused the change in his position is that he came to understand that imagination is not an obstacle but an essential element of psychic dynamism. Epistemology thus represents two dialectical activities, intellectual and imaginative, which should form the rhythm of life (Bachelard, 2000). Hence, Bachelard (2004) claims, "Without the help of poets, what can a philosopher, weighted down with years, do if he persists talking about imagination? He has no one to test. He would immediately get lost in the labyrinth of tests and counter-tests" (Bachelard, 2004, p. 25).

Inspired by Bachelard's ideas, Kuhn developed a theory of paradigm shifts that shed additional light on a new conception of science and scientific knowledge. Kuhn spent about 15 years studying the history of science that resulted in his famous *The Structure of Scientific Revolutions* (1962). He came to the conclusion that the development of science is not a linear and cumulative process. Some theories can be contradictory. His central concept is that of a paradigm whose definition entered most etymological and philosophical dictionaries as a "constellation of beliefs, values, and techniques shared by the members of a given scientific community" (Runes, 1983, p. 240).

In his seminal work, *The Structure of Scientific Revolutions* (1962), Kuhn maintains that some paradigms are general and encompassing, while others guide scientific thinking within specific areas of study. A paradigm is essential in the process of observation and experiment:

> Paradigms provide scientists not only with a map but also with some of the directions essential for map-making. In learning a paradigm the scientist acquires theory, methods, and standards together, usually in an inextricable mixture. Therefore, when paradigms change, there are usually significant shifts in the criteria determining the legitimacy both of problems and of proposed solutions. (Kuhn, 2000, p. 519)

A scientist cannot avoid bringing a definite belief system into the area of study. Kuhn observed that early stages of most sciences went through "pre-paradigm periods" characterized by conceptual chaos and competing views of nature. Paradigm debates always involve the question: "Which problems is it more significant to have solved? Like the issue of competing standards, that question of values can be answered only in terms of criteria that lie outside of normal science altogether, and it is that recourse to external criteria that most obviously makes paradigm debates revolutionary" (Kuhn, 2000, p. 519). When the majority of the scientific community accepts a paradigm, this newly accepted paradigm becomes a "warrant"—a mandatory way of approaching problems ("normal science"). A new and radical theory is not an addition to the existing knowledge but its interruption.

Kuhn's theory of paradigm shifts reinforces the general assumptions held by the twentieth-century philosophers of science—that our knowledge of the world is essentially fallible and, if acquired, it can only represent the best explanation available. Any new discovery can potentially lead to a dramatic shift in our view of the world's picture. This new understanding of science proposes an expanded notion of reason supported by a hermeneutic and a pragmatic logic. Charles S. Peirce (see Chapter 2), for instance, regarded the knowledge of science not as "the truth" but only as its approximation. "Truth" thus represents the effectiveness of our knowledge as demonstrated by the effectiveness of our action. Peirce also believed that knowledge was a communal achievement and that the community ("scientific community," as he would have it) had to make a decision to accept or reject a given paradigm of knowledge.

Considering the multifaceted constellation of existing beliefs, epistemological pluralism is the position from which one ought to approach the question of methods in both natural and human sciences. Contemporary inquiry often represents *syncretic* research which "proposes something more than the use of multiple systems of inquiry: it proposes the additional step of syncretizing the results of the multiple inquiries into a unified and integral result" (Polkinghorne, 1983, p. 254). For instance, German philosopher Otto Apel (b. 1922) proposed syncretic research in psychoanalysis in a form of "tacking," or "zigzagging," whereby the researcher "first is engaged in the research process, then distances himself from it, analyzes and reevaluates his position, and then returns to be a participant of the research again" (Polkinghorne, 1983, p. 255). Jurgen Habermas (b. 1929) developed the project that syncretized hermeneutic and empirical sciences to create guidelines for the logic of a critical science, and this will be the focus of our further discussion.

The Fallen Skies of Epistemological Certainty

"Positive" Knowledge Dethroned

The foundationalist assumptions of scientific knowledge, as enshrined in the philosophical works of Descartes and Locke, dominated epistemological discourses in the West for a long time. These assumptions have culminated in the positivist conception of science which held that only those things of which we are absolutely certain can be counted as knowledge. However, at the turn of the twentieth century, the "fallen angels" of logical positivism were overpowered by the new forces coming from several movements in the philosophy of science (see Chapter 2). Logical positivism was dethroned as supposedly the only valid scientific paradigm by the new developments in nuclear physics and microbiology. The nature of science and its scope have changed dramatically through the expansion of the boundaries of scientific inquiry which shifted radically from positivistic and reductionist models. An understanding of science by Anglo-American and Continental philosophers shifted entirely from the positivist to the post-positivist conception of science. The pioneering philosophers of science who championed the cause of questioning the absolute certainty of positivistic science were Bachelard, Kuhn, Frank, Popper, and Feyerabend, among a few others. Karl Popper (1902–1994) was one of the first to contest the claims of positivistic science by raising questions of scientific method that posit observation as its stepping-stone leading to theoretical formulations.

Paul Feyerabend (1924–1994) provided radical criticism of positivistic scientific methodology in his seminal work, *Against Method: Outline of an Anarchistic Theory* (1978). *Against Method* begins with Feyerabend's celebrated quote: "Science is an essentially anarchic enterprise: theoretical anarchism is more humanitarian and more likely to encourage progress than its law-and-order alternatives" (Feyerabend, 2000, p. 493). Feyerabend insists on the fact that science is not and cannot be governed by a system of firm, unchanging, and absolute principles and that all methodologies have their limits. The history of science "does not just consist of facts and conclusions drawn from facts. It also contains ideas, interpretations of facts, problems created by conflicting interpretations, mistakes, and so on" (Feyerabend, 2000, p. 495). To put it differently, there is no single theory that agrees with all the facts in its domain. In agreement with Bachelard and Kuhn, Feyerabend asserts that history clearly shows us that "epistemological breaks" have been necessary to propel scientific progress. Accordingly, pluralistic methodology becomes a necessity when comparing rival theories and ideas. Feyerabend's principle of methodological anarchism finds its utmost expression in the following statement: "[T]he idea of a fixed method, or of a fixed theory of rationality, rests on too naïve a view of man and his social surroundings. [It is clear that] the only one principle that can be defended under *all* circumstances and in all stages of human development is the principle: *anything goes*" (Feyerabend, 2000, p. 502).

"Anything goes" is the principle that can be leveraged against the backdrop of the debate formulated by the skeptics who believed that there could be only two propositions of knowledge—apodictic and problematic (see the discussion above). It follows then that a proposition can be either "infallible and beyond doubt or dubious and, therefore, not *episteme*" (Polkinghorne, 1983, p. 12). However, and as Feyerabend so vigorously claims, there can be indeed "assertoric" propositions that stand between apodictic ("infallible") and problematic ("dubious"). Assertoric propositions, although "supported by evidence," still "remain open to future confirmation and correction as more experience is gained" (Polkinghorne, 1983, p. 12). It follows then that between the extremes of absolute certainly and absolute uncertainty, "statements of knowledge can be judged against each other, and some of them can be accepted and used as the base for action while others can be rejected" (Polkinghorne, 1983, p. 13). The acceptance of assertoric knowledge as a legitimate goal of science "has reopened a possibility for alternative epistemological frameworks" (Polkinghorne, 1983, p. 12). Pertaining to the disputable nature of knowledge claims is the fact that knowledge is being developed in a "historical and cultural context, and it is subject to the limitations of the conceptual and technical tools of its situation" (Polkinghorne, 1983, p. 242).

A new understanding of science based on the fallibilistic and conditional nature of knowledge ushered in the development of pluralistic epistemologies. Although originated much earlier in time (see Chapter 2), hermeneutics was perhaps one of the most potent movements that challenged the notion of knowledge that was restricted to specifically the rationalist domain. *Understanding* (*verstehen* in German) becomes hermeneutic knowledge. The upper-case letter "U" underscores the importance of the notion. Without a capital letter "U," understanding refers to any kind of comprehension. Yet when capitalized, the word denotes a "specific type of understanding, the comprehension of meaning" (Polkinghorne, 1983p. 217). *Understanding* thus becomes a way of knowing and a method whereby researchers apprehend the meaning and translate it into a variety of forms of data to serve the purposes of their research.

Hermeneutics emphasizes the "embededness of knowledge in historically particular and contingent vocabularies" (Westphal, 2006, p. 416). Philosophical hermeneutics of Heidegger and Gadamer represent, by far, one of the most influential anti-positivist responses. Heidegger, for instance, repudiates foundationalism in his account of the hermeneutic circle. He draws distinctions between linguistic and prelinguistic interpretation of the text. To him, interpretation is always *seeing-as*. There is, in other words, an a priori understanding before we enter the circle, and it is, in fact, our understanding of ourselves. Every act of interpretation thus presupposes our understanding of ourselves as a thrown projection in our dealings with things. Heidegger admits that knowledge does have foundations, but "the basis of the linguistic expressions that are the bearers of truth or falsity are not those representations that are epistemically privileged, [but rather] practices that are not truth bearing" (Westphal, 2006, p. 424). Heidegger makes practice foundational to his epistemology and looks for a more primordial conception of truth which he often labels as "unconcealment" (along with some other terms).

Jurgen Habermas extended the hermeneutic tradition to the study of social theory, thus providing a sharp criticism of positivistic science. Habermas' ideas, along with those of other twentieth-century critical and postmodern philosophers, represent a concerted effort to deconstruct the very notion of episteme as a hegemonic construct in advanced Western powers.

Episteme Deconstructed

Critical hermeneutics positions Habermas within the milieu of the Continental postmodern/poststructuralist contemporary thinkers such as Jean-Francois Lyotard (1924–1998), Gille Deleuze (1925–1995), Michel Foucault (1926–1984), Jean Baudrillard (1929–2007), Jacques Derrida (1930–2004), and Julie Kristeva (b. 1941), among a few others, who have been performing deconstructive works and situated themselves within the postmodern outlook, which views itself as essentially different from modernism. Loyard's description of postmodernism as "incredulity toward metanarratives" (as cited in Rose, 1991, p. 55) puts deconstruction in perspective. Hence the project of deconstruction has been primarily about deconstructing metanarratives of any sort, including epistemological frameworks. Particularly, deconstructive works focus on delineating the political, social, and economic influences on what knowledge is accepted as valid and objective.

The history of postmodern outlook can be traced to nineteenth-century British artists. In the beginning of the twentieth century, the label of postmodernism was attached to a broad movement in art also known as "post-impressionist" or "post-industrial." Nietzsche is considered by many a presage of postmodern thought, which he expressed as the crisis of modernity [of his time] and the advent of a new age of *Übermensch* (see Chapter 2). The modern era is typically associated with the rise of natural sciences and the decline of the centralized power of Christendom (predominantly Catholicism). Secular movements within the Age of Enlightenment are also referred to the modern era. A modernist was regarded as a person committed to the modern age who believed that "traditions must be overthrown or redefined in order to do justice to the new forms of experience" (Scruton, 1996, p. 2). English-speaking philosophy is "modern, but not modernist. French philosophy [. . .] (e.g., Derrida, Foucualt) is modernist, without being particularly modern, i.e., without basing itself in the assessment of arguments, or in the desire to build on established truths" (Scruton, 1996, p. 2). At the turn of the twentieth century, the label "postmodern" was adopted by several French thinkers who had been sparking the debates of the "arching questions of the human spirit" (Scruton, 1996, p. 3).

The concern with these debates was unavoidable for Jurgen Habermas. In his opus magnum *Knowledge and Human Interests* (1972), Habermas brings forth the following three major theses: that (1) "*achievements of the transcendental subject have their basis in the natural history of the human species;*" (2) that "*knowledge equally serves as an instrument and transcends mere self-preservations;*" and (3) that "*knowledge-constitutive interests take form in the medium of work, language, and power*" (Habermas, 1972, pp. 312–313).

Especially important for educational inquiry, Habermas further draws distinctions regarding the three different modes of research associated with human interests. First, in the *empirical-analytic sciences*, "knowledge is [...] predictive knowledge. However, the *meaning* of such predictions, that is their technical exploitability, is established only by the rules according to which we apply theories to reality" (Habermas, 1972, p. 308). Further, the *historical-hermeneutic sciences*

> gain knowledge in a different methodological framework. Here the meaning of the validity of propositions is not constituted in the frame of reference of technical control. [. . .] Theories are not constructed deductively and experience is not organized with regard to the success of operations. Access to the facts is provided by the understanding of meaning, not observation. (Habermas, 1972, p. 309)

And finally, the "systematic *sciences of social action*, that is economics, sociology, and political science, have the goal [. . .] of producing nomological knowledge" (Habermas, 1972, p. 310). Habermas vehemently emphasizes that a critical social science will never be satisfied with such an outcome. It should be "concerned with going beyond this goal to determine when theoretical statements grasp invariant regularities of social action as such and when they express ideologically frozen relations of dependence that can in principle be transformed" (Habermas, 1972, p. 310). The methodological framework that Habermas proposes for determining the meaning of the validity of critical propositions of this type of inquiry is established by *self-refection* ("reflexivity"). Self-reflection designates an emancipatory cognitive interest.

Habermas' emancipatory and self-reflective practices incite social imaginations of postmodern and poststructuralist thinkers. Foucault (1967), for instance, proposes a metaphor of *heterotopia*, denoting a concept of human geography (place, space, dwelling, etc.). Heterotopia represents a *real* space (as opposed to utopia) which allows for generating non-hegemonic conditions of "otherness." Foucault maintains that there are *real* places in every culture and in every civilization that are formed in the very founding of society, which are "something like counter-sites, a kind of effectively enacted utopia in which the real sites, all the other real sites that can be found within the culture, are simultaneously represented, contested, and inverted" (Foucault, 1967, p. 3). Foucault's concern is with the spirit of individual and social imagination that should spur the societal and political change in an oppressive society.

Jacques Derrida, another prominent figure in postmodern and poststructuralist movement, is known for his radical hermeneutics. Derrida's main thesis is, "nothing is outside the text." This means, epistemologically, that "being must always already be conceptualized," and, ontologically, that "the thing itself is a sign" (Westphal, 2006, p. 430). In maintaining that there will always be at least two interpretations of interpretation [of the text], Derrida not just overcomes metaphysics, he essentially abolishes it. The critique of logocentric principle in the history of Western philosophy finds its ultimate expression in the philosophy of Derrida that can be briefly captured in the notions of identity and difference, or in other words, of continuity and being *deferred*. Derrida coins the word *differance* to convey both the difference and deferral. There is no knowledge as such, concludes Derrida, and its use-value becomes a mere production for "sale."

Jean Baudrillard's (1929–2007) postmodern critique of social realities in advanced Western powers is expressed through his extravagant images of simulacra and hyperreality. Assuming that we are the inhabitants of a postmodern world where the demarcation lines between what is real and what is not are simply impossible to draw, then, as Baudrillard suggests, most of us are confined to a hyperreality of Disneyland, a "perfect model of all the entangled orders of simulation":

> This imaginary world is supposed to be what makes the operation successful. But, what draws the crowds is undoubtedly much more the social microcosm, the miniaturized and *religious* reveling in real America, in its delights and drawbacks. [...] The objective profile of the United States [...] may be traced throughout Disneyland [...]. All its values are exalted here, in miniature and comic-strip form. Embalmed and pacified. Whence the possibility of an ideological analysis of Disneyland: ... digest of the contradictory reality. But this conceals something else, and that "ideological" blanket exactly serves to cover a *third-order simulation*: Disneyland is there to conceal the fact that it is the "real" country, all of "real" America, which *is* Disneyland. (Baudrillard, 1999, p. 485)

Baudrillard urges individuals to reawaken their self-consciousness and break away from illusions, deceptions, and oppressive influences of omnipotent and transcendent powers of politics, ideology, religion, or consumerism.

The domino effect of critical poststructuralist Continental philosophers produced a vibrant constellation of Anglo-American thinkers. Critical feminists who followed in the footsteps of their foremothers such as Simone de Beauvoir (1908–1986) ushered in several movements critical to the development of gender and identity issues in contemporary educational inquiry. Sociologist Dorothy Smith (b. 1926), for instance, argued that women experience the world differently from men, since men encounter the world "already processed" (e.g., meals prepared, laundry done), while the work of women is "the processing of the raw material" into a form "suitable for consumption" (Longino, 2006). Psychologist Carol Gilligan "criticized her colleague Lawrence Kohlberg's account of moral development as resting too much on a pattern ascertained from male samples" (Longino, 2006, p. 330). Educational psychologist Mary Belenky and her colleagues suggest that "women learn through connection rather than separation"; and they claim this as a "way of knowing" (Longino, 2006, p. 330).

One of the consistent themes running through the feminist rethinking of the subject of knowledge is the "insistence on its embodiment" (Longino, 2006, p. 331), which concerns the mind-body problem in Western philosophy. The disembodied self is a "Cartesian masculine subject." It is in fact displaced onto the bodies of "feminized and primitivized Others—European women and nonwhite women and men—who are thereby epistemologically disfranchised" (Longino, 2006, p. 332).

Haraway (1999) contributed to the feminist and postmodern critique of the philosophy of science as an essentially masculine project. Along with this critique, Haraway deconstructs the mythology of a unified women's movement on the basis of her argument of our "fractured identities":

> There is nothing about being "female" that naturally binds women. There is not even such a state as "being" female, itself a highly complex category constructed in contested sexual scientific discourses and other social practices. Gender, race, or class consciousness is an achievement forced on us by the terrible historical experience of the contradictory social realities of patriarchy, colonialism, and capitalism. (p. 540)

Haraway's concern is with feminists' "lapsing into boundless difference" and "giving up on the confusing task of making partial, real connections"; some differences are "playful; some are poles of world historical systems of domination. 'Epistemology' is about knowing the difference" (p. 543).

Embodiment is an important construct to delineate standpoint epistemologies championed by Donna Haraway in her essay, *Situated Knowledges* (1988). Standpoint epistemology represents an analysis of some Marxist ideas regarding the position of workers as opposed to "capitalists." Workers' understanding of their condition gave them privilege over capitalists, and this superiority could be regarded as both epistemological and political. Additionally, sexual division of labor in childbearing provided the basis for the opposed structuring of material life of women and men. Although the standpoint epistemological assumptions shared the above Marxist-based ideology, they failed to account for women's diversity and particular locations of female oppression (Longino, 2006).

Another dimension of the embodiment of the knower is the denial of any essential difference between subjects and objects of knowledge. With this regard, reflexivity takes on an especially important dimension, i.e., "the knower's awareness of her assumptions and values and of the ways in which these affect her beliefs and theorizing" (Longino, 2006, p. 334). Feminist epistemologists are convinced that current social arrangements "assign epistemic privilege to occupants of one social position," and that feminist standpoint theory "seeks to reverse the assignment and grants epistemic privilege to those in subordinated, socially unprivileged positions" (Longino, 2006, p. 338). Whichever the case, the postructuralist feminists are working vehemently toward to the demise of the positivistic rhetoric of science (Lather, 2004).

Worth noting is the fact that poststructuralist position steers away from feminism's tendency to make generalizations based on the experiences and accounts of Western, white, middle-class women. Instead, it looks at "the intersection of the identity categories: race, class, gender, sexual orientation, ethnicity, nationality, age, wellness, etc" (St. Pierre & Pillow, 2000, p. 7). The issue of woman's subjectivity continues to be challenged by poststructuralist feminists who place a greater emphasis on language and discourse that shape the ways women experience oppression (St. Pierre & Willow, 2000). Poststructuralist feminists question the very possibility of finite definitions:

> If "woman" is defined once and for all, then there is no hope of a reconfiguration that might offer different, strategic possibilities for ethical, political, and relational work. What kind of women and what kinds of feminism might we fail to produce if we define "woman" and "feminism" once and for all? (St. Pierre & Willow, 2000, p. 8)

One of the strengths of poststructuralism lies in its ability to continue to "reinvent itself strategically, shifting and mutating given existing political agendas, power relations, and identity strategies" (p. 8). Epistemic privileges and deconstructive practices are central to the critical race theory (CRT) framework. Critical race theories emerged in the 1980s as a reaction to critical legal studies and launched a critical examination of American society and culture in the intersections of race, law, and power. Later these theories included in the context of their investigations the constructs of gender, ethnicity, national identity, and sexual orientation CRT studies which ground themselves in the human and civil rights struggles for justice, and equal opportunity for historically oppressed and disadvantaged groups in the U.S. (Ballard & Cintron, 2010; Bell, 2008; Delgado & Stefanic, 2001; Essed & Goldberg, 2001). Ballard and Cintron (2010) identify three elements of critical race theory: microaggressions, creation of counter-stories, and development of counter-spaces. Microaggression is defined as "a type of subtle abuse aimed at minorities that can be visual, verbal, nonverbal, conscious, or unconscious" (p. 15). The creation of counter-stories is presented as "archives, testimonies, or discussions that marginalized groups use to respond to stories previously espoused by the dominant group" (p. 16). Finally, the development of counter-spaces is seen as a "means of conveying stories of experiences that have not been told, as well as a way to assess and counter dominant stories" (p. 16).

Critical race theory's concern is centered on W. E. B. Du Bois' (1868–1963) account of "double consciousness" as a "complex and constant play between the exclusionary conditions of social structure marked by race and the psychological and cultural strategies employed by the racially excluded and marginalized to accommodate themselves to everyday indignities as well as to resist them" (Essed & Goldberg, 2001, p. 5). Critical racial theories exert a significant influence on the humanities and social science scholarship, especially critical ethnicity studies (Gaspar de Alba, 2003; Noriega, 2000; Saldivar, 1990).

Wedded to the cause of critical theories are the issues of queer studies whose task is to challenge "those U.S. legal and social structures that privilege heterosexuality, patriarchy, white supremacy, and class advantage, with the legal and social liberation of sexual minorities—queers—as its principal focus" (Lugg, 2006, p. 178). The queer legal theory (QLT) emerged in the 1990s in response to some political and legal events, and it "does not expect the researcher to remain 'neutral' on issues of social justice and queer Americans" (Lugg, 2006, p. 177).

Disability studies provide a sharp critique of the social model of disability (Gabel and Peters, 2004). Recent developments in disability studies moved away from the objective-subjective dichotomy while adopting a postmodern position that provides a new space to deconstruct the notion of disability itself. Particularly, Gabel and Peters (2004) employ the postmodern perspective to critique medical and functionalist models of disability which marginalize and pathologize disability. Resistance theory is yet another powerful tool that adds to the deconstructive theory and practice of disability studies "to transgress, disrupt, and confront while also constructing a disability-centered notion of beauty and desire" (Gabel & Peters, 2004, p. 593).

Resistance is inherently political, and the above discussion on its theorizing and practical application provides an indispensable forum for educators to consider their inquiry along the lines of critical theories intersecting socio-economic class, race, ethnicity, gender, ability, or lifestyle issues pertaining to social justice.

Epistemological Pluralism on Equal Footing: Non-Western Ways of Knowing

Our quest to know often leads us to explore uncharted territories populated with different peoples having many and variegated beliefs. These beliefs form a "structure of great complexity, with innumerable changing elements that reflect our continuing experience and thought, our actions and emotions, our learning and forgetting, our inferring and accepting, our revising and rejecting, our speaking and listening" (Audi, 2003, p. 336). An apparent diversity of worldviews is indicative of the fact that we live in the world of "pluralistic epistemologies" (Polkinghorne, 1983). According to Ogilvy (1977), there is "not *one truth* which corresponds to *reality*. Instead, there are *some truths* which hold within communities" (as cited in Polkinghorne, 1983, p. 250). Epistemological pluralism hinges on the notion of context, or community that allows for an "understanding that is greater than the understanding of any one point of view" (Polkinghorne, 1983, p. 251). Epistemological pluralism incites the inquiry that can "reap significant methodological benefits from using multiple procedures for its research designs" (p. 252).

Whereas (for the most part) several preceding centuries were marked by the dominance of some epistemologies and the silencing if not subjugation and ridicule of others, this century (let us hope for the most part) brings to the forefront the power of knowledge unleashed from all four corners of the world on equal footing. The history of an epistemological journey of what can be labeled as "non-Western" traditions carries a record of extraordinary achievements and glory on the one hand, and colonialism and suppression on the other.

It should be noted that the terms "non-Western" and "Western" denote a great deal of ambiguity and confusion. If considered geographically, "non-Western" (as opposed to "Western" or "Western European") applies to most of the world's countries along with their inhabitants. It is estimated, for instance, that there are 196 countries in today's world (Glennon, 1995) (the number varies between 193 and 195 in other sources), out of which, only 44 are officially recognized as "Western European." If taken in political and economic terms, both "Western" and "non-Western" elicit the same amount of ambiguity. "Western" often refers to either Western European, or North American and Western European, or to both, designating several countries in Europe and North America with advanced economic and technological systems ascribed as dominant (perhaps until very recently) within the scope of a global economy. The same countries are often regarded in opposition to "non-Western" because of the history of colonialism. However, the term "Western European" is especially ambiguous due to its re-emergence after WWII, and after the Cold War fought by the U.S. and its allies against the former Soviet-bloc European countries. With the dissolution of the USSR, the political implication of the term lost its meaning, yet it remains popular.

Today's Europe is essentially different from what it was even some 50 or 60 years ago. There are 44 northern, southern, western, and eastern European countries on the world map; out of these 44, only 9 are recognized by the UN as "Western," and out of those 9, probably less than half have been responsible for the history of foreign invasions, slavery, and colonialism. Moreover, many European countries, in their remote and recent historical past, have been fighting for liberty and independence from their neighbors. Ukraine has been separated from Russia since the early 1990s but is now engaged in a brutal war against Russia fighting for its independence anew.

Evidently, the history of European revolutionary ideas and events continues to inspire social and political activism throughout the world. This brief and certainly superficial tour of European history reminds us of some facts that are important to consider when addressing non-Western traditions. And it is from the position of the general context of vast diversity and complexity between and within the world's cultures that we approach non-Western ways of knowing. Both the scope of this book and the space limit of its printed edition allow for the inclusion of some materials but not other materials.

Epistemological and Methodological Plurality Across Cultures

Being selective by no means implies privileging some perspectives over others. On the contrary, the premise of this book posits epistemological and methodological pluralism, which, at its core, recognizes and honors all cultures and their respective ways of knowing. The Eastern world abounds in rich and diverse philosophical thoughts. Chapter 2 outlines briefly Hinduism and Buddhism—the ancient philosophical traditions that originated in India. China is the birthplace of Taoism and Confucianism. Taoism begins with the anthology known as the *Daode Jing* (*Tao-te Ching*) and whose authorship had been ascribed to Laozi (Lao-tzu) who lived in China in ~ 5 BC. At the heart of his message is Tao, translated as "the Way." The Tao of Lao-tzu represents simultaneously the nature of reality, knowledge, and value perceived as a whole. From a Daoist or Taoist perspective, to be knowledgeable means to act in harmony with the Tao, or synchronize with natural rhythm of the universe. Actions that abuse consciousness may rebound and obtain their ecological retribution from persons and societies that have disrupted the equilibrium. Additionally, the Dao or Tao illuminates the principle of reciprocity wherein the outer world reflects the inner conditions and vice versa. Chinese teachers brought Buddhism to Japan. Particularly, Eisai (1141–1215) is considered to be the father of Zen Buddhism in Japan. The monk Dogen (1200–1253) is responsible for spreading Ts'ao-tung or Soto methods and teachings from China to Japan.

In the twelfth and thirteenth centuries, the movement known as the Qabbalah (Kabbalah) or Tradition (originated in Provence and Spain) revived the mystical strand in the Jewish tradition. The Qabbalists explore the techniques of meditation and ecstasy, especially Avraham Abulafia (1240–ca. 1291), who may have been influenced by Sufism or Islamic mysticism. Illuminationist, or Ishraqi, school of Persian philosophy, founded by the Sufi Sheikh al-Suhrawardi (1154–1191) used a linguistic connection between the concept of "Eastern-ness" (*mashriq*) and that of "wisdom" or "light" or "illumination" (*ishraq*). Both words are derived from *sharq*, meaning "the sunrise." Suhrawardi and his followers claimed that Light was the foundation of all existence. Knowledge of the truth is thus achieved through an intuition of Light—an "illumination." Rumi (1207–1273), a Persian Sufi mystic, is the key exponent of Sufism who believed that the ultimate center of human consciousness, our inmost reality, is the "heart" (*dil, qalb*). People's hearts are often "veiled" by innumerable levels of "dross" and "darkness." Transformation occurs when one's heart is completely purified. Love is, therefore, understood as a metaphysical and epistemological principle. Love must be experienced in order to be understood.

Mysticism and esoteric philosophy cross the geographical boundaries between the East and the West and represent an unbroken tradition from the Egyptians, Hebrews, and Greeks, through the Christian West, and continuing to the present. Central to esoteric world traditions is the system of "the One" that cannot be properly expressed in words and that has different interpretations specific to different cultures. The One is the supreme God that emanates in the form of the Intellect or Nous which further emanates in the Soul. It exemplifies the union of human beings with the Infinite. Gnosticism, the teaching of Gnostics, evokes the Sufi knowledge of the heart. Gnostics are said to have lived in AD 300 or AD 400. Gnosis is also known as the knowledge of the heart and its basic precepts are esoteric. "The terms *Gnostic* and *Gnosticism* are derived from the Greek word *gnosis*, which is usually (albeit somewhat misleadingly) translated as 'knowledge.' The knowledge the Gnostic seeks [. . .] is not rational knowledge. The Greek language distinguishes between theoretical knowledge and knowledge gained from direct experience. The latter is gnosis, and a person possessing or aspiring to this knowledge is a Gnostic" (Hoeller, 2002, p. 2). Hoeller (2002) proposes the term "insight" as opposed to knowledge to denote gnosis because it "involves an intuitive process that embraces both self-knowledge and knowledge of ultimate, divine realities" (p. 2). Gnosticism in the first century BC was represented by both Christian and non-Christian schools. Contemporary educational researchers may find it interesting that the hermeneutic tradition in interpretive research has to do, to an extent, with a non-Christian school of Gnosis known as Hermeticism—supposedly the original birthplace of Hermes.

Gnostics should be rightfully credited for their treatment of the feminine principle in the eschatological scheme of world events. *Sophia* is the name that personifies the Divine Feminine in Gnosticism and other esoteric traditions. Literally, "wisdom" in Greek, *sophia* is a female constitutive element of *philosophy* (see Chapter 2). Greek is a gendered language, and perhaps it is not coincidental that the word philosophy conveys the presence of a female principle in a nonetheless almost exclusively male domain. Gendered languages such as Greek or Ukrainian have myriads of words connoting female gender and thus carry empowering messages for women in their respective cultures. In fact, *Sophia* has been revealing herself to different people and under different disguises throughout the history of humankind.

Sophia appears in the Wisdom Books of the Old Testament as Chokmah. Gnostic Philo of Alexandria (ca. 20 BC—ca. AD 50) repeatedly used the concept of Sophia (on a par with Logos, Nous) drawing from the Old Testament. He claimed that God created Sophia in the beginning of creation and then together with Her created the entire universe. Greek philosophers wrestled with the questions of the origins of the world, the role of the divine wisdom-Sophia in the eschatological schemata, and the relationship between Sophia and Logos. Pythagoras, who is traditionally considered the first self-proclaimed "lover of wisdom," recognized Sophia in the Western philosophical tradition. In Plato's *Symposium*, *Diotima* (who might be Sophia personified) appears as the "great priestess of Mantineia" who "dictates to [her teacher, Plato] the ideal, idealized, and [the Platonic] concept of love" (Kristeva, 1987, p. 71). In contrast to the male-dominated structure of the possession-love, Diotima epitomizes the "uniting-love" principle, an "agent of synthesis," and the power of Phallus: "Diotima *is* it; she is that Phallus, even if she doesn't *have* it. She hands it over to the philosopher whose task is to possess it, to conquer it, and to use it to enslave or educate" (Kristeva, 1987, p. 74). Contemporary feminist scholars may find the Gnostic Sophia, if translated into secular imagery, refreshingly empowering.

Mystical world traditions teach us that all living things are one in their inner nature, which can explain compassion:

> Our propensity to identify with one another, to feel with and for one another, which if we were ultimately separate would be either inexplicable or mistaken—and it is compassion that is the foundation of ethics. Our fundamental intuition that the way to treat other people is as we ourselves would wish to be treated is grounded in the metaphysical truth that we and they are the same. (Magee, 1997, p. 453)

Metaphysical beliefs permeate indigenous and aboriginal cultures. Indigenous and aboriginal are often used interchangeably to refer to the people and cultures native to North and South America, Africa, Australia, and Oceania. *Native*, *aboriginal*, and *indigenous* typically identify people inhabiting particular geographical territories from the earliest times or from before the arrival of colonists. In the Americas, for instance, the Toltec culture (~ eighth century) was native to Mexico and preceded the Aztecs in the tenth century. The Incas in Peru have been known since the ~thirteenth century. The Mayan civilization dates back to ~2000 BC. Each of these cultures has left a heritage of sophisticated cosmological systems, myths, rituals, and traces of scientific, technological, and artistic advances. The Toltec were known as "women and men of knowledge" (Ruiz, 2004). They were masters (*naguals*) and students. *Naguals* were forced to conceal the ancestral knowledge-wisdom because of European conquest and misuses of personal power by a few students (Ruiz, 2004). Yet the knowledge was passed through generations of *naguals*. The result of believing in the truth is "goodness, love, happiness" (Ruiz, 2004, p. 19). The Toltec truth, the "story," needs to be "experienced to become legitimate" (Ruiz, 2004, p. 23).

The beliefs of the people residing in the vast areas of the Pacific Ocean represent an array of diversity as well as common patterns. The words *mana* (sacred power associated with gods; holy forces of nature) and *tabu* (or taboo) (that which is forbidden), for instance, are common to most of the Pacific region's inhabitants (Smart, 1998). The Polynesian religion distinguishes between the spiritual (invisible) world and the world of experience (seen), with the two worlds being interconnected. The use of practices such as rituals, magic, witchcraft, wearing masks, and body-painting are common to many cultures in Oceania. Essential to most aboriginals of Australia is the concept of the Dreaming, or Dreaming Time, which can be rendered as yet another way of knowing.

Shamanism originated among the Tunguso-Manchurian people to whom the word *saman* meant "he or she who knows" (Grof, 2006, p. 29). Shamanism is at least 30 to 40 thousand years old. The term also refers to Siberian native healers and it has been widely used for a variety of native healers in different parts of the world who have been popularly known as "medicine men, witch doctors, sorcerers, or wizards" (Grof, 2006, p. 29).

Plurality, depth, and scope of knowledge developed over thousands of years by indigenous peoples throughout the world and are evident in their ways of living. Indigenous knowledges are also diverse in themselves and unique to given cultures, geographies, and societies (Barnhardt & Kawagley, 2005). They have been passed through generations primarily through "storytelling, ceremonies, songs and dances from generation to generation" (Price, 2010, p. 2).

For the most part of their history, the cultures of Africa were viewed by Western colonizers and missionaries as "primitive, backward, and in need of radical reconstruction" (Brown, 2004, p. 4). And most of what has been known through literature about traditional African philosophical thought emerged through Eurocentric characterizations of African cultures (Brown, 2004). African conceptual languages have been replaced with "theoretical idioms from the West" (Appiah, 2004, p. 23). Yet throughout the same history of colonialism, the people of African descent have long engaged in philosophical thought of their own. Traditional African thought was indigenous to sub-Saharan cultures prior to the infusion of Islamic, Judaic, and Christian ideologues (Brown, 2004). Its fundamental feature is

> that there is more to reality and to the realm of experience than that which is readily accessible through empirical inquiry, and that one can acquire an understanding of natural phenomena by appealing to experiences whose characterizations are not empirically confirmable but are nonetheless warrantably assertible. The warrant is rooted in a felt sense that there are spiritual components to nature that influence experiences and perceptions. Underlying this perspective is a commitment to the existence of unobservable entities that can act as causal agents. (p. 159)

Within the realm of traditional African worldview, a person consists of a body made from the "blood of the mother, an individual spirit [*sunsun*] which is the main bearer of one's personality, and the *okra* [from which *sunsun* derives from the father at conception, the kind of a life force sent to a person from Nyame, the high god, and departs the body at death]" (Appiah, 2004, p. 28). In contrast, Western rationalism interprets a person as consisting of a body and a mind (or brain). However, many Europeans and Americans—and Africans—believe that the "departure of the mind from the body is death, and that the mind, released from the body, renamed the "soul," survives somehow, perhaps even somewhere" (Appiah, 2004, pp. 28–29). This seems like a "different theory—*sunsun* and *okra* are dual non-bodily entities, [of] which the mind is one" (Appiah, 2004, p. 29).

The belief in the existence of a spiritual world is not unique to African cultures. Native Americans, for instance, embrace the notion that there are "non-observable" life forms (spirits) that can reside in birds, bears, or streams. The beliefs of many cultures that have been regarded as "inferior" to those of modern Western European views show more commonalties than differences regarding the nature of the universe and human beings. The knowledge of indigenous societies derives from multiple sources, including traditional teachings, empirical observations, and revelations (Castellano, 2008). While traditional indigenous knowledge (a set of absolutes about the nature of reality and being) has been transmitted through generations without questioning, the empirical knowledge is gained through careful observation (e.g., knowledge of ecosystems).

Indigenous "revealed knowledge" is acquired through "dreams, visions, and intuitions that are understood to be spiritual in origin" (Castellano, 2008, p. 24). To understand what the beliefs of African or Native American people are, one needs an investigation that "challenges the ways in which research is conducted *on* Indigenous communities, rather than *with*, or *by* Indigenous communities and researchers" (Langdon, 2009, p. 9). Most aboriginal people who write about aboriginal knowledge have spent a "good deal of their lives interacting with mainstream society and see a need to make explicit those elements of their culture which are at risk if being lost" (Castellano, 2008, p. 31). The knowledge that these cultures can share with us will be a "living fire, rekindled from surviving embers and fueled with the materials of the twenty-first century" (Castellano, 2008, p. 34).

Most Indigenous peoples are currently undergoing "major social upheavals as a result of transformative forces beyond their control"; many of their values, beliefs, and practices are "recognized as being just as valid for today's generations as they were for generations past" (Barnhardt & Kawagley, 2005, p. 9). The process is reciprocal:

> Native people may need to understand Western society, but not at the expense of what they already know and the way they have come to know it. Non-native people, too, need to recognize the coexistence of multiple worldviews and

> knowledge systems, and find ways to understand and relate to the world in its multiple dimensions and varied perspectives. (p. 9)

Indigenous epistemologies continue to transform contemporary realities of Western advanced societies in the fields of medicine, health, law, politics, and education (Dei et al., 2008). The legacy of ancient worldviews, no matter how glorious or painful it might have been, represents a multifarious and at times surprisingly unified picture that finds its mythological expression in a poetic image of the necklace of the Vedic goddess Indra ("Indra's net"). The necklace is made of shining jewels, all interconnected. "It is told that if we take one jewel and look at it, we'll see the reflection of all others, infinite in number. Each of the jewels reflected in one and it reflects all others simultaneously; thus there is an infinite reflecting process occurring" (Robertson, 2009, p. 145). A similar account of a holistic view of the universe is found in the Hwa Yen school of Buddhism.

> The story is told that the Empress Wu, who was unable to penetrate the complexity of Hwa Yen literature, asked Fa Tsang, one the founders of the school, to give her a practical and simple demonstration of the cosmic interrelatedness. Fa Tsang first suspended a glowing candle from the ceiling of a room the entire interior of which was covered with mirrors, to demonstrate the relationship of the One to the many. Then he placed in the center of the room a small crystal and, showing how everything around it was reflected in it, illustrated how in the Ultimate Reality the infinitely small contains the infinitely large and the infinitely large the infinitely small, without obstruction. (Grof, 1985, p. 75)

These ancient Indian and Chinese legends illustrate a holonomic principle of the universe signifying the unity of the whole and its parts. Interestingly, a similar principle was described by German philosopher and mathematician G. W. von Leibniz (1646–1716) in one of his major works, *Monadology* (1714). Likewise, contemporary scientists contemplate the unity principle of the universe. David Bohm (1917–1992), a co-worker of Einstein, who made important contributions to theoretical physics, philosophy, and neuropsychology, believed that "matter and consciousness cannot be explained from, or reduced to each other. They are both abstractions from the implicate order, which is their common ground, and thus represent an inseparable unity" (Grof, 1985, p, 76). Edgar D. Mitchell, the lunar pilot for NASA's Apollo 14 space mission, recalls his experience in space: "I could see the stars, see the separateness of things, but felt an inner connectedness of everything. It was personal. It was wild. It was ecstatic. And it made me ask myself, well, what kind of a brain-mind-body is this that reacts to this vision, this sighting? And it made me realize that our story of ourselves as told by science was probably incomplete, and maybe flawed" (Brown, 2005, p. 56).

Ad Infinitum: New Horizons and Possibilities with Artificial Intelligence

Artificial Intelligence (AI) or Artificial Generative Intelligence (AGI), initially intended as a tool to help amplify knowledge, may have inadvertently become a deconstructive and revolutionary tool, redefining data from how we once knew it and disrupting political, economic, and social structures (Blais & Jungdahl, 2019). Alan Turing is widely believed to have laid the foundation of what became known as artificial intelligence. He was an English mathematician. The Turing Test involved assessing a computer and a human being in separate rooms on the same set of questions and comparing their respective performance. The computer ended up besting the human player, answering more quickly and accurately the same set of questions given to the human player. Through his imitation game, also known as the Turing Test, Turing posited that a computer can be said to possess intelligence if it can mimic human behaviors, including thoughts and actions (St George & Gillis, 2023). Though Turing's prediction that computers would be able to play the imitation game by 2000 has yet to come pass, his work has largely been viewed as the foundation for the development, expansion, and explosion of machine learning and deep learning (Oppy, 2021). While Turing's groundbreaking work laid the foundation in computer science for AI or AGI to emerge, others like Charles Babbage, Howard Aiken, John McCarthy, and scientists who gathered at Dartmouth College for a conference have been widely credited to have tilled the ground for AI exploits to flourish and enable its promises to bear the fruits (Kavanagh, 2019; Mills, 2023). In a nutshell, Artificial Intelligence is embodied by machines (computers and supercomputers) that perform a wide range of tasks with little assistance from human beings, once they have been coded. Essentially, these machines and software tools are programmed to simulate human intelligence; and, once trained through deep learning (DL) and machine learning (ML) through large, complex, and diverse datasets, they become endowed with reasoning and decision-making capabilities that can surpass or supersede human intelligence (Blais & Jungdahl, 2019; Clocksin, 2003). DL is especially fascinating as it is designed like "neural networks" and engineered to mimic how the human brain functions and performs (Mills, 2023, p. 7). Particularly, DL draws upon massive amounts of data from different sources, learns and extricates patterns in these data, and uses them to not only describe but also to predict behaviors and prescribe actions. According to West and Allen (2018), these machines think and behave like human experts in any given field. In many cases, their algorithms perform computations and calculations better and faster than humans can, while automating data analysis and discovery processes accurately and consistently (Gil et al., 2014; Mazzolin, 2020; Minsky, 1966).

Today, AI or AGI has a wide range of applications in various aspects of life and society, including education, computing, aviation, business, supply chain, spy craft, warfare, healthcare, data science, and more (Musib et al., 2017; West & Allen, 2018). The aura of optimism about AI's current impact is so high that its potential applications are touted as limitless (Mazzolin, 2020). As a result, the U.S. government, and governments from around the world for that matter, have taken a keen interest in AGI that is matched probably only by their interest in nuclear armament. In fact, Blais and Jungdahl (2019) review various initiatives that the U.S. government has undertaken to ensure it stays ahead of the curve. These include "enacting a series of policies meant to foster AI-related technologies into the defense and national security sectors" (p. 108). That initiative has manifested in "AI-investment and development . . . and access to federal data" (p. 108) aimed to prepare not just federal workers but all workers across the U.S. economy. Similarly, the U.S. Intelligence Committee (IC) has prioritized the development and deployment of AI-powered supercomputers, automated weapon systems, and unmanned aerial vehicles (UAV) (Blais & Jungdahl, 2019; Musib et al., 2017).

Perhaps, most relevantly for the *Paradigms of Research* project, the burnished optimism about AI's capabilities and its applications in academic disciplines and practices raises many salient questions with far-reaching ramifications for research and higher education Decker (2023), Mills (2023), and Staat (2023) highlight ways in which AI has impacted education and underscore the urgency for educators and scholars to get ahead of the curve. Mills (2023) describes and discusses many ways college campuses have already encountered AI, noting: "Examples include installing bots to answering frequently asked questions on websites, automated machinery in industrial laboratories, and robots welcoming students onto campuses . . ." (p. 1). Additionally, he beckons educators to eschew oscillating and to enthusiastically engage AI and all its promises. Similarly, Decker (2023) provides a blueprint for how educators can leverage AI tools in assignment and assessment designs while engineering curiosity, passion, creativity, and ingenuity in the learning process. For instance, she describes "AI-powered" tools that are currently used to help identify students who need support and students who are prone to suicide ideation. More importantly, Decker points out AI-directed programs such as Khan Academy, Mia Learning, and Pixar in a Box that effectively help teachers personalize learning for different student groups. Finally, Staat (2023) who wrote extensively on the subject led the charge with his editorial work in *Digital Directions*, arguing cogently that AI, as a form of technology, has transformed what was once considered normal and has in fact infiltrated higher education. Hence, the task of educators and higher education professionals is not to tether or hinder AI but to intelligently engage it and curve with it, so to speak, to harness its exploits and potentials.

Perhaps, one of the most consequential intersections of AI and higher education lies in data science, big data, and data analytics. This intersection carries salient implications for the enterprise of knowledge and research in education as a corollary. Scholars and data scientists recognize the saliency of big data, data science, and data analytics, acknowledging its impact on the pursuit, acquisition, and the use of knowledge. Kruse et al. (2016) define big data from the purview of 4 Vs—*volume*, *velocity*, *variety*, and *veracity*, noting: "Big data is commonly defined through the 4 Vs: volume (scale or quantity of data), velocity (speed and analysis of real-time or near-real-time data), variety (different forms of data, often from disparate data sources), and veracity (quality assurance of the data). The first 3 Vs are found in most literature [2, 3], and the fourth V is a goal [4]" (p. 38). As such, big data is being mined and applied in a lot of disciplines and business practices. Accordingly, Cao (2017) notes: "From the disciplinary development perspective, recognition of the significant challenges, opportunities, and values of big data is fundamentally reshaping the traditional data-oriented scientific and engineering fields. It is also reshaping those nontraditional data engineering domains such as social science, business, and management" (pp. 1–2). This presents scholars and researchers an immense opportunity to generate data-informed theories and hypotheses. Particularly, by parsing and molding this AI-powered data, researchers can link theoretical insights to data and triangulate conclusions, which will make relevant impact on educational research and practices, policies, business operations, and decision-making processes in society.

Searching the Known and the Not-Yet Known: The Wonder Continues

Despite our phenomenal excursions and groundbreaking exploits, past and present, into vast epistemological terrains, what can we, as humans, really know about the world around us? The *truths* about it both tempt and elude. The twentieth-century paradigm shifts in "hard" sciences can be looked at through the prism of an ancient Chinese saying: "To be uncertain is uncomfortable, but to be certain is ridiculous" (Boyd, 2012). Albert Einstein's theories of relativity (1905, 1916), quantum mechanics, the discovery of DNA and the ensuing advancements in biology, chemistry, physics, and mathematics have irrecoverably transformed our thinking about the universe and ourselves in terms of certainty of knowledge. Quantum mechanics, more so than other discoveries of the twentieth century, was the "first crack in the wall of the naïve determinism" and produced a domino effect rendering all methods of encryption "obsolete" in quantum computation, which in turn made us wonder how "our grandchildren will manage to keep their secrets" (Rota & Crants, 2000, p. 479). Quantum mechanics raised the questions regarding the prediction of the events at the subatomic level. Matter was no longer conceived as to be comprised of solid atoms; the atom itself was divided into constitutive particles held by different forces. At the subatomic level, particles did not obey to fixed mechanical laws. Quantum mechanics made us give up not only the conventional reality of the particle picture of electrons, but the nature of reality itself—no longer completely predictable, causal, and ordered.

What will the twenty-first century hold? Perhaps it will be as "much an age of philosophy as an age of science," wherein they become equal partners in "our project of understanding the world" (Rota & Crants, 2000, p. 491). In the history of Western and non-Western worlds alike, chaos, creativity, and transformation were understood as forming the fabric of a spontaneous cosmos. The principles of multiplicity, diversity, and seemingly random occurrences as the inheritance of many ancient traditions echo similar principles of contemporary fractal geometry, holographic images, and chaos and complexity theories. The new sciences of chaos and complexity and the study of nonlinear dynamic systems have opened venues for Western scientists to consider the pathways toward the interconnected system of a *conscious* universe.

Much like their alchemist counterparts of the "dark ages," contemporary scientists are on the quest to solve the mysteries of the universe. Today we are witnessing the "beginning of a restructuring of our idea of what a scientific theory should be. The old prejudice that all science should be eventually "reduced" to physics was prodded by the simplistic positivism that truculently dominated the philosophy of science in the latter half [of the 20th] century, and that we can now safely relegate to the dustbin of history" (Rota & Crants, 2000, p. 480). With almost 2,500 years of history on its record, contemporary science consists of "extending only incrementally what we can do, or what we can know. But now and then, unpredictably yet inevitably, an event occurs that crystallizes a new insight and reshapes how we perceive things" (Crease, 2003, p. xvi):

> *We choose to examine a phenomenon which is impossible,* absolutely *impossible, to explain in any classical way, and which has in it the heart of quantum mechanics. In reality, it contains the* only *mystery.*
>
> —Richard Feyman (as cited in Crease, 2003, p. 191).

For thousands of years, science and philosophy have shared the "thrill of discovery" and perceived an "intimate connection between the true, the beautiful, and the good, seeing these as 'entangled,' [...] inseparably bound up together in a common and deeply lying origin" (Crease, 2003, p. 216). Yet, the world is never fully transparent to us; the world that we want to explore is a "largely unknown entity," and we certainly must "keep our options open" (Feyerabend, 2000, p. 496). As long as we continue the pursuit of knowledge, moving from one location to another and allowing ourselves to be led upward, we can "achieve a more intimate connection with ourselves and the world, and thereby become more human" (Crease, 2003, pp. 216–217).

> *The scientist does not study nature because it is useful; he studies it because he delights in it, and he delights in it because it is beautiful. If nature were not beautiful, it would not be worth knowing, and if nature were not worth knowing, life would not be worth living.*
>
> —Henri Poincaré (as cited in Crease, 2003, p. 217)

Science, philosophy, and spirituality have been important forces in the history of humanity. Each operating within its own "language games," they continue to tread the path toward new insights today as they have been for thousands of years. Whether there is a possibility for convergence of different pathways in pursuit of knowledge remains to be seen as the twenty-first century unfolds. Living in today's world (unless one continues to do so in complete isolation) means dwelling in places within a *globalized* world and, by virtue of a readily available and diverse means of communication and travel, as well as experiencing both virtually and physically its pluralistic milieu. Coincidently, this also means recognizing, on equal footing, diverse worldviews from "quantum-relativistic physics, consciousness research, and neurophysiology" to the "ancient and Oriental spiritual philosophies, shamanism, aboriginal rituals, and healing practices" (Grof, 1985, p. 91). Even if it is against our wishes, a worldview is clearly emerging which may as well be envisaged as global epistemological pluralism.

References

Appiah, A. K. (2004). Akan and Euro-American concepts of the person. In L. M. Brown (Ed.), *African philosophy: New and traditional perspectives* (pp. 21–34). Oxford University Press.

Arendt, H. (1998). *The human condition*. The University of Chicago Press.

Audi, R. (2003). *Epistemology: A contemporary introduction to the theory of knowledge* (2nd ed.). Routledge.

Bachelard, G. (2000). *The dialectic of duration* (M. McAllester Jones, Trans.). Clinamen Press.

Bachelard, G. (2002). *The formation of the scientific mind: A contribution to a psychoanalysis of objective knowledge* (M. McAllester Jones, Trans.). Clinamen Press.

Bachelard, G. (2004). *The poetics of reverie: Childhood, language, and the cosmos* (D. Russell, Trans.). Beacon Press.

Ballard, H., & Cintron, R. (2010). Critical race theory as an analytical tool: African American male success in doctoral education. *Journal of College Teaching and Learning*, *7*(10), 11–23.

Barnhardt, R., & Kawagley, A. O. (2005). Indigenous knowledge systems and Alaska native ways of knowing. *Anthropology and Education Quarterly*, *36*(1), 8–23.

Baudrillard, J. (1999). Simulacra and simulations: Disneyland. In C. Lemert (Ed.), *Social theory: The multicultural and classical readings* (pp. 481–486). Westview Press.

Bell, D. A. (2008). *Race, racism and American law*. Aspen Publishers.

Blais, J. R., & Jungdahl, A. M. (2019). Artificial intelligence in a human intelligence World. *American Intelligence Journal*, *36*(1), 108–113. https://www.jstor.org/stable/27066342

Boyd, T. (2012). The clarity of coincidence. *Quest*, *100*(2), 44–45.

Brown, D. J. (2005). *Conversations on the edge of the apocalypse: Contemplating the future with Noam Chomsky, George Carlin, Deepak Chopra, Rupert Sheldrake, and others*. Palgrave.

Brown, L. M. (2004). Understanding and ontology in traditional African thought. In L. M. Brown (Ed.), *African philosophy: New and traditional perspectives* (pp. 158–178). Oxford University Press.

Castellano, M. B. (2008). Indigenous knowledges in global contexts: Multiple readings of our world. In G. J. S. Dei, B. L. Hall, & D. G. Rosenberg (Eds.). *Indigenous knowledges in global contexts: Multiple readings of our world* (pp. 21–36). University of Toronto Press.

Clocksin, W. F. (2003). Artificial intelligence and the future. *Philosophical Transactions: Mathematical, Physical and Engineering Sciences*, *361*(1809), 1721–1748. http://www.jstor.org/stable/3559219

Crease, R. P. (2003). *The prism and the pendulum: The ten most beautiful experiments in science*. Random House.

Decker, K. (2023). Artificial intelligence and education. In D. Staat (ed.), *Digital directions: Artificial intelligence pathways for higher education* (pp. 11–25). Rowman & Littlefield.

Dei, G. J. S., Hall, B. L., & Rosenberg, D. G. (Eds.). (2008). *Indigenous knowledges in global contexts: Multiple readings of our world*. University of Toronto Press.

Delgado, R., & Stefanic, J. (2001). *Critical race theory: An introduction*. NYU Press.

Essed, P., & Goldberg, D. T. (Eds.). (2001). *Race critical theories: Text and context*. Wiley-Blackwell.

Feyerabend, P. (2000). Against method. In S. Rosen (Ed.), *The philosopher's handbook* (pp. 493–502). Random House.

Foucault, M. (1967). *Of other spaces.* http://foucault.info/documents/heteroTopia/foucault.heteroTopia.en.html

Gabel, S., & Peters, S. (2004). Presage of a paradigm shift? Beyond the social model of disability toward resistance theories of disability. *Disability and Society, 19*(6), 585–600.

Gaspar de Alba, A. (2003). *Velvet barrios: Popular culture and Chicana/o Sexualities.* Palgrave.

Gil, Y., Greaves, M., Hendler, J., & Hirsh, H. (2014). Amplify scientific discovery with artificial intelligence. *Science, 346*(6206), 171–172. https://www.jstor.org/stable/24917255

Glennon, L. (Ed.). (1995). *Our times: An illustrated history of the 20th century.* Pub Overstock Unlimited.

Grof, S. (1985). *Beyond the brain: Birth, death, and transcendence in psychotherapy.* SUNY Press.

Grof, S. (2006). *The ultimate journey: Consciousness and the mystery of death.* MAPS.

Habermas, J. (1972). *Knowledge and human interests* (J. J. Shapiro, Trans.). Beacon Press.

Haraway, D. (1999). The cyborg manifesto and fractured identities. In C. Lemert (Ed.), *Social theory: The multicultural & classic readings* (pp. 539–543). Westview Press.

Hoeller, S. A. (2002). *Gnosticism: New light on the ancient tradition of inner knowing.* Quest Books.

Johnson, S. (1998). Skills, Socrates and Sophists: Learning from history. *British Journal of Educational Studies, 46*(2), 201–213.

Kavanagh, C. (2019). Artificial intelligence. In *New tech, new threats, and new governance challenges: An opportunity to craft smarter responses?* (pp. 13–23). Carnegie Endowment for International Peace. http://www.jstor.org/stable/resrep20978.5

Kenny, A. (2010). *A new history of Western philosophy.* Oxford University Press.

Kristeva, J. (1987). *Tales of love* (L. S. Roudiez, Trans.). Columbia University Press.

Kruse C., Goswamy R., Raval Y., & Marawi S. (2016). Challenges and opportunities of big data in health care: A systematic review. *JMIR Med Inform*, 4(4), e38. https://medinform.jmir.org/2016/4/e38

Kuehn, M. (2006). Knowledge and belief. In K. Haakonssen (Ed.), *The Cambridge history of eighteen-century philosophy* (Vol. 1, pp. 389–425). Cambridge University Press.

Kuhn, T. (2000). The structure of scientific revolutions. In S. Rosen (Ed.), *The philosopher's handbook: Essential readings from Plato to Kant* (pp. 503–519). Random House.

Langdon, J. (Ed.). (2009). *Indigenous knowledges, development and education.* Sense Publishers.

Lather, P. (2004). Critical inquiry in qualitative research: Feminist and poststructural perspectives: Science "after truth." In K. deMarrais & S. D. Lapan (Eds.), *Foundations for research: Methods of inquiry in education and social sciences* (pp. 203–215). Lawrence Erlbaum.

Lehrer, K., & Paxson, T. D. (1999). Knowledge: Undefeated justified true belief. In L. Pojman (Ed.), *The theory of knowledge: Classic and contemporary readings* (pp. 153–156). Wadsworth Publishing.

Longino, H. E. (2006). Feminist epistemology. In J. Greco & E. Sosa (Eds.), *The Blackwell guide to epistemology* (pp. 327–353). Blackwell.

Lugg, C. A. (2006). On politics and theory: Using an explicitly activist theory to frame educational research. In V. A. Anfara, Jr. & N. T. Mertz (Eds.), *Theoretical frameworks of qualitative research* (pp. 175–188). SAGE.

Magee, B. (1997). *The philosophy of Schopenhauer.* Oxford University Press.

Mazzolin, R., & Centre for International Governance Innovation. (2020). Artificial intelligence and keeping humans "in the loop." In *Modern conflict and artificial intelligence* (pp. 48–54). Centre for International Governance Innovation. http://www.jstor.org/stable/resrep27510.10

Mills, P. (2023). Artificial intelligence background. In D. Staat (ed.), *Digital directions: Artificial intelligence pathways for higher education* (pp. 1–10). Rowman & Littlefield.

Minsky, M. L. (1966). Artificial intelligence. *Scientific American, 215*(3), 246–263. http://www.jstor.org/stable/24931058

Moser, P. K. (2006). Foundationalism. In R. Audi (Ed.), *The Cambridge dictionary of philosophy* (2nd ed., pp. 321–323). Cambridge University Press.

Moser, P. K., Mulder, D. H., & Trout, J. D. (1998). *The theory of knowledge: A thematic introduction.* Oxford University Press.

Musib, M., Wang, F., Tarselli, M. A., Yoho, R., Yu, K.-H., Andrés, R. M., Greenwald, N. F., Pan, X., Lee, C.-H., Zhang, J., Dutton-Regester, K., Johnston, J. W., & Sharafeldin, I. M. (2017). Artificial intelligence in research. *Science, 357*(6346), 28–30. https://www.jstor.org/stable/26399366

Noriega, C. (Ed.). (2000). *The Chicano studies reader: An anthology of Aztlan, 1970–2000.* UCLA Chicano Studies Research Center.

Oppy, G. (n.d.). Turing test. *Stanford Encyclopedia of Philosophy.* https://plato.stanford.edu/entries/turing-test/

Papineau, D. (1996). Philosophy of science. In N. Bunnin & E. P. Tsui-James (Eds.), *Blackwell companion to philosophy* (pp. 290–324). Blackwell Publishing.

Pojman, L. P. (Ed.). (1999). *The theory of knowledge: Classic and contemporary readings* (pp. 153–156). Wadsworth Publishing.

Polkinghorne, D. E. (1983). *Methodology for the human sciences: Systems of inquiry.* SUNY Press.

Polkinghorne, D. E. (2004). *Practice and the human sciences: The case for a judgment-based practice of care.* SUNY Press.

Price, M. W. (2010). Indigenous taxonomy, ethnobotany and sacred names. In P. Boyer (Ed.), *Ancient wisdom, modern science: The integration of native knowledge in math and science at tribally controlled colleges and universities* (pp. 1–13). Salish Kootenai College Press.

Robertson, R. (2009). *Indra's Net: Alchemy and chaos theory as models for transformation.* Quest Books.

Rose, M. A. (1991). *The postmodern and the postindustrial: A critical analysis.* Cambridge University Press.

Rota, G. C., & Crants, J. T. (2000). Introduction: Ten philosophical (and contradictory) predictions. In S. Rosen (Ed.), *The philosopher's handbook: Essential readings from Plato to Kant* (pp. 473–491). Random House.

Ruiz, M. (2004). *A Toltec wisdom book: The voice of knowledge.* Amber-Allen.

Runes, D. D. (Ed.). (1983). *Dictionary of philosophy.* Rowman & Littlefield.

Saldívar, R. (1990). *Chicano narrative: The dialectics of difference.* University of Wisconsin Press.

Scruton, R. (1996). *Modern philosophy: An introduction and survey.* Penguin Books.

Smart, N. (1998). *The world's religions* (2nd ed.). Cambridge University Press.

St. George, B., & Gillis, A. S. (2023, April). *Turing test.* https://www.techtarget.com/searchenterpriseai/definition/Turing-test

St. Pierre, E. A., & Pillow, W. S. (Ed.). (2000). *Working the ruins: Feminist poststructural theory and methods in education.* Routledge.

Staat, D. (2023). *Digital directions: Artificial intelligence pathways for higher education.* Rowman & Littlefield.

West, D., & Allen, J. (2018, April). *How artificial intelligence is transforming the world.* Brookings Institute. https://www.brookings.edu/research/how-artificial-intelligence-is-transforming-the-world/

Westphal, M. (2006). Hermeneutics as epistemology. In J. Greco & E. Sosa (Eds.), *The Blackwell guide to epistemology* (pp. 415–435). Blackwell.

Winkler, K. P. (2006). Perception and ideas, judgment. In K. Haakonssen (Ed.), *The Cambridge history of eighteen-century philosophy* (Vol. 1, pp. 234–285). Cambridge University Press

Chapter 3 Paradigms and Educational Research: Weaving the Tapestry

Antonina Lukenchuk and Eileen Kolich

Paradigmatic Diversity and Educational Research

This chapter lends itself to the nexus of the issues concerning the notion of paradigm, the underpinning and, at times, misconceived assumptions of the nature and various types of educational research, and the value of philosophical inquiry into the underlying principles and constructs of research in human sciences. Our purpose is to establish a chain of interrelated links between epistemological and methodological questions that can lead to a more integrated and broader view of educational research.

One of the points of departure regarding educational research that we took in Chapter 1 was to position it, first and foremost, within the tradition of *human science* research. This tradition has a long history in the West, which is significant to recall because of the great deal of ambiguity surrounding more recent use of the word *science* and its place within the classification of arts and sciences. The word *science* is derived from *scientia* (Latin for knowledge) and can be defined as (1) an "intellectual and practical activity encompassing the systematic study of the structure and behavior of the natural and physical world through observation and experiment," (2) a "particular area of this . . .," (3) a "systematically organized body of knowledge of a particular subject," and (4) a "knowledge of any kind" (Stevenson & Lindberg, 2010, p. 1564). This extended definition of science can be applied to education whose disciplinary boundaries include an intellectual and practical activity aimed at a systematic study of human phenomena. The science of education seeks knowledge and understanding of multitudes of complex issues pervading the realm of human affairs—cultural, social, political, moral, religious, and so forth.

In the West, until about the Industrial Revolution, the above concerns comprised the domain of philosophy, the task of which was to provide a systematic and all-encompassing account of the nature of the universe and human being in physical and metaphysical terms. Educational issues were integrated within the hierarchy of arts and sciences, all of which served overall philosophical goals. Most ancient and modern philosophers did not differentiate their activities as philosophical, scientific, or educational. Socrates, Plato, Aristotle, Confucius, Rumi, to name a few, were all great teachers in their own right. Milesian philosophers (6 BC Ionia, which is present-day Turkey), who became known as the first scientists, taught that life and nonlife, and matter and spirit were all one.

The scientific discoveries and technological advancements following the Industrial Revolution provided an impetus for a separation between and compartmentalization of arts and sciences as well as for a shifting role of philosophy from its royal to a supplementary status serving the purposes of individual disciplines. The eighteenth-century philosopher David Hume attempted the inception of a science of human nature based on observable and measurable moral behavior, which eventually gave rise to behavioral sciences (Polkinghorne, 1983, 2004). The nineteenth-century German historian Droysen marked the distinction between *erklären* (explanation) (as in natural sciences) and *verstehen* (understanding) (as in human sciences), a distinction that presaged methodological debates in educational research. Further, in nineteenth-century Germany, Dilthey coined the word *Geistenwissenschaft*, which cannot be exactly translated into English. It is composed of *vershehen* (German for understanding) and *Wissenschaft* (German for science, learning, or knowledge). The science of understanding, also known as hermeneutics, has thus become a counterpoint to a natural science, the traditional purpose of which was explanation (see Chapters 1 and 2).

At the turn of the nineteenth century, in the West, social sciences emerged as an attempt to study individuals and their behavior within societal groups at the micro- and macrolevels, for example, sociology, anthropology, economics, and political science. Durkheim, Weber, and Marx were the architects of grand social science projects that still continue to provoke the social and political imaginations of contemporary thinkers (Lemert, 1999). August Comte attempted an ambitious positive social science that did not withstand the test of time. By the second half of the twentieth century, all positivistic undertakings in natural and social sciences had failed. The time became ripe for a new vision of science and the methods of scientific inquiry.

Methodological debates surrounding natural and human sciences entailed the revisionist conceptions of knowledge and scientific method from positivistic to post-positivistic (see Chapters 1 and 2). Einstein's relativity theory and quantum mechanics presented major challenges to the positivistic view of science. By the mid-twentieth century, the rejection of positivism by the philosophers of science, and their ensuing consensus that science could no longer produce certain knowledge, signaled radical changes in the understanding of methods applied to the study of human phenomena. Knowledge was conceived as fallible and subject to questioning, rejection, or acceptance as the best explanation available (temporary warrant) by a community of inquirers in a particular field of study.

Accordingly, the new conception of science assumed a critical stance toward scientific progress as an accumulation of and/or addition to the existing body of knowledge. Instead, the acquisition of knowledge represented the process of evolutionary change of paradigms competing for the best explanation of phenomena, accompanied by the process of occasional revolutionary epistemological breaks (paradigm shifts) that could invalidate the previously accepted warrants of knowledge. The tools of traditional scientific method were no longer sufficient to apply to an expanded notion of reason that included "systems logic, hermeneutic logic, pragmatic logic, the understanding and explanation of field theory, organic systems, linguistic statements, and consciousness" (Polkinghorne, 1983, p. 243). Since natural sciences were no longer restricted to the production of indubitable knowledge and, therefore, open to methodological alternatives, human sciences in turn became more receptive to the methods that could provide the most appropriate access to the study of human beings who present the most complex kinds of problems.

Feyerabend's proverbial anything goes (see Chapter 2) propels the idea that it is no longer possible to rely on fixed methods of investigation in any type of research. Methods are "no longer considered correct or right in themselves"; instead, they should be "appropriate . . . in relationship to the kind of question being addressed" (Polkinghorne, 1983, p. 273). The above statements underscore our position on knowledge and methods in educational research that can be generally expressed as an epistemological and methodological pluralism. Epistemological pluralism necessarily entails the recognition of diverse beliefs and practices found in today's world cultures and societal groups, and these beliefs and practices should be recognized and legitimized on equal grounds with those that have been [historically] given exclusive privilege, authority, and power, namely with the Western epistemologies (see Chapter 2).

In the previous chapters, we employed a number of metaphors to convey our messages with regard to educational inquiry, knowledge, and the research process. Chapter 1 opens with a spirited discussion of philosophy as a form of inquiry, a pursuit of wisdom or knowledge, which is intrinsic to a human being. Educational inquiry is a pursuit of knowledge writ at large driven by the primordial eros—an unsettling desire that accompanies the level-headed logos. Passionate search for wisdom can be translated into a tapestry of the world's cultural beliefs imbued within their original definitions: *jñāna* in Hinduism, the *Tao* in Chinese philosophy, *ishraq* in Persian tradition, *Sophia* in Gnosticism, and others (see Chapters 1 and 2). Passion is the gateway to things imagined that have inspired the most daring projects in the history of humankind, and philosophers and scientists alike can testify to the passion's triumph over the levelheadedness of reason in their pursuit of knowledge. Nietzsche and Poincaré may have little in common except their shared conviction that life is not worth living if it is not for the pursuit of creating art or discovering nature's wonders.

Alas, there is so much we do not know. There are perhaps as many holes in the spider web of our knowledge of the universe as there are stars in it radiating luring light from above. Like philosophers and scientists, educational researchers venture on passionate journeys to discover what the twenty-first century holds.

So, what are the ways of knowing available for educational researchers to pursue their projects in this day and age? The analysis of numerous philosophical and educational sources pertaining to epistemology and philosophy of science (see Chapters 1 and 2) allowed us to identify six paradigms of educational inquiry encompassing a great variety of beliefs, theories, assumptions, and practices. The number of identified paradigms is contingent on epistemological boundaries and is open to alternatives. The constitutive elements of each paradigm were delineated by taking into consideration existing scholarship on epistemology, philosophy of science, philosophical foundations of research, the accompanying vocabulary, and our own understanding of the conception of paradigm. The six paradigms identified for the purpose of this book are empirical-analytic, pragmatic, interpretive, critical, poststructuralist, and transcendental.

Table 3.1 depicts a typology of these six paradigms and their corresponding conceptual repertoire, epistemologies, methodologies, and selected methods. To fill in each cell of the table, we selected the terminology that is most frequently and widely used in philosophical and educational sources and captures the most important constitutive elements of each delineated paradigm. It is important to mention that the six paradigms are not completely autonomous entities; instead, most of them exhibit conceptual relationships that can be either strong or weak. Figure 3.1 portrays these relationships wherein solid lines demonstrate strong links and broken links, weak links. The description of the paradigms pertaining to Table 3.1 will be accompanied by comments on the paradigmatic relationships in reference to Figure 3.1.

There are numerous definitions of *paradigm* and contemporary educational researchers and scholars disagree on the use of the term. For instance, Yu (2006) prefers *tradition*' to *paradigm* based on his association of the term with Kuhn's definition of *paradigm* (see Introduction and Chapters 1 and 2). Yu claims that Kuhn's definition inevitably leads to an incommensurability thesis. However, if we look closer at Kuhn's argument about competing paradigms of science in the history of Western philosophy of science, it becomes clear that the incommensurability thesis does not apply to competing paradigms across different sciences. It is only within a particular field of study such as physics, where the thesis of incommensurability can be applied—some theories become obsolete in time, others remain credible within limited parameters, yet other theories can become completely overturned.

Our understanding of *paradigm* includes but is not limited to Kuhn's definition. Many educational researchers (e.g., Anfara & Mertz, 2006; Merriam, 2002) use a variety of terms in reference to paradigm: theory, theoretical framework, conceptual framework, model, lenses, a set of ideas, guiding principles, or perspectives. We consider all of these definitions under the umbrella term *conceptual repertoire*. Conceptual repertoire is a figurative expression that means an "endless list of conceptual ingredients," comprising a particular paradigm of research and resembling a list of musical pieces whose endless and different configurations can generate multiple productions. Tapestry of beliefs (see Chapter 1) is another metaphor to convey the same idea. The conceptual repertoire cell consists of ideas, concepts, theories, philosophies, ideologies, traditions, perspectives, and practices (see Table 3.1).

Paradigm (from the Greek *para*, beside, and *deigma*, example) is an "example, a model, a worldview, a theory, or a methodology" (Stevenson & Lindberg, 2010, p. 1269). Other dictionary definitions of paradigm include "example, archetype, beau ideal, chart, criterion, ensample, exemplar, ideal, mirror, model, original, pattern, prototype, sample, standard" (Kipfer, 2010, p. 588). Introduction provides a definition of paradigm derived from several dictionaries, resulting in a paradigm pyramid construct (see Figure I.1). For the purpose of this book, we employ a threefold definition of paradigm: (1) a system of inquiry, (2) a model, and (3) a way of knowing.

Polkinghorne (1983) identifies three major paradigmatic possibilities for human science research: deductive-hypothetical, pragmatic, and existential-phenomenological and hermeneutic systems of inquiry. Our use of paradigm as a system of inquiry refers to such overarching historical and philosophical traditions (macro constructs). Based on this definition, five of the six paradigms were identified: empirical-analytic, pragmatic, interpretive, critical, and transcendental (see Table 3.1). Inquiry is a broad term that can designate any research project as an "act of asking for information," posing a "question," and conducting an "official investigation" (Stevenson & Lindberg, 2010, p. 897). We consider this broad meaning of inquiry as integral to our understanding of paradigm as a system of inquiry, which can be subsequently extended to an act of posing research questions within a "set of [beliefs] connected [as] parts forming a complex whole" and following an "organized scheme or method" (Stevenson & Lindberg, 2010, p. 1763).

Our second use of paradigm as a model is based on the assumption of it as a micro construct, such as, for instance, a specific theory that can underpin an individual research project, or a theoretical model that can emerge as a result of conducting an individual research project (e.g., grounded theory). The chapters in Part II of this book demonstrate various microlevel paradigms positioned within the macrolevel overarching systems of inquiry (see Table 3.2). Finally, we conceive of paradigm as a discursive way of knowing that doesn't necessarily fit in within a well-delineated model or system of inquiry. Poststructuralist falls within this definition of paradigm.

The following detailed description of the six paradigms provides insights into the ways we conceptualize each of them individually and in relation to each other. The first row in Table 3.1 shows the interconnections between a paradigm and its constitutive ingredients. The arrow that extends from the cell paradigms onward points to the conception of paradigm as encompassing conceptual repertoire, epistemologies, methodologies, and methods. The arrows that spread from the methodologies cell to the right and to the left point to epistemologies, conceptual repertoire, and methods as constitutive elements of methodology. Thus, the first row in Table 3.1 provides an organizational framework for the description of each paradigm.

Empirical-analytic paradigm acquires its label from the long-standing traditions of Western rationalism and empiricism as well as the relevant educational research positions of materialism and behaviorism. Positivism exerted its influence on this paradigm for a relatively short time and was repudiated in the second half of the twentieth century. It is no longer acceptable to equate this paradigm with positivistic research (Yu, 2006); however, some educational researchers continue to do so (e.g., Hesse-Biber & Leavy, 2011; Lather, 2004; Pascale, 2011). Habermas (1972) distinguishes empirical-analytic sciences whose purposes are prediction and control. Polkinghorne (1983) refers to this paradigm as empirical, deductive, or deductive-hypothetical. Creswell (2003) singles out a similar paradigm he identifies as post-positivistic.

Paradigms *as* **Systems of Inquiry** **Models** **Ways of Knowing**	Corresponding **Conceptual Repertoire** ideas, concepts, theories, philosophies, ideologies, traditions, perspectives	Corresponding **Epistemologies** types of knowledge and knowledge claims	Corresponding **Methodologies**	Selected **Methods** within corresponding methodologies
Empirical-analytic	rationalism, empiricism, materialism, behaviorism, *positivism (minimal and short-lived influence)	probabilistic, fallible, formal, theoretical, approximation to *truth* (small "t") warrant	quantitative can be critical	experimental, quasi-experimental, correlational, survey, causal-comparative, ex post facto
Pragmatic	pragmatism, empiricism, rationalism, experimentalism, instrumentalism, utilitarianism, materialism	provisional, fallible, best possible explanation, trial-and-error, warrant	quantitative, qualitative, or mixed can be critical	grounded theory, action and practitioner research, case study, various quantitative and qualitative methods
Interpretive	existentialism, phenomenology, hermeneutics, constructivism, ethnomethodology, symbolic interactionism	understanding (*verstehen*), description, interpretation, meaning-making, contextual	qualitative often coupled with critical	great variety of methods: e.g., case study, [auto]-ethnography, narrative, phenomenology, unobtrusive methods (content, text, discourse analysis), visual, arts-based research

Critical	neo-Marxism, critical theory, feminism, critical race and ethnicity theories, queer theory, disability studies, social reconstructionism, social and political activism	emancipation, advocacy, consciousness-raising, social and political transformation, standpoint epistemologies, contextual	predominantly qualitative can be quantitative or mixed	various qualitative, quantitative, or mixed methods
Poststructuralist	antifoundationalism, postmodernism, *simulacra*, chaos and complexity theories, social and political activism	deconstruction of *episteme* as the only true knowledge, epistemological anarchism, discursive, contextual, socially and politically transformative	predominantly qualitative and critical	experimentation with various methods and ways of representation (textual and visual), unobtrusive methods
Transcendental	foundationalism, Western and non-Western metaphysical systems, world esoteric and spiritual traditions, Gnosticism, most indigenous and aboriginal traditions	ultimate Truth (capital 'T'), finite, intuitive, emotive, spiritually, socially and politically transformative, body-mind-soul unity, revelation	predominantly qualitative can be critical	variety of qualitative methods

Table 3.1: Typology of Paradigms as Major Systems of Inquiry, Models, and Ways of Knowing, and Their Corresponding Conceptual Repertoire, Epistemologies, Methodologies, and Selected Methods

Scientific also stands for empirical-analytic research paradigm (e.g., Cohen et al., 2008) and its use is appropriate as long as a post-positivistic conception of science is implied. The term that is most frequently used to designate this paradigm is *quantitative* (e.g., McMillan, 2008)

Empirical-analytic research in education yields probabilistic, formal, theoretical, explanatory, and warranted truths/knowledge claims obtained as a result of experiments, analysis of variables, or causal-comparative studies within the theoretical boundaries delineated by each individual project. Although the purpose of empirical studies is to produce foundational knowledge, it can be at best weak foundationalism (see Chapters 1 and 2). Until about the 1970s, empirical-analytic research held an epistemological and methodological privilege over other systems of inquiry in human and social sciences, and it remains highly influential among contemporary educational researchers. Part II features several quantitative research projects described further in this chapter. Empirical-analytic paradigm exhibits several links with other paradigms (see Figure 3.1). In epistemological terms, it is closely linked to pragmatic paradigm, hence a solid line depicting a strong link. Although rare, empirical studies can also be critical in terms of their research purposes. A broken line shows a weak relation between empirical-analytic and critical paradigms (see Figure 3.1).

Pragmatic paradigm is important to distinguish because of its unique position on knowledge claims Polkinghorne (1983) defines, via Peirce (see Chapters 1 and 2), as trial-and-error truths that withstand the test of experiment, time, and utility. Pragmatic truth is not a justified belief in a strict epistemological sense, but rather the effectiveness of knowledge demonstrated by the effectiveness of action (Polkinghorne, 1983). Pragmatic truths are warranted assertions that have to be agreed upon and accepted (or rejected) by a community of inquirers. Creswell (2003) singles out pragmatic paradigm as problem-centered and action-oriented and as such it is highly appealing to practitioner and action researchers. Conceptually, pragmatism has the strongest connection with empirical-analytic paradigm and tentative connections with interpretive and critical paradigms (see Figure 3.1). Precisely because of these links, pragmatism is often positioned as an in-between and

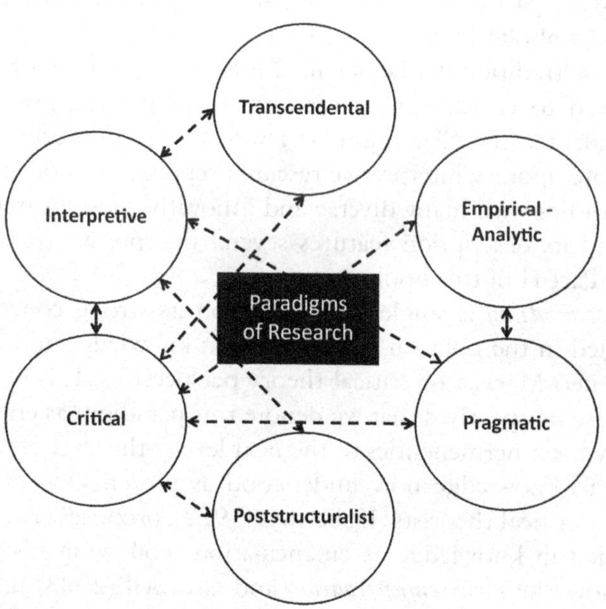

Figure 3.1: Conceptual Relationships Between the Paradigms of Research

reconciliatory paradigm (between supposedly pure empirical-analytic and interpretive paradigms) (see Johnson & Onwuegbuzie, 2004). Pragmatism is an overarching paradigm undergirding a variety of qualitative, quantitative, and mixed-methods research projects.

Interpretive paradigm has roots in several traditional arts and sciences: anthropology, psychology, sociology, political science, linguistics, and philosophy. Polkinghorne (1983) provides a sophisticated analysis of the origins of this paradigm in the existential-phenomenological and hermeneutic systems of inquiry (see Chapters 1 and 2). Germinating from several nineteenth-century European movements, existential-phenomenology and hermeneutics represented the strongest anti-positivist response (Polkinghorne, 1983) that triggered radical changes in the conception of science, knowledge, scientific method, and appropriate methodologies for the study of human phenomena. *Phenomenological* (or descriptive) and *hermeneutic* (or interpretive) are the historical terms associated with this paradigm. Other terms for it found in research textbooks are *interpretivist*, *qualitative*, or *naturalistic*, which are often used interchangeably. Habermas (1972) distinguishes historical-hermeneutic sciences that aim at knowledge as understanding. *Understanding* (capital *U*) underscores the nature and type of knowledge uniquely attributed to this paradigm. Lather (2004) identifies this paradigm as understanding. Similarly, Creswell (2003) emphasizes understanding as part of constructivist paradigm, which is synonymous with interpretive. Symbolic interactionism and ethnomethodology sprang from the interpretive tradition (Cohen et al., 2008). Interpretive paradigm is most strongly linked to critical, and tentatively to pragmatic, poststructuralist, and transcendental (see "Paradigmatic Diversity and Educational Research" section). Contemporary interpretive research represents a flourishing field of qualitative studies with many diverse and innovative designs (see Table 3.1). Table 3.2 and its description features several interpretive research projects presented in Part II of this book.

Critical paradigm is singled out based on its strong conceptual repertoire grounded in the political perspectives on knowledge and research and especially in neo-Marxist or critical theory perspectives. It is by the association with these perspectives that we denote this paradigm as critical. Critical epistemology takes hermeneutics to the next level—the level of emancipation with regard to knowledge now understood as power. One of the leading contemporary critical theorists, Habermas (1972), proposes critical social science grounded in knowledge as emancipation. Following his lead, Lather (2004) employs the term *emancipatory* and Creswell (2003) uses *advocacy/participatory* to identify this paradigm. Lather (2004) reminds educational

Chapter №	Title	Author	Paradigm	Methodology	
				Theoretical Frameworks Perspectives Models	**Design & Instruments**
Ch 4	*Narratives of Black Female Elementary School Teachers: Navigating the Normative Discourse of Whiteness*	Thera Tilmon	Interpretive & Critical	Critical Race Theory Black Feminist Theory Intersectionality Transcendental theories	*Qualitative* Narrative Counter-narrative Interviews Observational & Self-Reflective Notes
Ch 5	*Sociocultural Perspectives of First Generation Asian Indian Leaders in U.S. Higher Education AnEthnographic Study*	Matthew Woolsey	Interpretive	Sociocultural Lens Bicultural, intercultural, and global perspectives on leadership	*Qualitative* Ethnography Biographical narrative Interviews Field notes Documents Artifacts
Ch 6	*Toward the Inclusion of LGBTQ+ Students of Color: A Case Study of Public High Schools in the Midwest*	Joanne Yonan	Interpretive & Critical	Critical Race Theory Intersectionality Queer Theory	*Qualitative* Case Study Interviews Field Notes Documents Artifacts
Ch 7	*Navigating Adverse Childhood Experiences for More Effective Learning and Student Well-Being*	Amy Kendryna	Interpretive & Critical	Ecological Model of Human Development Social-Ecological Model Ethics of Care Attachment Theory; Social Justice Theory	*Qualitative* Case Study Interviews Observations Field Notes Documents Artifacts Visual Materials

Ch 8	*Is There a Model for Success? A Grounded Theory Approach to Exploring the Facets of Sustainable Professional Employment among the Graduates of Clinical Exercise Physiology Programs*	Regina Schurman	Interpretive & Pragmatic	Model of Sustainable Professional Employment for Clinical Exercise Physiologists	*Qualitative* Grounded Theory (Glaser) Interviews Documents
Ch 9	*Critically Engaged Curriculum: A Call for Action to Elementary Public-School Teachers*	Cheryl Jean DeRoo	Interpretive & Critical	Theory of Change Theory of Social Justice	*Qualitative* Case Study Interviews Observations Documents Artifacts
Ch 10	*Greek Parents' Perspectives and Experiences regarding their Children's Learning and Social-Emotional Difficulties*	Eirini Adamopoulou	Empirical-Analytic	Ecological Perspective Social-Emotional Learning	*Quantitative* Survey Design Test of Psychological Adaptation Parent Survey
Ch 11	*Speech-Language Pathologists' Barriers to Providing Services to the Deaf and Hard of Hearing Children Ages Two to Nine*	Irene S. Garcia-Benavides	Interpretive & Critical	Sociocultural Theory (Vygotsky) Concept of Language Deprivation	*Qualitative* Case Study Demographic Survey Interviews Observational & Self-Reflective Notes

Ch 12	*A Paradigm of Critical Discourse Analysis on Neoliberalism: The Case of Haiti as a Neophyte*	Baudelaire K. Ulysse	Critical (theoretical)	Critical Discourse Analysis Ideologies of Neoliberalism	Analysis of semantic macrostructure Analysis of subtle structure Analysis of global and local discourse forms Analysis of specific linguistic realization (hyperbolas) Analysis of content
Ch 13	*Narratives of Grit by African American Women: Standing Tall Against Racial Microaggressions While Advancing to Community College Senior Leadership Positions*	Toya Michelle Webb	Interpretive & Critical	Critical Race Theory Black Feminist Theory Micro-aggressions	*Qualitative* Narrative Counter-Narrative Interviews Documents Artifacts Visual Materials
Ch 14	*Locked Gates and Chain-Link Fences: A Generational Phenomenological Story of Disability*	Sharon Duncan	Interpretive & Critical	Critical Theory Disability Studies Hermeneutics Phenomenology	*Qualitative* Phenomenology Interviews Documents

Table 3.2: Positioning Part II Chapters within the Paradigms of Research

researchers that the key issue is "how to bring scholarship and advocacy together in order to generate ways of knowing that interrupt power imbalances" (p. 208). Critical paradigm is linked conceptually with all others in terms of its research purposes, and its strongest connection is with the interpretive system of inquiry. Critical inquiry is exceedingly popular among educational researchers, and it inspires an array of research and scholarly projects in feminism, critical race and ethnicity, queer, and disability studies. Table 3.2 and its description in the next section feature several critical inquiry chapters.

The four paradigms that have been described thus far share several important features. First, they encompass major methodologies employed in current educational research (Creswell, 2003, 2012) with various terms ascribed to them. In epistemological terms, all four paradigms designate knowledge claims as provisional, contextual, and contingent. This means that the knowledge/truth that is produced as a result of the research projects conducted within these paradigms is "constructed within [particular] conceptual systems" and is "relative to time and place" (Polkinghorne, 1983, p. 3). Given the characteristics of the knowledge claims of these four paradigms, poststructuralist and transcendental paradigms represent their counterparts, each in their own terms. Between themselves, transcendental and poststructuralist paradigms are epistemological opposites and there is absolutely no connection between them (see Figure 3.1).

Poststructuralist can be best described as a discursive way of knowing due to its complete rejection of foundational knowledge. Poststructuralism is an essentially anti-foundationalist project seeking to deconstruct episteme as the only true and privileged knowledge. There is no knowledge as such, according to poststructuralist thinkers; all that we have is text and its endless interpretations—the copy of the copy of the copy, *simulacra*, or *hyperreality* (see Chapters 1 and 2). The poststructuralist way of knowing is conceptually at odds with many structured models of inquiry, yet its representatives ally with emancipatory research agendas proposed by critical researchers. Poststructuralist research does not stand on its own ground—which it resists and rejects—and is typically conducted within interpretive and critical inquiries. Poststructuralist feminist research is especially appealing to educators (e.g., Lather, 2004, 2008; St. Pierre & Pillow, 2000). Poststructuralist thinkers generate innovative ways of conducting research by experimenting with expressive means and genres such as art, literature, cinematography, or digital imaging. Although elusive in terms of its own definition and suspicious of structured approaches to research, poststructuralism is important to singling out creative ways of generating research projects that stir our social imaginations.

Finally, we distinguish *transcendental paradigm* as truly unique among the constellation of contemporary educational research paradigms. It represents a metaphysical alternative to all other paradigms (which are grounded in a materialistic conception of reality) in that it posits the existence of the ultimate reality and Truth (capital letter *T*) and asserts the importance of reason and intuition, or revelation, as the ultimate ways of knowing. What follows from this position is that reality and a human being have at least two dimensions: physical and metaphysical, or body and mind, as in most ancient and classical philosophical traditions. Some similar non-Western traditions identify a threefold conception of the universe and a human being: body, mind (soul), and spirit (see Chapters 1 and 2). Transcendental paradigm deals with the issues of spirituality. *Transcendental* is a conditional term that we use to designate an array of traditions, ranging from Western mysticism to aboriginal and indigenous beliefs. *Transcendental* means "relating to a spiritual or nonphysical realm" (Stevenson & Lindberg, 2010, p. 1838). The word also evokes Transcendentalism, an idealistic philosophical movement begun in New England in the 1830s. Its major representatives, Ralph Waldo Emerson (1803–1882) and Henry David Thoreau (1817–1862), believed in the divine order of nature and humanity and held progressive views on abolitionism, feminism, and communal living. *Transcendental* can be interpreted in both religious and secular terms. In either case, it implies the existence of an internal moral compass according to which a human being establishes her or his relations with others and the surrounding world. Immanuel Kant (1724–1804) calls this compass a "categorical imperative," or a sense of moral obligation. Metaphysical arguments are not easy to discard. Contemporary professional philosophers continue to wrestle with a metaphysical conundrum and its sources: consciousness and freedom (Scruton, 1996). Self-consciousness presents us with a "peculiar idea of unity," which Kant described as a "transcendental unity of apperception" (Scruton, p. 226).

The issues of spirituality are rarely explored by educational researchers, and when they are, the studies focused on these issues are typically conducted in conjuncture with interpretive or critical (or both) types of research. For instance, Dantley (2005) contends that faith grounds contemporary educational leadership when it is inclusive and politically effective. He aligns faith with leadership, specifically with transformational leaders who wrestle with undemocratic practices such as tracking and ability grouping, inequitable funding, and high-stakes testing. According to Dantley, these leaders exercise faith as they "envision schools grounded in democracy and social justice but they labor to bring about what they have created by faith into existence" (p. 11). Tisdell's (2000) study seeks to determine "how spirituality influences the motivations and practices of a multicultural group of women adult educators who are teaching for social change" (p. 67). Tisdell positions her research within the critical and poststructuralist feminist framework, and she discovers that spirituality is elusive as well as all-encompassing and is a force that "gives meaning and coherence to life" (p. 86). And it is this compelling realization that adds an immense value to the participants' efforts to teach for social change.

The examples of research projects presented in Part II do not intersect with either the transcendental or poststructuralist paradigms directly. However, tentative links with the transcendental paradigm, for instance, can be established in the content of Chapters 4 and 14 has an implicit poststructuralist ring to it.

The description and graphical representation of the six paradigms identified for the purposes of this book are yet another conceptual version, among others, of educational research. These paradigms do not exhaust all possibilities, yet we believe that they are sufficiently encompassing in terms of existing educational research alternatives. A different number of paradigms can be potentially identified. Ours is not a matter of concern with the number but, more effectively, with the purpose of this paradigm journey to broaden the conception of educational inquiry and the spectrum of its methodological choices.

Toward Methodological Pluralism

Although the fierce battles between positivistic and post-positivistic camps of philosophers are the remnants of the past, today's researchers continue to debate the issues surrounding appropriate methods of educational inquiry whereby placing positivism in the center of debates. For instance, Howe (2009) posits the existence of a tacit form of positivistic research (new scientific orthodoxy) that presumably is still thriving in educational research. Yu (2006) would question this and similar statements on the grounds of persisting misconceptions and misrepresentations of positivism in educational research (see Chapters 1, 2, and the discussion above).

Current research in hard and soft sciences is engaged in multischematic and multi-paradigmatic inquiries choosing among available and often competing methodological alternatives (Polkinghorne, 1983; Yu, 2006). Epistemological and methodological pluralism, which is the reality of the day, calls into question any assumption of certainty regarding the knowledge of the world and any fixed method designed to unravel all its mysteries. The existing theoretical frameworks and methods in educational research do not represent impervious to criticism or annihilation models but rather alternative and multiple paradigms of research, each of which can represent the best available and most *appropriate* model for individual inquiry, and each of which can be eventually subject to questioning and rejection. Choosing appropriate paradigm(s) for a particular research project is the key to the project's successful planning, that is, selecting appropriate methodologies and that project's subsequent implementation.

Relevant to our discussion on research methodologies is the question of definitions. The terms *methodology* and *methods* are often used synonymously, even though they have very distinct meanings and purposes. Both words have their origins in Latin and their etymology partially was addressed in Chapters 1 and 2. Consulting the etymology of many terms that we use in education is essential to their proper understanding. The roots, prefixes, or endings of these terms often bear important connotations that, if not accounted for, could create controversies and debates around their use (and these occur fairly often among educational researchers and scholars). *Method*, for instance, designates

> particular activities that are used to achieve research results. Methods include various experimental designs, sampling procedures, measuring instruments, and the statistical treatment of data. The word *method* retains the mean of its etymological roots. It is made up of the root words *meta* and *hodos*: *meta* means "from" or "after," and *hodos* "journey." The word *method* is thus a "going-after" or "a pursuit." [I]t is a pursuit of knowledge. (Polkinghorne, 1983, p. 5)

deMarrais and Lapan (2004) define method as specific research techniques used to gather evidence about a phenomenon, and it typically utilizes such research tools as surveys, observations, interviews, and the like. Bogdan and Biklen (2007) define *method* as "consistent with the logic embodied in the methodology" (p. 35).

Methodology, on the other hand, reflects an overarching process or plan for researching phenomena. Methodology includes the root word *logos*, which has a rich history beginning with Greek philosophy where it was used to refer to the principle of reason, the source of world order and intelligibility (see above). Methodology is "the examination of the possible plans to be carried out—the journeys to be undertaken—so that an understanding of phenomena can be obtained" (Polkinghorne, 1983, p. 5). Methodology is typically informed by major systems of inquiry, or paradigms, and includes under its umbrella definition specific ideas or theories as part of the conceptual repertoire and corresponding epistemological positions and methods. Epistemological and ontological assumptions ought to be especially carefully crafted since they have a significant impact on how we generate knowledge (Pascale, 2011).

deMarrais and Lapan (2004) reiterate a similar position claiming that our assumptions about what we believe knowledge is "are embedded in methodological discussions, and therefore have consequences for how we design and implement our research studies" (p. 5). For example, ethnographic research can be grounded in a range of epistemological and methodological positions such as symbolic interactionism or critical theory (deMarrais & Lapan), cultural and cognitive anthropology, or feminism (Creswell, 2012). Specific theoretical assumptions about how one defines culture are certainly paramount for ethnographic research (deMarrais & Lapan). Determining which methods to use (e.g., observations, interviews, document analysis, etc.) should first be based on a thorough review of methodologies, which addresses phenomena that can be studied as the method emerges in a related way. Thus, it is imperative that researchers qualify their inquiries by demonstrating how their research is connected to larger theoretical and philosophical dispositions on knowledge that often constitute a system or tradition of inquiry—paradigm (e.g., empirical-analytic, pragmatic, interpretive, critical)—that provides a substantive context for situating and crafting a credible research plan (methodology) that is aligned with appropriate activities and tools for collecting and analyzing data (methods).

Selecting a methodology and accompanying methods can be a daunting task for novice researchers, given the varied and sometimes unique ways in which the overarching research paradigms and methodologies are interpreted by the respective researcher, authors of research methods texts, and articles addressing methodological assumptions. It should be noted that the assumptions of what research is in the field of human and the social sciences has changed significantly over the last several decades. The repudiation of positivism and subsequent changes in the understanding of scientific method, along with the emergence and growing popularity and legitimacy of interpretive methodologies, have changed the nature and scope of educational research.

Although over the years interpretive (qualitative) research has gained proper recognition and place within the constellation of methodologies in social and human sciences, many contemporary educational researchers and scholars continue to debate the nature of the scientific method, which supposedly puts a demarcation line between more scientific quantitative research and its less scientific qualitative counterpart. Moreover, many partisan researchers on both sides of the debate continue to misrepresent positivism by associating it with quantitative research. It is imperative for educational researchers to develop a deeper and clearer perspective on the philosophical underpinnings of quantitative inquiry. We rely primarily on Yu (2006) to demystify positivism in general, especially its misconceived relation to quantitative research. Yu presents a detailed analysis of positivism, its history and its relevance or absence thereof to quantitative methods of analysis:

> While positivism has been universally rejected by philosophers of science over the past fifty years, the current textbooks still either associate quantitative methods with positivist ones or cover quantitative methods within a positivist frame of reference. Despite the fact that newer epistemologies and methodologies, such as post-positivism, critical realism, and critical multiplism, have been discussed in numerous books and articles, the debate regarding the paradigm of quantitative methods seems to be trapped in a time warp. (p. 23)

There are several reasons for the misunderstanding of the relationships between positivism and quantitative research:

> The misunderstanding is due to the association between the one-way reductionism endorsed by certain logical positivist and quantitative methods. In addition, quantitative research includes time-series analysis, repeated measures, and other trend-based inquiries, and thus it is inaccurate to describe quantitative research

> as merely orienting towards outcomes and lacking the process orientation. (Yu, 2006, p. 24)

Further, the perception that quantitative research assumes static reality is attributed to the myth that logical positivists are realists, which is conceptually erroneous. Whereas from a positivistic standpoint reality is equated with experience, quantitative researchers typically posit objective reality as the point of departure for pursuing research. Logical positivism represents conventionalism, relativism, and subjectivism—a position that is essentially antirealist (Yu, 2006). Yu contends that at the ontological, epistemological, and methodological levels, "the Fisherian School, the Neyman/Pearson School, the Bayesian school, the Resampling School, and the Exploratory Data Analysis (EDA) school are fundamentally different, and to some extent are incompatible" (pp. 24–25). This statement clearly supports the epistemological and methodological pluralism position relevant to quantitative *and* qualitative methods as well as the methods *within* each of these categories.

Positivists' major principle of verification represents another dilemma with regard to misconceived relations between positivism and quantitative research. The principle of verification concerns statements of meaning and posits that a statement is meaningless if verification is not possible. Therefore, if statistical methods that are applied cannot yield verifiable results, the effort is useless. In the tradition of quantitative research, there is no evidence that any major quantitative researchers subscribe to this radical epistemology. For example, Cronbach, the famous statistician who introduced Cronbach coefficient Alpha and construct validity, did not restrict his inquiry to only verifiable materials in the logical positivist sense. When Cronbach contemplated the problem of causal inferences in research, he did not employ LISREL or other quantitative causal modeling techniques. Instead, he looked to the more qualitative methods of the ethnographer, historian, and journalist (Yu, 2006). Statistical methods do not provide verification in the logical positivist sense:

> The logic of statistical hypothesis testing is not to verify whether the hypothesis is right; rather, the logic is to find the probability of obtaining the sampled data in the long run given that the null hypothesis is true. However, if we put any theory in the perspective of the "long run," *nothing can be conclusively verified* [our emphasis]. (Yu, p. 29)

In agreement with Yu (2006), we contend that many educational researchers incorrectly attribute causal inferences to logical positivism. Quantitative methods, which include randomized experiments, quasi-experiments, meta-analysis, and structural equation modeling, are not compatible with the anti-cause notion of logical positivism. Yu further argues that it is questionable to attribute positivist reductionism to quantitative research. The history of positivism shows how the originators of many statistical methods—which are still widely used in quantitative research— such as Pearson and Fischer, initially adopted positivistic assumptions predominant at that time. Yet shortly after the overall repudiation of positivism, most if not all scientists abandoned its positions (see Chapters 1 and 2). The point that logical positivism is not—and cannot be—the modern scientific paradigm can hardly be overestimated. Positivistic assumptions of science have become obsolete by default due to the scientific and technological advancements of the recent century, and current methods of going after knowledge are not a matter of certainty but rather a choice that can yield the best explanation or understanding among the existing alternatives.

Various schools in quantitative research utilize different assumptions and could be treated as independent traditions; therefore, methodological pluralism is encouraged by quantitative researchers:

> What is needed is to encourage researchers to keep an open mind to different methodologies by allowing research methods being driven by research questions, while retaining skepticism to examine their philosophical assumptions of various research methodologies instead of unquestioningly accepting popular myths. (Yu, 2006, p. 43)

The perspectives provided by Yu (2006), Polkinghorne (1983), and Ozman and Craver (2008) suggest the need for (1) carefully scrutinized philosophical frameworks, (2) utilizing a syncretic process that incorporates a multi-paradigmatic approach to educational research, and (3) exploring new philosophical directions in an effort to maximize the potential of the researcher's inquiry.

In this chapter, we illustrate how 11 burgeoning researchers coming from various fields of educational study have approached their respective projects using various epistemological and methodological perspectives informed by specific overarching systems of inquiry in an effort to gain a more in-depth understanding of their research and its ramifications (see chapters in Part II). The works of these authors originated from their dissertation research projects that effectively represent inquiries into significant human problems and the attempts to solve them. Table 3.2 exhibits the approach that we take to position the chapters in Part II within the four major paradigms of research: empirical-analytic, pragmatic, interpretive, and critical. In what follows, we provide a brief analysis of these chapters focusing on how specific types of knowledge, theories, and theoretical orientations are linked directly with the steps of the research process.

For instance, Eirini Adamopoulou (Chapter 10) conducted her study within the empirical-analytic paradigm and employed a nonexperimental, descriptive survey design. Eirini's intent was to describe a specific phenomenon: Greek parents' perceptions and experiences about their children's learning and social-emotional challenges in elementary school. Her survey included a large sample of parents who reside in different areas of Greece. In addition to the survey, she used the Test of Psychosocial Adaptation where parents rated their children's social-emotional learning functioning. The study was guided by Bronfenbrenner's ecological systems theory. Using the ecological perspective, she explored the impact of Greek society's limiting factors, constraints and opportunities, and the general environment. The large data sets, the multiple perspectives, and the statistical measures provided a wealth of information that enabled Adamopoulou to gain a depth of knowledge that informs and yet remains fallible and subject to further improvement.

The pragmatic paradigm is the overarching framework shaping Regina Schurman's research in Chapter 8. Schurman selected a grounded theory design for her study because she saw the need for a broad theory or explanation for her particular inquiry. The study reflects qualitative grounded theory and is firmly positioned within the pragmatic tradition. Pragmatism, which reflects Peirce's process of inquiry (abduction, deduction, and reduction), parallels the process Schurman utilized as she wrestled with her research inquiry. The grounded theory design fits her research purposes and questions and is sensitive to the individuals in her setting. Schurman used semi-structured and unstructured interviews with the participants who had graduated from the clinical exercise physiology program. She stayed close to the data in this design by continually analyzing one set of responses that led to an analysis of the next set. Schurman appropriated the Glaserian version of grounded theory that was best aligned with her research purposes to address the employment challenges faced by graduates of clinical exercise physiology programs. Her study resulted in a model of sustainable professional employment that captures the processes that guide graduates to management positions in healthcare systems.

It should be noted that the pragmatic paradigm underpins mixed-methods studies. This paradigm holds a worldview "that focuses on the outcomes of research, that include the actions, situations, and consequences of inquiry" (Creswell, 2012, p. 22). Pragmatism is an exceedingly practical and applied research philosophy (Creswell, 2003). The pragmatic worldview incorporates multiple methods that would best answer the research questions, utilize quantitative, qualitative, or mixed methods for collecting data, address practical applications of ideas, and emphasize the importance of the research problem as the context for conducting the research (see Tables 3.1 and 3.2). In recent years, mixed-methods research has gained relative popularity because its purpose is to reach convergent validity or a stronger warranted assertion. Johnson and Onwuegbuzie (2004), for instance, provide a compelling position regarding the role of mixed-methods research and the need to promote the importance of the pragmatic viewpoint as researchers strive to inform practice with a perspective that reflects inductive and deductive approaches.

Several chapters in Part II present studies conducted within the traditions of interpretive and critical research: ethnography, autoethnography, phenomenology, narrative, case study, and critical discourse analysis (see Table 3.2). For instance, in Chapter 5, Matthew Woolsey selected an ethnographic approach as a framework to shape his exploration of first-generation Asian Indian leaders because it directly addresses his intent to discover how individuals in different cultures and subcultures respond to and make sense of their lived experiences (see Table 3.2). Ethnography is an effective way to understand social reality by directly observing behaviors and interacting with others within the research setting. Woolsey specifically wanted to know which salient features in their backgrounds enabled and nurtured their viability both in India and in the United States especially. He was also interested in identifying the key motivators that influenced Asian Indian expatriate college and university leaders to pursue higher education leadership positions in the United States.

Woolsey actively pursued data to inform his inquiry. He spent hours observing participants, maintaining field notes and reflections, using thick descriptions to establish credibility and capture behavioral nuances, and studying signs in the language (semiotics) that reflect a "stratified hierarchy of meaning structures" (Bogdan & Biklen, 2007, p. 30). He made every effort to become part of the culture in order to gain the trust and the respect of his participants and, moreover, to be able to "understand" what is communicated verbally and silently because he possesses "the insider's view" (Bogdan & Biklen, p. 31) and now has acquired shared meaning.

The critical paradigm has gained special dominance, drawing from the politically transformative events of the Civil Rights and counterculture movements. The political and philosophical ideas and events reflective of this paradigm's epistemological and philosophical underpinnings have given rise to such forms of educational inquiry as feminism, critical race, ethnicity, and queer theories; disability studies; critical discourse and semiotic analyses; and postmodern and poststructuralist inquiries. Critical inquiries are strongly aligned with the interpretive tradition, and this is evidenced in the works of Thera Tilmon (Chapter 4), Joanne Yonan (Chapter 6), Amy Kendryna (Chapter 7), Cheryl Jean DeRoo (Chapter 9), Baudelaire K. Ulysse (Chapter 12), Toya Michelle Webb (Chapter 13) and Sharon Duncan (Chapter 14).

The aforementioned authors have chosen various methodological approaches to explore critical issues within their respective studies. Four of them chose case studies (Chapters 6, 7, 9, & 11) that allow for exploration of real-life contemporary contexts that involve individuals or small groups and organizations bounded by time and place (Creswell & Poth, 2018, p. 96). Case studies typically involve lengthy periods of time spent in particular settings and multiple sources of data collected for the purpose of making a comprehensive case. Thus, Joanne Yonan (Chapter 6) has made a case for advocacy for LGBTQ+ high school students of color in the school district when she has been working for a number of years witnessing the events of discrimination and stereotyping, some of which had resulted in tragic circumstances.

Amy Kendryna (Chapter 7) is a passionate advocate for children with adverse childhood experiences (ACEs). She has dedicated several decades of her life working as an elementary school principal and dealing with numerous cases of ACEs within her school district. Resulting from the years of Amy's leadership and research is the Social-Ecological Model (Figure 7.1) that offers invaluable insight and direction to all those on the path to advocacy for children with ACEs. Cheryl Jean DeRoo shares her path as elementary school leader and passionate advocate for civic engagement through the case study conducted within her school district. Cheryl delves deep into the roots of activism, social justice, and theories of change to understand, reimagine, and promote civic engagement among the teachers, school leaders, and other educational professionals with the purpose of creating lasting and permanent changes in the U.S. school system that can serve the needs of all students toward equity and social justice.

Irene Garcia-Benavides' case study stands out, among others, as one that focuses on professional roles and responsibilities of language and speech pathologists providing services to the deaf and hard of hearing children ages two to five. Unique as it were, Irene's case unfolds a spectrum of issues that arise out of practice of many professionals that serve the needs of these children, as well as the barriers that need to be overcome to provide more effective services. Irene makes a compelling case about the medical vision of the speech-language pathology as being detrimental to proper language acquisition of deaf and hard of hearing children.

Part II features two distinguished examples of critical narrative research by Thera Tilmon (Chapter 4) and Toya Michelle Webb (Chapter 13).

Narrative has gained prominence as tradition and qualitative research methodology since at least the end of the twentieth century (Creswell & Poth, 2018). Narrative has roots in the ancient tradition of storytelling in various cultures, as well as more defined disciplines of literature, history, anthropology, sociology, and socio-linguistics (Creswell & Poth, 2018). Wedded to the narrative tradition is its critical bent of counter-narrative that provides a way for the researchers to present experiences that are contradictory to commonly accepted viewpoints (Goodall, 2010).

Thus, Thera Tilmon ventures on the counter-narrative journey exploring the experiences of elementary school teachers navigating the normative discourses of whiteness when teaching African American students. Toya Michelle Webb (Chapter 13) weaves together powerful narratives of African American women acquiring senior leadership positions in community colleges, while overcoming hidden or overt microaggressions on their path. Toya's personal narrative adds to the valuable insights and unique experiences of the nine participants of her study.

Baudelaire K. Ulysse (Chapter 12) employs critical discourse analysis (CDA) that reflects a number of theories, sampling procedures, and analytic frameworks (Pascale, 2011) to explore his overarching research question: How is the current engine of economic globalization, or the global economy, being propelled by neoliberalism as the dominant discourse? Ulysse is committed to fair-mindedness, freedom of academic practice, and a genuine interest in the human condition, and his passionate commitments drive his thinking and actions. His analysis of the discourse of neoliberalism is informed primarily by the critical theory perspective. Through the use of CDA, and the process inherent within the tool, he has been able to dissect and decipher these texts and resources, determine the underlying messages associated with neoliberalism, and discuss these findings within the context of his research intent. Ulysse's study is a compelling case of the potential of unobtrusive methods of analysis (Hesse-Biber & Leavy, 2011).

Duncan's research (Chapter 14) is done in the intersections of phenomenology and critical inquiry into disability studies (see Table 3.2). Her overall intent is to raise awareness of the lived experiences of individuals with disabilities and the impact these experiences have on their families. As Duncan shares the lived experiences of her participants, she inserts specific connections between the story and the research intent. Her purpose is to identify key themes that ground the phenomenology of disability in specific critical intentionalities as portrayed through the participants' experiences. Duncan reaches her ultimate research purpose as she elevates the level of readers' awareness so that able and disabled can meet at the fence and open the gate.

The above projects, rendered through the context of major theoretical frameworks of educational inquiry, provide ample opportunities for novice researchers to enhance their skills of data analysis, inferring meaning from individual lived experiences, creating theoretical models to improve practice, and emancipating consciousness to fight for social justice, and along the way, to learn to position research projects within appropriate paradigms. Journeying through a variety of research exemplars and paradigms inevitably leads to broadening one's horizons in terms of epistemological and methodological pluralism.

Paradigms of Research: Mapping the Final Journey

British philosopher, mathematician, and educator Bertrand Russell (1872–1970) believed that the value of philosophy can be found in the effects upon those who study it. Many philosophers have attempted to provide definite answers to the fundamental questions concerning the nature of the universe and human being without much success. The value of philosophy, therefore, should be sought in its very uncertainty. Philosophy has its chief value "through the greatness of the objects which it contemplates, and the freedom from narrow and personal aims resulting from this contemplation" (Russell, 1993, p. 4). It has to be studied

> not for the sake of any definite answers to its questions, since no defined answers can, as a rule, be known to be true, but rather for the sake of the questions themselves; because these questions enlarge our conception of what is possible, enrich our intellectual imagination and diminish the dogmatic assurance which closes the mind against speculation; but above all because, through the greatness of the universe which philosophy contemplates, the mind also is rendered great, and becomes capable of that union with the universe which constitutes its highest good. (p. 5)

Collingwood (2005) is critical of the excesses of the modern utilitarian mentality that suppresses emotions and ridicules superstitious beliefs in the irrational. He appeals instead to the intuitive and imaginative powers of our primordial being. Bachelard (2005) echoes in turn by exclaiming that when imagination works, everything works!

Educational researchers pride themselves on implementing the projects that serve practical purposes and solve daily human problems. Yet they also conceive of the value of educational inquiry in posing the questions that enlarge our conception of what is possible and what enriches our intellectual and social imaginations. Imagination is the gateway into the known and the unknown, the mysterious spark that instigates our thinking and desire to pursue daring projects. Imaginative thinking frees us from the constraints of prescriptive rules and standards that dictate how to conduct research projects. Like philosophy, research begins in wonder. Wondering and imagination take precedent over calculation and precision in launching successful and gratifying inquiries, and those of us who have ever experienced this, know *for sure* that it is true. Figure 3.2 has *wonder* as its heart center. Emanating from wonder are research questions, hypotheses, methods, epistemologies, theoretical frameworks—all the ingredients of the research process that are informed by the six paradigms. Figure 3.2 captures the image of the paradigm tapestry as a multi-paradigmatic and holistic representation. Each of the six paradigms envelopes corresponding epistemological assumptions and major research designs. Intersecting the cells of the paradigms are the passages with the inscription "re-search process," which intends to convey the idea that the

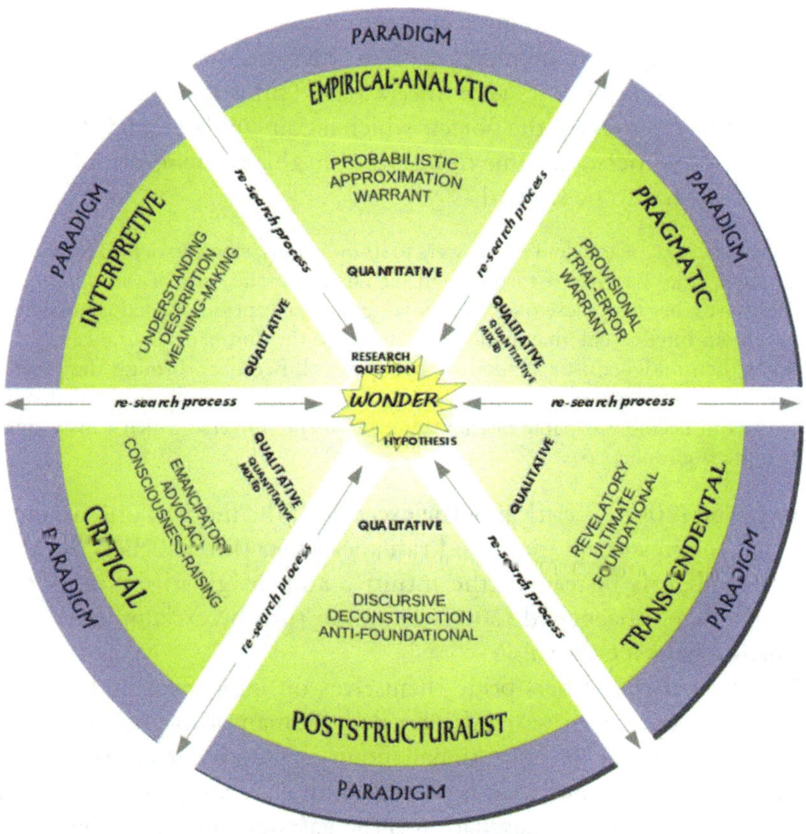

Figure 3.2: Paradigms of Research: Mapping the Final Journey

research process is informed from the beginning to end by specific paradigms and that it is circular in nature. Its circular nature is explicated in the word itself: *re*-search, meaning searching all over again. It implies that our knowledge of the world and human phenomena is never complete. The end of any research process, no matter how strongly it can be grounded in foundational knowledge, signifies a new question emerging from the results, and thus the process continues. Open spaces between the paradigms on the outer circle connote the holes in our knowledge and infinite possibilities of its pursuit through multidimensional and diverse paradigmatic research processes. The circle is never complete and the re-search process remains open.

Our paradigm journey ends on the pages of this chapter. It is final, but not complete or finite. We have endeavored this quest out of the desire to broaden our conception of what is possible in educational inquiry and to enlarge our intellectual imagination of it. We are grateful to the readers who joined in along the way. The search for truth begins with wonder at its heart center and continues as we speak.

References

Anfara, V. A., Jr., & Mertz, N. T. (Eds.). (2006). *Theoretical frameworks of qualitative research*. SAGE Publications.

Bachelard, G. (2005). *On poetic imagination and reverie* (C. Gaudin, Trans.). Spring.

Bogdan, R. C., & Biklen, S. K. (2007). *Qualitative research for education: An introduction to theory and methods* (5th ed.). Pearson.

Cohen, L., Manion, L., & Morrison, K. (2008). *Research methods in education* (6th ed.). Routledge.

Collingwood, R. G. (2005). *The philosophy of enchantment: Studies in folklore, cultural criticism, and anthropology*. Oxford University Press.

Creswell, J. W. (2003). *Research designs: Qualitative, quantitative, and mixed methods approaches* (2nd ed.). SAGE Publications.

Creswell, J. W. (2012). *Educational research: Planning, conducting and evaluating quantitative and qualitative research* (4th ed.). Pearson.

Creswell, J. W., & Poth, C. N. (2018). *Qualitative inquiry research designs: Choosing among five approaches* (4th ed.). SAGE Publications.

Dantley, M. (2005). Faith-based leadership: Ancient rhythms or new management. *International Journal of Qualitative Studies in Education, 18*(1), 3–19.

deMarrais, K., & Lapan, S. D. (Eds.). (2004). *Foundations for research: Methods of inquiry in education and social sciences*. Lawrence Erlbaum.

Goodall, H. L. (2010). *Counter-narrative: How progressive academics can challenge extremists and promote social justice*. Left Coast Press

Habermas, J. (1972). *Knowledge and human interests* (J. J. Shapiro, Trans.). Beacon.

Hesse-Biber, S. N., & Leavy, P. (2011). *The practice of qualitative research* (2nd ed.). SAGE Publications.

Howe, K. R. (2009). Epistemology, methodology, and education sciences: Positivist dogmas, rhetoric, and the education science question. *Educational Researcher, 38*(6), 428–440.

Johnson, R. B., & Onwuegbuzie, A. J. (2004). Mixed methods research: A research paradigm whose time has come. *Educational Researcher, 33*(7), 14–26.

Kipfer, B. A. (Ed.). (2010). *Roget's international thesaurus* (11th ed.). Collins.

Lather, P. (2004). Critical inquiry in qualitative research: Feminist and poststructural perspectives: Science "after truth." In K. deMarrais & S. D. Lapan (Eds.), *Foundations for research: Methods of inquiry in education and social sciences* (pp. 203–215). Lawrence Erlbaum.

Lather, P. (2008). (Post)feminist methodology: Getting lost OR a scientificity we can bear to learn from. *International Review of Qualitative Research, 1*(1), 55–64.

Lemert, C. (1999). *Social theory: Multicultural & classic readings*. Westview.

McMillan, J. H. (2008). *Educational research: Fundamentals for the consumer* (5th ed.). Pearson.

Merriam, S. B. (Ed.). (2002). *Qualitative research in practice: Examples for discussion and analysis*. Jossey-Bass.

Ozmon, H. A., & Craver, S. M. (2008). *Philosophical foundations of education* (8th ed.). Merrill Prentice Hall.

Pascale, C.-M. (2011). *Cartographies of knowledge: Exploring qualitative epistemologies*. SAGE Publications.

Polkinghorne, D. E. (1983). *Methodology for the human sciences: Systems of inquiry*. SUNY Press.

Polkinghorne, D. E. (2004). *Practice and the human sciences: The case for a judgment-based practice of care*. SUNY Press.

Russell, B. (1993). The value of philosophy. In J. Perry & M. Bratman (Eds.), *Introduction to philosophy: Classical and contemporary readings* (pp. 2–5). Oxford University Press.

Scruton, R. (1996). *Modern philosophy: An introduction and survey*. Penguin.

St. Pierre, E. A., & Pillow, W. S. (Eds.). (2000). *Working the ruins: Feminist poststructural theory and methods in education*. Routledge.

Stevenson, A., & Lindberg, C. A. (Eds.). (2010). *New Oxford American dictionary* (3rd ed.). Oxford University Press.

Tisdell, E. J. (2000). Spirituality and emancipatory adult education in women adult educators for social change. *Adult Education Quarterly, 50*(4), 308–335.

Yu, C. H. (2006). *Philosophical foundations of quantitative research methodology*. University Press of America.

Part II Paradigms as Educational Research Exemplars

Chapter 4 Narratives of Black Female Elementary School Teachers: Navigating the Normative Discourses of Whiteness

THERA TILMON

Our ancestors told stories before the written word was developed and long afterward. They used stories to inform, teach, inspire, and motivate. Stories came in many forms, including orature, songs, chants, proverbs, and body language. They provide insights into social phenomena and the human condition. They are important to our history, our future, and our identity. This research stems from my story. A story in which I was often still and silent, in spaces where no one shared my culture or skin color. Spaces in which I was seen but not heard. Spaces in which I struggled to find my place and my sense of being and self. At times, the distance my color afforded me allowed me to size up the group before engaging with it, like testing the water before jumping in, and no one noticed. My color allowed me to be, at times, invisible and ignored. Maybe I enjoyed something about that experience because I continued to find myself in white space. I almost feel comfortable there or it just became familiar. There was also this nameless feeling, which I now know is "cultural alienation." I learned much about the culture and history of the people I shared white space with, but I had a "limited knowledge base of [my own] cultural history" (Shujaa, 2003, p. 182). The difference I felt in white space surpassed my skin color and extended into culture and identity.

I spent much of my life, both in childhood and adulthood, feeling a sense of separateness, pondering my identity, and contemplating how much I would endure, identify, and accept the dominant culture around me (Shujaa, 2003).

I asked myself, subconsciously, how much I would take and how long this would last. In my home as well, I learned to be respectful, invisible, and quiet. I learned not to stick my neck out or ask too many questions. Between the education I experienced at school and the conditioning I experienced at home, I wondered if I would ever find my voice.

With the shortage of Black teachers in America, many Black students like me do not have that cultural and racial connection or understanding in their classrooms. I often consider how my identity development, self-esteem, and overall education would have been different if I had a teacher who looked like me. These thoughts and discussions stir up deep emotion. I find it hard to defend race talk without getting angry and having tears in my eyes. But alas, I am meant to be the expert; it is expected and assumed that I will speak up in White education spaces. As a result, some teachers walk on tiptoes around me, biased in their view of Black women being angry, loud, and confrontational.

As a child, I experienced microaggressions that I did not recognize and, therefore, internalized. Microaggressions are the everyday racist events that occur throughout the lived experiences of many African American people (Doharty, 2018). Microaggressions are subtle, preconscious, or unconscious degradations and putdowns that quietly denigrate people of color (Allen, 2010); (Doharty, 2018). Microaggressions are the passive and commonplace abusive behaviors that marginalize groups, usually groups that are outside the dominant normative group. They can be verbal, physical, non-verbal, inferred, or explicit. These microaggressions contributed to my internal struggle with my Blackness.

In addition, I received confusing messages about how a Black woman should act and feel from my parents, the predominantly White community I grew up in, the media, and many other factors. In my teen years, I felt confused about my Blackness and did not experience that typical "Black experience" depicted on television and in movies. I struggled to understand what it all meant and whether I was truly "Black enough." My parents, who I would now describe as "assimilators," did not help with that clarification. Instead, they transmitted conflicting models. I had no Black teachers to counterbalance the narrative. My friends, mainly White, also had ideas about my Blackness that were based on stereotypes and prejudices. My search for my identity cost me academically as I tried to assimilate as much as possible, only to realize that my skin color could not be changed. In other cases, I rebelled and "tried on" other identities like "justice queen" and "Afro-punk." Most of the time, I conformed and acculturated into Whiteness, creating safe spaces for my White friends and associates that made them feel comfortable, ignoring my needs for comfort and belonging. This process of acculturation allowed me to live and work in White spaces and become "non-threatening and racially innocuous" (Liu et al., 2019, p. 143). This process may have protected my relationships and encounters with White people but damaged my emotional and physical health.

Whiteness is a part of the racialization of humans that defines human beings by their skin color. In the United States, Whiteness takes on another dimension and continues to construct new definitions centered on dominance. Whiteness includes the process of naturalization, which defines White as the norm from which all other races are defined and even ranked. "One of the most powerful and dangerous aspects of whiteness is that many (possibly the majority) of white people have no awareness of whiteness as a construction" (Gillborn, 2009, p. 55). In America, Whiteness transcends racial identity and has evolved into notions of supremacy.

Blackness is the state of belonging to a group defined by the color of their skin, usually a darker shade with components of melanin. In the United States, there is a dominant narrative that places constraints on Blackness, defining, creating, and re-creating Blackness (Acuff, 2018). Blackness is the identity of being Black within a White dominant society. "Racial identity is about shared social status, not shared individual characteristics" (Zuberi & Bonila-Silva, 2008, p. 7). In this study, I wondered about my Blackness and how our shared racial experiences benefit my student's growth. I wondered about whether other Black teachers connect with their students the way that I hope I do. I wondered how they navigate the systems they work under and how they find the balance between the standardization movement rooted in the White narrative and the needs of their students. It is from the lens, that this study was born.

The purpose of this study was to examine the counter-narratives of identity by Black female elementary school teachers within the discourse of Whiteness that remains dominant in the U.S. culture in general and the U.S. public-school system (Lawrence & Tatum, 1999); (Matias & Newlove, 2017). Specifically, I explored the stories of six Black female teachers that illuminate the experiences of success and discrimination, achievement and oppression, and the building of supportive connections with their Black students.

The following overarching research question guided this study: What are the counter-narratives of identity voiced by Black female elementary school teachers within the dominant narrative of Whiteness in U.S. elementary public schools?

Additional secondary questions were:

- How do these teachers navigate the dominant narrative of Whiteness when serving Black students?
- How do these teachers connect with and support their Black students?

Methodological Approaches

My research is centered on telling the stories of Black women. Black women sit in the intersection of Blackness and femaleness, a position that "others" Black women in multiple ways. Othering stems from a dichotomous way of thinking, an either/or process that categorizes people and ideas by their differences. Othering is the social construction of the stranger, the outsider, the other. The others in a society or group can never truly belong. Others stand outside the norms and can threaten the moral and social order of the dominant group. In this way, others define the margins of what is normal; they are the boundaries (Collins, 1991, p. 68).

In this research, I examined not only the stories of Black women as they have experienced racism and sexism, navigated through Whiteness, and realized their own identity, but I also included my counter-narrative. By telling the stories of the experiences of others, I analyzed those experiences in relation to the educational institution. By including my own story, I provided an autobiographical account and reflection through a critical-race lens (Solorzano & Yosso, 2009).

Defining how the "Black experience" contributes to or detracts from the teaching experience, particularly with Black students, required revealing patterns and understanding and interpreting the lived experiences of the teacher-participants. These lived experiences provided a complex web of intersecting identities and experiences that qualitative research addressed in a dynamic process. The analysis of these stories allowed me to understand how all those factors collectively affect participants and students. The research was about exploring the emotional side of the issues in question. These are emotions that are not easily quantified or revealed through quantitative measurements. As a participant researcher, the process of fieldwork or naturally engaging in the process also lent itself to qualitative research. My experiences are a part of the data collection process, combined with the experiences of the participants. Qualitative researchers are interested in "people's subjective interpretations of their experiences, events, and other inquiry domains" (Ravitch & Mittenfelner, 2021, p. 10). My research centered on those experiences, and the stories told by participants were woven with my story.

Identity and intersectionality are also key components in my research and my quest for a deeper understanding of the experiences of Black teachers of Black children. Qualitative research positions the investigations squarely in the participants' lived experiences, bringing this understanding into the light. Qualitative research contributed to the goals of my research to "develop counternarratives to dominant cultural knowledge and normative narratives that circulate in everyday life" (Ravitch & Mittenfelner, 2021, p. 12). The methods I used to tell those counter-stories revolved around critical theories. The power of storytelling was the main data-gathering tool.

Theoretical Lens

This study is positioned within the overarching interpretive and critical paradigms of research. An interpretive paradigm seeks to understand, interpret, describe, or make meaning. It seeks to understand how people engage in meaning-making throughout their daily lives and it draws on the patterns and processes that individuals use to assign meaning (Leavy, 2017). The critical paradigm falls under this category; however, a critical paradigm takes interpretation to the level of "emancipation with knowledge now understood as power" (Lukenchuk, 2013, p. 70). A critical paradigm critiques the power dynamics in society and how that power contributes to the lived experiences of individuals within that society, specifically the interactions between the privileged and the nonprivileged. A critical framework renders that "our lives are mediated by systems of inequity, such as classism, racism, and sexism" (Shields, 2012, p. 4). In addition, the goal is to raise awareness, urge reflection, and lift some of the unheard voices. The intent is to provide and explore multiple perspectives to "identify underrepresented voices and challenge commonly accepted truths" (Shields, 2012, p. 6). A critical lens examines, interrogates, and re-imagines. This qualitative study was informed by critical race theory (CRT), Black Feminist Theories (BFT), Theories of intersectionality (IST), and transcendental theories. (TST).

CRT raises the consciousness of both the researcher and the reader to gain understanding and advocacy for underrepresented members of society. The theory aims to promote social justice and equity through the interpretations of the meaning of Black lives (Creswell & Poth, 2018). Following the branches of CRT, it is important to note that my research is not intended for the "consumption and self-understanding" of the dominant culture. In contrast, using the storytelling methodology, my research gives voice to Black teachers and is, therefore, intended for Black teachers. CRT "questions long-held beliefs in Western methodologies and research that has long disparaged

Black people as a 'problem'" (Leonardo, 2013, p. 63). In that sense, I hope my research is more of a celebration than an indictment. By recording the first-hand narratives of Black teachers, a marginalized group in our society, a different voice can be seen as privileged, and perhaps a new light on the standing and status of these teachers and the lives they touch is revealed and felt by other teachers like them. (Leonardo, 2013, p. 604). Leonardo explains that "subjects live race reality as a relation between their objective and subjective world" (Leonardo, 2013, p. 600). As participants told their stories through narrative inquiry, they did so with their interpretation and perspectives of the world. Through the process of narrative inquiry, stories were revealed. These voices are crucial to our understanding of the Black teacher to Black student dynamic. Critical race theory also examines the social constructs of what knowledge is important, what interests are being served, how power is distributed, and what voices are revealed.

This research followed a Black feminist approach. "Black women bring forth critical perspectives about vulnerability and struggle, resilience and resistance, and love and justice" (Evans-Winters, 2015, p. 129). True to a critical-race approach, my research revolved around the Black feminist theory. This allowed the insights and experiences of Black women to provide the data for the research. A Black feminist approach was the lens from which all the research was being viewed. A lens that "provides a conceptual model for understanding how racism, sexism, and classism intersect to constrain women's bodies and psyches" (Evans-Winter, 2015, p. 133). The experiences, knowledge, and meaning that the participants provided gave voice to Black women to claim and define their realities. According to Evans-Winter (2015), this approach "fosters dialogue for understanding power and privilege" (p. 134) and an understanding of how Black women teachers navigate White supremacy in our school systems and their classrooms.

Part of the Black feminist approach involved the inclusion of my own story as I reflect on my experiences and bring my insights into the research process. Black feminist theory questions the thinking that research should be objective. "Black feminism maintains that research with women and racial/ethnic minorities at the center of the analysis is necessarily subjective, with the intent of promoting social change, self-knowledge and empowerment, or community uplift" (Evans-Winter, 2015, p. 135). Although every Black woman has a different story to tell, they all share "experiences and some form of oppression characterized and related by their class, race, or gender, by their existence as women" (Dillard, 2012, p. 60). With this understanding, my research uncovered many of those experiences and revealed the processes by which Black women navigate through them.

An intersectionality framework includes consideration of multiple influences in an individual's life. Numerous social identities, such as race, ethnicity, gender, and class intersect. "Intersectionality refers to the fluid process inherent in holding two or more social identities that are situated within a historical context" (Jackson et al., 2012, p. 14). The combined experiences provide context for different understandings and meanings for different people. The lived experiences of Black women involve "converging systems of race, class, and gender oppression" (Romm, 2010, p. 220). When investigating the lives and experiences of Black women, it is impossible and impractical to try to separate these converging factors. Black women approach racism and discrimination differently and often according to their class, status, and other factors. This called for an intersectional analysis of the participants' experiences as they worked through "intersecting discrimination" (Romm, 2010). The perspectives gained through participants' stories centered on the multiple social identities that intersect their lives.

The transcendental theories are transformative from a spiritual, metaphysical approach as they seek to explain current symptoms of trauma and subconscious influences. The approach is to link the spiritual influences, unique to a group of people, with advocacy to interpret power imbalances. It is about making space for the mind, body, and spirit in the work. Both the researcher and the participants brought their whole selves to the work, recognizing that the "mind, body, and spirit are intertwined in their functions of maintaining the wellbeing of the individual and community" (Dillard, 2012, p. 81). I conscientiously sought to understand how the spiritual, social, traumatic, and life experiences motivated and influenced the actions of Black women, giving meaning and understanding to the Black experience. Using transcendental theories is about looking beyond the everyday experiences to what lies beneath those experiences. The theory involves explaining what is happening and why it is happening. What are the influences that create that action, emotion, and reaction? A transcendental approach also puts aside any preconceived notions "allowing the true meaning of phenomena to naturally emerge with and within their own identity" (Sheehan, 2014, p. 10). The challenge for me, a participant in the research, was to put aside any notions of reality that I experienced, allowing for new insights and new understandings. An act of reciprocity happened in this research—understanding that "the researcher and the researched are changed in the process of mutual teaching and learning" (Dillard, 2012, p. 81).

Narrative Research Design

Qualitative research design is an ongoing, fluid process. As Ravitch and Mittenfelner (2021) explain, in qualitative research, the "data collection processes are not linear, but rather recursive, iterative, and inductive—with processes that build on and influence each other" (Ravitch & Mittenfelner, 2021, p. 106). Therefore, the design process cannot be dictated or predetermined. Qualitative researchers provide an interpretation of a participant's interpretation of their lived experiences.

Counter-Narrative

The counter-narrative challenges the dominant discourse and the majoritarian narrative. A majoritarian narrative "privileges Whites, men, the middle and/or upper class, and heterosexuals by naming these social locations as natural or normative points of reference" (Solórzano & Yosso, 2009, p. 28). Instead of simply responding to the common narrative, I used counter-narratives to challenge the notions that Black people's views, preferences, and experiences are not normal or acceptable. The counter-narratives challenged and shifted the White privileged perspective on its head and lifted the voices of historically misrepresented and silenced voices (Milner, 2007). The counter-narrative focused on "disrupting and extending what it means to be normal" (Milner, 2007, p. 389). Instead of maintaining the common narrative about what is normal and whose voices are important, the counter-narrative allowed the participants to name their reality. It made the experiences of the oppressed visible and centered, thus normalizing their experiences and their voices.

My research uncovered and centered the stories of Black women, with an understanding that Black women sit in the intersection of Blackness and femaleness, a position that others Black women in multiple ways. Although I recognize that each person's story is different, telling their stories is important. The counter-narrative is as it implies—the other narrative—or perhaps we could say the narrative of the other. In my research, I examined not only the stories of Black women as they have experienced racism and sexism, navigated through Whiteness, and realized their own identity, but I also included my counter-narrative. By telling the stories of the experiences of others, I was able to analyze those experiences in relation to the education institution. By including my own story, I provided an autobiographical account and reflection through a critical-race lens (Solórzano & Yosso, 2009).

Participants

This study uplifted the voices of Black elementary school teachers. The criterion for participants was that they are elementary public-school teachers who self-identified as Black, African American, or of African Ancestry. These teachers also needed to teach in a school where their classrooms are populated by more than 30% Black students. Additionally, I included participants from various levels of teaching experience from different public elementary schools to gain multiple perspectives and understandings. Six participants accepted the invitation to participate. I began the process of selecting participants using a purposeful and convenient sampling strategy. Purposeful sampling "provides context-rich and detailed accounts of specific populations and locations" (Ravitch & Mittenfelner, 2021, p. 83), which was essential for answering my research questions. The sampling was purposeful because I wanted to deliberately identify the best candidates for my research. The sampling was convenient sampling because it identified participants that I had access. Some were fellow teachers in my school district. This factor is important because my research calls for in-depth, personal interviews. Trusting relationships needed to be established to provide the data required by the research questions. I required time to develop a rapport with participants; therefore, they needed to be accessible. A snowball sampling strategy was employed as I looked to identify new participants from conversations with already identified participants (Leavy, 2017). In my experience, I have noticed that there are few Black teachers in the district compared to White teachers. Black teachers many times form strong bonds with other Black teachers, providing a safe place for solidarity and friendship. Therefore, using a snowball strategy introduced me to Black teachers in the area doing amazing work I was unaware of. One of those teachers agreed to participate in the study.

Once potential participants were identified, I began an informal email correspondence to develop a rapport. Rapport is important in the narrative inquiry process because it is through relationships that the participants will "relate and live through stories that speak of their experience" (Caine et al., 2013, p. 577). These experiences could be painful or traumatic, leaving the participant vulnerable and possibly apprehensive. The more trust we had before the interview, the more in-depth the interview could be and the more valuable the data. Once participants informally agreed to participate in the study, I emailed a formal letter of invitation and a consent form.

Sources of Data and Data Collection Strategies

Narrative interviews are well suited for my research into Black lives and the Black lives of teachers who teach Black students. These interviews provided the bulk of the data for this research and the substance for the interpretative narratives. With the information that was shared, I was able to craft the stories of these teachers' lives as well as my own life experiences in a rich and important tradition that traces back to our ancestors. For many of us, as was revealed in the stories participants told, storytelling proved to be their first language, an ancestral language and methodology passed down from generation to generation and revived often in their daily lives and teaching experiences. This legacy of Black feminism has allowed us to "survive with such spiritedness the assault on our bodies, social institutions, countries, and our humanity" (Edwards, 2018, p. 86). Sharing our stories helped us to share our survival.

The ability to tell our stories is at the heart of narrative inquiry because it "makes visible alternative knowledge often silenced and/or contested" (Grady et al., 2018, p. 153). In many ways, sharing our stories is an act of resistance against the dominant narrative. Dillard (2012) describes it as an act of (re) membering that "is a response to the false divisions created between mind, body, and spirit . . . a response to our ongoing experiences and understanding of difference and identity" (p. 17). The key was to discover and uncover the stories of Black teachers. "Studying persons is to study beings existing in narrative and socially constituted by stories" (Leavy, 2014, p. 197). Stories, however, do not happen in isolation. By combining the stories of the Black teachers in my research, I better understood the connections between experiences, emotions, and instruction. Narrative inquiry also presents reflective, creative, and emancipatory possibilities as well as the production of knowledge (Grady et al., 2018). The goal of the narrative inquiries was to provide multiple experiences outside of my own experience as I sought new understandings. This goal committed me to know other stories to hear and record conditions that may not mirror my own (Dillard, 2010). By asking the correct open-ended questions, rich authentic stories of the lived experiences of the participants were told. I conducted one in-depth interview with each participant that lasted at least 2 hours per participant. I followed up with a couple of short questions via email for a few gaps I found in the research. In all cases, the participants provided a wealth of data and insights. No follow-up interviews were necessary.

The interviews I conducted and the stories I retold required an intensive interview approach. Romm (2010) describes an intensive interview as "a way of generating in-depth talk in relation to experiences/cognitions relevant to discussions around racism" (p. 215). The methodology of this type of interview can be regarded as a mutual effort between the researcher and the participant, much like a conversation as previously referenced. To begin this conversation, I asked the participants to share stories of their lives, from childhood to adulthood; describe how race and gender have affected or have not affected their lives and careers; and reflect on how factors such as spirituality, microaggressions, and racism have impacted their identity development. In the intensive interviews, the participant and the researcher engage "in a mutually humbling experience, where each understands our limitations in speaking for the other" (Dillard, 2012, p. 80). The experiences of the participants revealed troubling, painful, and sometimes repressive experiences. The interviewee's experiences and the retelling of those experiences were also triggering for me, the interviewer. In this sense, we were both vulnerable. We both needed to be introspective, open, and willing to relive those experiences to handle this. As the participants did relive and retell their stories, a wide range of responses happened. For some participants, the retelling promoted healing as they gained mastery of their experience and were unburdened. For others, the retelling process was perhaps triggering. These variables can very well dictate the flow of the interview and the questions asked. This required an active-interview approach rather than a passive approach. The interviews were semi-structured because the research aimed to understand the lives of the participants from their perspectives. The goal was to elicit the story (Kvale & Brinkman, 2009).

Memoing and Journaling

After each interview, I wrote a quick memo that included some observational notes and reflections. Direct observation of the interview video provided further context and understanding of the stories told. In many cases, the stories participants told can be lived in what they say as well as what they do not say (Caine et al., 2013). This process involved observation of body language, facial expressions, and other meaningful cues to generate my understanding. Throughout the research process, I also journaled my thoughts, reflections, and observations. This journal was included in the data as a representation of the personal side of the data collection process. A journal is an "introspective record of the fieldwork" (Spradley, 1979, p. 93) that provided me a tool to consider my biases, feelings, and spiritual connections.

Data Analysis and Interpretation

Critical qualitative data analysis includes analysis and interpretation in the process of finding meaning. The analysis comes into play as the qualitative researcher summarizes and organizes the data. Interpretation comes into play as the researcher finds or makes meaning. This recursive process blends the two, as the researcher flows back and forth between analysis and interpretation (Leavy, 2017). The process of data analysis begins with the coding process. I began by highlighting the data—after multiple readings, selecting which segments should gain more importance than other segments, and determining which stories, plots, story elements, or characters assist in describing the environment and experiences of the Black teachers. I scanned for and highlighted the nuggets of information that helped me explain how things are and how they got that way, moving beyond descriptions to deeper understanding (Wolcott, 1929). Using a sort of values coding, I coded the text with the drivers, stresses, supports, and influences in the participants' lives based on the interview questions. I asked what the drivers were that motivated the teacher-participants. I looked at what the stresses were that got in the interviewee's way, redirected them, or re-established their purpose. I also looked at what supports helped build the interviewee up, what kept them going, and what protected them in their careers. I looked at what were the influences that contributed to the interviewee's way of thinking, doing, and knowing. I wondered if there was a climactic event that shifted their thinking, their approach, or their choice of where to teach. I highlighted the facts and the transcripts that provided clues to the mystery of Black teachers.

After each interview was highlighted and key story elements were identified, I combined the interviews with observations, memos, and other data to create a more complete narrative based on the participants' experiences (Allaire, 2018). Additional coding on the narratives involved identifying themes and subthemes. In vivo coding "prioritizes and maintains participant's language" which allows "codes to develop organically" (Leavy, 2017, p. 151). In vivo coding added another crucial element of the thematic analysis.

The highlights, themes, and transcripts were then organized by the participant and sorted by the initial emerging themes. This allowed for additional themes to emerge, initial themes to change, and subthemes to be identified. This third phase of coding resulted in a type of "findings display" that was graphic in nature. It made the overlapping ideas as well as the gaps visual. This type of graphic composition could also be useful in highlighting aspects of the study (Wolcott, 1929). Visualizing the data in new ways provided new insights and revealed new themes and subthemes.

The highlights and graphic compositions from interviews were then compared to the highlights from the memos and journal entries to find additional patterns or counter-patterns. I asked myself the main question: What do the stories and facts have in common and where is that one story that takes a different path or against the noticeable grain? I looked for the "broader framework of interpretative and evaluative processes" as a sort of shared interpretation (Romm, 2010, p. 225). The analysis of the data included a process of "looking across data sources" and finding meaning in the complexity of the sources. This looking across data sources began as the first sources of data were gathered and continued throughout the research process. Moving in cycles between storying, re-storying, interpretation, analysis, interpretation, re-storying, and so on. Each part of the process informed the others as data was gathered, interpreted, and analyzed. The analysis involved finding or interpreting the connections between the sources of data in a search for meaning. Leavy (2017) explains that qualitative research analysis includes "the systematic reduction of content, analyzed with special attention to the context in which it was created, to identify themes and extract meaningful interpretations of the data" (Leavy, 2017, p. 146). In narrative research, most of the data are generated from participant interviews. This "text" is investigated to uncover the meanings embedded in the text.

Qualitative analysis can be formative, offering flexibility in the research, such as reflections on the research questions. The analysis can also be summative as the researcher combines multiple theories, perspectives, and stories into new learning or understanding. The goal is to look for "different relationships and frames for data" (Ravitch & Mittenfelner, 2021, p. 244). For example, by interpreting and analyzing each narrative interview as I traveled through the process, I reflected on the environment, the research questions, and the responses of the participants at that moment. To arrive at the meaning, to solve the mystery, involves "surrendering to the data" and allowing the data to reach their optimum depth to find meaning (Wolcott, 1929, p. 28) By going with the flow of data, alternative research questions were identified, and some questions were omitted on the spot as they had already been answered through conversation. Each interpretation of the interviews and the participants' stories were then combined in a more summative way to share perspectives and come to a more holistic understanding.

Interpretation is an ongoing process with qualitative research, particularly with narrative inquiry. Although much of the data gathered in narrative research are descriptive, an interpretative element still exists throughout the inquiry process. As the researcher, I offered an interpretation of the stories related to me and told by me. My observations and memos also lent themselves to an interpretive quality. Despite all efforts to relay the lived experiences of my participants honestly and accurately, everything was presented through my interpretive lens.

Stories Told to Me

The narrative stories that were shared with me took on an interpretive lens from the participants' points of view before they were transcribed or put to pen. As they expressed their thoughts and narrated their stories, or in other words "re-story," they reflected on and interpreted their own stories. I, as the researcher, in turn, reflected on the stories they told me and reflected on and interpreted the retelling (Clandinin & Connelly, 1989). In the reconstruction of the telling of their stories, the interpretations were refined between me and the participants. These stories also provided themes related to how the participants navigated Whiteness or perceived racism and Blackness.

My Story Told

My story was also a part of the research, interpretation, and analysis process. My narratives were lived, told, and retold in the research. "Thus, the narratives of participant and researcher become ... a shared narrative construction and reconstruction through the inquiry" (Clandinin & Connelly, 1989, p. 11). My re-story was an interpretation of my past, present, and future experiences. In the analysis phase, however, I supported those interpretations with triangulation, discussions with critical friends, and other analytic means.

Interpretation also came into play as the data was gathered and analyzed. Interpretation helped to answer the question: "What does it all mean?" Interpretation looked for patterns, links, concepts, and themes. This process included triangulation, which involved multiple data sources (Leavy, 2017). Combining all the data gathered in this triangulation provided a holistic view of the research questions.

Stories Told, Lives Lived: Introducing the Participants

This research explores the lived experiences and storylines of six Black women teachers in my quest to understand better how Black women teachers navigate through whiteness. Their voices tell the stories of their lives, from childhood to the present, their entrance into teaching, their experience, and their understanding of who they were and who they are today. The stories presented are the counter-narratives this research sought to undercover, answering the overarching research question as well as the secondary questions I sought answers to. I began the work with a biographical sketch of each participant, a chronological birds-eye view of their lives. The stories are then analyzed, revealing themes and subthemes that help answer the research questions.

The participants that were chosen and agreed to participate in this study are all dedicated, hardworking Black female teachers. All but one is currently teaching in schools with a high percentage of Black students. One participant is retired after teaching for more than 30 years in a predominantly Black and Latinx school district. These educators are solid and resilient. They are compassionate, warm, funny, and a joy to interview. These ladies opened their lives and hearts to me in all the interviews. They shared information that surprised me, enlightened me, and inspired me. I found myself in their stories, sharing their joy and trauma. Each participant was given a pseudonym to protect their identity.

Discussion of the Findings

One of the discoveries that revealed itself in the data was the commitment to teaching that the participants displayed. All are devoted and dedicated to the education of Black students and the elevation of Black people in their communities and beyond. Although the participants were at different levels of their identity journey, they share a common thread in terms of responding to the powerful calling to give back and uplift. Each in their own way they provide advocacy and activism. Their stories provide the counter-narrative to how individual lived experiences, such as those of the participants of this study, can challenge and handle othering, form their own notion of Black skin love, and develop their own unique Black identity.

Counter-Narrative of Identity

The common narrative of Black women is based on a set of stereotypes that were developed specifically to dehumanize Black women. The counter-narratives presented in this study reveal the contradiction. Many of their stories included a thread of reverence and honor to the Black women in their lives and Black people in general. Threads of Ancestral greatness appeared throughout their stories and found themselves in different parts of their lives and identities.

The participants recognized the history and legacy of the Diaspora. Many of the participants, for instance, were connected to their ancestry in America. Most of the participants also hold their religions and spiritual practices as sacred and although they may not recognize it, the suppressed and demonized elements of African traditional religions are woven into the Black churches that many of them include in their understanding of themselves as black people, Black women. Many of them spoke about the music they enjoy in Church and about the power of the music. The participants' sentiments about church and spirituality align with the findings of Hamilton-Mason (2009) when they indicated many Black women rely on their faith or spirituality.

Safe Haven: Response to Othering

Each of the participants included elements of their stories that explained how they responded to the process of othering. In all their stories, there was an element of safe haven. A place where they felt valued, human, seen, and heard. Some found this in the same neighborhoods and churches they attended their entire lives and some created communities of their own. These shelters of love and support provide the tools needed to manage the dehumanization process that exists outside their havens. These havens follow the historical pathways from slavery, in which Black women were aware of the larger community, extending beyond their own nuclear family, to an entire community. These teachers bring their entire community with them as they venture out and navigate through their lives and careers. These experiences provide convincing evidence that many Black teachers continue to enter the teaching profession with the intent to uplift the entire community.

Black Skin Love Starts with a Strong Foundation

In all my interviews with participants, there was an overarching sense of Black pride and self-love. For some, that love was always there and for others, it grew over time. The length of the journey to self-Black love was found in the strength of their Black foundation. The participants who had a strong foundation of Blackness struggled less with their identity and found battling racism and stereotypes easier as well. Even the participants that grew up in solid Black communities and experienced poverty still describe a strong connection and love for their Blackness. The women who had those strong Black foundations also seemed to experience less exposure to the stereotype trap. They had less instances of feeling silenced, unable to express their thoughts or stand up to injustice. They had less examples of RBF racial battle fatigue (Acuff, 2018) Although they could site examples of their experiences with the anticipation of discrimination as Canady (2016) explained was a stress-inducing experience, the coping mechanisms they had in place were strong enough to relieve much of that stress. The safe havens that include the workplace also provide fewer microaggressions among the participants. The findings from this study are consistent with what Jones and Day (2018) explain as the socialization of Black girls in Black communities that prepare them better for race-based social and political obstacles, responding to stereotypes, and even assuming family responsibilities.

For the participants of this study who did not grow up in established Black neighborhoods, there was confusion and uncertainty about Blackness. These experiences were very different from the participants who grew up in solid black neighborhoods and felt validated throughout most of their lives. For them, there was an instant sense of pride that never seemed to waver in their lives. There was no question or confusion about their Black identity. Another finding is that the participants who grew up surrounded by Blackness experienced less childhood racial trauma and microaggressions. Their first encounters with explicit racism were well into their teens or adulthood when they were already armed with a shield of Black love to help them move through those experiences. This speaks to the need to maintain Black neighborhoods, retain more Black teachers in those neighborhood schools, and support Black children in Black skin love.

The Journey to Strong Identity

Williams-Washington and Mille (2018) explain that the depth of harm from collective trauma depends on the individuals' sense of identity. The data in this study supports that idea as participants with the strongest sense of Black identity showed fewer symptoms of RES (residual effects of slavery), such as low self-esteem and feelings of inferiority. Some of the participants spent much of their young lives in the pre-encounter stage of racial identity development. As Cross (2016) explained individuals in this state focus on enculturation to remove the label of other. For some the journey was trying to find the right balance between Black and White—just the right amount of assimilation to fit in but still maintain a Black identity. Other participants seemed to skip that stage altogether and spent much of their early years in the encounter stage, where they saw glimpses of racism and inequity but understood their Blackness as significant and important.

All the participants show evidence that they eventually evolved into the immersion/emersion stage where they realized the depth of oppression and racism which led them to the final stage of racial identity—internalization. At this stage, the participants showed that they developed a strong positive self-image, developing Black pride in the recognition of oppression, microaggressions, and racism. It is interesting, however, that all the participants arrived at this place of strength, some taking longer than others. The journey to a strong Black identity in many ways mirrored the journey outlined by Jones and Day (2018). The study showed black women at different phases of the journey from identifying as a woman first, to identifying as a Black person first, to understand that you are simultaneously both. The participants all fell into different identity types. These results validate that Black women are not a monolith and display varying dimensions or levels of Black identity, as identified by Jones and Day (2018) and Cross (1971).

Navigating the Dominant Narrative of Whiteness

Examining how the participants navigated the dominant narrative was also an attempt to see how Black women come to understand and relate to their common experiences of being Black in a society that denigrates and others Black women. This study examined how Black women grapple daily with a conscious and unconscious awareness of their race and gender. Coming from a Black feminist theory, the study places Black women at the center and examines how they cope with the intersectionality of their lived experiences. This navigation includes a survival plan or road map. The road map for many of the participants included a career path that supports collective responsibility, haven communities, spiritual awareness, and special friendships.

Survival Plan A: Career Path That Disrupts the Narrative

White supremacist culture (WSC) focuses on personal success rather than community success. The participants present an alternative, leading more toward an African indigenous culture that focuses on collective responsibility and community cohesion. Almost all the participants started their working lives chasing the WSC dream of money and material success. They all realized, after varying degrees of time, that they couldn't ignore the calling forever. They eventually had to find a way to contribute to the community instead of competing within it. The participants who grew up in strong Black communities spoke fondly of the sense of community and the education that they received in these areas. This is an example of what Collins (1991) wrote when she discussed "cooperative networks" that were created for survival under the harsh realities of slavery and endured long after. It is those enduring networks that the participants all sought in their careers.

Survival Plan B: The Safety of Blackness: Validation, not Mitigation

As WSC has continued to find ways to suppress Black people, the participants all spoke to how they found or created communities to support each other and lift all Black people. They each described how they created a sort of insulated bubble that includes community, church, and family. In some cases that community is the community they grew up in and in some cases, it is the community that they created. But in either case, their community is filled with people like them, either people from the same culture or people with the same mindset. So, one of the ways they navigate whiteness is by returning to the safety of blackness. Fueling themselves with that armor of culture allows them to go out into a WSC culture, experience racism, and microaggression, and know that they have a safe place to land and return to. The safety of Blackness and familiarity also extended to where the participants chose to teach, in Black communities with mostly Black students. The amount of societal pressure, racism, and oppression the participants experienced was lessened because of this cultural safety bubble. Although each participant had that one unforgettable moment when they first experienced racism or saw the glaring discrepancies between what it means to be White in America as opposed to being Black in America, they found healing in the safe Black spaces they created. One of the main things that these communities provide is validation instead of mitigation. In these validating spaces, they are not just tolerated or accepted. Their needs are not ignored or lessened. Instead, they find validation and peace. Reliance on the community as a coping strategy bares out in the research that Davis (2019) encountered. The community provides Black women with the validation they need and a place to be their true authentic selves.

Survival Plan C: Spiritual Awareness

This study provides evidence to support the research that many Black women's survival plan includes a spiritual place or practice that transcends their everyday lives. It could be an organized religion or a universal spirituality. All but one of the participants showed how they find peace within faith in a realm higher than themselves. Four of the participants state the Black Christian Church is one of the safe places that gives them comfort, rejuvenation, and validation. This study revealed how the Black Christian Church serves as more than just a place to worship. There is evidence that these Churches also provide fellowship, friendship, guidance, and support.

Survival Plan D: Special Friends

The majority of the participants spoke about how conversations with other Black women provide them a place to cope, heal, protect their mental health, and build identity. Much of the data collected also shows that these Black women value their friends as protectors of their mental health. They are also selective about who those friends are. Only two of the participants used professional mental health providers when things got especially difficult for them. These relational supports provided the participants with mental health support as well as solace. The data provides the evidence to conclude that Black women tend to "value relational supports rather than mental health services" (Hamilton-Mason et al., 2009, p. 466)—this is in response to the stereotypes and legacy of struggle—we are expected to be strong, so Black women deny the existence of mental health challenges and are reluctant to seek professional help.

Connecting and Supporting Black Students

A major revelation in the research demonstrated how the participants were unified in their love and respect for Black students as well as their commitment to high expectations. They all spoke about how they are tougher on Black students because they know what they will face upon graduation and in the real world. All the participants provided evidence to support the conclusion that Black teachers recognize the advantage of their race and skin color when teaching Black children. They understand how important they are in their role and are committed to their work.

Teacher Identity: A Benchmark for Effectiveness

Much of the connection between Black teachers and Black students begins with the identity development of the teacher. As we know from the research, teachers' identity is wrapped up in how they navigate through various racial and religious communities. The data revealed, as explained above, that the communities that participants navigate through are essential to their identity as Black women. They each, in their own ways, bring those values and beliefs into their school communities (Hodges & Cady, 2012). The depth of these values and beliefs stems from the strength of the teachers' self-worth and how they see themselves as Black women. As Kelchterman (2009) pointed out, teaching is not a neutral endeavor. The data collected in this study supports that concept. Like many Black teachers before them, the participants took on different degrees of racial advocacy challenging the status quo. The participants also saw themselves as uplifters, working to prepare Black students for the future in a WSC world (Lewis, 2008). There is evidence to the conclusion that Black teachers recognize the significance of their place in the educational lives of Black children. Each participant explained how Black children benefit academically, find love and support, and experience validation from them.

Teacher Efficacy: The Importance of Blackness

All the teachers/participants saw value in their Blackness, particularly when teaching Black students. Blackness provides cultural bonds, stronger relationships, and a higher level of commitment to Black students. This study supports the ideas of Farinde (2016), who described how Black teachers can bridge the gap between cultural identity and academic identity with Black children. The participants also recognized that sharing the same cultural/racial identity allowed for a natural bond between students. Authenticity also proved to be an important ingredient as many of the participants explained how being their authentic self-helped to foster stronger relationships, trust, and respect between themselves and their students. This study also revealed how many Black teachers and black students interact. They push these students harder so they're tougher on their black students because they know that the rest that the world at large will be tougher on them. Because of their experiences they understand the value of education and the value of rising above the norm. Sharing a cultural identity and presenting yourself in an honest and authentic way provides children a place where they know they fit in, and they trust you. It is a crucial point in establishing relationships with students.

Longevity: Teachers That Stick Around

One interesting and somewhat surprising detail that came from this study is while many Black teachers come in highly motivated and then quickly get discouraged due to the invasion of WSC, the Black teachers in this study revealed a strong commitment to the profession. Even beyond their love of teaching, they each had a strong tie to the district in which they teach and the children they serve. Even the youngest teacher in the study was committed to staying in the district in which she started teaching, with already 6 years in.

Another surprising trend that came from the study is that the participants did not have countless stories about racism or microaggressions. This indicates that they are either blind to these occurrences or the insulated bubbles they created work so well that they don't have too many incidents. These results are contrary to some of the research conducted by Rinker and Lawler (2018) and Williams-Washington and Mills (2018) among others, that show the depths of long-term racial trauma. Although the symptoms do depend on the level of Racial Identity, current experiences and historical knowledge (Williams-Washington & Mills, 2018). All the participants in this study enjoy the benefit of all those aspects.

Conclusions

Black women teachers face many obstacles and barriers as they strive to be productive and successful leaders and educators of Black children. Navigating the dominant narrative of Whiteness and WSC while also serving Black students can be a challenging and daunting task. The Black women in this study are showing up every day to do just that—as they prepare to battle their own racist demons and answer their calling to make a difference in the lives of Black children. These women wear invisible armor that is stronger than steel and they carry an invisible shield that protects them and their students from harm. Their armor is their communities, and their shields are their connections. The armor is made of solid, loving, and supportive communities. It is studded with Black church, Black friendships, Black love, and Black power. The shields are made of strong connections—tied to their spiritual selves, tied to their ancestral greatness, and tied to the young lives they teach and inspire.

Armor of Community: Black Teachers, Black Students, Black Schools

One conclusion that is revealed in this study is that Black students thrive when they are in Black schools with Black teachers and Black cultural experiences. The attempt to integrate schools and eliminate Black teachers and culture from the curriculum has harmed our children. The mission was never to leave our communities behind, but rather to have the resources to compete on an even playing field while maintaining the love and support our communities provide our children. The plan was never to assimilate, it was to validate who we are as Black people and ensure that our children feel valued and important. This study revealed a perfect example of how effective Blackness can be to inspire Blackness.

The stories illustrated the strength and power of Black excellence and how much easier it is to reach a high level of Black understanding and Black love when you are surrounded by a community of Blackness. For Black teachers to be effective and for Black children to thrive, we need to create environments in which Black culture is not simply tolerated or even just accepted. Blackness needs to be validated in the same way that Whiteness is validated, every day and in every way. This process becomes easier and almost automatic when children are surrounded by Blackness in their communities.

Answering the Call

One way that Black women can respond to this need is to answer the call to become the educators' Black children need and deserve. That process begins, however, with self-reflection and examination of their individual identity. As Black men and women go about their lives living in their black skin, a certain amount of Black pride and validation must take place first. It is that pride that allows Black teachers to overcome the legacy of slavery, handle generational and societal trauma, and adequately serve Black children. You can't teach what you don't know. So as a Black teacher, you first must know yourself as a Black person, a Black woman. You must answer the call with an authentic, unapologetically Black voice that allows you to bring your full self to the classroom and your full self to the fight for equity and justice. Your students need to see you as the real deal—a fighter for validation, a champion of excellence, and a loyalist that never gives up on them. If you are going to answer the call, you must answer it with passion, enthusiasm and more than anything Black love.

This study followed the lives of six Black female elementary school teachers through a process of narrative research. It examined their identity development, socialization, and career paths. In addition, the data revealed glimpses into the spiritual, social, and traumatic aspects of teaching while Black as well as the intersection of race and gender.

The participants in this study were all examples of dedicated Black teachers that are committed to Black excellence in their students and communities. The data retrieved contradicted many of the stereotypes that dehumanize Black women. The data showed strong spiritual connections, a powerful link to created and evolved communities as power centers or safe havens, and the benefit of a strong foundation of Blackness to protect you from harm. This study also revealed the tool kit for thriving in education as a Black educator. It showed how creating cooperative networks, living, and working in validating spaces, being spiritually aware, and having a close set of Black friendships, work together to strengthen a teacher's sense of self and survival in a white supremacist culture.

At the heart of this study was the connection between Black teachers with a strong sense of self and Black children who are developing their own identity. This is the most significant part of the research as it speaks to the so-called achievement gap and how Black teachers make a difference. It illuminates the idea that Black Teachers matter in the lives of Black children. This study does not compare Black teacher effectiveness with white teacher effectiveness, and it isn't an indictment on white teachers. It is more about the brilliance and celebration of Black teachers. It is a testimony to responding to the call for teaching, giving back to their community, and validating Black lives, including their own.

References

Acuff, J. (2018). Confronting racial battle fatigue and comforting my Blackness as an educator. *Multicultural Perspectives*, *20*(3), 174–181. https://doi.org/10.1080/15210960.2018.1467767

Allaire, F. S. (2018). Themes from a narrative analysis of native Hawaiian experiences in science, technology, engineering, and mathematics. *Journal of Ethnographic & Qualitative Research*, *12*(3), 173–192.

Allen, Q. (2010). *Racial microaggressions: The schooling experiences of Black middle-class males in Arizona's secondary schools. Journal of African American Males in Education*, *1*(2), 125–143, 19.

Caine, V., Estefan, A., & Clandinin, D. J. (2013). A return to methodological commitment: Reflections on narrative inquiry. *Scandinavian Journal of Educational Research*, *57*(6), 574–586. https://doi.org/10.1080/00313831.2013.798833

Clandinin, D. J., & Connelly, F. M. (1989). *Narrative and story in practice and research* (p. 25) [Descriptive, evaluative/feasibility].

Collins, P. H. (1991). *Black feminist thought: Knowledge, consciousness, and the politics of empowerment*. Routledge.

Creswell, J. W., & Poth, C. N. (2018). *Qualitative inquiry & research design: Choosing among five approaches* (4th ed.). SAGE.

Cross, W. E. Jr. (1971). *The Negro-to-Black conversion experience: Toward a psychology of Black liberation* (pp. 20, 13–27). Black World.

Cross, W. E. Jr. (2016). *Meaning-making, internalized racism, and African American identity*. SUNY Press.

Davis, S. M. (2019). When sistahs support sistahs: A process of supportive communication about racial microaggressions among Black women. *Communication Monographs*, *86*(2), 133–157. https://doi.org/10.1080/03637751.2018.1548769

Dillard, C. (2012). *Learning to (re)member the things we've learned to forget: Endarkened Feminisms, spirituality, & the sacred nature of research and teaching*. Peter Lang.

Doharty, N. (2018). "I FELT DEAD": Applying a racial microaggressions framework to black students' experiences of Black History Month and Black History. *Race Ethnicity and Education*, *22*(1), 110–129. https://doi.org/10.1080/13613324.2017.1417253

Edwards, K. T. (2018). Stories of migration: Passing through, crossing over, and decolonial transgressing in Academyland. In *Black Women's Liberatory pedagogies*. Palgrave Macmillan.

Evans-Winters, V. E. (2015). Black feminism in qualitative education research: A Mosaic for interpreting race, class, and gender in education. In V. E. Evans-Winters & B. L. Love (Eds.), *Black feminism in education: Black women speak back, up, and out*. Peter Lang.

Farinde, A. A., Allen, A., & Lewis, C. W. (2016). Retaining Black teachers: An examination of Black female teachers' intentions to remain in K-12 classrooms. *Equity*

& Excellence in Education, *49*(1), 115–127. https://doi.org/10.1080/10665684.2015.1120367

Grady, G. O., Clandinin, D. J., & O'Toole, J. (2018). Engaging in educational narrative inquiry: Making visible alternative knowledge. *Irish Educational Studies*, *37*(2), 153–157.

Hamilton-Mason, J., Hall, J. C., & Everett, J. E. (2009). And some of us are braver: Stress and coping among African American women. *Journal of Human Behavior in the Social Environment*, *19*(5), 463–482. https://doi.org/10.1080/10911350902832142

Hodges, T. E., & Cady, J. A. (2012). Negotiating contexts to construct an identity as a mathematics teacher. *The Journal of Educational Research*, *105*(2), 112–122. https://doi.org/10.1080/00220671.2010.529956

Jackson, J. S., Caldwell, C. H., & Sellers, S. L. (Eds.). (2012). *Researching black communities: A methodological guide*. University of Michigan Press.

Jones, M. K., & Day, S. X. (2018). An exploration of Black women's gendered racial identity using a multidimensional and intersectional approach. *Sex Roles*, *79*(1–2), 1–15. https://doi.org/10.1007/s11199-017-0854-8

Kelchtermans, G. (2009). Who I am in how I teach is the message: Self-understanding, vulnerability and reflection. *Teachers and Teaching*, *15*(2), 257–272. https://doi.org/10.1080/13540600902875332

Kvale, S., & Brinkman, S. (2009). *Interviews: Learning the craft of qualitative research interviewing* (2nd ed.). SAGE Publications.

Lawrence, S. M., & Tatum, B. D. (1999). White racial identity and anti-racist education: A catalyst for change. In E. Lee, D. Menkart & M. Okazawa-Rey (Eds.), *Beyond heroes and holidays: A practical guide to K-12 anti-racist, multicultural education and staff development* (p. 12). Network of Educators on the Americas.

Leavy, P. (2017). *Research design: Quantitative, qualitative, mixed methods, arts-based, and community-based participatory research approaches*. The Guilford Press.

Leonardo, Z. (2013). The story of schooling: Critical race theory and the educational racial contract. *Discourse: Studies in the Cultural Politics of Education*, *34*(4), 599–610.

Lewis, E. (2008). Race, power, multipositionality. *Interventions*, *10*(3), 20.

Liu, W. M., Liu, R. Z., Garrison, Y. L., Kim, J. Y. C., Chan, L., Ho, Y. C. S., & Yeung, C. W. (2019). Racial trauma, microaggressions, and becoming racially innocuous: The role of acculturation and White supremacist ideology. *American Psychologist*, *74*(1), 143–155.

Lukenchuk, A. (2013). *Paradigms of research for the 21st century: Perspectives and examples from practice* (Vol. 436). Peter Lang.

Matias, C. E., & Newlove, P. M. (2017). The illusion of freedom: Tyranny, whiteness, and the state of US society. *Equity & Excellence in Education*, *50*(3), 316–330. https://doi.org/10.1080/10665684.2017.1336951

Milner, H. R. (2007). Race, culture, and researcher positionality: Working through dangers seen, unseen, and unforeseen. *Educational Researcher, 36*(7), 388–400. https://doi.org/10.3102/0013189X07309471

Ravitch, S. M., & Mittenfelner, N. (2021). *Qualitative research: Bridging the conceptual, theoretical, and methodological* (2nd ed.). SAGE.

Rinker, J., & Lawler, J. (2018). Trauma as a collective disease and root cause of protracted social conflict. *Peace and Conflict: Journal of Peace Psychology, 24*(2), 150–164. https://doi.org/10.1037/pac0000311

Romm, N. R. A. (2010). *New racism: Revisiting researcher accountabilities.* Springer Science +Business Media.

Sheehan, S. (2014). A conceptual framework for understanding transcendental phenomenology through the lived experiences of biblical leaders. *Journal: Emerging Leadership Journeys, 7,* 11.

Shields, C. M. (2012). Critical advocacy research: An approach whose time has come. In S. R. Steinberg & G. S. Cannella (Eds.), *Critical qualitative research reader* (pp. 2–12). Peter Lang.

Shujaa, M. J. (2003). The widening gap between education and schooling in the post 9/11 era. *The Journal of Negro Education, 72*(2), 179. https://doi.org/10.2307/3211167

Solorzano, D. G., & Yosso, T. J. (2009). Critical race methodology: Counter-storytelling as an analytical framework for educational research. In E. Taylor, D. Gillborn, & G. Ladson-Billings (Eds.), *Foundations of critical race theory in education.* Routledge.

Spradley, J. (1979). *The ethnographic interview.* Holt, Rinehart and Winston.

Williams-Washington, K. N., & Mills, C. P. (2018). African American historical trauma: Creating an inclusive measure. *Journal of Multicultural Counseling and Development, 46*(4), 246–263. https://doi.org/10.1002/jmcd.12113

Wolcott, H. F. (1929). *Transforming qualitative data: Description, analysis, and interpretation.* SAGE Publications.

Zuberi, T., & Bonila-Silva, E. (2008). *White logic, white methods: Racism and methodology.* Rowman & Littlefield.

Chapter 5 Sociocultural Perspectives of First-Generation Asian Indian Leaders in U.S. Higher Education: An Ethnographic Study

MATTHEW A. WOOLSEY

> What do I think of Western civilization? I think it would be a very good idea.
> In truth there are as many religions as there are individuals. (Suri, 2011)
>
> —Mohandas Gandhi

I have a nomadic spirit, an indelible curiosity to discover other walks of life unlike my own. Living to learn in another part of the state, country, and world has formed who I am today. Of these influences, none had a more profound impact on my life than the time I spent in India immersing myself in its culture. The people, aromas, food variations, music, religious festivals, chaotic but organized traffic, colors, elephants in the streets, and so much more triggered an indescribable passion within me to learn more. Subsequently, my India persuasion led me to this academic juncture of exploring the individual perspectives of Asian Indians in their interpretive journey that brought them to serve as leaders in what to them was a foreign country—the United States of America. While I have a desire and appetite to discover the ways of life of peoples in lands unlike mine, I wonder whether Asian Indians have the same compulsion with regard to the United States, with, moreover, a drive to become a leader.

* * *

> What you think you become. (Suri, 2011)
>
> —Mohandas Gandhi

Background of the Study

A striking feature of U.S. higher education is the high participation rate of Asian Americans as professionals in that employment sector. As of 2010, Asian American Pacific Islanders made up 7.2% of the total faculty population inclusive of Asian Indians (National Commission on Asian American and Pacific Islander Research in Education, 2010, p. 11). In terms of Asian Indians employed in U.S. higher education, there are more than 5,000 serving as faculty in U.S. post-secondary institutions (U.S. Census Bureau, 2004). With all this effort to attract Asian Indians to U.S. colleges and universities, less than 1% of all institutional presidents are of Indian descent (Yamagata-Noji, 2011). Why is this the case? And, for those Asian Indians who made it to higher education leadership roles, what were the contributing factors? What might the implications of these factors be for other Asian Indians who may aspire to similar positions of leadership?

Taking the Leap

History shows waves of Indian diaspora over time steadily manifesting into sizeable populations across the United States with recent reports of nearly three million Asian Indians in the country (U.S. Census, 2010). Indians who make the conscious decision to fully embrace the American way of life still find some link to their cultural roots (Kakar, 2007). As I reflect on my own experiences working in India as a team leader and trainer, I find it necessary to delve into the cultural nuances of Indian culture if I expect to achieve any level of success. In essence, making this cross-cultural leap requires recognition and effort to learn cultural norms and mores (Hofstede, 2001), incorporate a genuine willingness to learn the unspoken (tacit) culture (Li & Scullion, 2010), and embrace leadership competencies on both local and global dimensions (Cohen, 2007). What does this cross-cultural leap look like for Asian Indians coming to the United States?

Research Purposes and Questions

The study of leadership within the context of U.S. higher education covers the gamut from trait, contingency, and behavioral theories to modern frameworks, including transformational, collaborative, and social constructivism. Particular to Asian Indians in higher education, the bulk of research focuses on the influx of Asian Indian students, and where focus on leaders does occur, studies tend to aggregate all Asians with Caucasian or Other designations (Teranishi et al., 2009). In fact, Museus states, "Asian Americans in the field of higher education . . . have been relatively excluded from higher education research and discourse" (Museus & Chang, 2009, p. 95).

The purpose of this study is to acquire an in-depth understanding of a complex world of sociocultural influences and interactions in which Indian expatriates pursue positions of leadership in U.S. higher education. I seek to answer the question: How do Indian expatriates view their highest professional attainments in U.S. higher education from their sociocultural perspectives? In an effort to unpack this main question, I am led to the following questions.

- What are the defining features of the Indian expatriates' backgrounds that sustain their *shakti* (life force) in India and especially in the United States?
- What ultimately motivates them to pursue higher education positions of leadership in the United States?

Leadership Inquiry into Asian Indians in U.S. Higher Education

> A man is but the product of his thoughts. (Suri, 2011)
>
> —Mohandas Gandhi

The stretch of general leadership research, defined as the Transactional age, harkens back to the Industrial Revolution (1830–1978) and focused on deliberate traits, the one-man, hero approach to defining leadership (Stogdill & Coons, 1957). Soon thereafter, the shape of leadership study began to explore the interchange between the leader and follower with the eminent goal for the leader to get the follower to achieve something under the headings of behavioral and contingency theories (Yukl, 2010). The late 1970s and early 1980s ushered in the Transformational leadership age recognizing the value of all working together toward a common goal, which is largely attributed to Burns's seminal book titled *Leadership* (1978). The debate about who plays the true influential role in this configuration continues with further examination. One thing is certain—leadership is no longer a title-honored concept, but rather one based on high moral standards, trust, devotion to followers, the ability for all to lead where social constructs influence self in relation to others, and the circumstances at play (Bass, 1990; Northouse, 2010).

Leadership studies of Asian Indian leaders migrating to the United States shows, from a business perspective, concerted effort required for leaders to make a successful leap. The work of Hofstede (1980, 2011) illustrates five cultural dimensions of difference—power distance, individualism, masculinity, uncertainty, avoidance, and long-term orientation—and Indian and U.S. cultures most notably differ in power distance and long-term orientation. Results from the Global Leadership and Organizational Effectiveness (Chhokar et al., 2008) initiative describe American and Indian leaders as action oriented with similar approaches to work, but they differ in the value Indian leaders put on self-reflection compared to their American counterparts. Studies indicate Indians migrating to the United States experience a shift in values (Budhwar et al., 2008), while other research shows that Western tools for testing may have limitations in accurately measuring leadership style (Dalton & Wilson, 2000).

The U.S. higher education leadership inquiry landscape covers theoretical frameworks from trait to social constructivism (Bensimon et al., 1989; Komives & Woodard, 2003). Recent trends indicate education leaders will need to demonstrate a set of nimble characteristics as technology and global influences pressure the academy. Contemporary research in U.S. higher education is beginning to focus on Asian leaders, though aggregated together with no discrimination between Asian origins (Teranishi et al., 2009).

* * *

> Truth is by nature self-evident. As soon as you remove the cobwebs of ignorance that surround it, it shines clear. (Suri, 2011)
>
> —Mohandas Gandhi

As a frequent visitor to India I became affectionately connected with and inquisitive about the Indian people, culture, and ways of life. I participated in religious activities and built relationships with locals, which led to home invitations. These relationships were based on trust with individuals whom I call my friends; trust is fundamental to relationship building in India. My personal disposition for a culture almost the opposite of my Western roots drives my desire for knowing, understanding, and interpreting the underpinning reasons that drive Asian Indians to lead in a world figuratively and literally opposite from their own.

Methodology

Qualitative Inquiry: Discovering Leadership Phenomenon Meaning

To examine the leadership phenomenon of a specific group of Asian Indians in U.S. higher education, I employed qualitative methodology, which deals with "multiple realities" and is flexible in nature to address the "shaping influences and value patterns experienced by the researcher" (Lincoln & Guba, 1985, p. 40). While describing the experiences of a group of Asian Indians as they see it, I attempted to create a holistic account and reconstruct the reality of cultural influences on their leadership journey (Creswell, 2009). Through these multiple forms of realities, the result was an emergent framework that renders this phenomenon meaningful and of practical value.

Qualitative research has been identified as a preferred method for leadership studies (Drath, 2001; Uhl-Bien, 2006; Yukl, 1989; Parry, 1998). The Relational Leadership Theory (RLT) approach posits a framework "for the study of leadership as a social influence process through which emergent coordination (e.g., evolving social order) and change (e.g., new approaches, values, attitudes, behaviors, ideologies) are constructed and produced" (Uhl-Bien, p. 668). With this premise, the discovery of context as it pertains to leadership further supports the need to deeply explore perceptions and interpretations through a qualitative approach.

Higher education is a unique, complex culture in which academic leaders fill a critical and influential role (Kezar, 2009; Rhoads & Tierney, 1992). To do this effectively, qualitative epistemology requires me to seek understanding that goes beyond making causal linkages. Lincoln and Guba (1985) state that dialogue between the research participants and me brings to the fore "myriad mutual shapings" where my understanding is reliant on an appreciation of the descriptive structures that emerge from our interactions (p. 152). I challenged myself to persist with genuine curiosity, to dig deeper opening myself to other "forms of order" about Asian Indian leadership in higher education (Shank, 2006, p. 208).

Ethnography: Depicting the Journey

In this study I utilized ethnography as the approach because it examines the human experiences of their journey to leadership as described by the participants. Extensive observation and field notes are required while collecting artifacts and representative cultural materials. Ethnographers are the recorders of life activities for those under study where inquiry is intimate, focusing on life influences like family, friends, socioeconomic structures, and religion (Hesse-Biber & Leavy, 2011).

Ethnography derives from the field of anthropology where researchers went "native" by immersing themselves in the foreign culture, seeking understanding of customs, cultural patterns, norms, beliefs, and behaviors. Since then the concept of *culture* has migrated to the study of *cultures* representing a group sharing common values, beliefs, and life experiences (McMillan, 2008). Flick (2009) emphasizes the criticality of the researcher "going native" to gain an inside perspective of the studied culture while systematizing "the status of the stranger at the same time" (p. 229). The common ground for this study is lived experience as a member of Indian culture and the impact these life experiences made on the selected individuals.

An ethnographic design is somewhat vulnerable given the interpretative and observational methods employed by the researcher. However, in cases where "interpersonal relationships, social structures, creative products, and so on ... are under examination, quantitative methods simply are not appropriate" (Leedy & Ormrod, 2010, p. 135). Further, the ethnographic design is useful for educational research when it is incumbent on the researcher to collect "multiple sources of information and [spend] considerable time in the field" gathering information when evaluating the credibility of findings purported by the study (Creswell, 2008, p. 493).

Sociocultural Lens: Elucidating the Experiences

The process of finding meaning implies a learning process. Wertsch (1985) states that sociocultural perspectives take this a step further where "social contexts and interactions play in the construction of meaning ... we cannot understand the individual without understanding the social and historical context in which he or she lives" (as cited in Lattuca & Stark, 2009, p. 156). Sense-making, self-interpretation, and language are all influenced by culture where "cognitive processes are ... cultural processes because they are situated in, and thus created by, relevant interpersonal, social, cultural, institutional, and historical contexts" (Lattuca & Stark, p. 156).

Sociocultural research tends to focus on the interpretation of identity formation after joining a community (Lewis & Moje, 2003, p. 1979). The intent of this project was to examine participant self-reflection and interpretation first from an Indian perspective, and then moving to their adjustment to American culture and their experience in U.S. higher education. By doing this, the discovery not only addressed past experiences but also explored "how they shape identities related to the conflict and tension that is always present in such communities" (Lewis & Moje, p. 1979).

The participants of this study were asked to reconstruct their life stories through a semi-structured interview. Throughout the inquiry, I continued posing these questions to myself: "What happens in the translation of reality into text? What happens in the retranslation of texts into reality or in inferring from texts to realities?" (Flick, 2009, p. 75). While the researcher is dependent on the subject's narrative, the aim is not to discern factual processes. This biographical narrative "becomes a mimetic presentation of experiences, which are constructed in the form of a narrative for this purpose—in the interview" (Flick, p. 81). Instead of mirroring reality, applying mimesis means interpretation happens from not only the subject's narrative but a construction by the researcher and reader as well.

Data Collection Strategies

Interviews

A major source of data collection for this study came from semi-structured interviews typical of ethnography (McMillan, 2008). Interviews provided me the advantage of asking the respondent to "reconstruct the past, interpret the present, and predict the future" (Lincoln & Guba, 1985, p. 273). The interviewer in a semi-structured approach uses open-ended questions to set the general direction of the dialogue, but the participant controls the discussion, requiring flexibility on the part of the interviewer (Cohen et al., 2008).

I interviewed five Asian Indian expatriate collegiate leaders at the vice-presidential and presidential levels. Given the nature of this study where human interaction between the researcher and participant is necessary, a small sampling for in-depth analysis until reaching saturation is optimal (Creswell & Clark, 2011; McMillan, 2008). Creswell and Clark recommend four to ten participants typical of ethnographic research. The criteria stipulated participants must have:

- Grown up in India at least through their secondary education; and
- Served at the vice president level or higher in U. S. higher education.

A potential candidate list was generated from personal contacts combined with the snowball technique where additional participants were identified. Twelve individuals matched the criteria and seven were invited to participate, five individuals were subsequently interviewed. Interviews ranged from one to two hours each and took place within the participant's office space, except for one who was in-between positions at the time of data collection. Institutions were located in the East Coast and Midwest. Participant composition included a female at the vice president level, a female president, and three males at the president level.

Field Notes

Field notes, in the form of journaling, "are the data that you gather to make sense of your research setting, and they serve as an aid in writing your research results" (Hesse-Biber & Leavy, 2011, p. 216). My journal entries contain both retrospective and most current memories. While in India, dating back to 2006, I witnessed a myriad of activities and celebrations transforming my perceptions and beliefs about the Indian way of life. I adopted Van Maanen's methodology (1988) called ethnographic impressionism. Van Maanen posits that time away from the field results in a more holistic and complete picture of experiences. My intent was to provide "thick descriptions" incorporating direct quotes, sensory observations such as smells and visuals, along with my feelings and emotions (Hesse-Biber & Leavy, 2011), which contributes to the trustworthiness of this study (Lincoln & Guba, 1985).

Documents and Artifacts

Ethnographic study lends itself to multiple forms of data, enriching the overall contextual interpretation of the phenomenon in question. Some argue there is not one way for recording field observations. Thus, pictures, documents, and video are considered elements of valid data collection (Hesse-Biber & Leavy, 2011). In addition to my journal entries, documents such as pictures, India Internet resources, a video I recorded featuring a typical drive to work each morning in India, and other leadership resources are contained on my website portal capturing my learning journey through this process.

Ethical Considerations of Ethnographic Research

With qualitative research, trustworthiness (credibility) is what gives the study merit. To be deemed trustworthy, the study must be transparent, have consistency-coherence, and communicability (Rubin & Rubin, 1995). Transparency relates to the manner in which data were collected; consistency references the extent the researcher investigated inconsistent responses, achieving coherence by describing conflicting points of view; and communicability means that the reader is able to contextualize the experiences as described by the subjects (Rubin & Rubin).

Qualitative research assumes multiple realities and it is the researcher's role to translate the interpretation of the subjects being studied (Merriam & Simpson, 1995). Internal validity guided my data analysis. The ultimate goal is to present that reality as accurately as possible by implementing various procedures. One way to ensure research credibility is through triangulating data sources and research techniques. Interviews, documents, and artifacts are meant to triangulate my data sources and to illuminate themes of discovery pertaining to events, facts, and interpretations about key factors and competencies for future Indian natives in pursuit of U.S. higher education leadership. Hesse-Biber and Leavy (2011) recommend looking for emergent themes within the text, then comparing artifacts and field notes to confirm consistency.

I made use of member checking after the interviews were transcribed and themes identified. Member checking is a common practice requiring the researcher to compile interview results and ask participants to confirm their reflections were accurately captured; in my case, one participant made minor revisions to the transcript (Creswell & Clark, 2011). Member checking is the most valuable approach to establishing credibility, and can be done in both formal and informal methods throughout the data collection process (Lincoln & Guba, 1985).

I sought feedback from a colleague, which proves to be an effective way to ensure credibility (Flick, 2009). I engaged a colleague to independently review the anonymous transcripts and that colleague subsequently confirmed my results (McMillan, 2008).

In an effort to maintain a balanced way of my own engagement in the study, of who I am, what I am experiencing, and my subsequent interpretations of the information before me, I maintained reflective dialogue; this approach is often termed *reflexivity* (Flick, 2009; Lincoln & Guba, 1985). Lincoln and Guba recommend the researcher engage in daily journaling, capturing logistical observations, reflecting on self in relation to values and areas for further exploration, and recording ongoing decision-making about methodology. My personal reflections through the written word added to the collection of data for triangulation and illuminated places where I potentially may have been self-imposing my own sociocultural perspective on my participants.

Data Analysis: Making the Connections for Understanding

I began data analysis by transcribing the interviews and coding for themes and categories. I did my first round of descriptive coding manually by hand and then went back to adjust for consistency (Saldana, 2009). All 240 codes called *nodes* were transferred into NVivo9, a qualitative data analysis software tool designed specifically for qualitative research to assist in categorization of content. Digital audio recordings from participant interviews, field notes, and artifacts were subsequently uploaded, resulting in a multidimensional picture for analysis.

Information was categorized as either emic or etic data. The emic and etic data were then assembled into "families of codes" representing "setting and context subjects' definitions of a setting, subjects' perspectives about other people and aspects of a setting, process changes over time, activities, events, and techniques subjects use to accomplish things, and relationships and social structures" (McMillan, 2008, p. 284). The key here was to let the data form the codes, beginning from the specific and moving to the general as multiple layers of analysis were required for robust results (Creswell, 2009). Researcher interpretation required me to go beyond describing the complex themes and digging deeper for understanding.

The data analysis process yielded nine themes specific to this community of practice with seven particular to leadership and two others related to their journey alone and "going to the other side" while linking back to their roots. What follows is the description and representation of the research findings and results from the lives of Dr. Rajan, Dr. Gupta, Dr. Moorthy, Dr. Arora, and Dr. Agarwal.

* * *

> There are times when you have to obey a call which is the highest of all, i.e., the voice of conscience even though such obedience may cost many a bitter tear, and even more, separation from friends, from family, from the state, to which you may belong, from all that you have held as dear as life itself. For this obedience is the law of our being. (Suri, 2011)
>
> —Mohandas Gandhi

Exploring the Other Side Alone, Linking Back

Warren Bennis (2009) states, "Those who travel farther from home learn even more" (p. 84). Exploring "the other side" is a vital aspect with this group of Asian Indians. Filled with an inquisitive spirit, these individuals sought to reach a new land and soared in their new environment. Not only did they literally travel the expanse from East to West, they also embraced the American form of higher education and crossed the chasm from academic to administrative roles. Through each lived experience, the texture of each person's journey became vivid, revealing challenges and triumphs, testing and developing methods for navigation.

A number of participants used the word *alone* when describing elements about themselves whether it was their travels to America, leaving family as a child to attend school, or the work they enjoy as executives here in U.S. higher education. On the surface this makes sense, but in some ways it points to their ability to navigate between groups while preserving their individual identity. To move from where they were in their life required a strategy to permeate any perceived boundaries. A solo-spirit may just be one secret ingredient to their life success.

Hofstede (1980, 2001; Hofstede et al., 2010) describes India as a collectivist society where people help each other and do everything possible to save face. American culture is much more individualistic. Could there be an insight here for Asian Indians who describe themselves as "alone?" Perhaps this descriptor has been part of who they are from birth, which, even though living in a collectivist society as defined by Hofstede (1980, 2001), gave them the skills needed to navigate the Indian ways before moving to the United States. In essence, relocating to the United States provides the perfect entre for them to preserve the alone dimension, but successfully navigate boundaries to get things done. For them, becoming vulnerable, realizing skill strengths and gaps, and approaching the challenge with an eagerness to learn served a transformative platform into a new life construct.

Going to the other side has now mutated into a new career phase as some of the participants are now reconnecting with their India ethnic roots. Dr. Moorthy is forging academic agreements with Indian higher education institutions by which students may transfer to the United States and complete a baccalaureate degree within three years. Dr. Arora is increasing professional ties with Mumbai business leaders. In all cases, each participant makes it a priority to return to India for various reasons but is resolute in the proclamation that he or she is more American than Indian.

Immigrant Mentality: Asian Indian Self-Identity

In the beginning, self-actualization through acculturation and the refining of self-identity coalesced into an immigrant mentality of being American first. This insight bucks research findings asserting first-generation Asian Indians identify as Indian first (Farver, Narang, et al., 2002; Farver, Xu, et al., 2007; Hickey, 2006). Born into a society with predetermined roles and a set of societal expectations, all formed an affinity for collectivism, maintained allocentric components in America "where the self and the family are integral, rather than separate, concepts" (Farver, Narang, et al., 2002, p. 340), but naturally absorbed elements of the individualistic American way of life. This assimilation into American culture netted the best of their Indian roots and positively impacted U.S. higher education leadership execution—leading with care for the home and family.

Work Hard: Pull to Serve and the Power of Encouragement

Working hard and responding to the "pull" gives these leaders the resolve that they are fulfilling their calling by not dwelling on the next strategic career move. This Gandhian approach links tightly back to Indian culture heavily influenced by Hindu constructs where one's role is assigned, all reinforced through ancient Indian teachings of heroism in the Ramayana and Mahabharata epics (Butt, 2004). Steeped in a life with values for doing the right thing, education was a catalyst for each person to elevate their role within society (Bhattacharya & Schoppelrey, 2004). Dr. Moorthy sees this "a calling from God to serve others ... not as much aspirational, but something that sort of tends to pull you." By working hard and doing the right thing, all participants subscribed that the "pull" to the next life challenge presented itself, but all in one way or the other had to be encouraged before pursuing the next career move. This need for encouragement poses an incongruous paradigm since Asian Indians tend not to encourage others (Kakar et al., 2002).

Education: Constant Learner

The genesis for academic achievement in each participant's story was fueled by external stimuli, namely his or her mother, who positioned education as a form of insurance toward a future of prosperity. Dr. Rajan said her "mother made it very clear to my sister and me ... that in order to have insurance of some kind ... and that insurance for us was our education." Wrapped in this motivation to succeed academically, education was a source credited for shaping their self-identity. This identity resulted in a search for truth as they migrated to the United States and becoming scholars in their academic fields. As life experiences synthesized, the "pull" factored into their work ethic, and education served as a catalyst by which each assumed formal administrative posts that led toward executive leadership positions with a drive to make a difference.

Credibility: Links to Teaching and Research

Leading U.S. higher education institutions demands leaders skilled across a portfolio of business-savvy competencies (Bolman & Gallos, 2011; Fullan & Scott, 2009; Waugh, 2003). This community of practice emphasized that while leadership roles can be taxing, maintaining credibility through continued scholarly actions was paramount. Dr. Gupta and Dr. Agarwal profess their admiration for learning and teaching and see these as critical parts of who they are. As president, Dr. Agarwal never really left teaching. Dr. Rajan blocks time on her calendar to meet with her laboratory research team. Dr. Rajan and Dr. Agarwal team-teach at their institutions while Dr. Moorthy remains engaged as a guest lecturer and publishes. The challenge is for leaders to strategically allocate time specific to scholarly activities.

Intolerance for Risk Aversion: Principles and Values

Asian Indian leaders are intolerant of academic leaders who avoid risk as the easy way out to evade potential public institutional scrutiny. Propelled by a spirit of exploration into new worlds, all participants spoke fondly of their formative years in India where they assumed their predestined role and achieved academic success while absorbing fundamental lessons shaping their values. "Entrepreneurial," "rebel," and "competitive" were some of the self-subscribed descriptors about who they are. In many ways, to explore in a highly rigid and structured society such as India is not commonplace since one typically lives within his or her birth role in a given community (caste) (Chhokar et al., 2008). This has changed considerably since the lifting of Licence Raj in 1991 (government laws established in 1947 composed of strict business regulations to control the economy), but for each of them, such exploration was rather novel in the 1960s and 1970s. Dr. Arora referenced Gandhi's essay on the Bhagavad Gita that explained while life may be predestined (dharma), all of us are still active participants and through good actions, actions will bring good. The implication here is that action requires risk taking, a concept strongly promoted by Gandhi's leadership during the liberation movement.

Research indicates people living in cultures with strict prescriptions for life activities and requirements for achieving favor with God, like Christianity in the United States, tend to be risk averse (Miller, 2000). Asian Indians come from a society where religion tends to be more fluid and one's religious journey offers more options about how to achieve a happy life on Earth and after (Bacon, 1999; Falk et al., 2010). Taking risks is more acceptable as long as decisions are moral- and value-laden.

Permeate Boundaries: Relational Constructs

Living in a land interfacing with and engaging in customs and traditions of multiple faiths blurred boundaries for these Asian Indians, allowing for different religions and faiths to manifest together. The Hindi phrase, *Vasudheive Kutumbakam*, means the "whole world is my family." The consideration of the "whole world is my family" influences their perception about the concept of networked relations that extend beyond the immediate, nuclear construct. Dr. Rajan emphasized that "being an Indian you are used to larger groups, larger interactions and networks." Asian Indian executives consider all members of the academic community family—students, staff, faculty, alumni, neighboring community, and the board—no matter role, position, title, or any other designation.

Velvet Glove, Steel Hand: Communication with Action

Communicating with conviction, maintaining a tempered demeanor, fully listening to contrasting points of view, and making bold moves based on core principles is an earmark approach for this community of practice. To circumvent negative perceptions by others about his composed communication style, Dr. Arora said that leaders require a consciousness about the principles at stake as a gauge for implementing a firm communication style. He went on to say, "When people feel the velvet glove they think that you're going to be easy to push around … But when it comes to the important things, you really have to stick to the principle and not be folding and compromising."

* * *

Going Forward

> Be the change you want to see in the world. (Suri, 2011)
>
> —Mohandas Gandhi

Asian Indians need to encourage others and pull them along. The message for all is to work hard in the moment and do so with a positive mindset. Likewise, Asian Indians need to seek out leadership training for constant refining, which can be done through internal institutional programs or external venues such as educational conferences and organizations. Time and energy must be devoted to sense-making in a world of mixed messages about ethical leadership that will ultimately mitigate any unwarranted compromises.

People know when a person has their interests in mind no matter the given situation (Salovey & Mayer, 1990). Asian Indians have an opportunity to increase influence by collaborating with others, developing relationships, and doing so in overlapping places to incite positive change. Fostering these relationships requires a communication approach that works with Americans who tend to speak loudly and with emotionality (Varma, 2004).

Learning is a foundational dimension and the search for truth can only promote good in all leadership activities. When truth is at the core, Asian Indian leaders have the opportunity to not only discover new paradigms but also make positive differences in the lives around them and build an external network for support and guidance. Being a leader often causes one to compartmentalize and guard certain emotions, requiring time and a place for emotional venting without fear of reprisal to maintain balance.

My Journey, "On the Other Side"

Going to the other side is a metaphorical phrase descriptive of my life journey where the other side stimulated an unquenchable thirst to explore and learn. From my early years, education became a way for me to distinguish myself from the crowd, opening doors for opportunities unbeknown to me at the time. Primary education helped me hone leadership skills in student organizations while I dove into my studies and became skilled in communication and music.

My time at Washington State University (WSU), located on the other side of the state of Washington in relation to my hometown, nurtured this ongoing affinity for education and leadership development. WSU served as a catalyst to my venture in seeing the world, and from there I seized the opportunity to learn and help others, culminating in a career in student affairs. As I forged onward to West Virginia University on the other side of the country, I quickly learned that while part of the same country, a cultural shift came into play because life constructs and perceptions were different from my West Coast mindset. After six years of student affairs work, I made the choice to go to the other side and give the corporate world a chance.

Life on the other side of the planet struck a chord with me because my travels to India exceeded anything required as a work obligation. Education has always been about finding truth—truth as a result of learning about the world and the interpretations other human beings have about truth—and sorting through to create a holistic frame to guide how I live my life. My passion for working with others, my insatiable appetite for learning, and my affinity for cultural interludes have brought me to this intellectual exercise where India, leadership, and education converged.

Along the way, I have featured quotes from one of the most transformational leaders in the modern era, Mohandas Gandhi. Gandhi was heavily influenced by his readings of Hindu, Christian, Buddhist, and Muslim texts, as well as his experiences with racism in South Africa and with the British legal system, and then he developed it into the nonviolent movement after reading Tolstoy, Thoreau, and others. His life, his calling, his "pull" to serve literally changed the livelihood of an entire nation, inspiring people the world over since his walk on Earth to present day. Gandhi's voice had resonance, reaching all factions of Indian society, friend or foe, culminating in action for the greater good. As I continue along this life journey, I hope my voice and actions, big and small, somehow influence the world around me for the better.

References

Bacon, J. (1999). Constructing collective ethnic identities: The case of second generation Asian Indians. *Qualitative Sociology, 22*(2), 141–160.

Bass, B. M. (1990). *Bass and Stogdill's handbook of leadership: Theory research and managerial application.* Free Press.

Bennis, W. (2009). *On becoming a leader: The leadership classic revised and updated.* Perseus.

Bensimon, E M., & Neumann, A. (1993). *Redesigning collegiate leadership: Teams and teamwork in higher education.* Johns Hopkins University Press.

Bensimon, E. M., Neumann, A., & Birnbaum, R. (1989). *Making sense of administrative leadership: The "L" word in higher education* (ASHE-ERIC Higher Education Report No. 1). George Washington University.

Bhattacharya, G., & Schoppelrey, S. L. (2004). Preimmigration beliefs of life success, postimmigration experiences, and acculturative stress: South Asian immigrants in the United States. *Journal of Immigrant Health*, *6*(2), 83–92.

Bolman, L. G., & Gallos, J. V. (2011). *Reframing academic leadership.* Wiley & Sons.

Budhwar, P. S., Woldu, H., & Ogbonna, W. (2008). A comparative analysis of cultural value orientations of Indians and migrant Indians in the USA. *International Journal of Cross Cultural Management*, *8*(1), 79–105.

Burns, J. M. (1978). *Leadership.* Harper & Row.

Butt, J. (2004). *Visions of service: An introduction to five of the world's great religions, with excerpts from the sacred writings and questions for study and reflection for those engaged in service.* International Partnership for Service-Learning & Leadership.

Chhokar, J. S., Bordbeck, B. C., & House, R. J. (2008). *Culture and leadership across the world: The globe book of in-depth studies of 25 societies.* Psychology.

Cohen, E. (2007). *Leadership without borders: Successful strategies from world-class leaders.* Wiley & Sons.

Cohen, L., Manion, L., & Morrison, K. (2008). *Research methods in education* (6th ed.). Routledge.

Creswell, J. W. (2008). *Educational research: Planning, conducting, and evaluating quantitative and qualitative research* (3rd ed.). Pearson.

Creswell, J. W. (2009). *Research design: Qualitative, quantitative, and mixed methods approaches.* Sage.

Creswell, J. W., & Clark, V. L. P. (2011). *Designing and conducting mixed methods research* (2nd ed.). SAGE.

Dalton, M., & Wilson, M. (2000). The relationship of the five-factor model of personality to job performance for a group of Middle Eastern expatriate managers. *Journal of Cross-Cultural Psychology*, *31*, 258.

Drath, W. (2001). *The deep blue sea: Rethinking the source of leadership.* Jossey-Bass.

Falk, C. F., Dunn, E. W., & Norenzayan, A. (2010). Cultural variation in the importance of expected enjoyment for decision making. *Social Cognition*, *28*(5), 609–629.

Farver, J. M., Narang, S., & Bhadha, B. R. (2002). East meets West: Ethnic identity, acculturation, and conflict in Asian Indian families. *Journal of Family Psychology*, *16*(3), 338–350.

Farver, J. M., Xu, Y., Bhadha, B. R., Narang, S., & Lieber, E. (2007). Ethnic identity, acculturation, parenting beliefs, and adolescent adjustment. *Merrill-Palmer Quarterly*, *53*(2), 184–215.

Flick, U. (2009). *An introduction to qualitative research* (4th ed.). SAGE.

Fullan, M., & Scott, G. (2009). *Turnaround leadership for higher education*. Jossey-Bass.

Hesse-Biber, S. N., & Leavy, P. (2011). *The practice of qualitative research* (2nd ed.). SAGE.

Hickey, M. G. (2006). Asian Indians in Indiana. *Indiana Magazine of History, 102*, 118–140.

Hofstede, G. (1980). *Culture's consequences: International differences in work-related values*. SAGE.

Hofstede, G. (2001). *Cultures' consequences: Comparing values, behaviors, institutions, and organizations across cultures*. SAGE.

Hofstede, G., Hofstede, G. J., & Minkov, M. (2010). *Cultures and organizations: Intercultural cooperation and its importance for survival*. McGraw-Hill.

Kakar, S. (2007). *Indian-ness*. Little India.

Kakar, S., Kakar, S., KetsdeVries, M. F. R., & Vrignaud, P. (2002). Leadership in Indian organizations from a comparative perspective. *International Journal of Cross Cultural Management, 2*(2), 239–250.

Kezar, A. (2009). *Rethinking leadership in a complex, multicultural, and global environment: New concepts and models for higher education*. Stylus.

Komives, S. R., & Woodard, D. Jr. (Eds.). (2003). *Student services: A handbook for the profession* (4th ed.). Jossey-Bass.

Kouzes, J. M., & Posner, B. Z. (1995). *The leadership challenge*. Jossey-Bass.

Lattuca, L. R., & Stark, J. S. (2009). *Shaping the college curriculum: Academic plans in context*. Jossey-Bass.

Leedy, P. D., & Ormrod, J. E. (2010). *Practical research: Planning and design* (9th ed.). Pearson.

Lewis, C., & Moje, E. B. (2003). Sociocultural perspectives meet critical theories: Producing knowledge through multiple frameworks. *International Journal of Learning, 10*, 1979–1995.

Li, W., & Scullion, H. (2010). Developing the local competence of expatriate managers for emerging markets: A knowledge-based approach. *Journal of World Business, 45*, 190–196.

Lincoln, Y. S., & Guba, E. G. (1985). *Naturalistic inquiry*. SAGE.

McMillan, J. H. (2008). *Educational research: Fundamentals for the consumer* (5th ed.). Pearson.

Merriam, S. B., & Simpson, E. L. (1995). *A guide to research for educators and trainers of adults* (2nd ed.). Krieger.

Miller, A. S. (2000). Going to hell in Asia: The relationship between risk and religion in a cross-cultural setting. *Review of Religious Research, 42*(1), 5–18.

Museus, S. D., & Chang, M. J. (2009). Rising to the challenge of conducting research on Asian Americans in higher education. *New Directions for Institutional Research, 142*, 95–105.

National Commission on Asian American and Pacific Islander Research in Education. (2010, December 20). *Reports & publications*. http://www.nyu.edu/projects/care/docs/2010_CARE_Report.pdf

Northouse, P. G. (2010). *Leadership: Theory and practice* (5th ed.). SAGE.

Parry, K. W. (1998). Grounded theory and social process: A new direction for leadership research. *Leadership Quarterly*, *9*(1), 85–105.

Rhoads, R. A., & Tierney, W. G. (1992). *Cultural leadership in higher education*. National Center on Postsecondary Teaching, Learning, and Assessment.

Rubin, H. J., & Rubin, I. S. (1995). *Qualitative interviewing: The art of hearing data*. SAGE.

Saldana, J. (2009). *The coding manual for qualitative researchers*. SAGE.

Salovey, P., & Mayer, J. D. (1990). Emotional intelligence. *Imagination, Cognition and Personality*, *9*(3), 185–211.

Shank, G. D. (2006). *Qualitative research: A personal skills approach* (2nd ed.). Pearson.

Stogdill, R. M., & Coons, A. E. (1957). *Leader behavior: Its description and measurement*. Ohio State University, Bureau of Business Research.

Suri, R. P. (2011). *Inspiring quotes of Mahatma Gandhi* [Kindle version]. Retrieved from Amazon.com

Teranishi, R. T., Behringer, L. B., Grey, E. A., & Parker, T. L. (2009). Critical race theory and research on Asian Americans and Pacific Islanders in higher education. *New Directions for Institutional Research*, *142*, 57–68.

Uhl-Bien, M. (2006). Relational leadership theory: Exploring the social processes of leadership and organizing. *Leadership Quarterly*, *17*, 654–676.

U.S. Census Bureau. (2004). *Fact sheet for Asian Indian alone or in any combination and U.S. 2004 American community survey*. https://www.census.gov/

U.S. Census Bureau. (2010). Retrieved from https://www.census.gov/

Van Maanen, J. (1988). *Tales of the field: On writing ethnography*. University of Chicago Press.

Varma, R. (2004). Asian Americans: Achievements mask challenges. *Asian Journal of Social Science*, *32*(2), 290–307.

Waugh, W. L. (2003). Issues in university governance: More "professional" and less academic. *The ANNALS of the American Academy of Political and Social Science*, *585*(84), 84–96.

Wertsch, J. V. (1985). *Vyotsky and the social formation of mind*. Harvard University Press.

Yamagata Noji, A. (2011, July 6). *LEAP/APAHE leadership development program in higher education* [Paper presentation]. Annual Leadership Development Program for Higher Education, Kellogg West Conference Center, Pomona, CA, United States.

Yukl, G. (1989). Managerial leadership: A review of theory and research. *Journal of Management*, *15*(2), 251–289.

Yukl, G. (2010). *Leadership in organizations* (7th ed.). Pearson.

Chapter 6 Toward the Inclusion of LGBTQ+ Students of Color: A Case Study of Public High Schools in the Midwest

JOANN YONAN

> There is no such thing as a single-issue struggle because we do not live single-issue lives.
>
> —Audre Lorde (BlackPast, 2012)

Students crowd around my room; it is the fifth period, and the juniors are having lunch. They are laughing, teasing, and chatting away just like any other high school adolescents. As I open the door, they rush in, load up their music, and start dancing. These students come to my room almost every day because they do not feel comfortable in the school lunchroom. As the music blares, I remind my students, "Keep the noise down." I know that the discipline office will expect them to be in the lunchroom if the noise gets loud. The students hush down quickly because the lunchroom is one place they want to avoid.

The high school lunchroom should be a welcoming place where students can eat and have downtime with their friends. However, for lesbian, gay, bisexual, transgender, questioning+ (intersex, asexual, pansexual, agender, genderqueer, bigender, gender variant, and pangender) students of color, finding inclusion is an elusive event. According to the 2019 GLSEN (Gay, Lesbian, and Straight Education Network) survey, 94% of the students of color who identify as LGBTQ+ (lesbian, gay, bisexual, transgender, questioning+) have experienced bullying at least once, and 60% have repeatedly been harassed, bullied, or experienced name-calling (Zongrone et al., 2020). Statistics for LGBTQ+ students who are White experience similar percentages of bullying, but they do not experience harassment based on their race, nor are they typically blamed for violations against them (Burdge et al., 2014; Kosciw et al., 2018).

For many LGBTQ+ students of color, having to navigate between race, heterosexism, and genderism daily takes a toll on their physical and psychological well-being (Moradi et al., 2009). Repeatedly experiencing microaggressions manifests in 48% of LGBTQ students of color having regular school absences compared to 21% of White LGBTQ+ students. Without considering trauma, missing school lowers a student's grade point average and raises the dropout rate by 5% to 10% (Zongrone et al., 2020). More concerning is the 21% rate of attempted suicide for LGBQ+ non-transgender and, even worse, a 37–40% rate for students who identify as transgender students (Zongrone et al., 2020).

LGBTQ+ students of color represent the most bullied group of students in American high schools (Diliberti et al., 2019; Pew Research Center, 2013). Bullying is a malicious act, and psychologists believe it is an event that can be a lasting memory, creating future isolation and reduction of self to the point where the bullied no longer allow themselves a voice (Espelage & Swearer, 2008; Farrington & Baldry, 2010; Ryan, 2010; Ryan et al., 2010). Adolescence is the time when self-esteem, sense of identity, and voice are constructed. That is why having a supportive and inclusive environment is crucial for LGBTQ+ students of color (Kosciw et al., 2020). The World Health Organization (WHO, 2017) states that an individual's environment influences the changes taking place during adolescence and those changes will affect that person for a lifetime. For LGBTQ+ students of color, this is specifically important because so many students report severe anxiety and depression at an alarmingly high rate (Platt, 2020). For these students, the high school environment is often the framework for creating emotional instability and a future life of low self-esteem and confidence, two qualities necessary for success in adulthood.

All high school students feel insecure and vulnerable at some time during their adolescence; however, LBGTQ+ students are the most vulnerable demographic that struggles to survive these formative years. Kosciw et al. (2020) identify this segment of American high school students as representing the highest percentage of bullying and attempted suicides. Moreover, even less is known about the experiences of LGBTQ+ students in the context of race because these students face more than one disenfranchisement (Toomey et al., 2017). LGBTQ+ students of color encounter more marginalizing experiences associated with sexual and gender identities along with race and ethnic background, exposing them to heightened institutional and interpersonal racism, heterosexism, and transphobia. Even worse, they are exposed to violence and sexual abuse at a time when they are extremely fragile and searching for their place in the world (Kosciw et al., 2018).

Looking at these severe statistics, one must wonder what public schools are doing to address our LGBTQ+ population. According to Kosciw et al. (2018), a GSA (Gay-Straight Alliance) creating anti-bullying policies and allowing for safe spaces keeps students safer in school, but is this enough? Cleary (2018) identifies the importance of educators creating an environment of inclusion: "Educators often suspect that the social world of adolescents is beyond their reach and out of their control, but that's not really so; teachers have leverage because they set the tone for their schools that indirectly shape their students' future" (p. 1).

The research of Robinson and Espelage (2011) suggests that educators are the most influential in making students feel included by finding correlations between educators and the messages received from adults, peers, and themselves. According to Robinson and Espelage (2011), teachers are the key message shapers who build student inclusion. The GSLEN surveys present statistics for the last seven years that show that establishing a gay-straight organization in school provides opportunities for education and advocacy that reduces harassment and bullying by students' non-LGBTQ+ counterparts (Kosciw et al., 2020). Further, Latinx lesbian and homosexual students experience a 20% reduction in harassment while African Americans experience a 12% reduction; however, for bisexual students of color, this result is much less, with a 7% reduction in cases. For the transgender community of color, GSA produced little change in harassment, bullying, and discriminatory discipline, indicating that this sector of LGBTQ+ is not participating or it has no impact on this demographic of students.

LGBTQ+ students of color are falling behind their peers academically. They have lower GPAs (grade point averages) and are twice as likely not to attend school regularly (Kosciw et al., 2020). Further, this sector of students often experiences poverty, homelessness, depression, and lack of proper medical care (Gates, 2017; Goldstein, 2016). Ten years into the future, LGBTQ+ adults of color will be the majority, representing an estimated 60% of the LGBTQ+ population or 10 million people. (American Psychological Association [APA], 2019). As a result, our education institutions must address this fragile sector of America, or 10 million US adults could continue to struggle with the same issues they experienced as adolescents. (APA, 2019). That is why it is imperative for educators to address LGBTQ+ issues for students of color so they can build a bridge of equity for all students.

Building classroom communities for LGBTQ+ students of color improves attendance, academic grades, and graduation rates (Marx & Kettrey, 2016). This is particularly true for students with multiply marginalizing experiences, such as, students of color who have alternative sexual identities. Several studies (e.g., Kosciw et al., 2020; Kosciw et al., 2018; Marx & Kettrey, 2016) claim schools that show support for LGBTQ+ students through active LGBTQ+ organizations, and support an anti-bullying policy see a greater retention of students who graduate and go on to attend college. In addition, students who report feeling included have fewer incidents of bullying and reports of suicidal thoughts (Kosciw et al., 2018; Marx & Kettrey, 2016). According to Parent et al. (2013), changes in the school environment through SAGA (Straight and Gay Alliance) groups and anti-bullying policies mainly address LGBTQ+ White, middle-class students. It appears from the Zongrone et al. (2020) and the African American Trevor Report (Price-Feeney, 2020) that classroom curriculum and norms provide more inclusive support. The question becomes, how can norms, policy, and curriculum create inclusion and belonging for LGBTQ+ students who experience multiple societal marginalization within society?

Positionality Statement

I embarked on this journey of researching the experiences of LGBTQ+ high school students of color after taking a class in epistemology and discovering the concept of Intersectionality. Intersectionality provided answers to the confusion I have felt for much of my life about why I felt unaccepted. Having an immigrant background, being ADD, and being a female in STEM does not always fit with the status quo. Crenshaw's (2017) theory of intersectionality explains that societies have multiple points of oppression that exist in American society. Intersectionality relates to everyone who experiences discrimination and exclusion, and being a teacher, I realized that extended societal oppression, particularly seen in marginalized individuals, is trauma.

As a high school teacher, I always reflect upon my students' social, emotional, and mental well-being, particularly those who are being pushed out by the system. Kosciw (2020) surveyed the LGBTQ+ student population, resulting in LGBTQ+ students of color reporting the highest levels of ostracization by other students and faculty. Russel and Horn (2017) reviewed juvenile prison demographics and found that LGBTQ+ students of color are experiencing the school-to-prison pipeline at a much higher rate than other demographics of students. Thinking back over the years of teaching LGBTQ+ students of color, I am heartbroken imagining their struggles weighing on their future success. At the first read, I questioned Russel and Horns' findings, and then I discovered that Kosciw et al. (2020) also collected data showing that LGBTQ+ students of color experience regular school discipline, disparaging grades, lengthy periods of isolation and do not finish high school.

The purpose of this qualitative case study was to explore the teacher practices intended to offset oppressive behavior and build classroom inclusion for LGBTQ+ urban high school students of color. The underlying narratives need to be heard, and the K-12 public system needs to know of the practices that pioneering teachers have implemented to offset the oppression these students experience. The following research questions guided this study:

1. What are the issues that LGBTQ+ students of color experience when attempting to find inclusion within an urban high school context?
2. What teacher practices in the classroom can remove barriers to inclusion for LGBTQ+ students of color?
3. How can the addition of LGBTQ+ students of color into the curriculum play a role, if any, in building inclusion for these students?

Throughout this chapter, I utilized the following terminology and definitions to provide a shared common understanding:

- *Asexual*: A person who does not experience sexual attraction, but may experience other forms of attraction (e.g., intellectual, emotional) (Human Rights Campaign, 2018).
- *Bisexual*: This term originally meant attraction to both males and females. However, since the 1990s, according to the LGBT network, bisexuality is currently defined as a person who likes all types of sexual identities and the term is no longer restricted to the ideal of just male and female (LGBT Network, 2021).
- *Binary*: The societal categorization of people as male or female only (Human Rights Campaign, 2018).
- *Gender Non-conforming*: A term created in 1991 by Lisa Diamond, Susan Bonner, and Janna Dickenson describing how one's self-concept deviates from societal norms of masculine or feminine (Merriam-Webster, n.d.).
- *Queer*: An umbrella term that was a derogatory term during the 1940s and 1950s meant to describe a sexual orientation, gender identity, or gender expression that does not conform to dominant societal norms. The LGBT community now uses it as a neutral or positive term to mean people who have sexual orientations the exist in and out of the sexual binary (Human Rights Campaign, 2018).

- *Questioning*: A person who is in the process of understanding and exploring what their sexual orientation and/or gender identity and gender expression might be (Human Rights Campaign, 2018).
- *Transgender*: A person whose gender identity and/or expression are not aligned with the gender they were assigned at birth. "Transgender," in the late 1990s, became an umbrella term under the LGBTQ community to encompass many identities related to gender nonconformity (Human Rights Campaign, 2018).
- *Cis-gender:* A person whose gender identity and expression are aligned with the gender they were assigned at birth and is a term created by German sexologist Volkmar Sigusch in 1998 (McIntyre, 2021).
- *Heteronormative*: A person who identifies as their sex at birth and is emotionally and/or physically attracted to members of the opposite gender. This term was coined by Warner (1999) in *The Trouble with Normal*, a book that discusses what societies expect, demand, and allow when they consider relations between men and women to be the only normal sexual orientations.
- *Intersex*: An umbrella term used to describe a variety of conditions in which a person is born with reproductive and/or sexual anatomy that does not seem to fit the medical definitions of female or male (Planned Parenthood, 2021).

Theoretical Lens and Research Design

This exploratory study examined how high school students experience school from two intersecting points of oppression and how teacher practices addressed race and preferred identity to build inclusion for these students. Critical race theory (CRT), intersectionality, and queer theory shaped this study's purpose and research questions. CRT allows for a critique of societal and political norms. Queer theory disputes sexuality and gender expression occurring at birth; instead, it views sexual identity as fluid and changing throughout one's life (Wiggin & Watson, 2016). Queer theory refutes the assignment of gender and sexuality as standardizing humanness for the purpose of politicizing sexuality through the defining of alternative identities as divisive and disruptive to respectability (Plummer, 2004). Policing behavior benefits those who view society as harming those who want to embrace their identity. Queer theory embraces one's right to sexual ambiguity, stating that binary norms have no physiological or emotional position other than to control personal expression resulting in psychological and emotional trauma (Browne & Nash, 2014).

According to Walton and Cohen (2007), belongingness uncertainty depletes the energy children need to succeed in school. According to the theory of Intersectionality, identification with a certain group can set you up for lack of social bonds or equitable support and assistance because you do not conform to societal norms (Crenshaw, 2013). Walton and Cohen (2007) state that American LGBTQ youth are emotionally taxed and, therefore, lack the energy necessary for motivation and achievement in school. Within the framework of intersectionality, LGBTQ+ people of color have fewer ties, which thwarts their intellectual influence and voice. According to Cho et al. (2013), elements of power are embedded in language, disciplinary action, economics, and other signs. Intersectionality addresses those whose oppressive elements of power. According to GLSEN, identities considered subversive by Butler, such as body dysmorphia, receive the least amount of support from school staff, the highest level of harassment from fellow students, and increased disciplinary action in comparison to the cis-gendered identities of their counterparts.

Critical race theory and the framework of intersectionality disrupt the system that perpetuates race discrimination in America. CRT's five tenets uproot the American white social narrative of "meritocracy" that one can achieve by merits alone. CRT addresses the second-class citizenship of color that permeates our institutional system, such as inequitable education and justice for people of color. CRT is an ongoing ever, ever-evolving retort that challenges the status quo by questioning who is benefiting from America's social construct of color. CRT recognizes society's judgment of others based on skin color versus merits alone and the necessity of unseating the historical narratives to achieve equity for all.

Viewing education through the lens of CRT, intersectionality, and queer theory provide explanations for the achievement gap, the school-to-prison pipeline, and the dropout rate for students of color. Statistics show that transgender students of color are the most disciplined and the highest demographic in prison. Both theories support the necessity of hearing the counter story and the recognition that neither race, which is a social construct, nor sexual preference, which is an identity and not a subversive behavior, needs to be controlled. This qualitative study looks into the classrooms of teachers who alter the social narrative and the techniques they employ to achieve this change.

Case Study

A qualitative case study was used to provide an in-depth evaluation of teachers' praxis at one Midwestern urban high school known for building inclusion for their LGBTQ+ students of color. This study is considered exploratory because of the limited available data and the focus on finding practical solutions. Qualitative research studies individuals in their natural settings and attempts to make sense of or interpret phenomena in relationship to the meanings (Denzin & Lincoln, 2008). In this study, I explored how teachers within their natural school settings and their typical daily engagements influenced the student social environment. Therefore, marginalized students are given a place within the classroom. By utilizing the qualitative research approach, I looked below the surface and focused on what, how, and why questions related to the lived experiences of those involved in this study (Stake, 2010). Particularly, this research landed itself on the premises of an exploratory, intrinsic, and descriptive study (Creswell & Poth, 2018) as the most suitable design to explore the ways in which teachers build inclusion for LGBTQ+ students of color.

The site for this study was a Midwestern urban public high school. The participants were teachers with experience working with students of color who are LGBTQ+. The high school was selected because it was convenient and easy to access, making interview scheduling less burdensome. The participants were found by emailing all the teachers at one high school, explaining my research study, and asking if they would like to participate. From the teachers who responded, participants were sent a letter of consent if they had been teaching for more than ten years of service and if they had taught and are currently teaching LGBTQ+ students of color. I recruited a total of eight participants.

I employed several sources of data for this study: semi-structured interviews, field notes, documents, and artifacts. The utilization of multiple sources ensures data triangulation. Triangulation is the collection of data from at least three different sources to give greater breadth to the data and add validity to the study's accuracy (Saldaña & Omasta, 2018). The application of triangulation, or multiple data sources, can enhance the validation of the study findings. The purpose of the interviews was to evoke rich and thick descriptions of an observed episode, linkage, or explanation (Saldaña & Omasta, 2018). According to Saldaña & Omasta (2018), the researcher can use several methods from a predetermined list of questions and suggested topics for discussion or allow the interview to evolve based on the questions and responses of the participants. All the interviews were audio-recorded, transcribed, and sent to participants for accuracy verification.

For further verification, I kept a spiral notebook of self-reflective notes that I used during the interviews, and I wrote in the margins of the transcribed interviews to remember some of the side information and observations to mark down. These notes were used to build the rich and in-depth information I needed to remember about each interviewee. I also collected documents to show visual representation of the resources used by participants. The resources were examples of lessons and activities participants used to address and discuss racism and sexual identity in the classroom.

Data Analysis

Qualitative data analysis covers many approaches and methods to provide consistency and accountability of findings. This is why Creswell and Poth (2018) recommend following a process to provide a chain of evidence in case-study analysis that creates credibility for the results. The first step in my process was transcribing, cataloging, and sorting the data into different ways to identify patterns and points of intersection. My second step was using the interview questions to determine potential category themes. My third step was separating the data by person and by question. My fourth step was cutting the data into individual quotes and separating these by hand. Finally, I ran a word analysis to evaluate word choice to ensure I had separated the quotes and information into the correct themes. Studying the data and finding a general sense of the information, even writing down observations, or recording general thoughts. This coding method assisted me in summarizing, synthesizing, linking, and interpreting the data.

Validation Criteria and Ethical Considerations

Validity of qualitative research is often expressed through trustworthiness, authenticity, and credibility. Credibility refers to the truth of the findings, and dependability is the capacity for the findings to be repeated within the same context. In contrast, transferability demonstrates that the results can be successfully applied to other contexts (Creswell & Poth, 2018). Member checks were used to enhance the construct validity of the research findings (Yin, 2009). In this study, member checks examined their downloaded data, and then when their responses were separated into categories, I sent them to the participants again for approval. Confirmability, which is part of authenticity, shows that the responders shape the findings from the study and are not influenced by the researcher's bias, motivation, or interest (Creswell & Poth, 2018). This was performed through reflexivity and triangulation.

Reflexivity is a safeguard against potential researcher biases (Creswell and Creswell, 2018). Reflexivity is the awareness of the influence that researcher bias has on the topic and the participants who are being studied. Researchers should engage in active self-reflection and analysis of one's own preconceived ideas, assumptions, or biased thoughts precisely because researchers can exert unintentional influence on people or the topic being studied (Yin, 2018). To become aware of my biases, I have kept a spiral notebook of self-reflections focused on exploring my assumptions, emotional reactions, and cultural positions throughout the research process. Triangulation of data also helps in mitigating any researcher bias. For this reason, I used different sources of data such as interviews, written lessons, my journal of personal notes of thoughts, quotes of what I heard, feelings, and my personal metacognition of events, as well as personal and member checks to see if different sources provide similar results.

Discussion of the Findings

Listening to the stories of the eight participants allowed for a deeper understanding of praxis teacher utilize to build space for marginalized students. The teachers dialogue brought home the struggles to belong and the extra effort to succeed that students of color with non-hetronormative sexual identities need to be successful in urban public schools. Extensive analysis of interviews and additional sources of data has resulted in identification of three main themes: (a) "LGBTQ+ Students of Color: Confronting the Issues"; (b) "LGBTQ+ Students of Color: Building Inclusion Beyond Curriculum"; and (c) "Advocating for My LGBTQ+ Students of Color."

The first main theme was the common issues all participants witnessed while teaching LGBTQ+ students of color. The second is the praxis of each participant, which included altering the class environment and incorporating the LGBTQ+ narratives into the curriculum. Finally, all the participants felt that students of color need strong advocates from their teachers to set the tone of inclusion so all students build empathy and compassion for their fellow classmates. Throughout the interviews, participants in this study shared their educational best practices and methods to foster the inclusion and integration of LGBTQ+ students of color into their classroom communities.

Confronting the Issues

The participants admitted barriers that LGBTQ+ students of color experience in their school, which refer to being misidentified, insensitive remarks, teachers referring to them by their deadname, not being out to their family, being blamed because of the color of their skin, and not allowing them to use the bathroom of their choice. Every participant shared their strategy for change and agreed to start with three things. First, they acknowledged the importance of learning students' preferred names and pronouns. Some participants struggled with the guilt of misidentifying students; however, they felt strongly that teachers influence student change. Second, standing up to misidentification and insensitive remarks is paramount. Every participant stressed the importance of students being known by their preferred identity and having the support of at least one teacher to overcome derogatory comments or references to a student's former name. Further, knowing who is "out" to their parents is also important because teachers mentioned having outed students in the past. Third, the participants expressed the need to create classroom norms around how to show respect and speak to each other with respect.

All participants voiced methods of deliberate classroom interactions that build space for LGBTQ+ students of color. The participants emphasized that this requires correctly identifying students while recognizing ethnicity and culture. For instance, Betty, one of the participants, emphasized that having dark skin affects how people treat her. She feels that having pictures and quotes for all races, types of families, and sexualities lets students know she is open-minded and accepting. All participants support a classroom environment that fosters respectful, empathetic, unstructured conversations to create a safe space. Other participants felt that creating inclusive conversations happens when teachers deliberately build questions into the curriculum while maintaining normed boundaries based on respect.

The participants of this study pointed to several examples that illustrate the isolation of LGBTQ+ students of color. For instance, the participants witnessed staff members avoiding preferred names and pronouns, and a few even struggled to allow preferred bathrooms. Others could provide examples of staff members avoiding the LGBTQ+ issue because student family members were unaccepting. One participant even spoke about the uncertainty of how to approach students about their status when class members are uninviting. One participant spoke of teachers avoiding name changes because their parents did not accept their children using alternative names. Another participant discussed how the hue of one's skin color determines if LGBTQ+ students are accepted or ridiculed. The study participants mentioned that points of oppression are individual, and teachers should never assume or stereotype experiences; teachers must work to make their classroom a safe space where everyone is respected. All the participants stated that having different methods and practices to build inclusive classrooms for LGBTQ+ students of color is important because there is no perfect method. Every teacher in this study took time and reflection to find strategies that worked with the students they had at that moment to build environments of respect so that all voices could be heard.

Regarding the first research question, the findings of this study confirm that LGBTQ+ students of color experience a series of issues when navigating the school system, and the feeling of isolation is at the top of the list. The participants reported witnessing the isolation of LGBTQ+ students of color in their school. For example, observing staff members denying students access to the bathroom of their choice. Further, faculty failing to correct students who showed verbal disrespect through name-calling and shaming students based on their sexual identity and color. This confirms what Kosciw et al. (2020) found that gay high school students of color report the highest amount of isolation from students and teachers.

The other most commonly mentioned issue by the participants was that their LGBTQ+ students of color experience overt disrespect through derogatory comments, jokes, and insults that marginalize and isolate them from their classmates, which confirms what Dinkins and Englert (2015) found in their study. Another important component links the issues of isolation and disrespect that often get placed on the LGBTQ+ student for instigating the behaviors, especially if you're a student of color. Dinkins and Englert (2015) say that teachers often find themselves in uncharted territory when it comes to school policies and resources provided for teachers to resolve the unfair treatment of LGBTQ+ students of color in their schools. However, Dinkins and Englert (2015) state that teachers are the best resource for making a profound difference in how others see and treat LGBTQ+ students.

Beyond the Curriculum

Most participants felt that they must build multiple voices and perspectives into daily instruction, therefore exposing students to stories that counter the societal message. Not all participants agreed on how this happens in the classroom. One teacher supported it happening organically and indirectly through reading, writing, and class discussion, while the other two participants supported teaching the information directly. Further, participants in the language arts suggested using character development to bring out voices and articles on discrimination to create awareness and empathy for the struggles experienced by LGBTQ+ people of color. All participants agreed that the classroom curriculum should build-in humanity by including various identities, races, and cultures.

Another practice recommended by the participants was embedding LGBTQ+ and race-related issues in the curriculum. This practice confirms Blackburn's (2015) statement that students must compare their unique perspectives to those of "othered voices" through the curriculum to understand how societal values impact LGBTQ+ students of color. A participant, named Lisa emphasized this in her unit on synthesizing texts. Her unit, structured to counter discrimination around race and sexual identity, helping students to be better informed in discussing these issues. Kumashiro (2019) states that schools should challenge the myths and interpretations students experience outside school by including "othered" voices embedded into their disciplines. One participant mentioned using LGBTQ+ authors where students can compare content and context to recognize different voices and perspectives.

The participants differed in how they embedded the intersection of race and sexual identity into the curriculum based on developmental level. Some participants worked with older high school students and recommended that students discover the counter story through articles, books, and short stories written in the voice of an LGBTQ+ person of color. In contrast, others felt that some students need direct lessons around LGBTQ+ issues. One participant, a gay cis-gender science teacher, felt that students need to understand how genetic inheritance and preferred identity differ. All the participants felt that the LGBTQ+ community should be interjected into the curriculum around prior background and knowledge of the students in the room.

Beyond curriculum changes, participants stated that students need open and honest discussions between teachers and students. All the participants expressed that teachers need to develop open-ended questions that build conversations around race and the LGBTQ+ community. The participants felt that teacher-student communication is vital in creating critical open-ended questions and points of empathy and understanding with their peers. Participants who teach science said that including experiences that open their world makes them realize that life is not a monolithic event. Several participants maintained that honest questions about the gay community should be addressed immediately because that is where responses have the most impact. For example, in the story of Gordo, students had to discover the character from the context of the book. Teachers in this study emphasized that pressing students with critical questions to reveal the main character's identity created deeper and more thoughtful discussions.

Teachers who work with students stated that students talk together better when student-to-student discussions happen daily. She believes that discussions model how students should talk to each other, primarily how to embrace everyone's differences positively and empathetically. One participant insisted that it is the student-to-student discussions that make the difference. This participant believes that personalized voices build insight into individual and alternative perspectives that allow space for acceptance for LGBTQ+ students of color. All participants agreed that student-to-student discussion is the best method for building community inclusion. Every participant stated that unstructured peer conversations are better when students regularly discuss issues among themselves. At this level of interaction, students can safely and openly talk to each other. Adding in texts provides additional information about LGBTQ+ perspectives and creates more information for students to look through to find similarities with their peers.

Every participant in this study agreed that classrooms, where discussions around color and sexual identity happen teach students to be inclusive. Furthermore, they felt that organic and deliberate discussions are more impactful, as one participant stated, "Wonderings are understood best when addressed as they arise." Still, every participant shared the need for deliberate ideas to be inserted into the discussion. Overall, classrooms need practices and methods that build space for LGBTQ+ students of color by using proper pronouns, norming a classroom around respect, advocating for LGBTQ+ students of color, encouraging daily discussions among students, and incorporating gay voices and subjects of race through articles, readings, or teacher-led discussions.

Going beyond the curriculum, LGBTQ+ students of color often face challenges when navigating a high school system that may not be friendly or inclusionary. The findings of this study uncovered several issues ranging from teachers' hesitancy to use the students' preferred names and pronouns to the hidden prejudices on the part of their peers or the instances of overt disrespect through derogatory comments, jokes, and insults that marginalize and isolate them from their classmates. Most of the participants felt that having student-to-student daily discussions is important for building positive classroom rapport with their classmates.

This study supports Blackburn (2015), who demonstrated that LGBTQ+ students of color need their identities seen and recognized by their teachers and classmates for inclusion. The participants in this study stated that they altered their teaching methods by recognizing and building in situations where students felt empathy and compassion for students of color who are different because they have struggled with their LGBTQ+ identity. The teachers who participated in this study also created opportunities for student-to-student unstructured discussions where alternative voices could be heard; therefore, they are showing value and importance for marginalized students' voices so they would be heard.

One of the main findings of this study demonstrates the participants' struggle to build inclusion of LGBTQ+ students of color in their classroom settings and beyond. This finding confirms what Lee and Smith (2023) identify as the struggle to build inclusion in public schools when the classroom does not make room for alternative voices. The participants of this study felt that teachers need to daily build a place for students who have marginalized identities. The participants all felt that this comes from the consistent use of proper pronouns and preferred names. One of the inclusive practices that all participants created was an environment of respect through daily class discussions. In these discussions, the students practice sharing, with their tablemates or elbow partners, opinions about a class topic, a current event, or a puzzling situation. The participants mentioned that students need to know proper boundaries in classroom discussions by stating that students must be honest and truthful about their opinions, they must take turns sharing and listening, and when they disagree they place the disagreement on opinion but not the person. Stulberg's (2017) study on respecting and hearing alternative voices claimed that pushback must happen for LGBTQ+ students of color to gain the self-esteem and confidence to realize their authentic selves. The participants of this study stated that they practiced daily intra-student dialogue to deliberately teach students to interact in a respectful, inclusive classroom community.

Blackburn (2015) found that LGBTQ+ students of color need their identities seen and recognized by their teachers to feel part of the classroom. Every student wants recognition and support. That is why the participants stated that instructors confidently and regularly use a student's proper identity. Most participants stated that they do this immediately to ensure they determine student identities from a student survey or other methods. Then participants stated how important it is to correctly identify students properly within the first week. Teachers who misidentify students silently permit others to misidentify them (Kosciw, 2020; Delgado & Stefanic, 2012). The participants stated that students appreciate it when teachers work hard to properly name and identify students.

Next, participants believe in creating an environment of respect by teaching students how to correctly address their classmates and to practice daily class discussions, whereby students practice sharing with their tablemates or elbow partners. How the participants chose to do this differed, but the norms they stated that having in place was important to ensure respect remains consistent. Furthermore, the participants mentioned that students need to know proper boundaries in classroom discussions, stating that students must be honest and truthful about their opinions and that students must take turns sharing and listening so every student is heard. The participants confirmed that norming student-to-student discussion was where students build empathy for each other because they listened and reflected on what others said versus just debating, which contributes to Stulberg's (2017) study on respecting and hearing alternative voices as respectful pushback must happen in order for LGBTQ+ students of color to gain the self-esteem and confidence to stand up for their authentic selves. The participants of this study stated that they practiced daily intra-student dialogue with their students to deliberately teach how to interact in a respectful, inclusive classroom community.

The participants singled out several such practices regarding curricular practices. Classroom dialogue was the number-one method used to build inclusion for queer students of color, echoing the findings of Wiggin and Watson (2016), who found that teachers empower the voices of marginalized students with dialogue. Students cannot effectively build inclusion without knowing how to have respectful, structured dialogue. One of the participants in this study said that deliberate classroom conversations break down cliques and eliminate gossip, bringing the classroom into a more cohesive unit. All the participants felt that student-to-student conversations should be practiced daily so that every student feels heard and included.

Yet another method recommended by the participants was embedding LGBTQ+ and race-related issues into the curriculum. According to Blackburn (2015), students need to compare their unique perspectives to those of "othered voices" through the curriculum to truly understand how societal values impact marginalized people. The participants also emphasized that some direct instruction should be included in lessons and units so students are better informed about what it means to be LGBTQ+. Finally, the participants mentioned that putting students into the content and context enhances learning about the different voices and perspectives in the context of LGBTQ+ students of color.

Advocating for LGBTQ+ Students of Color

The importance of teachers' advocacy for these students can hardly be overestimated. Sewell (2019) says LGBTQ+ students of color suffer severe isolation in high schools because teachers do not consistently stand up for them. Gay students of color often choose their race over their sexual identity, particularly if they do not feel supported by the school (Sewell, 2019). Advocacy can be a daily practice in peer-to-peer discussions in which teachers deliberately include opportunities for honest, respectful discussions about marginalized students' experiences. Although the participants of this study limited their advocacy to classroom practices, they all agreed it is imperative to take advocacy beyond the school environment to the outside world that often mutes the voices of marginalized groups.

Participants deemed as particularly important is to stand up for any witnessed injustice. Students who are misidentified, insulted, or rejected in the classroom based on their race or sexual identity must be corrected immediately. The participants felt this must happen consistently and immediately to be effective. The findings of this study confirm that all involved believed that supportive teachers understand the importance of standing up for students' preferred pronouns and names (Sewell, 2019). Instructors must confidently take pride in correcting any person, staff, admin, or student, who mislabels any person within their school community (Sewell, 2019). Educators play a crucial role in building positive self-esteem and confidence in a student's identity, which is extremely important for LGBTQ+ students of color who typically are suffering.

The participants admitted that many staff members felt conflicted when using preferred names and pronouns because they did not want to draw attention to students with alternative identities, especially in the case of transgender students. However, all participants felt that many of their LGBTQ+ students of color were lonely and isolated at their school because their identity was not authentically known. The participants stressed that their best practices arose because they wanted their students to choose their authentic identity and to create an inclusive curriculum and environment where all members of the classroom address every student with respect for their identity. Every participant in this study mentioned how some teachers struggle to adopt the practice, which echoes what Delgado and Stefanic (2012) mentioned about the fear of pushing up against societal values or accepted "norms" are oppressive causing many people to remain silent. The participants were adamant about the importance of advocating for LGBTQ+ students of color.

The participants stated that high school students grow socially by discovering new ways to see the world other than their own perspective. Ashcroft (2012) found there is no better place than safe classrooms for vastly different students to exchange ideas, ask questions, and hear how "othered" students live and think about life, which is what the findings of this study confirm. Teacher-facilitated dialogue builds acceptance of every student by giving them space for a voice through the telling of their story. These statements are supported by the findings of Blackburn's (2015) study that confirmed the importance of fostering daily student-to-student conversations. In Brian's words, "Having real conversations between students about sexual orientation and/or color will change the environment from institutional to community because now everyone is learning to understand each other's perspective." All the participants supported student-to-student conversations as the place where real discussion and understanding occur.

The participants of this study asserted that building in marginalized voices takes practice and intentionality on the part of the teacher. Most participants agreed on how important daily discussion is to open students' minds to different lived experiences. One participant even stated that LGBTQ+ students of color have lived experiences that most high school students do not understand. As students explore other experiences outside their own, they build a base to honestly and authentically connect to the experiences of LGBTQ+ students of color, which may cause them to be less judgmental (Collins, 2019). Many participants shared how everyone's life is so unique that they may not see that LGBTQ+ students of color suffer from many points of oppression. That is why all participants felt that regular student-to-student conversations unmask and expose moments of oppression so that they are seen and discussed.

This study underscores the importance of always standing up for your students. Every participant in this study felt that we need to be real about our students lives and to reflect on how the societal messages can be crippling to students who are not fitting into the cookie cutter method of thinking. Just as the theories of this study require a call to action, the participants felt that instructors need to be the leaders in the classroom by standing up for every child's chosen identity, adding in stories and messages that are not often heard, and allowing space for students themselves to share their realities so that everyone sees the multidimensional aspect of humans and how they live.

This study gave space to instructors who work to underscore the importance of advocacy for LGBTQ+ students of color by teachers and leaders. The teachers who were the participants expressed their dedication to advocating for all their students, particularly LGBTQ+ students of color, recognizing not just the importance but, more so, the urgency of the cause. They all agreed on the need to deliberately put certain practices and methods into place to create space for LGBTQ+ students of color. The participants' expression of advocacy supports Crenshaw's (2002) call for educators to be creative in overcoming the system. Similarly, Lee (2023) appeals to teachers as activists who create space for empathy and community so that all students can be seen and heard.

Conclusions

All in all, the findings of this study confirm that students need honest conversations about LGBTQ+ and race to create inclusive discourse, which supports the conclusions of several studies by Ashcroft (2012), Blackburn (2015), and Sewell (2019), who stated that students who stand in the instruction of marginalized voices have a greater appreciation and richer understanding of how society misrepresents their humanity. The participants of this study expressed that students must stand in the context of many perspectives and lives through daily student-to-student conversations supported by practiced norms of respect. Kumashiro states in his 2019 study that schools must challenge the myths and interpretations students experience outside school through the inclusion of "othered" voices embedded into the curriculum. Clearly, and as the findings of this study confirm, students need to hear and ask hard questions about race and sexual orientation because the LGBTQ+ story has many perspectives, and everyone's story is unique. Finally, the participants of this study asserted that embedding the content of alternative lifestyles into the school curriculum humanizes LGBTQ+ communities and builds empathy for those historically marginalized by the system.

Recommendations for Educational Professionals

First and foremost, all educational professionals should be more aware of the vulnerability of LGBTQ+ students of color. The issue of sexual identity remains highly debatable in U.S. politics, mass media, and the broader public. It is a sensitive issue, especially when educating K-12 students. LGBTQ+ students of color have the highest rate of homelessness, suicidal ideation, and depression among high school students. Policymakers need to be more determined to reinforce legislation requiring schools to create policies that allow students to use their bathroom of choice and require teachers and staff to recognize students' preferred names and pronouns. I believe if the school does not support these students, then it sets up the most vulnerable students for a life of drug addiction, poverty, and possible imprisonment (Kosciw, 2020).

School leaders and teachers should advocate more fiercely for a curriculum that includes different cultural, ethnic, and sexual identities. School principals should make professional development sessions that focus on sexual identity mandatory. School leaders should instruct teachers to regularly call out students who misidentify or demean another student because of their identity. There should be a disciplinary school policy for students who do not want to address other humans respectfully and with kindness and respect. I believe if school leaders make space for their LGBTQ+ students of color, then it might create healthier students who understand other types of students better.

Teachers should make more effort to create an inclusive curriculum that does not leave out LGBTQ+ students of color. Teachers need to be deliberate about what students learn and what topics are discussed. Teachers must create space for students to respectfully and truthfully discuss the issues that LGBTQ+ students of color face. Best practices can include having regular classroom discussions among students as peers who learn from and about each other, including their sexual identities. Students should learn about the experiences of people who are different from them, particularly about the histories of people historically discriminated against in the United States.

Pre-service educational programs in higher education should emphasize the importance of identity for the LGBTQ+ community. Pre-service teacher educators should be better prepared to teach students who represent diverse cultural, racial, ethnic, gender, sexual orientation, or immigrant groups who have made enormous contributions to the United States. Since the LGBTQ+ community of color remains a minority group within the dominant discourse of heterosexuality, providing more space for the voices representing this group in teacher education curricula can make classrooms more inclusive. Finally, the more diverse and authentic voices are included in the professional and personal discourses, the more humane they become.

References

American Psychological Association. (2019). *Lesbian, gay, bisexual, and transgender persons & socioeconomic status.* https://www.apa.org/pi/ses/resources/publications/lgbt

Ashcroft, C. (2012). Literacy and sexuality: What's the connection? *Journal of Adolescent & Adult Literacy, 52*(7), 636–686. https://doi.org/10.1598/JAAL.52.7.9

Blackburn, M. V. (2015). *Interrupting hate: Homophobia in schools and what literacy can do about it.* Teachers College Press.

BlackPast, B. (1982/2012, August 12). *Audi Lorde, "Learning from the 60's."* BlackPast.org. https://www.blackpast.org/african-american-history/1982-audre-lorde-learning-60s/

Browne, K., & Nash, C. J. (2014). Resisting LGBT rights where "we have won": Canada and Great Britain. *Journal of Human Rights, 13*, 322–336. https://doi.org/10.1080/14754835.2014.923754

Burdge, H., Licona, A. C., & Hyemingway, Z. T. (2014). LGBTQ youth of color: Discipline disparities, school push-out, and the school-to-prison pipeline. *Gay-Straight Alliance Network and Crossroads Collaborative.* http://doi.org/10.13140/2.1.1362.6568

Cho, S., Crenshaw, K. W., & McCall, K. (2013). Toward a field of intersectionality studies: Theory, applications, and praxis. *Signs, 33*(4), 785–810.

Cleary, J. (2018, October). The number one factor in student success? Relationships with teachers. *Learning Science International.* https://www.learningsciences.com/blog/number-1-factor/

Collins, P. A. (2019). *Intersectionality: As a critical social theory.* Duke University Press.

Crenshaw, K. W. (2017). *On intersectionality: Essential writings*. The New Press.

Creswell, J. W., & Poth, C. N. (2018). *Qualitative inquiry & research design: Choosing among five approaches* (4th ed.). SAGE Publication.

Delgado, R., & Stefancic, J. (2012). *Critical race theory: An introduction* (2nd ed.). New York University Press.

Denzin, N. K., & Lincoln, Y. S. (2008). The discipline and practice of qualitative research. In *Strategies of qualitative inquiry* (3rd ed., pp. 1–43). Sage Journal.

Diliberti, M., Jackson, M., Correa, S., & Padgett, Z. (2019, July). *Crime, violence, discipline, and safety in U.S. public schools: Findings from the school survey on crime and safety: 2017–18* (NCES 2019-061). U.S. Department of Education. National Center for Education Statistics.

Dinkins, E., & Englert, P. (2015). LGBTQ literature in middle school classrooms: Possibilities for challenging heteronormative environments. *Sex Education, 15*(4), 392–405.

Espelage, D. L., & Swearer, S. A. (2008). Addressing research gaps in the intersection between homophobia and bullying. *School Psychology Review, 37*(2), 155–159.

Farrington, D., & Baldry A. (2010). Individual risk factors for school bullying. *Journal of Aggression, Conflict and Peace Research, 2*(1), 4–16. https://doi.org/10.5042/jacpr.2010.0001

Gates, G. J. (2017). LGBT data collection amid social and demographic shifts of the US LGBT community. *American Journal of Public Health, 107*(8), 1220–1222. https://ajph.aphapublications.org/doi/full/10.2105/AJPH.2017.303927

Goldstein, T. (2016). Border crossing in the classroom through performed ethnography. *Perspectives on Urban Education, 13*(1), 4–19. https://files.eric.ed.gov/fulltext/EJ1103885.pdf

Human Rights Campaign. (2018). *Glossary of terms*. https://www.hrc.org/resources/glossary-of-terms

Kosciw, J. G., Clark, C. M., Truong, N. L., & Zongrone, A. D. (2020). *The 2019 National School Climate Survey: The experiences of lesbian, gay, bisexual, and transgender youth in our nation's schools*. GLSEN. https://eric.ed.gov/fulltest/ED535177.pdf

Kosciw, J. G., Greytak, E. A., Zongrone, A. D., Clark, C. M., & Truong, N. L. (2018). *The 2017 School Climate Survey: The experiences of lesbian, gay, bisexual, and transgender youth in our nation's schools*. GLSEN.

Kumashiro, K. K. (2000). Toward a theory of anti-oppressive education. *Review of Educational Research*, 70(1), 25–53.

LGBT Network. (2021). https://lgbtnetwork.org/content/2017-impact-statement

Lee, A. F., & Smith, G. D. (2023). Where is the love, y'all? Punk pedagogy in high school choir. *Research in Education*. https://doi.org/10.1177/00345237231152605

Marx, R. A., & Kettrey, H. (2016). Gay-straight alliances are associated with lower levels of school-based victimization of LGBTQ+ youth; A systemic review and meta-analysis. *Journal of Youth and Adolescence, 45*(7), 1269–1282. https://doi.org/10.1007/s10964-016-0501-7

McIntyre, J. (2021). *Explainer: What does it mean to be "cisgender"?* The Conversation. https://theconversation.com/explainer-what-does-it-mean-to-be-cisgender-103159

Merriam-Webster. (n.d.). Gender non-conforming. In *Merriam-Webster.com dictionary*. Retrieved June 1, 2021, from https://merriam-webster.com/dictionary/gender%20nonconforming

Moradi, B., Mohr, J. J., Worthington, R. L., & Fassinger, R. E. (2009). Counseling psychology research on sexual (orientation) minority issues: Conceptual and methodological challenges and opportunities. *Journal of Counseling Psychology*, *56*(1), 5–22. (EJ827086). ERIC. https://eric.ed.gov/?id=EJ827068

Parent, M. C., DeBlaere, C., & Moradi, B. (2013). Approaches to research in intersectionality: Perspectives on gender, LGBT, and racial/ethnic identities. *Sex Roles*, *68*, 639–645.

PEW Research Center. (2013, June 13). A survey of LGBT Americans. *Social and Demographic Trends*. https://www.pewsocialtrends.org/2013/06/13/a-survey-of-lgbt-americans

Planned Parenthood. (2021). *What's intersex?* https://www.plannedparenthood.org/learn/gender-identity/sex-gender-identity/whats-intersex

Platt, L. C. (2020). The presenting concerns of transgender and gender nonconforming clients at university counseling centers. *The Counseling Psychologist*, *48*(3), 407–431. https://doi.org/10.1177/0011000019898680

Plummer, K. (2004). Queers, bodies and postmodern sexualities: A note on revisiting the "sexual" in symbolic interactionism. *Qualitative Sociology*, *26*(4), 515–530.

Price-Feeney, N., Green, A. E., & Dorison, S. (2020, October 6). *All Black lives matter: Mental health of black LGBTQ youth*. The Trevor Project. https://thetrevorproject.org/2020/10/06/all-black-lives-matter-mental-health-of-black-lgbtq-youth/

Robinson, J. P., & Espelage, D. L. (2011). Inequities in educational and psychological outcomes between LGBTQ and straight students in middle and high school. *Educational Researcher*, *40*, 315–330.

Russell, S. T., & Horn, S. S. (2017). Sexual orientation, gender identity, and school: Learning from the past, envisioning the future. In S. T. Russell & S. S. Horn (Eds.), *Sexual orientation, gender identity, and schooling: The nexus of research, practice, and policy* (pp. 377–389). Oxford University Press.

Ryan, C. (2010). Engaging families to support lesbian, gay, bisexual, and transgender youth: The family acceptance project. *The Prevention Researcher*, *17*(4), 11–13.

Ryan, C., Russell, S. T., Huebner, D., Diaz, R., & Sanchez, J. (2010). Family acceptance in adolescence and the health of LGBT young adults. *Journal of Child and Adolescent Psychiatric Nursing*, *23*(4), 205–213. https://doi.org/10.1111/j.1744-6171.2010.00246.x

Saldaña, J., & Omasta, M. (2018). *Qualitative research: Analyzing life*. SAGE Publications.

Sewell, J. P. (2019). Being black, male, gay and gifted. *Journal of African American Males in Education*, *10*(1), 39–57.

Stake, R. E. (2010). *Qualitative research: Studying how things work*. Guilford Press.

Stulberg, L. M. (2017). *LGBTQ social movements*. Polity Press.

Toomey, R. B., Huynh, V. H., Jones, S. K., Lee, S., & Revels-Macalinao, M. (2017). Sexual minority youth of color: A content analysis and critical review of the literature. *Journal of Gay & Lesbian Mental Health*, *21*(1), 3–31. https://doi.org/10.1080/19359705.2016.1217499

Walton, G. M., & Cohen, G. L. (2007). A question of belonging: Race, social fit, and achievement. *Journal of Personality and Social Psychology*, *92*(1), 82–96. https://doi.org/10.1037/0022-3514.92.1.82

Warner, M. (1999). *The trouble with normal: Sex, politics, and the ethics of queer life*. Free Press.

Wiggan, G., & Watson, M. J. (2016). Teaching the whole child: The importance of culturally responsiveness, community engagement, and character development in high achieving African American students. *Urban Review*, *48*, 766–798.

World Health Organization. (2017). *FAQ on health and sexual diversity; An introduction to key concepts*. https://www.who.int/

Yin, R. K. (2018). *Case study research and applications: Design and methods*. SAGE.

Zongrone, A. D., Truong, N. L., & Kosciw, J. G. (2020). *Erasure and resilience: The experiences of LGBTQ students of color*. GLSEN.

Chapter 7 Navigating Adverse Childhood Experiences for More Effective Learning and Well-Being

Amy Kendryna

The Reality of Adverse Childhood Experiences

This is a not-so-uncommon true story. Paul arrived at school in a taxi cab. It is late fall and the wind is cold on his bare arms. He didn't eat breakfast and no one said goodbye to him before he left for school. He is wearing the same shirt he wore for the last five days, and probably the same pants, and no socks. As he enters the school Mrs. S warmly says hello and Paul nods to her and goes into the commons for breakfast. He takes his breakfast and the cafeteria lady gives him another breakfast for a snack later that day. Another student makes fun of his shoes and he shrugs it off as the offending student leaves with a teacher. Another teacher asks how he is doing and he says OK. But his face shows he is not OK, he is unhappy and worn out.

He has a lot to be unhappy about, as he has endured many tragedies in his young life. His dad died from gun violence in Chicago and his mom is a drug addict and cannot care for him. She is trying to stay clean so she can have him back in her life, but it is a long, hard road. Paul is 11 years old, and in elementary school; his big six-foot frame hangs over the table as he eats the donut holes and cheese stick. Later that day the class had a local police officer come in to teach Drug and Alcohol Resistance Education (DARE). Paul looks around the room to see who is watching him, as he reaches for the DARE officer's gun, not to grab it, just to get attention from his classmates. He makes a "watch me" face while stretching his arm out and the officer backs up and Paul touches the gun. That evening several students tell their parents what happened and one parent calls the police and files a complaint. The DARE officer called me, the principal, and told me that he didn't even see the student touch the gun. Another police officer was assigned to investigate.

While Paul is waiting in the office he is telling me how much he wants to go back to living with his Aunt. Her house was the fifth DCFS and foster care placement in the last two years. His aunt took him in and then decided it was too difficult to take care of another person in her household. He had only been living with her for five months. She placed him back in the Department of Children and Family Services (DCFS) system. DCFS placed him in a homeless shelter until another foster parent could be found. The homeless shelter is 18 miles away and that is why Paul takes a taxi to school.

Adverse Childhood Experiences: Background

The Adverse Childhood Experiences (ACE) study was developed by two family physicians Anda and Felitti (2004), who first coined the term ACEs. They initially operated a weight loss clinic, where they discovered that many of their patients were using obesity to ensure against unwanted sexual advances. Almost all the non-responders to the weight reduction program Anda and Felitti (2004) assert had a history of sexual abuse. These significant findings led to the development of the ACE study.

Trauma, the researchers emphasize, can include any event that harms the body, self, or spirit and can regard a one-time or continual event. Trauma covers a broad range of hurtful experiences, including physical, sexual, mental, or emotional, and usually regards a combination. Anda and Felitti (2004) identify various common and less common kinds of trauma as ACEs.

The study's findings were profound, showing significant correlations between the number of traumatic childhood experiences and the amount of physical and mental distress experienced as adults (Anda et al., 2004).

Adverse childhood experiences (ACEs) are potentially traumatic events that occur in childhood (0–17 years) that can have negative, lasting effects on health and well-being as children and into adulthood. These experiences range from physical, emotional, or sexual abuse. Also included are aspects of the child's environment that can undermine their sense of safety, stability, and bonding such as growing up in a household with substance misuse, mental health problems, or instability due to parental separation or incarceration of a parent, sibling, or other members of the household (CDC, 2020).

Numerous studies indicate toxic stress and trauma lead to a decrease in the volume of the brain's hippocampus, corpus callosum, cerebellum, and prefrontal cortex. Decreased volume in these areas of the brain impact learning, memory, and executive functioning (Child Welfare Information Gateway, 2018). Trauma is also associated with major psychological disorders such as reactive attachment disorder, disinhibited social engagement disorder, post-traumatic stress disorder, acute stress disorder, adjustment disorders, and intermittent explosive disorder. In the classroom setting, the cognitive and psychological effects of trauma exposure are paired with difficulties in academic and social functioning. Goodman, Miller, and West-Olatunji (2011) determined students with histories of traumatic stress when compared to those without these histories, scored lower on standardized tests and were three times more likely to have an Individualized Education Program (IEP). Cicchetti (2010) found deficits in academic achievement were also prevalent for students with histories of maltreatment. In addition to academic underachievement, children with trauma histories display a wide range of externalizing and internalizing behaviors including irritability, aggression, withdrawal, difficulty with authority, and hyperarousal (National Child Traumatic Stress Network, 2017). These behaviors present themselves as early as preschool and have the potential to continue into adulthood (Shonkoff & Garner, 2012).

Child abuse and neglect are common. At least 1 in 7 children have experienced child abuse and/or neglect in the past year, and this is likely an underestimate. In 2018, nearly 1,770 children died of abuse and neglect in the United States. Children living in poverty experience more abuse and neglect. Rates of child abuse and neglect are five times higher for children in families with low socioeconomic status compared to children in families with higher socioeconomic status.

Children who are abused and neglected may suffer immediate physical injuries such as cuts, bruises, or broken bones, as well as emotional and psychological problems, such as impaired social-emotional skills or anxiety. Chronic abuse may result in toxic stress, which can change brain development and increase the risk of problems like post-traumatic stress disorder and learning, attention, and memory difficulties. ACEs are common across all populations.

The ACE study directed both professional and public attention to the impact of ten family-related adverse events occurring in childhood. Since then, the psychological harm caused by a wide variety of events and circumstances, including disasters, social violence, racism, and poverty, has received increasing attention (Carter & Blanch, 2019). Without proper interventions, the trajectory of life satisfaction for children with multiple ACEs is indeed very flat.

The Impact of Societal Woes

Students need to feel safe and have supportive relationships for social, emotional, and academic learning to occur. Students experiencing trauma, such as a public health crisis, weather disasters, or other disturbing events, may have been exposed to unpredictable schedules, inconsistent supervision, or food insecurity (CDC, 2020). These students desperately need school to be safe, predictable, and positive, especially if they have been displaced or are without utilities or basic comforts.

Childhood trauma often involves a negative reaction, called traumatic stress, following an overwhelming, upsetting, or frightening experience—called a traumatic event—that challenges a child's ability to cope. Many students suffer adverse childhood effects and in turn have difficulty accessing academic learning. According to Sachs, Murphey, and Moore (2013), approximately 1 in 10 students in the state of Illinois, have more than two ACEs. For some students the trauma event may be temporary (e.g., death of a pet), while for others the trauma event may be more long-term. Children with a strong support system can overcome trauma, but many students do not have strong support systems and struggle to regulate their emotions. Many teachers do not have the training for trauma-informed care and those who do may not see that their verbal and non-verbal interactions affect the students' learning. According to Craig (2016), "Trauma has the unfortunate effect of leaving children in the past, unable to move forward" (p. 32). The type of relationship and interactions the teacher has with a student who suffers from multiple ACEs, can hinder the child's learning, and worse, further traumatize the child. Children with adverse childhood experiences suffer on multiple levels, with a lack of social belonging being one of them. Many children become susceptible to loneliness, social anxiety, and clinical depression in the absence of belonging. Children who suffer multiple Adverse Childhood Experiences (ACEs) need specialized services and support to navigate and access school, learning, and life, successfully.

Problem Statement

It is important to continue to study ACEs and their impact on the students' academic performance and well-being. This research focused on beliefs, understanding, and actions of classroom teachers regarding students with ACEs because the classroom teacher is the gatekeeper to social-emotional supports and mental health services.

Research Purposes

This qualitative case study explored ways in which elementary public- school teachers identify their students with adverse childhood experiences and create a classroom learning environment conducive to the well-being of those students. As a result, the student would have a better chance to succeed in the areas of social-emotional and academic growth. While educators cannot change the fact that a child may suffer ACEs, they can provide a classroom environment that is trauma-informed and conducive to learning.

Theoretical Lens

Several theoretical perspectives helped shape this study's purposes, research questions, and the strategies for data analysis: Ecological Model of Human Development, Social-Ecological Model, Ethics of Care, Attachment Theory, and Social Justice Theory. The concepts of Adverse Childhood Experiences and Social-Emotional Learning were examined through the lens of these theoretical perspectives, all of which comprise an original integrated model displayed in Figure 7.1.

Through the middle of the diagram is the Ecological Model of Human Development and the Multi-Modal Social-Ecological Model. They mirror each other in that the broad categories are similar: self to individual; micro and meso to social environment; exto to systems-level and macro and chrono are not a part of the Multi-Modal Social-Ecological Model but are factors when examining Adverse Childhood Experiences (ACEs) and Social-Emotional

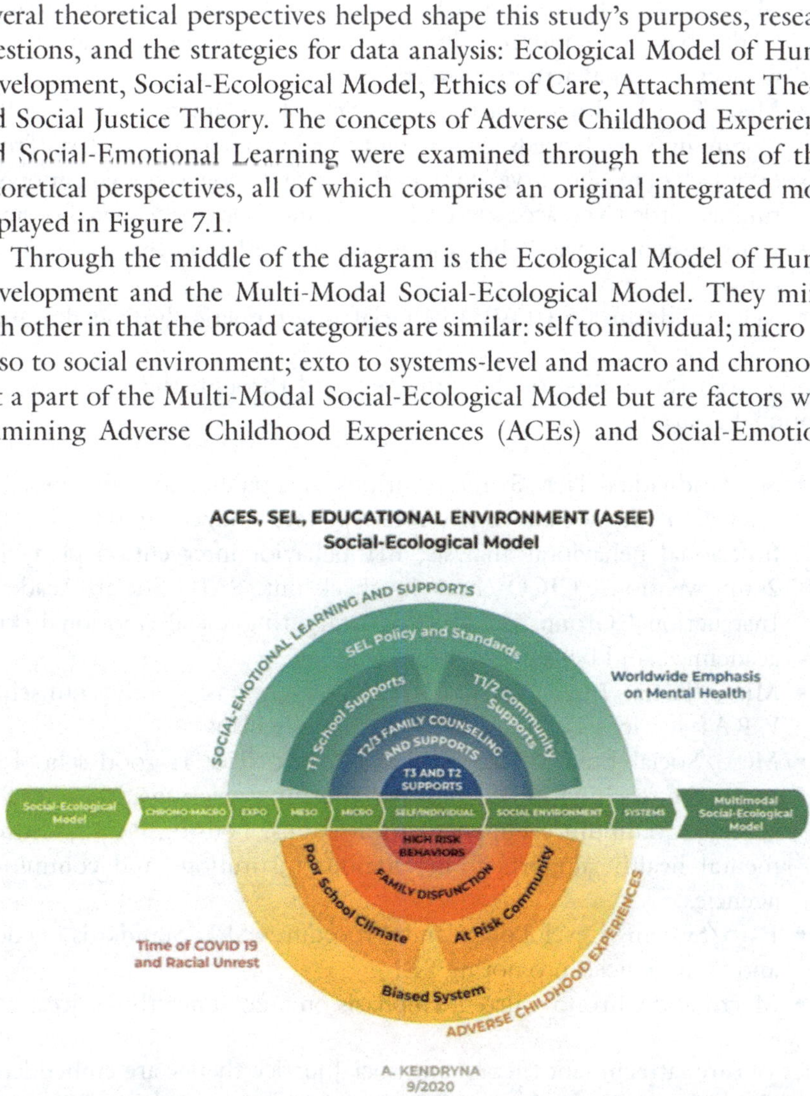

Figure 7.1: ACES, SEL, Educational Environment (ASEE) Social-Ecological Model

Learning (SEL). ACEs are delineated in the bottom half of the figure and SEL in the top of the figure.

Moving from the middle of the model outward through the lens of ACEs, the bottom half of the model includes:

- Self/Individual High-Risk Behaviors: cutting, attempted suicide, drug abuse, alcohol abuse, self-inflicted injuries.
- Micro/Social Environment-Family Dysfunction: violence, battered adults, battered children, adult drug and alcohol abuse, incarceration, neglect, criminal activity, poverty.
- Meso/Social Environment-Poor School Climate and Et-Risk Community: high needs schools, bullying, low academics, high staff turnover, lack of resources, violence, high crime rate, low employment opportunities, little to no access to health care, and food, inadequate housing.
- Exto/Systems-Level Policy and Procedures-inherent bias and systemic racism.
- Macro and Chrono-COVID 19, racial unrest, politically divided country.

Moving from the middle of the figure upward through the lens of Social-Emotional Learning:

- Self/Individual-Tier 3 interventions: hospitalization for psychiatric treatment, social work services-private and/or in school, FBA-functional behavioral analysis, BIP-behavior intervention plan, Tier 2 interventions: CICO-check in check out, SAIG-Social, Academic Instructional Groups: small groups targeting social-emotional skills, academics, and behaviors.
- Micro/Social Environment-Tier 3 interventions: family counseling, WRAP services Tier 2 interventions: family plans.
- Meso/Social Environment-School Climate: Tier 1: good school climate, the teaching of SEL lessons, morning meetings, monthly SEL survey; Community Supports: food banks, housing-PADS, shelters, mental health supports from religious institutions and community agencies.
- Exto/Systems-Level Policy and Procedures-SEL Standards, Federal and State policies promoting SEL.
- Macro and Chrono-Current emphasis on mental health services.

Ethics of care, attachment theory, and social justice theory are embedded in parts of this figure. For Ethics of Care and Attachment Theory: Micro and Meso/Social Environment-home, school, places of worship, clubs, groups, activities are all places where relationships are formed. Adult caregivers in those places can form positive attachments with children and contribute to positive relationships and build social-emotional skills. Those relationships can be just the opposite and create more trauma or adverse childhood experiences for the children in their care.

Nel Noddings' (2015) work, which takes ethics of care and applies it to the field of education, informed this study as teachers needed to care for and take care of students with ACEs. The social-emotional well-being of students needs to be monitored before any emphasis on academics can occur. If a teacher attends to the needs of the student, the student will be able to depend on the teacher. Some students may come to school not knowing how to attach to others because of traumatic events or abuse. It takes an informed teacher to notice this deficiency and choose to resolve it at least within the student-teacher relationship.

For social justice theory: Exto/Systems-Level (policy and procedures) and Macro and Chrono (societal values and time in history) are the levels where social justice theory is prevalent. While the outer levels of the diagram have less influence on the child than the levels closest to the child, the outer levels can still have an impact. People in positions of power and influence can determine if they are going to eradicate institutional bias and systemic racism or contribute to it. One of the tenets of trauma-informed care is to help create a happier, healthier, and more ethical society (Figley, 2012). This tenant is directly linked to social justice theory. While this study does not address larger societal issues like equitable monetary resources, access to health services, fresh food, and safe areas to live for all, there would be fewer stressors and children with a smaller number of ACEs. However, teachers can be advocates for children in their care, making sure the children who need it are provided with resources and kept safe while in the care of educators.

Case-Study Design

A case study was the most suitable design for this study's research purposes. Yin (2018) offers this twofold definition of a case study as a research method that (a) "investigates a contemporary phenomenon (the "case") in-depth" and (b) "within its real-world context, especially when the boundaries between phenomenon and context may not be clearly evident" (p. 15). This study was conducted in a real-world context of a classroom, seven out of eight observations were in a physical classroom and one was in a virtual classroom. It aimed at investigating the belief systems of teachers regarding how they view and interact with students with ACEs in great depth.

According to Stake (1995), "The first criterion should be to maximize what we can learn. Given our purposes, which cases are likely to lead us to understandings, to assertions, perhaps even to modifying generalizations?" (p. 4). Thus, this case study fitted within an instrumental type. The close examination of teachers' belief systems about students with ACEs deepened an understanding of how to educate the students more effectively.

Site and Participants

This study was conducted in a Midwestern suburban public elementary school. I have been the Principal of this school for the last ten years. Over the past five years, we have seen an increase in the number of children with multiple ACEs and increasing poverty in our community. The percentage of students who receive free or reduced lunch has gone from 13% to 37% within those ten years. All of the townhomes behind the school are now Section Eight housing. That transition started seven years ago. Three years ago, all of the teachers started teaching Second Steps, a tier-one, social-emotional learning program. This program is aimed at helping all students build social-emotional skills. While the participants saw the benefit of (this) SEL program with some of their students, many of the students with ACEs still react atypically in common situations and cannot regulate their emotions, resulting in students running out of classrooms, refusing to do classwork, crying, hitting others, and throwing items across the classroom. Even more seriously, the participants have seen an increase in students on anxiety medication and students who threaten to commit suicide at younger and younger ages in the last few years.

The participants of this study included five general education elementary teachers in grades kindergarten through fourth grade. I chose participants using purposeful sampling, with maximal variation and convenience (Creswell, 2012, p. 208). Saldana and Omasta (2018) agree that explicit intentionality and convenience of choosing the site and participants validate purposeful and convenience sampling strategies in qualitative research. The participants represented teachers with similar schedules or availability, and the most varied grade levels.

Sources of Data and Methods of Data Collection

Case-study research involves various methods of data collection. According to Yin (2018) for a qualitative case study, "there are six sources of evidence: documentation, archival records, interviews, direct observations, participant observation, and physical artifacts" (p. 114). For this case study, I conducted semi-structured interviews with five teachers; I made two observations of teacher-student interactions during class time and I recorded field notes. I collected artifacts and visuals that pertained to the teachers' understanding of ACEs and SEL. Multiple sources of data ensured triangulation, validated the findings and gave greater breadth or depth to the data (Saldana & Omasta, 2018).

Observations

At the beginning of this study, I conducted two observations of the participating teachers. Participant observation requires observing, listening, and using one's senses to take in and record the rich details as people interact with each other and their environment (Stake, 1995). The qualitative case-study researcher, during the observation, needs to concentrate on what constitutes a tally-what is key to the research-but also look for other factors that may be influencing the result (Stake, 1995, p. 62). The field notes included a record of any statement that highlighted the student-teacher relationship. The emphasis during the early stages of the observations was discovery (Bloomberg & Volpe, 2019). Observations allowed me to take detailed first-hand accounts of the specific phenomenon being studied.

Semi-Structured Interviews

Interviews are most commonly used in case studies and they played a key role in the data collection for this study. "Case study interviews resemble guided conversations rather than structured queries" (Yin, 2018, p. 118). Semi-structured interviews follow a line of inquiry that is aligned to one's case study but also allows for an open, non-threatening line of questioning that may help the researcher get deeper, richer data. Interviews can get to the *how* and *why* that is the focus of the research (Yin, 2018, p. 118). Interview guide (Appendix A) was used to stay on the topic of the inquiry but I was also able to add deeper questions from some of the participants, which resulted in richer data than I anticipated. The interview guide was developed to ascertain what the teacher knows about ACEs, how they affect student learning, what the teacher does to mitigate the harmful effects of ACEs, and advocate for the students.

Documents, Artifacts, and Visual Materials

The focus of this study was on the teacher. I took pictures of the teachers' classrooms hoping for an indication of the climate of the classroom. Stake (1995) contends that most studies find the need for some type of documentation.

Gathering "data by studying documents follows the same line of thinking as observing or interviewing" (Stake, 1995, p. 68). I took pictures of parts of the school to show the influence of the school community on SEL.

Strategies for Data Analysis

Analyzing case-study evidence includes organizing and displaying data in different ways, looking for patterns, insights, and concepts, developing an analytic strategy, considering analytic techniques, and addressing contradictory explanations and interpretations (Yin, 2018). Qualitative data analysis typically consists of several cycles of coding (Saldaña & Omasta, 2018). Saldaña and Omasta (2018) describe one of the four types of coding methods as In Vivo for coding qualitative data. IN Vivo coding only considers the responses from the interviewee, not the questions from the interviewer. To start the coding process, I began with a close reading of the transcript and open coding. I coded the data to determine the themes within the interviews and the observations. The interviews were coded by "aggregating the text into small categories of information" (Creswell & Poth, 2018, p. 190). Throughout the analysis, I looked for specific phrases that refer directly to ACEs, SEL, trauma, cues to the teacher-student relationship, and teacher as an advocate.

After determining the major themes and subthemes from multiple sources of data, I placed the themes in a graphic organizer to see if any other themes emerged. I reread the transcripts to see if there are any other emerging themes. Coding allows the researcher to summarize, interpret, synthesize, and extend alternative interpretations. The interviews and observations were put into a program called Dedoose, that made it easier for me to look for themes. Yin (2018) suggests that the researcher look back at the original questions and look at the evidence that addresses the original questions. Yin goes on to suggest that the researcher continue that process until all research questions have been examined. The themes that occur more frequently, across all of the data collected, should be given more weight in the analysis. Ultimately, I have created a model for ACEs, SEL, and the learning environment (ASEE), (Figure 7.1) to analyze the data.

Validation Criteria

I employed several criteria for validation of data analysis: reflexivity, triangulation, member checks, authenticity, and rich and thick descriptions. Reflexivity offered me the way to turn the problem of subjectivity in research into an opportunity (Finlay, 1998). The reflexive process can unfold new understandings.

Personal and methodological reflexivity should be included as an element of research and that without it the validity of the research could be undermined. Reflexivity is a safeguard against potential researcher biases therefore requires that the researcher stay conscious of biases, values, and experiences brought to the study. Reflexivity is an awareness of the influence that the researcher has on the participants and the topic. I have kept a journal of my reflections, thoughts, emotions, and assumptions throughout this research process.

A major strength of case-study data collection is "the opportunity to use many different sources of evidence. Case studies using multiple sources of evidence were rated more highly, in terms of their overall quality" (Yin, 2018, p. 126). One reason triangulation of data is important in case studies is to help the researcher get an in-depth look at a phenomenon in a real-world setting. In this case study, I used multiple data sources to obtain a more holistic understanding of the data and reasonable explanations of the phenomenon being studied.

Member checks are taking the data back to the participants and asking them to review the data collected to assure accuracy. "Member checks-taking data and tentative interpretations back to the people from whom they were derived and asking them if the results are plausible" (Merriam, 1998, p. 204). I used member checks when I sent the transcripts of the interviews to the participants for verification of accuracy. Using member checks helps the process to be transparent and credible. Additionally, rich and thick descriptions provide insights into the lived experiences. They help to create a picture in the reader's mind, to see the situation as clearly and as deeply as possible. "Generating a 'thick' description means the researcher needs to capture the details, emotions, and voice of the participant" (Creswell & Poth, 2018, p. 245). The authenticity and quality of educational research can be judged by the procedures used to address reliability, validity, and triangulation (Scott, 2007). Authenticity evokes a sense of what is real, real to the participant.

Discussion of the Findings

The circumstances under which persons are born can play an enormous role in who these persons can become as adults. There may always be an exception to the rule: a student who was once homeless can go to Harvard or a rich white man can end up in jail. But exceptions are just that, exceptions, and not the norm. Unfortunately, the norm for adverse childhood experiences (ACEs) is that nearly 18% of the population of children ages zero to 18, in the United States, has suffered two or more ACEs (Center for Youth Wellness, 2019). Suffering ACEs can derail a child's chance at accessing education.

Children who have suffered ACEs require additional support in and outside of the school setting. Brain science (Navalta et al., 2018) shows that, in the absence of protective factors, toxic stress damages children's developing brains. Toxic stress can arise in response to living for months or years with a screaming alcoholic father, a severely depressed and neglectful mother, or a parent who copes with life's frustrations by beating a child. While ACEs have been linked to poor health outcomes in adulthood, researchers are beginning to understand the mechanisms leading to disease and early death due to toxic stress and multiple exposures to trauma. Left unaddressed, toxic stress affects the fundamental biological functioning of the body and, in many children, healthy brain development.

Research indicates that "roughly 1 of 5 children have diagnosable mental health disorders but that roughly 70% do not receive indicated services" (Cook et al., 2015, pp. 166–167). The mental health issues surface in a variety of ways, such as, for instance, self-harming, aggressive behavior, criminal behavior, and low academic scores. These issues have important implications for children's health and well-being, including the need for increased attention toward the early detection and treatment of children affected by trauma. Prevention is the goal first and foremost, however it is illogical to believe that one or more school programs, whether behavioral or Social-Emotional Learning (SEL), can provide students with mental health issues or multiple ACEs the type of support they need. Social work and wraparound services provide the solution in cases where only 1–2% of students suffer from ACEs. In a school of 400, student wraparounds are possible for 4 to 8 families, however research shows that 9% of students have suffered three or more ACEs and that 13%–20% of those students have mental health issues. These families need this intensive type of service, but schools and most communities lack the resources to provide wraparound services for 35–80 families. I refer to these statistics because that is exactly what the participants of this study face. My study also revealed that if the participants and other teachers do not provide Tier Two services for students who need them, and they refer all of those students to the social worker, the students will not receive services at all because one social worker does not have the capacity for providing services to all students who need Tier Two and Tier Three supports.

Teachers can begin with a solid foundation of Tier One instruction in SEL, but monetary and personnel support are needed to develop a model of Tier Two support for students who struggle with trauma and mental health. In the history of American education, this is the first generation to recognize the ravages of child abuse and neglect and begin to act in response and this is also the first generation to begin to heal ourselves physically and psychologically from the harmful effects of ACEs. Through trial and error as well as research like that of Felitti et al. (1998), educators can constructively apply our new knowledge and skills to help all of our children. Let us consider the societal implications—if all children could have well developed social and emotional skills, then as adults they would be able to thoughtfully solve problems in nonviolent ways. The most important influence in a school setting is the person closest to the child: the teacher.

Adverse Childhood Experiences

Teachers, especially at the elementary level, are the adults who spend the most time with the school age child. Students with ACEs need more support than a good climate, even more than a Tier 1 intervention for SEL. The resources available make it impossible for social workers to meet with and conduct groups with 20% of the school population (CASEL, 2018). Teachers and other school staff should find ways to provide students with much-needed services. Though school social workers and counselors are often viewed as the primary providers of mental health services in schools. The participants of this study identify some ACEs as hypervigilance. To reiterate some of the participants' responses, the students didn't trust any adults and had an exaggerated startle response when someone came near.

Franklin et al. (2012) highlight the role that teachers currently play in delivering mental health services to children in schools. Though teachers typically co-deliver these services, according to Franklin, nearly 1 in 5 school-based mental health interventions are led solely by teachers. These data account only for the formalized delivery of interventions, like Tier One programming, in the schools and do not address the informal mental health support teachers provide on a daily basis (Franklin et al., 2012).

Social-Emotional Learning: We Need a Tier 2 Band Aid

I considered several theoretical models that address ACEs and I have developed my own, integrated ASEE model that puts an individual child in the center. The spheres of influence on the well-being of a child gradually decrease in their intensity during the process of that child's growth and development. Worth noting is the second sphere of influence, from the middle, that represents the family and the school. As stated above, school personnel and especially the classroom teacher have significant influence on a child.

Students with social-emotional skills have the ability to perceive emotions about themselves and others, understand them and regulate them. This in turn can promote intellectual growth (Solovey & Mayer, 1990). When teachers teach each student the five SEL skills, this can affect the climate of the classroom and school in a positive way. It is best if students are able to generalize the skills into all areas of their life, even outside of school. While most SEL programs have three tiers of suggested support, no SEL program specifically targets students with ACEs, but my ASEE model makes that direct connection for educators and other professionals.

The findings of this study revealed that the participants believed that it is part of their role as a teacher to help students address their social-emotional issues that prohibit them from learning. The participants admitted that they do not have a systematic way to identify students with ACEs, they learn by what they seek from previous teachers and from the children themselves. The participants stated that they did not have the training necessary to address the Tier Two and Tier Three supports needed. It was unclear if they believed that providing Tier Two and Tier Three supports was a part of their responsibility as a classroom teacher. The participants did not know how to advocate for students beyond their classroom, nor did some of them think it was beneficial. They felt the same way about policy, either disinterested or ineffectual.

Importantly, the results of this study echo the very precepts of the ethics of care (Noddings, 2015). The participants of this study are highly devoted to their craft and primarily to the children they teach. Put differently, they do care *for* their students a great deal. They understand the ACEs of their students and do their best to make sure these students find their school as a warm and welcoming environment. They have a deeper understanding and commitment to the well-being of their students, including students with ACEs. Such attitudes on the part of the participants of this study speak volumes to support the Attachment Theory (Bowlby, 1982). The closer the teacher is to the student, understanding the student, and knowing them deeply, the more the teacher is inclined to care *for* the child and provide supports

Mental Health and Well-Being

Mental health and well-being of children are indicators of future success, oftentimes more than academic adeptness. The study data confirm that the students with ACEs are more likely than not, to be the bully, or the victim, and the student with emotional and social maladaptations (CDC, 2020). The 2020 CDC report, "Preventing Adverse Childhood Experiences (ACEs): Leveraging the Best Available Evidence," indicates that about 61% of adults surveyed across 25 states reported that they had experienced at least one type of ACE, and nearly 1 in 6 reported they had experienced four or more types of ACEs. While educators cannot change the fact a child may suffer ACEs, they can recognize students with ACEs, provide a conducive climate, and Tier One and Tier Two supports, *if* the teacher is knowledgeable in these areas, which is what this study confirms.

With nearly half of all children experiencing at least one adverse childhood event ("Child and Adolescent Health Measurement Initiative," 2013b), teachers' approach to trauma in the classroom is critical. The findings of this study support the fact that a better understanding of teachers' knowledge and confidence in supporting students exposed to traumatic events can be instrumental in enhancing these students' well-being. Existing research suggests that teachers often feel unprepared to address the needs of this group of students (Alisic, 2012). This may or may not be true to all teachers; however, what this study affirms is the teachers' unwavering dedication to get to know their students with ACEs more and to provide them with the best services they can, even if they may not be fully aware of a variety of resources available to them.

The participants of this study all agreed that students come first, their needs, their access to education and most importantly their social-emotional needs. The students need to be ready to learn before learning can take place. A child who comes into school late, didn't eat breakfast because there was no food in the house, and is upset because her mother's boyfriend was yelling at her, is not ready to learn. The first place the child goes to is the classroom. If the teacher in that room does not recognize that the student is upset and is not aware of the ACEs the child has or has had, that child will not be able to access the learning needed to be successful for that day and in the future.

The participants could give examples of ACEs and could name a few students they knew who had ACEs. They identified the students' ACEs through talking to former teachers and sometimes from the parents or students themselves. As a matter of fact, there is no formal process for identifying students with ACEs. Once the teacher knows the student has ACEs the teacher waits for the student to act up, shut down, or run away before taking any action to address the ACEs.

All participants agreed that having a good classroom and school environment was vitally important for all students, especially those with ACEs. Teachers could name many things that make a good classroom and school climate: greeting students by name, knowing the students' likes and dislikes, singing and dancing as students come into school each day, attending to students' basic needs, and student choice. The participants of this study emphasized that classroom community building can promote school and civic engagement, which can result in improved academic outcomes

(Rimm-Kaufman et al., 2014). Knowing a student's culture and celebrating that culture can help all students feel good about themselves and their heritage. If teachers connect students' cultural assets and use them to teach academic skills and concepts, then the student starts with their funds of knowledge and can better understand the new material. This may provide access to resources for educational rigor for all students. Also, knowing the norms of a culture can stop actions that people of that culture may find offensive and for students with Aces, may be a trigger.

The participants of this study showed an immense knowledge about social-emotional learning and its paramount importance in the teaching-learning processes. All of the participants have morning meetings where students learn social-emotional skills and get to know each other. Some participants spoke about CICO, a Tier Two support for students who need someone to check in with another adult before class and at the end of the day. If students had greater needs the teachers said they would contact the social worker. Yet the participants did not make the connection between the levels of ACEs to the levels of SEL supports. In this regard, I questioned the reasons behind the lack of the connection between their extensive professional development, on the one hand, and their lack of awareness of SEL support resources, on the other.

Recommendations for Educational Professionals and Researchers

Considering the results of this study, several recommendations are worth noting. First and foremost, there needs to be a mandated systematic way of identifying students and families with ACEs. This could be completed by measuring students' social-emotional skills, habits, and mindsets, which, in turn, may be assessed through student self-reporting on surveys, teacher observations, or performance assessments. Whichever method of assessment is employed it needs to clearly identify whether children have or do not have ACEs.

While there exist surveys that assess the general climate of the school, a more specific survey needs to be developed and conducted to find out if the climate of the school helps or retraumatizes the students with ACEs. It is paramount for school teams to meet regularly to discuss the results of the survey and data that include attendance, discipline and special education referrals. School teams may want to reimagine the school day in order to include SEL in each part of the day based on the data from the survey on the students' needs, the survey that should be taken every week. Clearly, the students with high needs would need more time in terms of SEL supports. Tier two systems that have the capacity for large groups of students need to be funded and implemented. After-school and before school programs that have SEL supports and mentoring should also be a priority in order to connect youth to other caring adults.

For educators to be able to make informed decisions further research is needed to determine if teachers have the capacity to provide Tier Two supports within the structures of the school day to large groups of students needing Tier Two supports. Also, further research is needed to find out why teachers with extensive professional development in ACEs and SEL do not make the connection between the two.

Finally, various types of research can be employed to investigate the aforementioned issues further: a longitudinal study conducted in the same school district that would include all elementary schools; a mixed-methods research that could present a more comprehensive view of the state of affairs in the same school; a multi-site qualitative case study within several school districts that reflect broader diversity of demographics; or a comparative quasi-experimental research conducted in two schools with drastically different demographics. Regardless of methods employed, what ultimately matters is a concerted effort on the part of all stakeholders to engender the change that will alleviate the suffering of children with ACEs.

A Too-Common Ending

The police tell the principal that they have to arrest Paul, even though she has explained that he was only kidding, trying to get much-needed attention. The police officer takes Paul into the gym and handcuffs him. The principal starts crying and tells the police officers to take the handcuffs off. Paul tries to reassure the principal that it is OK. She screams that it is not OK and the police officer takes him to the squad car just outside the gym doors.

I tell this true story because this boy is one of many children who suffer multiple Adverse Childhood Experiences (ACEs). He is in need of specialized services and support to navigate school, learning, and life successfully. Nearly 35 million U.S. children have experienced one or more types of childhood trauma and are in schools.

I wonder how Paul's experience changed if he moved in with his aunt, who had a stable job, enough money to feed her family, free of alcoholism and who was able to express love and care to him? I suspect, very different. But what if the home experience was the same and his school experience was different? What if Paul's kindergarten teacher saw how the ACEs affected Paul and connected his family and him with critical support at an early age? What if Paul came into breakfast and met with a small circle of students and a counselor who spoke to them about what they were feeling that morning? If Paul went to class where a teacher warmly greeted him, knew about his circumstances and got to know him on a personal level? If classmates regularly gave kudos to each other? If Paul had access to a social worker whenever he was feeling overwhelmed? If all people treated Paul like the beautiful young man he is, and schools provided the support he and his family needed, then maybe he wouldn't have had the need to get attention by touching an officer's gun.

I have been an educator and administrator for the last 30 years. I have taught in public, private and military schools in several states across this country and in Puerto Rico. I have taught in schools where the parents of the children are multi-millionaires residing in the north shore of Chicago, Illinois, and in schools where the families live in houses with dirt floors, in the hills of northwest Pennsylvania. Many of the families in each situation have a common thread of trauma. Some families have support systems to help guide each member through the trauma on to mentally healthy lives, and others are not so lucky. I personally suffered several Adverse Childhood Experiences. While my family never went without food, shelter and clothing, a member of my family was alcoholic and my dad traveled a lot for his job. My younger brother, by 13 months, had juvenile diabetes and was in the hospital at least three times a year, since first grade. He passed away at the age of 27. There was constant stress in our house and a lack of supervision. On occasion there was corporal punishment, but no one called DCFS; this was a new agency in the 1960s.

School was my sanctuary and several adult relationships in elementary school helped me to see more possibilities for my life, beyond my current circumstances. Somewhere deep inside I knew I had to be a teacher, so I could help the students like me. As a teacher I saw many students who suffered from Adverse Childhood Experiences (ACEs). These troubled and often marginalized groups of students have atypical reactions to problems and disappointments. As an administrator, for the last 16 years, I have seen the number of students with ACEs climb and the severity of the ACEs go up.

Spanning my thirty-year career in education, I have always been deeply concerned about two groups of students: the externalizers known as the high flyers-students who have consistent behavioral issues, and the internalizers, the quiet students who appear unhappy, but are not behaviorally or academically on the school staff's radar. In getting to know these students personally, I find that many of them have experienced several adverse experiences (ACEs): divorce, loss of parent job, death of a family member, physical, sexual or verbal abuse, foster care, homelessness, and others. The more trauma, or higher the intensity, the child has experienced, the more likely the effects of the trauma will manifest itself either externally or internally. In my experience Tier One universal social-emotional intervention programs are not enough. Tier One instruction occurs with a whole class, teachers can introduce social-emotional skills to students using programs like Second Steps, and help emotionally stable students grow in those skills. It is not designed to and it does not help traumatized students to recognize their lack of skills nor provide needed intensive instruction. Teachers aware of a gap between student need and teacher ability are in a position to seek opportunities to improve their understanding of trauma and its influence on children's emotional, behavioral, and academic functioning. Much more work in the area of ACEs and SEL needs to be done.

References

Alisic, E. (2012). Teachers' perspectives on providing support to children after trauma: A qualitative study. *School Psychology Quarterly*, *27*(1), 51–59. https://doi.org/10.1037/a0028590

Anda, R., & Felitti, V. (2004). Childhood abuse, household dysfunction, and indicators of impaired adult worker performance. *The Permanente Journal*, *8*(1). https://doi.org/10.7812/tpp/03-089

Bloomberg, L., & Volpe, M. (2019). *Completing your qualitative dissertation*. SAGE.

Bowlby, J. (1975). Attachment theory, separation anxiety, and mourning. In S. Arieti (Ed.), *American Handbook of Psychiatry* (Vol. 6, pp. 290–308). Basic Books.

Carter, P., & Blanch, A. (2019). A trauma lens for systems change. *Stanford Social Innovation Review*, Summer 2019, 49–54.

CASEL Collaborative for Academic, Social, and Emotional Learning. (2018). *What is SEL?* http://www.casel.org/what-is-sel/

Centers for Disease Control and Prevention. (2020). *Preventing adverse childhood experiences (ACEs): Leveraging the best available evidence*. https://www.cdc.gov/index.html

Center for Youth Wellness. (2019). *ACEs and toxic stress science*. https://centerforyouthwellness.org/the-science/

Child and Adolescent Health Measurement Initiative. (2018). *National Survey of Children's Health (NSCH) data query*. www.childhealthdata.org

Cicchetti, D. (2010). Resilience under conditions of extreme stress: A multilevel perspective. *World Psychiatry*, *9*(3), 145–154. https://doi.org/10.1002/j.2051-5545.2010.tb00297.x

Cook, C. R., Frye, M., Slemrod, T., Lyon, A. R., Renshaw, T. L., & Zhang, Y. (2015). An integrated approach to universal prevention: Independent and combined effects of PBIS and SEL on youths' mental health. *School Psychology Quarterly*, *30*(2), 166–183.

Creswell, J. (2012). *Research designs: Qualitative, quantitative, and mixed methods approach* (4th ed.). SAGE.

Creswell, J. W., & Poth, C. N. (2018). *Qualitative inquiry & research design: Choosing among five approaches* (4th ed.). SAGE Publications.

Felitti, V. J., Anda, R. F., Nordenberg, D., Williamson, D. F., Spitz, A. M., Edwards, V., Marks, J. S. (1998). Relationship of childhood abuse and household dysfunction to many of the leading causes of death in adults. *American Journal of Preventive Medicine, 14*(4), 245–258. https://doi.org/10.1016/s0749-3797(98)00017-8

Figley, C. (2012). *Encyclopedia of trauma: An interdisciplinary guide*. https://doi.org/10.4135/9781452218595

Finlay, L. (1998). Reflexivity: An essential component for all research? *British Journal of Occupational Therapy, 61*(10), 453–456. https://doi.org/10.1177/030802269806101005

Franklin T. B., Saab, B. J., & Mansuy, I. M. (2012). Neural mechanisms of stress resilience and vulnerability. *Neuron, 75*(5), 747–761. https://doi.org/10.1016/j.neuron.2012.08.016. PMID: 22958817.

Goodman, R. D., Miller, M. D., & West-Olatunji, C. A. (2012). Traumatic stress, socioeconomic status, and academic achievement among primary school students. *Psychological Trauma: Theory, Research, Practice, and Policy, 4*(3), 252–259.

Merriam, S, B. (1998). *Qualitative research and case study applications in education*. Jossey-Bass.

National Child Traumatic Stress Network, Schools Committee. (2017). *Creating, supporting, and sustaining trauma-informed schools: A system framework.*

Navalta, C., McGee, L., & Underwood, J. (2018). Adverse childhood experiences, brain development, and mental health: A call for neurocounseling. *Journal of Mental Health Counseling, 40*(3), 266–278. https://doi.org/10.17744/mehc.40.3.07

Noddings, N. (2015). *Philosophy of education*. Routledge. ProQuest Ebook Central. http://ebookcentral.proquest.com/lib/nlu/detail.action?docID=5352127. 10.1037/0003-066x.63.9.852

Rimm-Kaufman, S., Larsen, R., Curby, T., Baroody, A., Merritt, E., Abry, T., & Wanless, S. (2014). Efficacy of the responsive classroom approach: Results from a three-year, longitudinal randomized control trial. *American Educational Research Journal*. https://doi.org/10.3102/0002831214523821

Sacks, V., Murphey, D., & Moore, K. (2014). Adverse childhood experiences national and state-level prevalence. *Child Trends*. https://doi.org/10.13140/2.1.1193.8087

Saldaña, J., & Omasta, M. (2018). *Qualitative research: Analyzing life*. SAGE.

Scott, D. (2007). Resolving the quantitative-qualitative dilemma: A critical realist approach. *International Journal of Research and Method in Education, 30*(1), 3–17.

Shonkoff, J., & Garner, A. (2012). Committee on psychosocial aspects of child and family health committee on early childhood, adoption, and dependent care and section on developmental and behavioral pediatrics. The lifelong effects of early childhood adversity and toxic stress. *Pediatrics, 129*(1), e232–e246.

Salovey, P., & Mayer, J. D. (1990). Emotional intelligence. *Imagination, Cognition and Personality*, *9*(3), 185–211. https://doi.org/10.2190/DUGG-P24E-52WK-6CDG

Stake, R. (1995). *The art of case study research.* SAGE.

Yin, R. K. (2018). *Case study research and applications: Design and methods* (6th ed.). SAGE.

Chapter 8 Is There a Model for Success? Exploring Sustainable Professional Employment among Clinical Exercise Physiology Program's Graduates

REGINA SCHURMAN

When I say that I am a clinical exercise physiologist, people usually think I am either a personal trainer or a physical therapist. While there is some overlap between the skill sets of clinical exercise physiologists, personal trainers, and physical therapists, there are important differences that set clinical exercise physiologists apart. Personal trainers and clinical exercise physiologists assess various indices of physical capability of their clients and develop exercise programs to improve deficiencies; however, only clinical exercise physiologists possess the training necessary to work with individuals who have a variety of chronic health conditions. Physical therapists work with a broad range of conditions that limit mobility (American Physical Therapy Association [APTA], n.d.) but usually do not work with a patient until an event has occurred whereas clinical exercise physiologists utilize exercise as a means of chronic disease prevention (CEPA, n.d.; Potteiger, 2011).

Unlike other healthcare professions such as nursing or physical therapy, clinical exercise physiology is relatively new. The work of Levine, Lown, and Hellerstein, who used exercise in the rehabilitation of cardiac patients, led to the establishment of cardiac rehabilitation programs in hospitals in the 1970s (Potteiger, 2011). Despite several decades of practice, it was not until 2010 that the Bureau of Labor Statistics finally created a separate Standard

Occupation Code (SOC) for exercise physiologists (U.S. Department of Labor, 2010). Between the confusion over what clinical exercise physiologists do and the delay in receiving government recognition, it is no wonder that the general public does not understand the scope of practice for clinical exercise physiologists.

Why would someone go into the field of clinical exercise physiology given all the challenges that the profession is facing? Clinical exercise physiology has its origins in anatomy, physiology, and medicine and thus appeals to students who want to better understand both the human body's response to exercise as well as the power of exercise to improve health (Potteiger, 2011). The practice of clinical exercise physiology is broader than that of personal trainers who typically only work with healthy individuals. While physical therapists are typically limited to treating a specific body part, clinical exercise physiologists look at the whole person as they work to manage chronic disease and promote lifestyle habits that enhance health.

The students who enter our master's clinical exercise physiology program at Benedictine University usually have the goal of obtaining full-time employment in the field after graduation. Most of them seek employment in cardiac rehabilitation or cardiac diagnostics departments at hospitals. Several of the adjunct faculty who teach in our program have full-time positions as managers of these types of departments at local hospitals. These individuals serve as exemplars when prospective students inquire about their prospects for finding employment post-graduation. How these individuals attained their career success despite competition from other professions as well as the lack of licensure for clinical exercise physiologists is unclear.

It is apparent that more than a master's degree is needed to be successful in the competitive job market in the field of clinical exercise physiology. Graduates face many challenges in securing positions due to the economy, healthcare reform, and a lack of license for their profession. However, in spite of these challenges, some students are able to secure professional employment with opportunities for future advancement. There seem to be other factors involved that allow these students to succeed in an adverse job market.

This study was needed since the profession of clinical exercise physiology does not have a clear career path like physical therapy or nursing. Marketing materials for clinical exercise physiology graduate programs state that exercise physiologists can be found in leadership roles in cardiac rehabilitation programs, fitness centers, and agencies. However, it is left up to the students to determine the best way to secure their desired career post-graduation.

The flash of insight that focused me on the substantive area of this study was the realization that there were several clinical exercise physiologists in the Chicago area who held management positions in hospitals. This was interesting because clinical exercise physiologists are not licensed, except in the state of Louisiana. However, this lack of licensure had not held back these individuals from achieving positions as managers in cardiac rehabilitation and cardiac diagnostic departments. The departments these clinical exercise physiologists manage have a mix of healthcare professions, including nurses, respiratory therapists, echocardiography technicians, and other licensed professionals. This insight led me on a process of abduction to form a hypothesis of how this was possible and to conduct a research study in a manner that generated a substantive theory to explain my observations.

The purpose of this study was twofold: (1) to describe the clinical exercise physiology profession from the perspective of its practitioners and the graduates of clinical exercise physiology programs and (2) to develop a model of sustainable professional employment that exhibits the processes that allow graduates from clinical exercise physiology programs to attain management positions in a healthcare system dominated by licensed professionals.

This study was guided by the following questions:

- What are the graduates' perceptions on sustainable professional employment within the clinical exercise physiology profession and the path to its highest attainment?
- What are the perspectives of clinical exercise physiology professionals on sustainable professional employment and what is the career path toward their highest professional attainment?
- What is the model that exhibits the processes that allow clinical exercise physiologists to obtain sustainable professional employment and to attain management positions in a healthcare system dominated by licensed professionals?

Theoretical Positioning of the Study

Pragmatism provided the foundation of this study in terms of methodological and epistemological assumptions. Pragmatism was selected because this study seeks to provide "practical solutions to practical problems" (Ozmon & Craver, 2003, p. 138). Clinical exercise physiology students seek guidance on how to best prepare themselves to attain sustainable professional employment in today's competitive job market. Identifying the factors that contribute to securing employment in the field and thus creating a model of sustainable professional development is one of the solutions offered by this study. Wedded to my pragmatic goals is the choice of a qualitative grounded theory that is rooted in the philosophical tradition of pragmatism. Qualitative methodology would allow the experiences of clinical exercise physiology practitioners to be captured and provide the opportunity to probe more deeply into themes that may be revealed during interviews.

Grounded theory method originated with Glaser and Strauss's 1965 publication of their research in *Awareness of Dying*. At the time of the development of grounded theory method, qualitative methods were viewed as inferior to quantitative ones (Glaser & Strauss, 1967). Therefore, Glaser and Strauss wanted to prove that there were forms of qualitative research that could have as much rigor as quantitative research (Bryant, 2009). In the publication of the grounded theory method their philosophical worldview was never explicitly defined, which perplexed many, including Bryant, since Strauss had a pragmatist background being from the Chicago School of Sociology.

The two founders of grounded theory method parted ways when Strauss published *Basics of Qualitative Research* with Corbin in 1990, a book which Glaser rebutted in his book *Emergence vs. Forcing: Basics of Grounded Theory Analysis* in 1992. Despite this split, the use of the method grew in popularity. In the 1990s, those using the method realized that the issues of the role of the researcher, induction, and prior knowledge needed to be addressed, and thus many argued that grounded theory method was based on interpretivism or constructivism (Bryant, 2009). However, using constructivism does not solve the criticisms of grounded theory method since constructivism has as its basis that knowledge depends on the participants' meanings rather than on an objective view of reality (Bryant; Creswell & Clark, 2011; Mills et al., 2006). A researcher's view of truth and reality can influence him or her to justify study outcomes based on the belief that knowledge was provisional and dependent on the participant's perspectives (Bryant). However, researchers are part of the research process and their humanness will influence the construction of knowledge (Mills et al., 2006).

Positioning grounded theory method in the framework of pragmatism resolves this lack of a solid epistemological footing (Bryant, 2009). Despite a lack of an explicit reference to American pragmatism in the writings of Glaser and Strauss, Strauss did stress that it was a key part in his intellectual formation because he was exposed to the writings of Dewey and James when a student in the 1930s (Bryant). Strauss referred to the influence of pragmatism on his work as "a red thread running through my work" (Bryant, para. 51). Bryant's reconsideration of grounded theory method in the worldview of pragmatism leads to a more cohesive method that can be defended and that turns "the red thread into a lifeline" (para. 58). When taking the pragmatist view that any theories or concepts developed should be judged by their "usefulness rather than their truthfulness," the features of grounded theory become more understandable in terms of generating substantive theory (Bryant, para. 61).

In selecting a method to perform the inquiry for this study, it was important that I choose one based on the scientific method in order to generate the substantive theory for my model. What Glaser and Strauss (1967) mean by substantive theory is that it was developed for a particular "area of sociological inquiry, such as patient care, race relations, professional education," as opposed to a conceptual area of sociological inquiry, such as "stigma, deviant behavior, formal organization" (p. 32). Glaser and Strauss (1967) label these theories as "middle-range" because they "fall between the 'minor working hypothesis' of everyday life and 'all-inclusive' grand theories" (pp. 32–33).

Clinical exercise physiology is a scientific field; therefore, the primary audience for this study is those accustomed to reading research articles that use solid quantitative research. This audience typically values hard numbers higher than the softer qualitative research often used in social sciences. Some of the problems associated with the use of qualitative data include producing a study full of "undisciplined speculation laced with interesting anecdotes" (Mullen, 1996, p. 63). By utilizing a method guided by pragmatism, it was possible to generate substantive theories and a model that can be judged by its practicality in helping subjects resolve their main concern (Bryant, 2009). This aligns with Dewey's view of knowledge as instrumental, which allows theories to best be considered as tools (Bryant). The theoretical model generated by this study is a tool for future practitioners in the field to guide them onto a path to sustainable professional employment.

Grounded theory method consists of the typical stages of analysis employed in traditional scientific inquiry. However, the process of inquiry begins with abduction, or that "flash of insight" (Bryant & Charmez, 2007). Founder of pragmatism C. S. Peirce (1839–1914) believed that abduction was the only type of inference that would allow the creation of new knowledge since both induction and deduction were rooted in the development of existing knowledge. Peirce "always saw abduction as a form of reasoning that develops from surprise or sudden flashes of insight" (Bryant, 2009, para. 93).

Glaser and Strauss were considered radical by positioning grounded theory method as an open-minded, inductive model. In the ensuing years, this has led to criticism of the method when researchers do not explicitly position the method in an appropriate worldview. Utilizing pragmatism as the philosophical worldview for this study, in conjunction with grounded theory method for data collection and analysis, yielded a model that is robust and truly grounded in the data (Merriam & Simpson, 1995).

Grounded Theory Method

Grounded theory method is intended to develop new theories, but what "a theory" means is ambiguous (Bryant, 2009). Theories span the range of those based on conjecture to those that have been extensively tested and challenged and yet still hold up (Bryant). By adopting an instrumental view of theories, it can be shown the ways a particular theory holds up in practice (Bryant). Theories developed with the grounded theory method are tied to the context in which the research is based, thus becoming substantive (Bryant). Glaser and Strauss (1967) explain that "generating a theory from data means that most hypotheses and concepts not only come from the data, but are systematically worked out in relation to the data during the course of the research" (p. 6).

A test of a theory or model generated with qualitative methodology is whether the findings will be applicable beyond the specific research subjects and setting (Bogdan & Biklen, 2007). I expect my model to hold up and be reproducible since it is grounded in the data due to the use of the scientific method as described by Peirce and Dewey. The relationship between theory and practice in a worldview of pragmatism lies in the utility of the theory in practice (Bryant, 2009). If the theory that is generated makes a difference in people's understanding and actions, then it is substantive (Bryant). The ultimate goal of this study was to make a difference in the career outcomes of the graduates of clinical exercise physiology programs.

Data Collection and Analysis Techniques

Grounded theory is unique because analysis of the data is done concurrently with data collection. The primary data for analysis were gathered through semi-structured and unstructured interviews with the participants—graduates from clinical exercise physiology programs practicing in the field. The codes that emerged from each interview were compared with previous interviews in order to guide the collection of additional data as well as to identify when enough data had been gathered (Merriam & Simpson, 1995). The goal of the data collection process was to gather sufficient information in order to identify common themes and generate a model of sustainable professional employment. I felt this method best revealed the factors that were involved in my study's participants achieving career success.

Qualitative semi-structured and unstructured interviews provided my main source of data because I wanted to understand my participants' unique journeys to their career success. An open-ended question asking the participants to describe their experiences from the time they started college to their current position began each interview. Questions were added to the later interviews to provide insight on themes that were revealed earlier in data collection, which is consistent with constant comparative analysis. Grounded theory method mandates that the researcher remain open to what is being said in order to observe and determine the main concern of the interviewees and how they were able to resolve it (Glaser & Holton, 2004).

A total of 21 interviews were conducted. Seventeen interviews were conducted with veterans in the field and four interviews were conducted with recent graduates of Benedictine University's program who aspired to higher positions within the healthcare system. By the time of the last few interviews, I felt I had gathered enough data since very little new information was revealed. This is consistent with Glaserian grounded theory method in that it proscribes interviews be conducted until saturation of the categories is achieved (Glaser, 1992, 1998).

Grounded theory method begins with Glaser's concept of *theoretical sensitivity*, which is essential to being able to generate concepts from data and turn them into theory. Glaser writes extensively on emergence, meaning concepts emerge from the data that in turn lead to the development of theories from the concepts that are identified. Development of grounded theory is based on taking the data collected and turning it into concepts referred to as *codes*. Theoretical coding begins with examining the data collected and grouping incidents into substantive categories. Substantive categories refer to particular aspects of the area being studied. These substantive categories are then examined to see how they might relate to each other in order to begin to develop the hypotheses that will eventually be turned into theory. Theoretical codes can be thought of as giving the big picture or a new perspective of what is occurring (Glaser & Holton, 2004, para. 47).

During open coding, the data are looked over carefully or line-by-line in order to determine what substantive codes can be found. Open coding can be thought of as the step where the story is broken apart so that the descriptive material can be reorganized into concepts (Mullen, 1996). The constant comparative method is one of the two foundational concepts of grounded theory, the other being theoretical sampling, which drives the development of the theory that emerges from the data. This is often referred to as a method to "tease out the similarities and differences in order to refine concepts" (Bryant & Charmez, 2007, p. 607).

Because grounded theory involves the simultaneous collection and coding of data, certain categories will become saturated earlier and this will help prevent the researcher from collecting redundant data (Holton, 2010).

Saturation refers to the point at which "no new conceptual properties or dimensions are emerging" (p. 27) and, therefore, no additional data need to be obtained for that category since one more indicator or incident will not expand on the theory being developed. Glaser describes the core variable as the category that emerges and can explain most of the variation surrounding the main concern of the study. The core variable serves the function of linking together as many other categories as possible. It is what provides "grab" for the formal theory that is being developed (Glaser & Holton, 2004, para. 54).

Memo writing is important in capturing the analyst's thoughts, hunches, and impressions about the data as they are coding or just after an interview. Memos provide a way to help bring out the emerging theory. These memos are not detailed notes; rather, they are theoretical descriptions. Upon reaching the point of theoretical saturation, the analyst takes the memos and sorts them. This is how the data that have been broken apart during all the coding processes can be put together to form a cohesive theory. Because there are no preconceived notions with classic grounded theory, this allows for a richer and more robust theory. The relevant literature is brought into the theory during this process. Parsimony is the key here—what is the simplest explanation of the resolution of the core concern expressed by the participants (Glaser & Holton, 2004, para. 66–70)?

The next step is sorting the memos in order to explain the most variation in the data with the least number of concepts. According to Glaser and Holton (2004), this will result in a theory that will be able to explain how the subjects are able to resolve "their main concern with concepts that fit, work, have relevance and are saturated" (para. 71–74). This goes back to the pragmatist view that theories should be viewed as tools and they should be judged by how well they help people resolve their main concerns (Bryant, 2009, para. 103).

I concur with Bryant that when grounded theory is based on a worldview of pragmatism, the theories and concepts generated are evaluated based on how applicable they are to certain situations (Bryant, 2009). Being able to generate a model out of my research that can be used to help counsel students to sustainable professional employment in the clinical exercise physiology profession reflects the pragmatic orientation of this study.

Turning Words into Theory

Classic grounded theory utilizes the participant's own words to derive the theory, therefore, generating an inductive, substantive theory. The process of analysis began with line-by-line coding that entailed examining the words of the participants and assigning codes to concepts conveyed. No predefined list of codes was used so as to avoid preconceiving what would be found in the data (Glaser, 1992). This first pass of coding the interview transcripts yielded numerous codes, many of them repetitious. These codes were compared and those that were very similar in terms of the concept they were trying to describe were combined. Then the categories were examined for their relationships with each other and how accurately they represented the participants' concerns. Codes were also examined to determine their best fit within the categories that were identified. This was an iterative process, and numerous additional passes of the data were made until it was felt that the categories derived accurately described the participants' observations.

It was during this interactive process that a core category appeared to emerge that represented the main concern of the study participants. Other categories also emerged that supported this core category. Eventually this process yielded 11 main categories as follows: *academic preparation*, *competitive job market*, *professional development*, *career satisfaction*, *professional identity*, *credentials*, *compensation*, *licensure*, *scope of practice*, *boundaries of expertise*, and *recognition of the expertise of clinical exercise physiologists*. The relationships among these categories were examined in order to produce a model that explains the key factors involved in the attainment of sustainable professional employment in the clinical exercise physiology field.

The development of the model of sustainable professional employment for clinical exercise physiologists has been central to my research purposes. The model reflects the processes involved in the journeys of successful clinical exercise physiologists, starting with their academic careers and culminating in an understanding of their current level of career satisfaction. In addition to deriving the factors that influenced their success, the challenges encountered in the practice of clinical exercise physiology were examined and are represented in the model.

The model created as a result of this study is pragmatic in the sense that it is a tool that can be used by others to address the concerns faced in practicing the profession of clinical exercise physiology (Bryant, 2009, para. 103). These categories form two main components of the model: (1) *the path to employment in cardiac rehabilitation and diagnostics environment*, and (2) *recognition of the expertise of clinical exercise physiologists*.

The Path to Employment

The bottom portion of the model shown in Figure 8.1 describes the process of becoming a successful practitioner in the field. The information derived from the interviews spanned many years. No matter the length of their

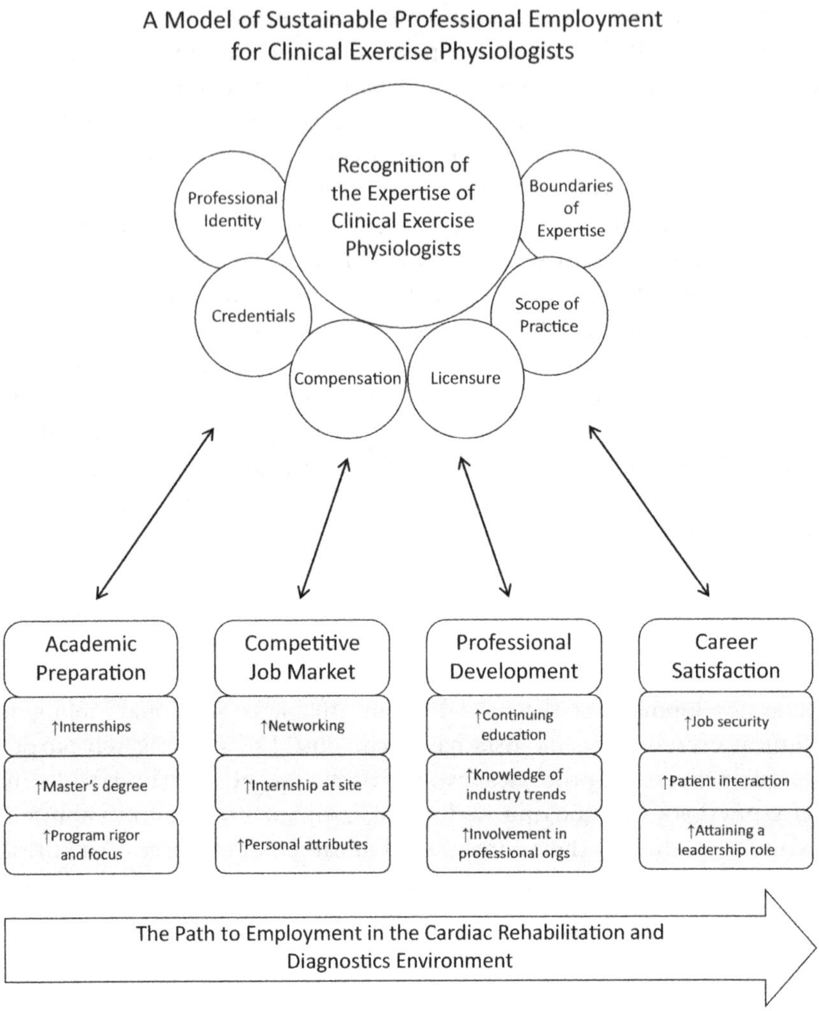

Figure 8.1: Model of Sustainable Professional Employment for Clinical Exercise Physiologists

journeys, all participants went through a process of transformation in order to become the successful practitioners they are today. No two participant's journeys were the same; however, there were many commonalities among them. All of the participants' journeys, *the path to employment in the cardiac rehabilitation and diagnostics environment*, consisted of four main categories: (1) *academic preparation*, (2) *competitive job market*, (3) *professional development*, and (4) *career satisfaction*.

Academic Preparation

In the Chicago area, a master's degree is usually required to secure a position in cardiac rehabilitation and diagnostics departments. Key components of academic preparation are clinical internships as well as the program of study's rigor. Nearly all of the study's participants felt that their internships were a critical component of their academic preparation (Ives & Knudson, 2007). The participants agreed that internships are a form of anticipatory socialization that allows a student to try on a career (Callanan & Benzing, 2004). It was through clinical internships that several of the participants discovered how much they loved the field of cardiac rehabilitation.

Hennemann and Liefner (2010) stress that an important component of an academic program is the development of competence. The goal of my participants when they have student interns is to have them as competent as regular staff by the end of their internship. *Academic preparation* is linked with the *competitive job market* through the networks that students begin to develop when they perform their internships. Many of the participants attained their first positions in the field through their internships.

Competitive Job Market

The next step in the path is entering the job market. The cardiac rehabilitation and diagnostics environment is very competitive in the Chicago area; thus, enhancing one's employability is key. Employability encompasses the "skills, understandings, and personal attributes" (Atlay, 2010, p. 19) that improve the chances that graduates will obtain employment in the occupation of their choice. Internships serve as a means for students to demonstrate their employability to potential employers.

My participants constantly emphasized the importance of networking, not only to enter the field but also their ability to advance within the field. Networking is a critical component in securing employment in addition to internships since both provide a means for students to demonstrate their competencies to potential employers (Sherman & Dyess, 2010). Henley's (1999) comment that "what you know counts, but who you know counts, too" was reflected in the number of instances where practitioners in this study obtained positions before they were even advertised.

Professional Development

Attainment of a position in the field is not the final step; those who hope to advance need to continue to invest in professional development. It is important to keep up with the changes in healthcare in terms of treatments, patient demographics, and insurance reimbursements that have a direct impact on participants' departments and, in turn, their job security. Continuing education is a means of lifelong learning and a way to develop professionalism (Garman et al., 2006). This study's participants utilized different approaches toward continuing education. Educational opportunities offered through professional societies are a common way that practitioners stay current in the field. *Professional development* is linked with the *competitive job market* primarily through the networks participants built through service in professional organizations.

Career Satisfaction

The culmination of *the path to employment in cardiac rehabilitation and diagnostics environment* is achieving satisfaction with your career choice. The vast majority of this study's participants had engaged in internships in the area in which they are currently employed. The awareness of the work environment produced by internships contributed to students making a commitment to the profession (Callanan & Benzing, 2004; Cranmer, 2006). Career success and fulfillment are a "function of the individual optimizing the 'fit' between their personal characteristics and their work environment" (Callahan & Benzing, p. 82). This was reflected in the passion that the successful practitioners exhibited when they spoke of their work with patients, which is also consistent with the findings of Ng and Feldman (2010) regarding the factors that contribute positively to a sense of well-being.

It Is a Profession! Recognition of the Expertise of Clinical Exercise Physiologists

A key concept in the development of grounded theory is that the researcher is to determine the main concern of the interviewee and how the person was able to resolve it (Glaser & Holton, 2004). This study's participants shared much information about their journeys, but the one key concern that kept emerging was the difficulty of having their expertise recognized by other healthcare practitioners. This main concern, or core category, is positioned in the center of the top section of the model presented in Figure 8.1. Surrounding the core category are the categories, or factors, that influence it. These supporting categories include *professional identity*, *credentials*, *compensation*, *licensure*, *scope of practice*, and *boundaries of expertise*. The model represented in Figure 8.1 also portrays the interrelationships between these categories and those that comprise *the path to employment in the cardiac rehabilitation and diagnostics environment.*

Professional Identity

Even though Brown (2000) argues that exercise physiology is not a profession, this study's participants felt that it *was* a profession. As part of the push for licensure to further establish exercise physiology as a profession, academic programs in clinical exercise physiology are being encouraged to attain accreditation. As part of accreditation, academic programs must demonstrate that their curriculum will ensure their graduates will possess a defined set of knowledge, skills, and abilities. Without this standardization it is hard for others to know what expertise a clinical exercise physiologist should possess. This results in a lack of a clear professional identity that works against attaining the *recognition of the expertise of clinical exercise physiologists* among those in the healthcare community.

In addition, clinical exercise physiologists are not united behind a single professional organization unlike other professions such as physical therapy. Only some of this study's participants were members either of the American Association of Cardiovascular and Pulmonary Rehabilitation (AACVPR) or the Illinois Society for Cardiopulmonary Health and Rehabilitation (ISCHR). However, these organizations do not represent those practitioners who work outside of cardiac rehabilitation. The lack of a single organization that actually represents all of clinical exercise physiologists hinders the attainment of the *recognition of the expertise of clinical exercise physiologists.*

Credentials

One way to address the current lack of a standardized curriculum is for practitioners to take certification examinations to prove that they do have the knowledge, skills, and abilities required of those who desire to work in the cardiac rehabilitation and diagnostics environment. Despite Keteyian's (1999) findings that certification examinations help address concerns from other healthcare professions regarding the academic preparation of exercise physiologists, this study's participants felt that examinations were of limited value because they only tested book knowledge. In addition, there was much confusion over what the differences were between the Exercise Specialist (ES), Clinical Exercise Specialist (CES), and Registered Clinical Exercise Physiologist (RCEP) certifications offered by the American College of Sports Medicine (ACSM).

Compensation

This study's participants are frustrated because they are paid less than nurses even though they have a higher level of education; they do not feel that their compensation reflects their expertise (Davis et al., 2001). Although Davis and colleagues and Ives and Knudson (2007) suggest that the employment of exercise physiologists might be favored over other licensed professionals such as nurses because of the salary differences, this was not consistent with what this study's participants reported. Due to the limits on scope of practice, nurses were still needed and, in fact, it was the versatility of nurses that made utilizing them preferable in cardiac rehabilitation and diagnostics departments despite their higher wages. Some of this study's participants suggested that licensure would increase the utilization of exercise physiologists.

Licensure

The lack of licensure for clinical exercise physiologists poses several problems. Of biggest concern to this study's participants is the lack of professional equality they feel when compared with other healthcare professionals. On a microlevel, they reported excellent working relationships with the other professions in their department, but on a macrolevel, there were concerns about the discrepancy in pay as well as limitations on what they could do as part of their jobs.

Related to *licensure* is *professional identity.* As a profession, we have not done a good job defining who we are and what we do since there are so many different career paths that clinical exercise physiologists can pursue. Berry and Verrill (2012) argue that "achieving licensure will finally enable the CEP to be viewed in the same light and with the same respect as other licensed health care professionals who work in the rehabilitation fields" (p. 37). Foster and Porcari (2012) outline the great difficulty involved in convincing legislators to support licensure due to the lack of evidence showing that large numbers of the general public are being harmed by the activities of unqualified practitioners. The points made by Foster and Porcari echo what this study's participants have mentioned—that we in the profession are not coming together to present a unified front in terms of minimal educational standards as well as working together with larger organizations, such as the physical therapists, to better define how our profession can work effectively with other professions in delivering patient care.

Scope of Practice

This category is related to *licensure* as part of the process of creating a practice act for a profession that defines those activities practitioners are permitted to engage in and what is prohibited. This study's participants repeatedly related how they were not able to perform certain activities, such as giving medications to a patient or taking orders from a doctor, due to the restrictions of the Nurse Practice Act. Several expressed frustration over how these restrictions limited their ability to service their patients. *Scope of practice* affects compensation because exercise physiologists are not able to function independently in cardiac rehabilitation. For smaller cardiac rehabilitation outreach sites, this often means that a registered nurse will be utilized since they are more versatile, thus keeping staffing to a minimum. Several of this study's participants suggested an expansion of scope of practice for clinical exercise physiologists could result in need for fewer nurses. This, in turn, could have a positive impact on *competitive job market.*

Boundaries of Expertise

Nancarrow and Borthwick (2005) found that professional boundaries are dynamic due to staffing shortages caused by changes in healthcare policies. Many of this study's participants reported a high degree of role sharing between exercise physiologists and nurses. The ability of clinical exercise physiologists to perform a wide variety of roles in the cardiac rehabilitation and diagnostics environment demonstrates their broad expertise. *Scope of practice* is related to *boundaries of expertise* since the scope of practice helps to define what should be expected of each profession. Regarding the scope of practice for exercise physiologists, ACSM mentions the use of exercise as a means of therapy for clinical situations such as those found in cardiac rehabilitation and diagnostics environments (Verrill & Keteyian, 2010). This study's participants felt that exercise prescription was best left to clinical exercise physiologists. Several participants believed patients were not being served well when cardiac rehabilitation programs only utilized registered nurses. They felt the lack of training for nurses in exercise prescription was a disservice to the patient.

Recognition of the Expertise of Clinical Exercise Physiologists

The main concern of this study's participants was earning recognition of their unique expertise from the other healthcare professionals. Many of this study's participants felt that they were being held back because they are not licensed professionals like nurses or physical therapists. As was previously discussed, there are several facets to this perception of a lack of recognition of expertise. A strong *professional identity*, such as that possessed by other professions, can help practitioners earn respect because it clarifies the role that the practitioner serves on the healthcare team. However, as was previously discussed, clinical exercise physiology practitioners are not unified behind one organization.

An acknowledgment of a practitioner's expertise is often demonstrated when they are paid in accordance with their *credentials*. However, the reality that a nurse with only an associate's degree has a higher starting salary than a clinical exercise physiologist with a master's degree makes some question their career choice. Other practitioners in this study take a more philosophical view—that it is more important to do something you are passionate about rather than earn a higher salary but not enjoy your work.

Licensure, despite being touted as a means to gain credibility and recognition, does not appear to be anywhere close to becoming a reality in the majority of states. Furthermore, this study's participants were mixed in their feelings regarding the benefit they would actually derive, and they questioned whether it would cause an additional burden, not only in terms of limits on the activities they could perform but also the expense practitioners would have to assume in attaining and maintaining a license.

Practitioners often feel that their unique expertise is not recognized due to the limitations imposed on their *scope of practice* by the Nurse Practice Act. This goes along with establishing *boundaries of expertise*. Clinical exercise physiologists have a significant investment in acquiring expertise in exercise prescription and the body's responses to the stress of exercise. They desire to utilize their expertise to provide better outcomes for their patients. While some of this study's participants feel that their expertise is recognized and sought out by other professions, it was not a sentiment that was shared by all.

The model of sustainable professional employment for clinical exercise physiologists generated by this study reflects the processes by which this study's participants have achieved their career success in addition to presenting their main concern of achieving recognition of the expertise of clinical exercise physiologists. This model shown in Figure 8.1 has been developed out of the analyses of the interviews that were conducted and has been further substantiated by relevant literature in the field. Arrows are used to represent how *the path to employment in the cardiac rehabilitation and diagnostics environment* interacts with *recognition of the expertise of clinical exercise physiologists*.

This model represents a pragmatic and inspiring tool to be used by practitioners in the field as well as those who hope to pursue new levels of career attainment. The inclusion of the perspectives of recent graduates into the creation of this model helps to strengthen its applicability to those students who seek to enter the field.

The original idea for this study started with a flash of insight when I observed so many exemplars in the field that had inexplicably overcome the challenges of the profession of clinical exercise physiology and attained career success. The use of grounded theory method revealed much about the preparation and practice of clinical exercise physiologists employed in the cardiac rehabilitation and diagnostics environment. I gained insight into the importance of clinical internships and the development of professional networks in attaining employment. I was dismayed to discover how widespread the lack of name recognition is for clinical exercise physiologists, even in a healthcare setting. Clinical exercise physiologists make significant contributions in cardiac rehabilitation due to their extensive master's level academic preparation that is the equivalent of nurses, dieticians, and physical therapists. Clinical exercise physiologists often work side-by-side with these professions, yet lack the recognition of expertise that licensure conveys. I was saddened to learn they are treated as the odd duck in the clinical environment because they do not exist independently despite being highly skilled (Foster & Porcari, 2012). Much work remains to unite our profession and elevate its standing in the healthcare setting.

References

American Physical Therapy Association. (n.d.). Who are physical therapists? http://www.apta.org/AboutPTs/

Atlay, M. (2010). *Introducing CRe8—The curriculum review 2008*. https://www.beds.ac.uk/

Berry, R., & Verrill, D. (2012). POINT: Licensure for clinical exercise physiologists—An argument in favor of this proposal. *Journal of Clinical Exercise Physiology, 1*(1), 35–38.

Bogdan, R. C., & Biklen, S. K. (2007). *Qualitative research for education: An introduction to theory and method*. Pearson.

Brown, S. P. (2000). Profession or discipline: The role of exercise physiology in allied health. *Clinical Exercise Physiology, 2*(1), 52.

Bryant, A. (2009). Grounded theory and pragmatism: The curious case of Anselm Strauss. *Forum: Qualitative Social Research, 10*(3). http://www.qualitative-research.net/index.php/fqs/article/view/1358

Bryant, A., & Charmaz, K. (Eds.). (2007). *The Sage handbook of grounded theory*. SAGE.

Callanan, G., & Benzing, C. (2004). Assessing the role of internships in the career-oriented employment of graduating college students. *Education & Training*, *46*(2), 82–89.

Clinical Exercise Physiology Association. (n.d.). *Consumer information: Clinical exercise physiology*. https://www.acsm-cepa.org/

Cranmer, S. (2006). Enhancing graduate employability: Best intentions and mixed outcomes. *Studies in Higher Education*, *31*(2), 169–184.

Creswell, J. W., & Clark, V. L. (2011). *Designing and conducting mixed methods research* (2nd ed.). SAGE.

Davis, S., Jankovitz, K., & Cooper, J. (2001). California cardiac rehabilitation practitioners and their staff preparation preferences. *Clinical Exercise Physiology*, *3*(2), 94.

Foster, C., & Porcari, J. P. (2012). COUNTERPOINT: Licensure for clinical exercise physiologists—A desirable goal with an elusive outcome. *Journal of Clinical Exercise Physiology*, *1*(1), 38–40.

Garman, A. N., Evans, R., Krause, M., & Anfossi, J. (2006). Professionalism. *Journal of Healthcare Management*, *51*(4), 219–222.

Glaser, B. G. (1992). *Emergence vs. forcing: Basics of grounded theory analysis*. Sociology.

Glaser, B. G. (1998). *Doing grounded theory: Issues and discussions*. Sociology.

Glaser, B. G., & Holton, J. (2004). Remodeling grounded theory. *Forum Qualitative Social Research*, *5*(2). http://www.qualitative-research.net/index.php/fqs/article/view/607

Glaser, B. G., & Strauss, A. L. (1965). *Awareness of dying*. Aldine de Gruyter.

Glaser, B. G., & Strauss, A. L. (1967). *The discovery of grounded theory: Strategies for qualitative research*. Aldine de Gruyter.

Henley, R. J. (1999). Enhancing what you know through who you know. *Healthcare Financial Management)*, *53*(12).

Hennemann, S., & Liefner, I. (2010). Employability of German geography graduates: The mismatch between knowledge acquired and competences required. *Journal of Geography in Higher Education*, *34*(2), 215–230.

Holton, J. A. (2010). The coding process and its challenges. *Grounded Theory Review*, *9*(1), 21–40.

Ives, J. C., & Knudson, D. (2007). Professional practice in exercise science. *Sports Medicine*, *37*(2), 103–115.

Keteyian, S. J. (1999). Trained in a discipline and practicing as a professional. Who we are, revisited. *Clinical Exercise Physiology*, *1*(2), 55.

Merriam, S. B., & Simpson, E. L. (1995). *A guide to research for educators and trainers of adults*. Krieger.

Mills, J., Bonner, A., & Francis, K. (2006). The development of constructivist grounded theory. *International Journal of Qualitative Methods*, *5*(1), 1–10.

Mullen, P. D. (1996). Cutting back: Life after a heart attack. In B. G. Glaser (Ed.), *Gerund grounded theory: The basic social process dissertation* (pp. 60–72). Sociology.

Nancarrow, S., & Borthwick, A. M. (2005). Dynamic professional boundaries in the healthcare workforce. *Sociology of Health & Illness*, *27*(7), 897–919.

Ng, T., & Feldman, D. (2010). Human capital and objective indicators of career success: The mediating effects of cognitive ability and conscientiousness. *Journal of Occupational & Organizational Psychology, 83*(1), 207–235.

Ozmon, H. A., & Craver, S. M. (2003). *Philosophical foundations of education.* Merrill Prentice Hall.

Potteiger, J. A. (2011). *ACSM's introduction to exercise science.* Lippincott Williams & Wilkins.

Sherman, R. O., & Dyess, S. (2010). New graduate transition into practice during turbulent economic times. *Journal of Nursing Education, 49*(7), 367–368.

U.S. Department of Labor, Bureau of Labor Statistics. (2010). *Standard occupational classification: 29–1128 exercise physiologists.* https://www.bls.gov/

Verrill, D. E., & Keteyian, S. J. (2010). Evolution of the clinical exercise physiologist. In J. Myers & D. C. Nieman (Eds.), *ACSM's resources for clinical exercise physiology: Musculoskeletal, neuromuscular, neoplastic, immunologic, and hematologic conditions* (pp. 280–287). Lippincott Williams & Wilkins.

Chapter 9 Civically Engaged Curriculum: A Call for Action to Elementary Public-School Teachers

CHERYL JEAN DEROO

We develop our positionalities early and often based upon our life experiences. The early school years of my childhood were spent in a stereotypical White, suburban neighborhood where mothers were nearly always at home ready to care for kids, clean, cook, and provide all of the daily necessities. The vast majority, if not all of the families on our block were White, and the school we attended matched the neighborhood. If there were other diverse ethnic groups, I cannot recall. Recent experiences have helped me to understand that my lack of knowledge was a convenient benefit of my White privilege.

As my dad's business grew, my parents also had outgrown the neighborhood and were ready to move to a larger home. We were not included in the search, but were pleased with our new living space. We moved to what was probably considered a higher-income neighborhood just outside of a small city. It had a community pool, tennis courts, and plenty of activity. We did not know it at the time, but our lives as school children would look much different. My older sister and I attended a middle school right in the heart of the downtown area of the city. The diversity in the student body took me by surprise. The mix of Black, White, and Hispanic students was new to me, and early on, I was quite uncomfortable. I recall the first day feeling overdressed and out of place, unsure of how or if I would ever fit in. My experiences would prove my initial reactions wrong. Though during this time period there were often visual and social racial divides in our school, it was also a time filled with opportunities for me to personally thrive. Those years did not bring us to have conversations about race, ethnicity, or inclusion; however, I grew in my relationships with all students while developing an interest in other races and cultures. In some people, the seed grows; in others, it does not. I believe this move had a profound impact on the person I would grow up to be.

As an elementary school principal, a majority of my time is spent inside classrooms observing teacher practices and student learning. Often these observations are done in a formal manner, while many times, I am informally assessing overall teacher practices. At times, it brought back memories of my own teaching career, while at other times, I was struck by the new, more interesting, and innovative practices that teachers had developed over the years. However, even the untrained eye would notice that most of the days are spent in the world of literacy and mathematics, with little time for social studies and science. Over the years, I saw social studies lessons here or there; however, they were primarily readings shared with the students, often in the form of a chapter from a 20-year-old textbook followed by a list of questions for students to answer. That brought back memories. Memories from my days in school when I was bored out of my mind reading words from a three-inch-thick social studies text that lacked interest to me and words ran together in a meaningless way. There has to be a better way! Where, I have often wondered, are the experiences? How can we find the time to make social studies curriculum more meaningful to students and create a connection to their personal lives?

It did not occur to me that becoming a school building leader would have me learn more about power and equity than I would about how children learn to read. That is exactly what happened over the past 15 years as an elementary school principal. It first struck me while opening our school doors for the first time during a local election. We only had a single precinct, but I was thrilled for the students to be able to have a chance to witness a real election. To my surprise, the polls were empty; very few voters came out to cast a ballot. I was certain that in the next presidential election year, we would see a much different story. Our first African American presidential candidate, Barak Obama, was running for office, while on the opposing side, a female, Sarah Palin, was attempting to fill the vice-presidential seat with John McCain as the presidential nominee. The students had been talking about the election and they were excited. Students were excited to share their voting choices, typically repeating the verbiage from the conversations heard at home. The election ended, and the curriculum moved on. Four more years of focus on textbooks, dry readings, and a lack of rigor. Yet increased testing practices, pressure from district leaders, and outdated materials continued to delay the change that I was hoping for—a curriculum based on real-life experiences, action, and problem-solving that would engage and inspire our students. This long-carried frustration and unfulfilled hope compelled me to embark on this study in the hope of contributing to civic research and student engagement.

Statement of the Problem

Today, across the media, Americans see civil unrest, distrust in government, and the nation divided among political lines. It is difficult to see any positive outcomes of continual conflict. Despite the current challenges in the United States, this conflict may be providing motivation for people to share their voices. Early voting results show record numbers of voters going to the polls. In a National Public Radio (NPR) interview, University of Florida professor Michael McDonald summarizes his voter-tracking information: "We continue to pile on votes at a record pace. We've already passed any raw number of early votes in any prior election in U.S. history" (Sprunt, 2020, para. 4). In addition, according to the Center for Information and Research on Civic Learning and Engagement (CIRCLE) (2020), youth activism and civic engagement are increasing.

While the increase in civic participation is a reason to hope for advocates of social studies education, the barriers created have continued to marginalize social studies curriculum, particularly in the early grades. These barriers can be based on federal and state mandates and testing but they also come from pressure at the district and school administrative levels (Pace, 2011). Pace (2011) points to previous research that affirms this is particularly the case with schools serving low-income populations: "Narrowing of curriculum occurs disproportionately in low-performing schools with large minority populations, thereby contributing to educational inequity in the name of narrowing the achievement gap" (p. 33).

For decades, academic scholars have recommended an integrated approach to the curriculum, particularly at the elementary school level: "More recently, content integration has received renewed interest in the Common Core State Standards (CCSS) and is a key component to CCSS" (Huck, 2019, p. 3). Integration, however, poses additional challenges for classroom teachers. Heafner (2018) explored perspectives of both teachers and an administrator on the move to an integrated ELA and social studies integrated curriculum model and found several challenges. Teachers, in Heafner's study, reported ambiguity and confusion due to limited training. Teachers also reported that a wide variety of hands-on materials were available yet there was little time to plan or work with grade-level teams, causing a lack of enthusiasm and frustration. Additionally, the administrator suspected a lack of teacher expertise in social studies itself as a concern for implementation (Heafner, 2018).

It is important then to determine how it is that teachers develop the professional agency to design and implement civically engaged curriculum. Despite the challenges that we face, with teacher training and preparation, I believe that civic engagement can—and should—begin in elementary school.

Research Purpose and Questions

The purpose of this case study was (a) to investigate ways in which elementary teachers develop their positionality with regard to civically engaged education and design and implement civically engaged curriculum, and (b) to examine the conditions under which these teachers can develop agency to advocate for action-oriented civic education. The following questions guided the study:

1. How do elementary teachers develop positionality with regard to civically engaged education?
2. How do they design and implement civically engaged curriculum within the constraints of federal, state, and district mandates?
3. What prevents them, if anything, from implementing civically engaged curriculum?
4. How can these teachers motivate their students to understand the importance of civic responsibility and engagement in civic learning?
5. What are the conditions under which these teachers can develop agency to advocate for action-oriented civic education?

Methodological Approach: Theoretical Lens

The theory of change and social justice theory are the perspectives that informed this study's research purposes, questions, and the entire research process. Teachers themselves design their day-to-day complex instruction based upon the criteria provided by their districts, states, and the federal guidelines. However, teachers report that they need far more planning time than they are afforded by their school districts (Merritt, 2016). Additionally, through collaboration, teachers can share their voices. "One of the major messages from Visible Learning is the power of teachers learning from and talking to each other about planning" (Hattie, 2012, p. 60). Thus, in this study, the use of teacher voice and collaboration lend themselves well to both the theory of change and to social justice theory.

The Theory of Change

The theory of change has long been associated with school reform and the times political and economic climate (Goodson, 2014). Progressive change models reflect the need to include educator voice within the change process in order to provide change that can represent all the people the school serves. Educators' areas of expertise serve as the primary voice within the change process, although that voice must represent the people they serve. In the United States, White teachers continue to represent the majority, while their students represent those of color. According to the statistics of the Institute of Education Sciences (IES) (2020), the majority of teachers were White in schools where a majority of students were Hispanic (54%), Black (54%), Asian (60%), or American Indian/Alaska Native (61%). These data show that in schools where a large percentage of teachers were White, the majority of their students were not White. Thus, it is paramount to acknowledge these teacher voices in a collaborative way.

Additionally, Hargreaves (1996) encourages researchers to acknowledge teacher voices without silencing the voices of students and parents: "Though silenced in research and in policy, teachers' voices often prevail inordinately within their own institutions, to the exclusion of students' and parents' ones" (p. 14). Through this research, I listened to the voice of the teacher, focusing on each person's life history and their current positionality in an effort to discover ways in which they motivated and engaged their students in action-oriented civic education.

Social Justice Theory

Social justice theory (SJT) primarily concerns itself with providing equitable and fair opportunities for all within society (Rawls, 1971). Within education, SJT finds common ground with the change model; its focus is the needs and interests of the students and the community in which they teach. "Educational content and processes are connected to social justice theories and practices by deliberate and explicit interventions tailored to specific students, communities, and society in contexts" (Bogotch, 2002, p. 3). Teachers need to address barriers that students may come across as they embark on new curriculum. Villegas (2007) reminds educators that although schools have made progress in the work of social justice, there needs to be continued effort to focus on inequities, making learning an active process that brings in former life experiences, helping students to build bridges to prior knowledge, and constructing understanding. These were the practices that I listened for and looked for throughout my data collection and analysis. For students, lessons embedded in social justice concepts allow for critical thinking and problem-solving for change.

Freire (1968/2000) promotes liberating action of the oppressed so that they may transform and recognize their current reality to bring about transformative change. Freire (1968/2000) suggests that "to achieve this goal, the oppressed must confront reality critically, simultaneously objectifying and acting upon that reality" (p. 52). Furthermore, Freire supports teachers acting as advocates in this liberation by eliminating the banking model of education that focuses on the teacher as the expert, and moving toward a model where problem-solving and transformation can occur.

Liberation is a praxis: the action and reflection of men and women upon their world in order to transform it. Those truly committed to liberation must reject the banking concept in its entirety, adopting instead a concept of women and men as conscious beings, and consciousness intent upon the world. They must abandon the educational goal of deposit making and replace it with the posing of the problems of human beings in their relations with the world (Freire, 1968/2000, p. 79).

Social justice theorists and change theorists continue to advocate for this transformative learning as critical elements for educational models. According to Brown (2004),

> Employing a critical, transformative pedagogy requires professors to be active facilitators and co-learners who go beyond simply meeting the expressed needs of the learner. Through a wide array of roles, methods, and techniques, they need to take on the responsibility for growth by questioning the learner's expectations and beliefs. Transformative learning is a process of critical self-reflection that can be stimulated by people, events, or changes in context that challenge the learner's basic assumptions of the world. (p. 87)

The use of change theory and social justice theory as the theoretical bases for my study provided me with a framework to connect previous research to this study.

Research Design: Case Study

Qualitative methods offer effective ways to design a study of teacher positionality, agency, and action-based civic curriculum. I employed a case-study approach to gain an in-depth understanding of the conditions that emerge across a variety of individual cases. According to Stake (1995), "qualitative case study was developed to study the experience of real cases operating in real situations" (p. 3). Yin (2018) further defines case-study research as "an empirical inquiry that investigates a contemporary phenomenon (the 'case') in depth and within its real-world context, especially when the boundaries between phenomenon and context may not clearly evident" (p. 15). A case-study approach allowed for a deeper insight into the real-life experiences of the teachers participating in my study and the curriculum they create.

Stake (1995) recognizes that holism is a special characteristic of all qualitative research, defining it as contextually well developed, bounded, resistant of reductionism and elementalism, and noncomparative. Stake (1995) additionally identifies that qualitative studies, and thus this case study, are empirical, interpretive, and empathetic. The design of this study focused on these aspects through observations, interactions, and interpretations, yet although intentional, the structure was responsive to the experiences as they occurred.

Stake (1995) further differentiates between instrumental and intrinsic case study. An instrumental case study is "a research question, a puzzlement, a need for general understanding, and a feel that we may get insight into the question by studying a particular case" (Stake, 1995, p. 3). Conversely, intrinsic case study is one in which the researcher is studying the case to fill a particular need: "We are interested in it, not because by studying it we learn about other cases or about some general problem, but because we need to learn about that particular case" (Stake, 1995, p. 3). This case study was instrumental in that its intent was to gain insight into questions of teacher positionality, agency, and their effects on the design of action-oriented civic curriculum.

Research Site and Participants

The site for this study was a public elementary school in a large suburban school district located approximately 30 miles outside of a major metropolitan city in the Midwest. The school was a diverse school with approximately 57% of the students coming from low-income households. Additionally, the students attending the school came from a variety of ethnic and cultural backgrounds with 51% of the students identifying as Hispanic, 28% White, 11% Asian, 6% Black, and 3% or less identifying as one of a variety of other races. The 33 different languages spoken in the homes of its families also indicated the diversity of the school. While the student body was diverse, the teaching staff was less so. The school had 23 classroom teachers, 16 of which identified as White and seven as Hispanic. At the time of this study, the school site was also the place where I was one of the administrators. The site was selected based on its convenience for me and its ease of access to the participants. Additionally, due to the fact that school remained online during the COVID-19 pandemic, this setting needed to be accessible both on site and in the virtual setting.

The main participants in this study and on the site were classroom teachers. Participants were sought out using purposive sampling. Saldaña and Omasta (2018) explain that most qualitative research employs purposive sampling, in which participants are deliberately selected because they are most likely to provide insight into the phenomenon being investigated due to their position, experience, and/or identity markers (e.g., demographics, such as gender, race/ethnicity, health status) (p. 96). The participants were selected based upon their willingness to volunteer for the study after being provided its information and its purpose. This method was based on a convenience sampling because all of the participants were from the school in which I served. Additionally, because teaching teams often have strong knowledge of one another's practices, I asked teachers to recommend those who they think may be good examples for the study. This network sampling allowed me to identify further participants for the study.

Data Sources and Methods of Data Collection

Interviews

Interviews have the advantage of allowing the researcher to gain specific knowledge of the participants' experiences, values, attitudes, and beliefs about topics that relate to the particular study (Saldaña & Omasta, 2018). As Merriam (1998) explains, "the main purpose of an interview is to obtain a special kind of information" (p. 71). Patton (1990) further clarifies that the researcher is seeking information that is "in and on someone else's mind" (p. 278). I conducted the teacher interviews using a semi-structured approach, leaving me with the ability to modify my questions throughout the interview and create a more conversational tone. The semi-structured approach allows the researcher to adjust the line of questioning throughout the interview based on the participant's response.

The interview allowed me to hear a teacher's voice, understand their historical background, and note any potential biases that the interviewee may have. The interview also allowed me to gather data regarding the participants' understanding of the curriculum, resources, and the participants' perceptions of student engagement within their lessons. The interviews consisted of primarily open-ended questions to lead us into a conversation.

It was important for me, as an administrator in the building, to be aware that I held a power that could affect the responses of my participants. According to Saldaña and Omasta (2018), "researchers should be aware that interpersonal dynamics will likely affect any type of interview; we encourage researchers to make efforts to create as equitable a relationship as possible" (p. 90). In this case, it was vital that I set a conversational tone in the interview and then held the interview in a space that was free of distractions. Additionally, as a researcher, making eye contact, paraphrasing, and adjusting my questions was important in order to build trust with the participant.

Observations

Observations comprise additional sources of data gathered from real-world situations and events. I conducted multiple-observations, focusing on the engagement of the civic curriculum design. As an administrator who frequently acts as an informal observer and classroom participant, I joined the classroom as a participant-observer in order to assume a more natural researcher role. This active role allowed me, as the researcher, first-hand experiences of the work of the participants in the study. Throughout the observation, I recorded field notes, including timestamps, in a journal and purposefully scheduled time after an observation to review and type up the notes to ensure clarity. As with the interviews, procedures limited the number of in-person observations; therefore, some observations were done virtually.

Documents and Artifacts

Throughout the research period, I gathered several documents and artifacts in an effort to gather additional evidence. I analyzed curriculum documents, classroom work samples, and photos collected from students doing the work. To further add to my analysis, I focused my data collection on the teacher's lesson design, whole classroom work products, and the teacher's perceptions of the students' thinking, rather than on the actual student work production.

Data Analysis and Interpretation

When reviewing data using a qualitative approach, as a researcher, I analyzed the data with a critical eye. The interviews were recorded, transcribed, and coded along with the field notes, documents, and artifacts. I then analyzed the data to look for themes.

I began condensing the data by coding both the narrative data (observations, field notes, and transcriptions) and the visual data (photos, journals, lesson plans, etc.). Because there were multiple sources of data, I asked the teacher-participants to take photos of engaging and doing projects, taking precautions to conceal all identities. These photos were used as documentation of the curricular work and as part of the conversations with teachers to help them to recall lessons and past student engagement. The photos remained unpublished and were used with parental consent. I chose photos at random, which ensured neutrality on my part as well as that of the classroom teacher.

Coding the data is a vital part of qualitative research. These data needed to be coded multiple times so as to narrow down the themes and to find patterns within the data. While looking for patterns, I purposefully noted the routines, rituals, roles, and relationships that appeared throughout, labeling them as I moved through the data. I used the participants' own words to ensure that their voice was heard throughout the research; therefore, one method of coding that I used was in vivo coding. According to Saldaña and Omasta (2018), when referring to in vivo coding, "this coding method utilizes the participant's own language as a symbol system for qualitative data analysis" (p. 121). Process coding, a means to analyze coding, was useful as I analyzed the participants' design and implementation of civically engaged curriculum. A third type of coding that I used to identify teacher positionality, motivation, and agency was that of values coding. It is particularly important, as Saldaña and Omasta (2018) remind researchers, that the researcher use multiple sources of data to corroborate the findings.

Validation Criteria and Ethical Considerations

To ensure valid research, I employed several tactics throughout the research process. Creswell and Poth (2018) summarize the many views and understandings of validation to say, "we consider 'validation' in qualitative research to be an attempt to assess the accuracy" (p. 259) of the findings, as best described by the researcher, the participants, and the readers (or reviewers). Lincoln and Guba (1986) apply rigor as a parallel to trustworthiness, both serving as criteria to establish credibility within the inquiry process. They propose the use of a variety of techniques, such as prolonged engagement with the phenomenon, triangulation, member checks, and thick descriptions to build upon the inquiry's credibility.

The use of interviews, multiple-observations, and the collection of various documents and artifacts provided me with a variety of ways and views in which to engage with my topic of research to gain a holistic understanding. Triangulation further ensured an accurate interpretation of the vast amount of collected data. Creswell and Poth (2018) advise that "typically, this process involves corroborating evidence from different sources to shed light on a theme or perspective" (p. 260). The multiple data sources utilized in this study allowed for effective triangulation.

Member checks provide an additional validation strategy for qualitative research. Stake (1995) describes the process as "the actor is requested to examine rough drafts of writing where the actions or words of the actor are featured, sometimes when first written up but usually when no further data will be collected from him or her" (p. 115). The member checks in this study were conducted at the end of each interview. Case-study research also requires thick and rich description as a means of validation. This helps the reader to visualize the environment and transfer learning to other settings. Merriam (1998) describes rich, thick description as "providing enough description so that readers will be able to determine how closely their situations match the research situation, and hence, whether findings can be transferred" (p. 211). The vivid imagery allowed me as the researcher to interpret the data within my field notes and provide me with clear, articulate data.

Throughout the research process, reflexivity is a key component of increasing validity with qualitative research. Saldaña and Omasta (2018) describe reflexivity as looking inward at the data. I worked to remain reflexive, taking note of how my personal biases may affect the outcome of the data. I served in a supervisory role in the district and had a preconceived notion that action-oriented civic education is a strong strategy that needs to be considered. These things remained at the forefront of my mind while reflecting on the data in order to minimize my personal biases.

Additional ethical considerations must be considered when collecting qualitative research data, including gaining permission to conduct the study from the school district that served as a research site. Stake (1995) cautions: "School districts usually have permission procedures that should be followed" (pp. 57–58). Additionally, to ensure that my research followed legal and ethical guidelines, I complied with the requirements of the Institutional Review Board (IRB) at National Louis University. Furthermore, I shared with all potential participants prior to beginning, the details of the study as well as what I hoped to learn. Once the details were shared, as per legal and ethical guidelines, I obtained consent from all participants in my research study using the informed consent document and made it clear that they could withdraw consent at any time. This process allowed for the protection of the privacy and confidentially of all subjects.

Yin (2018) maintains that "the study of 'a contemporary phenomenon within its real-world context' obligates you to important ethical practices akin to those followed in medical research" (p. 88).

Finally, confidentiality, which is closely tied to consent, was of utmost importance throughout the research process. According to Saldaña and Omasta (2018), "researchers should always clearly inform participants what (if any) measures will be taken to ensure their anonymity and the confidentiality of the information they share" (p. 193). Throughout this study, the school district and its study participants were identified with pseudonyms for the express purpose of protecting their identities.

Discussion of the Findings

Creating civic leaders among our children requires twenty-first-century students to engage in their learning. Levine and Kawashima-Ginsberg (2015) remind educators that such learning goes beyond developing rote skills. It requires skills in critical thinking, problem-solving, collaboration, communication, self-directed learning, and the development of an academic mindset (Levine & Kawashima-Ginsberg, 2015). As a young child, most of my school day was spent on memorizing content predetermined and controlled by the powers that be, likely from the perspective of the White male because they were the primary policymakers. Schools were in the business of disseminating information into the minds of children. It was only through personal experiences that I received a clear understanding of what it meant to be culturally responsive. Perhaps it was by accident, or perhaps it was the mindset of our family culture that brought me to take an interest in the diversity of the American people. Unfortunately, the instruction within my schools did not create or support this belief.

Schools originated with the mindset of the Common School Movement operating under the pretense of unity for all; however, in actuality, they began as exclusive institutions filled with segregation and one-sided political values (Boyte, 2003; Warren, 2001). Throughout the decades and through multiple school reform efforts, the government took on more control, implementing standards, testing, and other accountability measures. Despite the work of educators and researchers across the country who advocated for critical thinking, problem-solving, effective communication, self-directed learning, and the development of an academic mindset, these efforts did little to protect and create equality for all children, with each state determining its own curricular purpose (Kawashima-Ginsberg, 2015).

Today, the reality of this inequity has come out of hiding. Technology and cell phones make it easy to document real-world problems and concerns within communities. The burden to equalize education has been laid primarily in the hands of teachers as they work tirelessly to ensure that each child has access to a high-quality education (Darling-Hammond, 2019). This study reveals the strains on teachers and the uncertainty of creating a social-justice-oriented civic education model for elementary students, given the constraints that teachers face. What follows is the discussion of the findings of this study and the ways they contribute to existing research and scholarship on civically engaged curriculum and a variety of issue pertaining to it.

Reimagining Civically Minded Elementary Education

Learning takes place when students connect new knowledge with prior knowledge in an active, meaningful, real-world context. Dewey (1916/2011) reminds us that education must be a vehicle to create social change, and it can do so when combining social interest and relationships. Social reconstructionists, such as Schiro (2013), agree that students make meaning as a result of interaction and contact with experiences, people, and the environment. Thus, children become contributing members of society and become vehicles for potential change.

This study highlights the voice of teachers regarding creating a meaningful curriculum that connects students to the real world. The teacher-participants in this study brought unique experiences to their classrooms and, at the same time, shared some similarities in what brought them to determine the primary values they held explicitly in regard to teaching civics.

The key findings of this study can be summarized in several main statements. First, the participants affirmed that past relationships and early life experiences were critical to developing their own civic mindset. Each participant told stories of important role models who impacted how they came to develop their own values and thus better understand their role as teachers. Campbell (2012) explains, "such values are at least in part expressions of one's personal experiences and background" (p. 189). These experiences impacted teachers' positionalities, which gave them the agency to seek out social justice experiences for their students. Second, while the participants spoke of feeling the need to prioritize civic education, they also voiced the lack of professional training in social studies education. Participants pointed out that only one social studies course was required in their teacher training. Additionally, once they were hired as a school teacher, they received little training in social studies education and no training in civic instruction. Their primary means of understanding came from collaborating with colleagues.

Observations in classrooms revealed a direct correlation between social justice concepts and civic education. Although participants did not narrate where they received their knowledge in social justice, several did point to their dual-language training as a means of support for bi-cultural experiences. This brought me to notice my third point, that is, that teachers implemented social justice ideals as a way to create civic-minded individuals.

Third, the teacher-participants designed lessons to include real-life problems; however, they fell short on creating a curriculum that included action-based experiences. The participants indicated that the lack of action-based experiences primarily stemmed from a feeling that providing these kinds of experiences was just too difficult to manage due to barriers within the educational system. Educators "have often moved from being proactive and constructive, to reactive and compliant" (Goodson, 2014, p. 771). The teachers in this research study found it easier to be compliant with policies rather than to push and plan for field-based experiences.

Unraveling Positionality

Participants in this study recalled stories of their youth and early adulthood where they were exposed to people and ideas that differed from their own. Through church groups, their parents' career choices, and the reality of their community experiences, each could point to specific examples where they developed a passion for helping others. While teachers bring their personal stories, they must recognize that their accounts may be vastly different from those of their students. Thus, a teacher's positionality then is of utmost importance. Borrero et al. (2018) assert that "particular positionalities, such as those that allow critique of power dynamics in schools, may work to improve the educational outcomes of culturally diverse students as opposed to those positionalities that endorse dominant deficit beliefs about those students" (p. 458).

Ladson-Billings (1995) encourages teachers to get to know their students, their families, the cultures, languages, and the values that they bring. Each participant's classrooms were filled with students from diverse cultural and economic backgrounds, with the majority of them from low-income households. The Carnegie Corporation of New York and Circle (2003) highlight the disparity of political and civic knowledge in immigrant and low-income families: "Race and family income can predict political and civic knowledge, and family income, education, and gender can predict voting patterns" (p. 19). With regard to this study, classroom observations and participant interviews routinely pointed to relationships and inclusive curriculum as key to student understanding of civics.

Lessons in Schooling

Similar to the participants' home experience, each of them pointed to specific incidents in school that had an impact on their civic development. Interestingly enough, most experiences appeared to have unintentional consequences, creating strong civic-mindedness in each of them. It is surprising that the teacher who had the earliest experiences with action-based civic education, Kevin, was the only one who cited that they grew up in a high-poverty area. Researchers in the United States find a disparity of civic teaching among the neediest of schools (NCSS, 2013). However, Kevin's experiences growing up in Mexico supported the need for real-world connections that were meaningful to students. In Kevin's experience, the community and the school were very much integrated, supporting one another. The teacher gave no textbook or skill-builder civics lessons; instead, the civic mindset came from the families and shared responsibilities to maintain and support the school. Upon moving to the United States as a pre-teen, Kevin almost immediately was thrust into the idea of assimilation and a banking model of education. His home language was discarded in lieu of learning English as quickly as possible. Schooling looked and sounded completely different from the early experiences in Mexico. Banks (2017) recalls that schools contribute to failed citizenship when they teach through an assimilation approach to civic education by requiring minoritized students to deny their home culture and language. Kevin's experiences in Mexico and transitioning to the United States only solidified his need to create a civic experience for his students.

The other participants recalled relationships with specific teachers as key to their commitment to civic education. Each of them cited exposure to ideas, cultures, and beliefs that were different from their own as a key area of deep learning. Levine and Kawashima-Ginsberg (2015) advocate for a focus on "deep learning," which goes beyond content to skills building in critical thinking and problem-solving, collaboration, effective communication, self-directed learning, and the development of an academic mindset. For many students, these experiences will not naturally be present in their everyday experiences. Therefore, schools must create ways to embed multiple perspectives and views into daily instruction. The participants in this study pointed to the use of various texts and other media to recognize biases and different viewpoints in their classrooms. They also recognized student discourse to engage students in conversations about the social issues of today. Weinstein (2004) emphasizes that students must be taught to listen to multiple perspectives through cognitive conflict and the teaching of controversy and worldviews within the school curriculum. Stuteville and Johnson (2015) define this type of curriculum as cultural pluralism, where students learn about the values of other cultures in order to make their own decisions regarding whether they will accept or reject societal and political beliefs. This, Weinstein (2004) offers, is an important skill for students as they prepare for a political life in the adult world. While it may not be entirely possible to identify the impact of the participants' intentional use of inclusive pedagogy, the previous research points to the likelihood that the students in the participants' classrooms will be prepared for a civically active life.

Social Justice as the Key Element of Curricular Change

Throughout this study, elements of social justice were consistently featured in the daily instruction in each classroom. Practices such as debating ideas, reading about characters from various backgrounds, role-playing, hearing multiple perspectives, collaboration, and discussing today's controversy were essential to each teacher-participant. This finding speaks to what Banks (2017) refers to as an imperative for citizenship education. Banks advocates for a civics curriculum that reflects students' diverse backgrounds and incorporates essential aspects of their ethnic and community cultures.

Schools with low-income families also suffer when students are not exposed to problem-solving. Carnegie Corporation of New York and CIRCLE (2003) note the lack of overall civic knowledge, particularly in low-income families where discussions around politics are not common. The school participating in this study had a low-income population of 58% and was representative of many other schools across the state and the nation. Villegas (2017) asserts that teachers need to be prepared to teach for social justice in order to educate students in the knowledge and skills they will need to be successful in their adult lives. The participants in the study regularly spoke of deliberative practices to ensure that students shared their own voices and opinions, and ideas related to civic education topics. Without creating inclusive pedagogy, students are at a disadvantage and thus may be less engaged in their learning. As Danielson (2013) suggests, teachers need to plan appropriate learning activities to avoid gaps or misconceptions.

Professional development in social justice and civic education also were topics discussed throughout this study. As participants pointed to their own professional development, all of them agreed that the lack of training, from college through career-based professional development, left them uncertain and ill-prepared to develop lessons that included meaningful, active, civic engagement. The same sentiment is found in Levine and Kawashima-Ginsberg (2015), who claim that controversial issues boost students' knowledge and interest and are especially valuable for children from homes where there is not much political discussion. Teachers need the training to support students to engage in these discussions while facilitating the conversations.

When asked how they came to this understanding of civic education, teachers cited the standards laid out in the curriculum documents provided by the school district. This, in turn, corresponds to what Stuteville and Johnson (2015) note in their study when they claim that most of the standards across the United States were primarily written from a legalist position, a claim based on the presentation of factual material about law, structures of government, and how government works.

Upon reviewing each of the participants' grade level's curriculum documents, which are provided by the school district, each contained requirements of connecting the past to the present to ensure student understanding. All teacher-participants affirmed the value of connecting significant concepts and ideas of the past to current realities. Teachers planned ways for students to better understand the past and present by looking at topics from multiple perspectives. Teachers often compared and contrasted past events with current events to help students to think critically. Techniques such as role play, comparing and contrasting, and deliberation and debate were used to help students fully understand concepts. The active and deliberative lessons, which I observed and were also spoken of by the participants, provided a means for students to engage in meaningful, real-life connections with today's social and political patterns.

What seems to be missing from the lessons of the participating teachers in this study was an action-based pedagogy. This supports the work of Kawashima-Ginsberg (2015) who suggest that most teachers do not regularly use pedagogical techniques designed to build civic participation skills. Further, a similar conclusion can be made based on what Ladson-Billings (1992) stresses as the importance of teaching using culturally relevant pedagogy (CRP). In this regard, CRP requires academic success for all students while also developing cultural competence and critical consciousness skills. According to Ladson-Billings (1995), this can be done when students must engage in personally meaningful curriculum beyond the standards. Therefore, college teacher preparation programs and school district training must provide opportunities for the development of teachers' skills in action-based civic education, even for our youngest learners.

Creating Lasting and Permanent Change

Experts on change theory agree that the collective teachers' voice must be a part of long-term systems change to create change. Goodson (2014) asserts that teacher voice must not be ignored, while Hargreaves (1996) suggests that the voice must come from multiple teachers' stories and perspectives. The teacher-participants in this study cited the teacher voice as an important key to strong curricular practices. The participants of this study explained that the current curriculum lacked multiple teacher's perspectives, which required teachers to seek out one another as support for creating a meaningful curriculum for their students. Furthermore, the participants in this study added to their lack of resources limited training for social studies and no training for action-based civics. The participants recalled only a single college course; each focused on general methods of teaching social studies such as backwards design, which is consistent with what Fullan (2006) argues about the missing components in professional development regarding understanding what teachers actually do within the classroom to improve instruction. The participants in this study also mentioned that district professional development focused on the materials and standards rather than teaching practices for social studies education.

This study's participants also cited policy and interfering with action-based curriculum as problematic because the logistics for planning action-based curriculum was too complex to make it worthwhile. These teachers felt overwhelmed by the procedures required to have students leave the school building for any period of time, citing that all of the jumping through hoops was too difficult. This finding points to the ways in which teachers need to be encouraged in their endeavors to create a positive change.

Developing Teacher Agency: The Barriers Teachers Face

Mark et al. (2019) point to the work of researchers across the field to show that teacher agency can often be limited by mandates and accountability measures. Each participating teacher pointed to barriers in the educational system as reasons why they lacked the agency to take steps to ensure students take action. These barriers include the reality of the current pandemic, fear of parents' pushback, the lack of materials, an overabundance of standardized testing, lack of time, strict and overwhelming policies and guidelines, and minimal training. These findings echo what Biesta and Tedder (2007) explain as agency, which is not something that people have, but rather something that people do. The participants in this study appeared to have the agency to implement social justice practices into their lessons; however, they lacked the agency to engage students in action.

Parent pushback became a common fear for a few of the teacher-participants. With parents literally "in the room" with students during instruction, conversations were often taken out of context and became one-sided. The teachers reported that students did not always feel free to share their own ideas. When a student did share, a parent in the room with the student did not always appreciate the discussions that were taking place, arguing that these discussions were a way for teachers to push their own political agendas on their students. This was a risk that teachers often took because they espoused inclusive practices such as multi-perspective teaching, racial injustice, biases, and discussions around current events. The participant-teachers at times lacked the agency to promote some of these student conversations despite the risk to student learning. Pantić and Florian (2015) directly associate inclusive teacher pedagogy with teacher agency. They recognize that promoting inclusive practices and social justice implies the need to challenge and transform current structures and requires a willingness to take a risk to improve students' learning.

The study participants also cited time and procedures and policies as barriers to creating actual action-based lessons. Participants pointed to the district's short school day of only five instructional hours as a challenge to leaving school for any length of time. Furthermore, the transportation policy documents reviewed for this study show that going out of the school building for any reason would require a plethora of red tape. Teachers must obtain parent permission and charge expensive and unmanageable fees for the use of buses.

Additionally, chaperone guidelines, such as requiring background checks for volunteer supervisors and providing a male chaperone on each trip, caused additional stress for teachers. The teacher-participants in this study found that planning was less cumbersome when they were able to use video resources and readings to simulate field experiences. In this regard, Dewey's (1897) advice that students should take a hands-on approach by exploring their own interests within the community seems to withstand the test of time. Further, Schiro (2013) promotes democratic citizenship by acknowledging the work of social reconstructionists who maintain that students must take action through involvement with social issues directly within their environment in which the issue occurs. The Carnegie Corporation of New York and Circle (2003) emphasize students' engagement to live what they learn. Teachers cannot be held responsible when charged with engaging curricular practices without the support and resources needed.

The results of this study distinctly articulate the need for permanent and lasting change in the way elementary teachers engage students in action-based, real-life civic opportunities. However, as teachers and leaders, we must understand that without a restructuring of the school day and explicit teacher training, civics education curriculum will continue to be minimalized at the elementary school level. I believe that by continually leaving civic education behind, we are also leaving behind the leaders of tomorrow.

In Conclusion

The findings of this study surface some insights into the work that needs to be done at the public elementary school level to create sustainable action-based civic education. It is imperative to include civic education at the elementary school level, throughout the curriculum, not as an add-on but rather an integrated curriculum component. Furthermore, as my study verifies, civic education curriculum must include social justice and culturally relevant practices in order to engage all students and prepare them for future adulthood and citizenship.

Teachers cannot be expected to do this important work without support and training. Therefore, teachers need to receive training that focuses on applying civic education to the community in which their students live. Professional development needs to be carefully designed so that it meets the teachers where they are in regard to their own civic development. Needs of teachers may range from support with lesson design and development to planning and implementing field-based experiences for their students. It is vital that this training is not simply a "one and done" workshop, but rather training that is based upon a long-term training and implementation plan.

Teachers in the classroom live the work of student learning each and every day. However, as this study's teacher-participants pointed out, they are the experts in their field, but their voices are often limited, or worse yet, excluded from district change initiatives. To achieve transformative change, teachers' voices must be heard and taken into account, as a collective, in the curriculum writing process to ensure that all perspectives are included in the process.

Finally, mandated and unfunded educational policies must be discontinued. All educators and educational leaders must take action themselves to encourage policymakers, school board members, legislators, and advocacy groups to develop policies that encourage and adequately fund action-based, community-based civic education for elementary school children and their teachers.

I cannot remember a time when I did not want to be a teacher. As a very young child, I remember playing school, helping my teacher aunt, and dreaming of the day when I would stand at the head of the class, imparting knowledge to little ones. When I signed on to be a part of the business of education, I had no idea where the journey would take me. With experience comes wisdom. The complexity of teaching taught me that each child has their own wisdom to bring to the table. With that knowledge, the ultimate responsibility we have as educators is to allow that child to develop into a problem-solving, critical thinking, independent, and active citizen.

Over the 30 plus years that I have served in education, I have seen initiatives and practices come and go. Policies created by the dominant members of society do not consider the vast array of cultures and experiences that our students come to school with. Testing and accountability practices change with each administration, yet these practices and supporting policies continue to ignore the voices of teachers and minority groups. I have seen the responsibilities of educators increase tenfold with little benefit accruing to the students who should remain at the center of what we do. However, more than ever in this 2020–2021 school year, as we all witness a divided nation, it is clear that our students must be given the tools to create a future where all people matter. It is long-overdue time to rise up and use our voices, as educators and Americans, to fight for what is best for our kids.

All children have the right to live in a nation where they can participate and lead a responsible, engaged, active civic life, a nation in which all voices are heard through the policies that are made. Each person should learn to have concern for the future world while honoring the current space in which they live. As an educator, I believe that we have the opportunity and the responsibility to provide the space for teaching these democratic skills. As Justice Sandra Day O'Connor asserted: "The practice of democracy is not passed down through the gene pool. It must be taught and learned anew by each generation of citizens" (as cited in Levine & Kawashima-Ginsberg, 2017, p. 19). Rather than crossing their fingers and hoping for the best for the future, teachers must provide the space for students to develop the skills they need to create a world in which each of us can hold an equal voice.

Children learn both academic and social norms from an early age. The teacher-participants in this study shared stories about how their beliefs were formed from early childhood experiences. Unfortunately for all of us, social studies education, particularly inclusive and civics education, is often left to the high school and college years. The teacher-participants showed a strong interest in creating curriculum through the lens of social justice; however, they often felt paralyzed by the barriers presented and the lack of "how-to" knowledge regarding curriculum design.

This study provides teacher educators and curriculum leaders with ways to support new and seasoned teachers to develop and prioritize civically engaged curriculum for young learners so that each child will grow up to become active and engaged adult citizens. We must prioritize our children's future by ensuring that they have the skills, interest, and better yet, a growing commitment to lead our great nation equitably.

References

Banks, J. A. (2017). Failed citizenship and transformative education. *Educational Researcher, 46*(7), 366–377. https://journals.sagepub.com

Biesta, G., & Tedder, M. (2007). Agency and learning in the lifecourse: Towards an ecological perspective. *Studies in the Education of Adults, 39*(2), 132–149.

Bogotch, I. E. (2002, March 1). Educational leadership and social justice: Practice into theory. *Journal of School Leadership, 12*(2), 138–156. https://doi.org/10.1177/105268460201200203

Borrero, N., Ziauddin, A., & Ahn, A. (2018). Teaching for change: New teachers' experiences with and visions for culturally relevant pedagogy. *Critical Questions in Education, 9*(1), 22–39. (EJ1172314). https://files.eric.ed.gov/fulltext/EJ1172314.pdf

Boyte, H. C. (2003). Civic education and the new American patriotism post-9/11. *Cambridge Journal of Education, 33*(1), 85–100.

Brown, K. M. (2004). Leadership for social justice and equity: Weaving a transformative framework and pedagogy. *Educational Administration Quarterly, 40*(1), 77–108. https://doi.org/10.1177/0013161x03259147

Campbell, E. (2012, March 23). Agency in curriculum contexts. *Curriculum Inquiry, 42*(2), 183–190. https://doi.org/10.1111/j.1467-873x.2012.00593.x

Carnegie Corporation of New York & CIRCLE. (2003). *The civic mission of schools* [Report]. https://circle.tufts.edu/sites/default/files/2020-01/civic_mission_schools_2003.pdf

Center for Information and Research on Civic Learning and Engagement (CIRCLE). (2020). *2020 election*. https://circle.tufts.edu/

Creswell, J. W., & Poth, C. N. (2018). *Qualitative inquiry and research design: Choosing among five approaches* (4th ed.). SAGE.

Danielson, C. (2013). *The framework for teaching evaluation instrument*. The Danielson Group. https://www.danielsongroup.org

Darling-Hammond, L. (2019). *Investing for student success: Lessons from state school finance reforms* [Brief]. The Learning Policy Institute. https://learningpolicyinstitute.org/product/investing-student-success-school-finance-reforms-brief

Dewey, J. (1897). *My pedagogic creed* (No. 25). E. L. Kellogg & Company. https://books.google.com/books?hl=en&lr=&id=EgwVAAAAIAAJ&oi=fnd&pg=PP5&dq=Dewey+My+pedagogic+Creed&ots=MKl8ePIFmF&sig=CaYRgRQBHNh0Nk_Pwix1HimrSgo#v=onepage&q=Dewey%20My%20pedagogic%20Creed&f=false

Dewey, J. (2011). *Democracy and education: An introduction to the philosophy of education*. The Free Press. (Original work published 1916)

Freire, P. (2000). *Pedagogy of the oppressed* (M. B. Ramos, Trans.). Bloomsbury Academic. (Original work published 1968)

Fullan, M. (2006). *Change theory: A force for school improvement* (Seminar Series Paper No. 157). Centre for Strategic Education.

Goodson, I. F. (2014). Context, curriculum and professional knowledge. *History of Education, 43*(6), 768–776. https://doi.org/10.1080/0046760X.2014.943813

Hargreaves, A. (1996). Revisiting voice. *Educational Researcher, 25*(1), 12–19.

Hattie, J. (2012). *Visible learning for teachers: Maximizing impact on learning*. Routledge. https://doi.org/10.1080/02667363.2012.693677

Heafner, T. L. (2018). Elementary ela/social studies integration: Challenges and limitations. *The Social Studies, 109*(1), 1–12. https://doi.org/10.1080/00377996.2017.1399248

Huck, A. (2019). Elementary social studies content integration in CCLS: An analysis of content integration. *The Social Studies, 110*(1), 1–16. https://doi.org/10.1080/00377996.2018.1524359

Institute of Education Sciences. (2020, September). *Race and ethnicity of public school teachers and their students* (NCES 2020-103). National Center of Educational Statistics at IES. https://nces.ed.gov/pubs2020/2020103.pdf

Kawashima-Ginsberg, K. (2014, March). *Harry, Hermione, Ron and Neville—Portraits of American teenagers' extracurricular involvement, and implications for educational interventions* (CIRCLE working paper No. 80). Center for Information and Research on Civic Learning and Engagement (CIRCLE). https://circle.tufts.edu/

Ladson-Billings, G. (1992). Culturally relevant teaching: The key to making multicultural education work. In C. A. Grant (Ed.), *Research and multicultural education: From the margins to the mainstream* (pp. 106–121). Falmer Press.

Ladson-Billings, G. (1995). But that's just good teaching! The case for culturally relevant pedagogy. *Theory into practice, 34*(3), 159–165. https://doi.org/10.1080/00405849509543675

Levine, P., & Kawashima-Ginsberg, K. (2015). *Civic education and deeper learning: Deeper learning research series* [Report]. Jobs for the Future. (ED559676). ERIC.

Levine, P., & Kawashima-Ginsberg, K. (2017, September 21). *The republic is (still) at risk—and civics is part of the solution* [Brief]. Tufts University.

Lincoln Y. S., & Guba, E. G. (1986, June). But is it rigorous? Trustworthiness and authenticity in naturalistic evaluation. *New Directions for Program Evaluation, 30*, 73–84. https://doi.org/10.1080/19439342.2017.1306577

Mark, S., Id-Deen, L., & Thomas, S. (2019). Getting to the root of the matter: Pre-service teachers' experiences and positionalities with learning to teach in culturally diverse contexts. *Cultural Studies of Science Education, 13*, 453–483.

Merriam, S. (1998). *Qualitative research and case study applications in education: Revised and expanded from case study research in education* (2nd ed.). Jossey-Bass. (ED415771). ERIC. https://eric.ed.gov/?id=ED415771

Merritt, E. G. (2016). Time for teacher learning, planning critical for school reform. *Phi Delta Kappan, 98*(4), 31–36. https://kappanonline.org/time-teacher-learning-planning-critical-school-reform/

National Council for the Social Studies. (2013). *College, career, and civic life (C3) framework for social studies state standards: Guidance for enhancing the rigor of K–12 civics, economics, geography, and history.* https://www.socialstudies.org/sites/default/files/c3/c3-framework-for-social-studies-rev0617.pdf

Pace, J. L. (2011, Winter). The complex and unequal impact of high stakes accountability on untested social studies. *Theory & Research in Social Education, 39*(1), 32–60. (EJ920268). ERIC. https://eric.ed.gov/?id=EJ920268

Pantić, N., & Florian, L. (2015). Developing teachers as agents of inclusion and social justice. *Education Inquiry, 6*(3), Article 27311, 333–351. (EJ1209656). ERIC. https://eric.ed.gov/?id=EJ1209656

Patton, M. Q. (1990). *Qualitative evaluation and research methods* (2nd ed.). SAGE. https://doi.org/10.1002/nur.4770140111

Rawls, J. (1971). *A theory of justice.* Harvard University Press. https://doi.org/10.2307/j.ctvjf9z6v

Saldaña, J., & Omasta, M. (2018). *Qualitative research: Analyzing life.* SAGE. https://doi.org/10.1177/1090198118795018

Schiro, M. S. (2013, August 29). *Curriculum theory: Conflicting visions and enduring concerns.* SAGE Publications. (ED500227). ERIC. https://eric.ed.gov/?id=ED500227

Sprunt, B. (2020, November 1). *93 million and counting: Americans are shattering early voting records.* NPR. https://www.npr.org/2020/10/26/927803214/62-million-and-counting-americans-are-breaking-early-voting-records

Stake, R. E. (1995). *The art of case study research.* SAGE.

Stuteville, R., & Johnson, H. I. (2015, Summer). Citizenship education in the United States: Perspective reflected in state education standards. *Administrative Issues Journal: Connecting Education, Practice, and Research, 6*(1), 99–117 (EJ1104347). ERIC.

Villegas, A. M. (2007). Dispositions in teacher education: A look at social justice. *Journal of Teacher Education, 58*(5), 370–380.

Warren, D. (2001, Fall). Original intents: Public schools as civic education. *Theory into Practice, 27*(4), 243–249. https://doi.org/10.1080/00405848809543360

Weinstein, J. R. (2004). Neutrality, pluralism, and education: Civic education as learning about the other. *Studies in Philosophy and Education, 23*(4), 235–263.

Yin, R. K. (2018). *Case study research and applications: Design and methods* (6th ed.). SAGE.

Chapter 10 Greek Parents' Perceptions and Experiences Regarding Their Children's Learning and Social-Emotional Difficulties

EIRINI ADAMOPOULOU

Introduction

A major issue confronting the mental health service system for children and adolescents worldwide is the role of the family. Children, for the most part, cannot access services on their own; parents must provide permission, transportation, knowledge of available sources, and financial resources for a child to receive care (Farmer et al., 1997). Cultural and ethnic differences are associated with differences in parents' beliefs about children's problems, the pathways that lead youngsters into mental health care, the kinds of referral problems identified by parents when they do seek help, and the kinds of interventions for those problems preferred by parents (McMiller & Weisz, 1996). Therefore, efforts to advance mental health services for children and adolescents in a particular country should include an examination of parents' distinct cultural differences and perceptions regarding their children's mental health.

Greece is one of the countries with the smallest changes in the family system and one of the most traditional countries in the European Union (EU). This is evident by the numbers of marriages, divorces, single-parent families, families with three generations, and interactions with relatives compared to other European countries (Georgas et al., 2004). Studies of the functional elements of the Greek family indicated that the family functions expand to a larger kinship network of extended family members and close relatives (grandparents, uncles, in-laws, aunts, and cousins) with very frequent visits and telephone contacts (Georgas, 1997, 1999a, 1999b; Georgas et al., 2004). At the same time, the family institution continues to be the most important kinship group for Greeks (Georgas et al., 2004; Giotsa, 1999; Sutton, 2001). The Greek nuclear family and the traditional extended family have strong expectations for social uplifting and enhancement of family prestige through the academic success of their children (Georgas, 1988; Kataki, 1998; Madianos, 1989). Even though Greek parents seem to be very involved in anything that has to do with their children's schooling, there is limited research on their perceptions and experiences regarding their children's learning and social-emotional difficulties.

At the same time, there has been a general reluctance among Greek parents to acknowledge their children's psychological problems and seek professional help due to prejudice and lack of adequate information (Bouhoutsos & Roe, 1984; Tsiantis, 1993b). Tsiantis (1993c) notes that referrals for mental health services were usually made around serious incidents as children were brought to the mental health providers after they had experienced severe health or social-emotional episodes. Additionally, Greek parents of students with disabilities often denied the need for special education services because they did not want their child in a special school or class (Kassotakis et al., 1996; Vardis, 1994). One reason for this rejection might be that Greek society viewed special schools with prejudice because of their history, as students with severe disabilities were secluded and marginalized in special schools in the recent past (Zoniou-Sideri, 2000). Nevertheless, the number of special classes in mainstream schools has dramatically increased in the past two decades due to the special attention that has been given in the development of special education (Kassotakis et al., 1996; Nikodemos, 1994). Despite the recent educational laws concerning special education services and psychological services in Greek schools, the vast majority of the student population with special educational needs attends regular schools and programs, and could benefit from special education services (Hatzichristou, 1998; Kassotakis et al.; Nikodemos; Υπουργείο Εθνικής Παιδείας και Θρησκευμάτων, 2008). Koliadis (1994) notes that even though there has been an emphasis on learning difficulties in recent years in Greece, teachers and parents frequently viewed the weak student in reading and spelling, who might have also failed in other academic subjects, as a "bad and lazy student." Thus, it is imperative to explore how parents are evaluating their children's academic and social-emotional functioning in contemporary Greece. Additionally, it is important to explore the significance that Greek parents attribute to their children's problematic behavior in relation to the interventions they adopt to support their children's needs.

Furthermore, the particular geographical composition of Greece has favored the creation of distinct residential, demographic, and cultural features. There is an inequality in the available mental health services and school special education services because of the geographic remoteness, overcentralization of services, and lack of efficient coordination and personnel (Bouhoutsos & Roe, 1984; Dellassoudas, 1994; Gari & Sofianidou, 2000; Hatzichristou et al., 2007; Mazi et al., 2004; Tsiantis, 1993a, 1993b, 1993c; Vardis, 1994). Hence, not all Greek families have access to the same level of state resources and services. The availability of community-based resources can impact how Greek parents identify and what type of services they prefer to address their children's learning and social-emotional difficulties.

Purpose of the Study and Research Questions

The purpose of this study was to explore the perceptions and experiences of Greek parents whose children experience learning and social-emotional difficulties. Seven research questions were addressed by this study. The research questions were as follows:

1. What are the parents' perceptions of their children's learning and social-emotional difficulties?
2. What children's behaviors are the parents most concerned about?
3. What do the parents perceive as the causes of their children's learning and social-emotional difficulties?
4. Who do the parents consider as responsible for solving their children's learning and social-emotional difficulties?
5. What is the perceived burden that the parents experience due to their children's learning and social-emotional difficulties?
6. What are the parents' actions to support their children's learning and social-emotional difficulties?
7. What are the parents' views and experiences with the available community services to support their children's needs?

Research Methodology

Conceptual Framework

This study design was guided by an ecologic understanding of parents' perceptions and experiences, suggesting that a myriad of factors at the child, family, and environmental levels simultaneously impact Greek parents' understanding of their children's problems and what they do to try to solve them.

As Bronfenbrenner (1979, 1989) points out, influences on children's behavior and development extend from the immediate family to schools, friendship networks, relatives, neighborhoods, communities, and geographical locations. These influences need to be conceptualized in terms of both individuals and the nested set of ecosystems within which they develop and function. Following an ecological perspective, this study examined Greek society's limiting factors and resources, constraints and opportunities, and the general environment, which can promote or undermine students' well-being and academic competence in regular Greek schools.

Specifically, this study assumed that Greek parents' decision to seek and utilize help for their children was based on their perceptions of the nature of their children's problems, the causes, and responsibility for solving their children's learning and social-emotional difficulties, as well as the cultural norms of Greek society. Even though one can imagine a plethora of possible causes inducing children's learning and social-emotional difficulties, this study included four causes: child, family, school, and sociocultural factors. Using an ecological perspective, an attempt was made to explore factors not only deriving from the child him- or herself, but also factors deriving from his or her immediate environment such as the family, his or her wider environment formed by teachers, educational system, neighborhood, and even possible immigration from another country. In addition, the proposed responsible persons for solving children's difficulties were the child, family members, school professionals, and specialists. These persons emerge from the child's immediate environment to broader dimensions of his or her surroundings.

An additional important variable is the perceived burden that Greek parents might experience due to the child's learning and social-emotional difficulties. The parental perceived burden was measured in three aspects: personal experience, relationships with family members and friends, and the family's finances and everyday activities. This study also examined the parents' actions to support their children's learning and social-emotional difficulties beginning with their personal efforts and extending to the supporting sociocultural environment in terms of the informal sources (e.g., family) and formal sources (e.g., community services) available for receiving help.

Research Design

Traditional educational and psychological research has commonly followed one of the two research paradigms: empirical-analytic versus interpretive. This study used primarily a quantitative method, which is derived from empirical-analytic research paradigm. Although in this conception, knowledge comes from systematic testing of hypotheses through experimentation (or quasi-experimentation), this study was primarily exploratory and was not derived from systematic testing of hypotheses. Measurement (including psychological testing) provides an objective, interpretation-free record of empirical regularities (Maxim, 1999).

In quantitative research, inquiry begins with a specific plan, a set of detailed questions and/or hypotheses. Researchers seek facts and causes of human behavior and want to know a lot about a few variables so differences can be identified. They collect data that are primarily numerical, resulting from surveys, tests, experiments, and so on (Maxim, 1999). Most quantitative approaches manipulate variables and control the research setting. Quantitative research allows the researcher to generalize research findings, and provides precise, quantitative, and numerical data. In addition, the research results are relatively independent of the researcher, and it is useful for studying large numbers of people (Johnson & Onwuegbuzie, 2004).

This study used a descriptive survey design that involves the collection of data from the population of interest on a particular problem or issue (Ravid, 2005). Specifically, this is a nonexperimental quantitative research that used questionnaires with categorical and quantitative variables. This method was selected because it is a means to describe systematically, factually, and accurately the characteristics of an existing phenomenon or to document its characteristics (Belli, 2008; Maxim, 1999). In this study the phenomenon included Greek parents' perceptions and experiences regarding their children's learning and social-emotional difficulties in elementary schools. As there has been limited research in this field of inquiry, I selected a quantitative methodological approach to summarize large amounts of data and reach conclusions and generalizations based on numerical descriptions (Roberts, 2004). Studying a larger sample of parents provided an opportunity to explore trends from a diverse population from different areas of Greece. The quantitative methodology and, specifically, the completion of surveys, also addressed the issues related to the time constraints of conducting research in another country. Specifically, I was able to travel only for a two-week period during January 2009 to Greece to collect the data, which were later analyzed through the SPSS version 16.0 for Windows in order to derive the numerical findings. Thus, there were time economics gained in this approach during the collection of the data and the use of accepted statistical analysis methods. Another advantage of this method is that it offered the possibility of collecting data anonymously.

However, quantitative research cannot capture the meanings people attach to the activities and events in their world as qualitative research can

(Roberts, 2004). To offset this limitation, I included narrative data (open-ended questions and open responses) in the quantitative study. I collected the quantitative data using a Likert scale on two structured questionnaires about parents' perceptions and experiences regarding their children's learning and social-emotional difficulties. The qualitative data included two open-ended questions and open responses on the same questionnaire completed by the same number of participants (parents) who completed the quantitative items. The quantitative data and their analysis enabled further exploration of the research questions. The embedded qualitative responses enhanced our understanding of Greek parents' perceptions and experiences regarding their children's learning and social-emotional difficulties. Thus, using the qualitative methods complementary to quantitative method I was able to validate and expand on the quantitative findings of the survey (Creswell & Plano Clark, 2007).

For the purposes of this research, the parents completed the Test of Psychosocial Adaptation of Preschool and Elementary Children (Test of Psychosocial Adaptation), where they evaluated their children's learning and social-emotional functioning, and the Parent Survey, which explored their perceptions and experiences regarding their children's learning and social-emotional difficulties. The Test of Psychosocial Adaptation of Preschool and Elementary Children is a rating scale that was developed recently in Greece to identify the skills or deficits in the social and emotional domains, and the personal, interpersonal, and school adaptation of a child (Hatzichristou et al., 2008). The Parent Survey was created based on the themes identified by the literature review. A pilot study was conducted to explore the use of the Test of Psychosocial Adaptation with Greek parents, to ensure and develop the questions of the Parent Survey, and examine the procedures of the study.

Procedure

With the permission of the Greek Ministry of Education and Religious Affairs, 30 primary schools were asked to participate in the study from five different areas of Greece. Primary schools in Greece covers 6 years of elementary education between the ages of 6 to 12 (Georgas, 1988; Hatzichristou et al., 2007; Vlachos, 2004). Nineteen primary schools from four different areas of Greece agreed to participate in the study resulting in a 61.29% permission rate. These areas represent different population densities and cultural and socioeconomic diversity. Parents were asked to complete the Test of Psychosocial Adaptation and the Parent Survey and return it to the school. The questionnaires were self-administered by parents.

Of the 1,000 questionnaires that were distributed to parents through their children's schools, 298 were returned, which resulted in a 29.8% response rate. The majority of the questionnaires (*N* = 209; 70.1%) were gathered from 15 schools in the capital city region of Athens. The schools in the area of Athens belong predominately to the northeast suburban school district (63.7%). Eight-nine questionnaires (29.9%) were returned from three rural areas: one school from a city in the northeast part of Greece, one school from a small town in the south of Greece, and two schools from an island in southeast Greece.

Participants

The sample of this study consisted of 298 parents of elementary students aged 6 to 11 years old. The majority of parents were female (*N* = 235; 78.6%) and in 25 cases both parents completed the questionnaires. The majority of the participants' ages ranged from 30–39 years (*N* = 129; 43.1%) to 40–49 years (*N* = 144; 48.2%). In terms of education, 134 mothers (44.9%) completed lyceum/college or technical school and 122 mothers (40.9%) held an undergraduate/graduate degree. Forty-eight percent of the fathers graduated from lyceum/college or technical school (*N* = 143) and 95 held a undergraduate/graduate degree (31.9%). Compared with the monthly minimum wage in Greece, the majority of the participants had a middle- to upper-class monthly income (Eurostat, 2009). With regard to housing, the majority of participants owned their house or apartment.

Model for Data Collection and Analysis

This study included two phases of data analysis. In the first phase of the data analysis, the responses of 298 Greek parents of elementary school students, aged 6 to 11 years, on the Test of Psychosocial Adaptation and on the first part of the Parent Survey were analyzed. Data from these two measures assessed children's learning and social-emotional difficulties and Greek parents' concerns and accessed services.

In the second phase of the analysis, 105 of the 298 Greek parents' responses on the second part of the Parent Survey were examined. The sample of the 105 parents was selected because their ratings on the Test of Psychosocial Adaptation identified their children with significant behaviors at least 1 *SD* below or above the mean. In this part of the Parent Survey, parents reported (1) the causes and responsibility for solving their children's difficulties; (2) parental perceived burden; and (3) actions, as well as (4) the use, likelihood to use, and barriers in accessing community services regarding their children's learning and social-emotional difficulties.

Discussion of Research Findings and Results

Prevalence and Types of Children's Learning and Social-Emotional Difficulties Based on parents' ratings on the Test of Psychosocial Adaptation, 35.2% of Greek elementary students aged 6 to 11 years experienced significant learning and social-emotional difficulties. Greek parents rated higher those behaviors that are more obvious and noticeable, especially in interpersonal relationships and groups on the Test of Psychosocial Adaptation. By contrast, parents had the tendency to rate the internalized behaviors of their children as significant when they were accompanied by externalized behaviors. Consequently, results from the Test of Psychosocial Adaptation suggest that Greek parents gave importance to children's social aspect of behavior and underreported introvert behavior.

Greek Parents' Concerns and Accessed Services

Almost one-third of Greek parents from the total sample of participants reported having concerns over their children's behavior and only 13.1% responded in the Parent Survey that they have accessed services. Even though parents reported mostly concerns over their children's social-emotional difficulties (e.g., anxiety, socialization, anger, and low self-esteem), the majority of their accessed services included support for their children's learning difficulties (e.g., dyslexia). From the parents who accessed services, only a small number reported a variety of other types of services for their children (e.g., occupation and play-based therapy).

Child's Responsibility

About a half of the parents appeared to consider their children's character as an important cause of their children's learning and social emotional difficulties. This finding suggests that when parents attribute responsibility to their children for their problematic behavior, they consider these difficulties as part of their temperament, an innate characteristic. This was also reflected in parents' responses regarding who is responsible for solving their children's difficulties in these areas, where almost 60% of the parents attributed responsibility to their children for improving their behavior. This indicates that some parents regard children as responsible both for causing their learning and social-emotional difficulties and for solving these problems. In conclusion, when Greek parents believed that children's character caused their behavior, they held children accountable for changing and ameliorating their learning and social-emotional difficulties.

Parents' Role

More than half of the parents did not believe they were mainly responsible for children's learning and social-emotional difficulties. The role of parents was more important in parents' opinions about who is responsible for solving or improving their children's problems. Around 80% of parents indicated that both parents should have the responsibility for solving or improving their children's behavior. Furthermore, in accordance with their perceptions about the responsibility for solving children's learning and social-emotional difficulties, parents indicated a greater preference for the use of personal actions and positive incentives to support their children over other interventions. Parents also did not ask the recommendations or support of their extended family for their children's challenges. The level of personal burden Greek parents experience due to their children's learning and social-emotional difficulties might also explain their preference for personal actions to support their children's needs. Specifically, almost half of the parents indicated a significant general level of family impact, especially on their personal competence as parents, as a results of their children's learning and social-emotional difficulties. Hence, the high level of these parents' personal and family burden can influence their actions and type of intervention implemented—in this case their preference for personal efforts.

Educational System

Another important finding is that more parents (n = 40%) attributed responsibility of their children's learning and social-emotional difficulties to the current structure of the Greek educational system than to the teachers' methods (n = 26.7%). One other interesting aspect was that even though 60% of parents indicated teachers or school personnel as responsible for improving their children's behavior, only one-third of Greek parents reported that they had consulted a teacher or other school personnel to support their children's needs.

Mass Media

It is notable that half of the participants indicated that television, movies, and video games were significant causes of their children's learning and social-emotional difficulties. For some parents these ratings might be an indication of their concerns about their children's overexposure to these programmings. This finding also underlines the important role of parents in limiting the amount of exposure their children have to television, movies, and video games to improve their children's behavioral challenges.

Sociocultural Factors

Greek parents did not attribute their children's learning and social-emotional difficulties to sociocultural and environmental factors such as low family income, type of neighborhood, speaking a second language, or recent immigration from another country. It should be noted that the majority of parents had children who were born in Greece (98%) and had not experienced immigration and second language acquisition challenges. In terms of the neighborhood, the majority of participants came from the northeastern suburban area of Athens, which includes mainly middle- and upper-class families who owned their house or apartment. Thus, the majority of the parents in this study appeared not to consider the socioeconomic conditions in which they live to have a negative impact on their children's behavior or the reverse.

Community Services

Overall, a very small number of Greek parents indicated that they had accessed community services to support their children's learning and social-emotional needs (responses ranged from 1% to 5%). Of these community services, private clinicians appeared to be the preferred service for parents (n = 13.3%). At the same time, parents reported an increased likelihood to use community services. Private clinicians were again the service with the highest future utilization based on parents' reports (n = 21.9%). It is significant that almost one-third of the parents reported that the lack of knowledge about the services, the time it takes to initiate services and long waiting lists, and the lack of specialists were barriers in the access of community services. These numerous barriers can limit children's access to community mental health care.

Conclusions

The results of this study are subject to the limitations of any self-report survey. Despite the limitations, this study provided useful information as there is little evidence and research in this domain. These research findings can provide professionals with information regarding the help Greek parents prefer when conducting assessment and implementing interventions. Finally, this information can contribute to a model of mental health delivery system that includes parents and provides culturally sensitive and effective services to Greek children.

References

Belli, G. (2008). Nonexperimental quantitative research. In *Lapan*. http://media.wiley.com/product_data/excerpt/95/04701810/0470181095-1.pdf

Bouhoutsos, J. C., & Roe, K. V. (1984). Mental health services and the emerging role of psychology in Greece. *American Psychologist, 39*, 57–61.

Bronfenbrenner, U. (1979). *The ecology of human development: Experiments by nature and design*. Harvard University Press.

Bronfenbrenner, U. (1989). Ecological systems theory. In R. Vasta (Ed.), *Annals of child development* (Vol. 6, pp. 187–251). JAI.

Creswell, J. W., & Plano Clark, V. L. (2007). *Designing and conducting mixed methods research*. SAGE.

Dellassoudas, L. G. (1994). Ειδική επαγγελματική κατάρτιση: Προτάσεις για την αναβαθμισή της [Special professional development: Recommendations for its advancement]. In M. Kaila, N. Polemikos, & G. Filippou (Eds.), *Ατομα με ειδικές ανάγκες* (Vol. 1, pp. 206–221). Ελληνικά Γράμματα.

Eurostat. (2009). *Population and social conditions: Minimum wages in January 2009*. Eurostat, Beate CZECH.

Farmer, E. M. Z., Burns, B. J., Angold, A., & Costello, E. J. (1997). Impact of children's mental health problems on families: Relationships with service use. *Journal of Emotional and Behavioral Disorders, 5*, 230–238.

Gari, A., & Sofianidou, E. (2000). Δομή και λειτουργία φορέων διάγνωσης και αντιμετώπισης διαταραχών παιδικής και εφηβικής ηλικίας. Παρουσιάση, σχολιασμός, και σύνθεση προτάσεων ομάδων εργασίας [Structure and function of providers of diagnosis and care of child and adolescent disorders: Presentation, comment, and synthesis of recommendations from working teams]. In A. Kalantzi-Azizi & I. Besevegis (Eds.), *Θέματα επιμόρφωσεις ευαισθητοποίησης στελεχών ψυχικής υγείας παιδιών και εφήβων* (pp. 105–112). Ελληνικά Γράμματα.

Georgas, J. (1988). An ecological and social cross-cultural model: The case of Greece. In J. W. Berry, S. H. Irvine, & E. B. Hunt (Eds.), *Indigenous cognition: Functioning in cultural context* (pp. 105–123). Martinus Nijhoff.

Georgas, J. (1997). Ψυχολογικές και οικολογικές διαστασείς στη δομή και τη λειτουργία της οικογένειας [Psychological and ecological dimensions in the structure and function of family]. In J. Tsiantis (Ed.), *Βασική Παιδοψυχιατρική. Εφηβεία* (Vol. 2, pp. 101–143). Εκδόσεις Καστανιώτη.

Georgas, J. (1999a). Ecological theory in social psychology. *Psychology, 6*(2), 111–123.

Georgas, J. (1999b). Family in cross-cultural psychology. In J. Adamopoulos & Y. Kashima (Eds.), *Social psychology and cultural context* (pp. 163–175). Sage.

Georgas, J., Gari, A., & Mylonas, K. (2004). Σχέσεις με συγγενείς στην ελληνική οικογένεια [Relationships with relatives in the Greek family]. In L. M. Mousourou & M. Etratigaki (Eds.), *Ζητήματα οικογενειακής πολιτικής: Θεωρητικές αναφορές και εμπειρικές διερευνήσεις* (pp. 189–225). Gutenberg.

Giotsa, A. (1999). Ο προσωπικός χώρος και η γειτονιά: Διαπολιτιστική έρευνα σε γειτονιές της Γενεύης, της Αθήνας και της Κεφαλλονιάς [Personal space and neighborhood: Cross-cultural research in neighborhoods of Geneva, Athens and Kefallonias]. *Psychology*, *6*(2), 124–136.

Hatzichristou, C. (1998). Alternative school psychological services: Development of a data-based model in the Greek schools. *School Psychology Review*, *27*(2), 246–259.

Hatzichristou, C., Polychroni, F., Besevegis, G., & Mylonas, K. (2008). *Εργαλείο Ψυχοκοινωνικής Προσαρμογής Παιδιών Προσχολικής και Σχολικής Ηλικίας* [*Test of psychosocial adaptation of preschool and elementary children*]. Υπουργείο Εθνικής Παιδείας και Θρησκευμάτων-ΕΠΕΑΕΚ.

Hatzichristou, C., Polychroni, F., & Georgouleas, G. (2007). School psychology in Greece. In S. R. Jimerson, T. D. Oakland, & P. T. Farrell (Eds.), *The handbook of international school psychology* (pp. 135–145). Sage.

Johnson, R. B., & Onwuegbuzie, A. J. (2004). Mixed method research: A research paradigm whose time has come. *Educational Researcher*, *33*(7), 14–26.

Kassotakis, M., Papapetrou, S., & Fakiolas, N. (1996). Φραγμοί στην εκπαίδευση και την επαγγελματική αποκατάσταση των ατόμων με ειδικές ανάγκες [Barriers in the education and professional development of people with special needs]. *Διαστάσεις του κοινωνικού αποκλεισμού στην Ελλάδα: Κύρια θέματα και προσδιορισμός προτεραιοτήτων πολιτικής* (Vol. 1, pp. 449–473). Εθνικό Κέντρο Κοινωνικών Ερευνών.

Kataki, C. (1998). *Οι τρεις ταυτότητες της ελληνικής οικογένειας* [*The three identities of the Greek family*] (8th ed.). Ελληνικά Γράμματα.

Koliadis, M. (1994). Οργανωτικά-διοικητικά σχήματα και ψυχοπαιδαγωγικά μοντέλα αντιμετώπισης των μαθησιακών δυσκολιών στο χώρο του σχολείου [Structural-administrative schemas and psycho-pedagogic models for the intervention of learning difficulties at school]. In M. Kaila, N. Polemikos, & G. Filippou (Eds.), *Ατομα με ειδικές ανάγκες* (Vol. 1, pp. 290–301). Ελληνικά Γράμματα.

Madianos, M. J. (1989). *Κοινωνία και ψυχική υγεία* [*Society and mental health*]. Εκδόσεις Καστανιώτη.

Maxim, P. S. (1999). *Quantitative research methods in the social sciences.* Oxford University Press.

Mazi, M. S., Nenopoulou, S., & Everatt, J. (2004). Dyslexia in Greece. In I. Smythe, J. Everatt, & R. Salter (Eds.), *International book of dyslexia: A guide to practice and resources* (pp. 103–108). John Wiley & Sons.

McMiller, W. P., & Weisz, J. R. (1996). Help-seeking preceding mental health clinic intake among African-American, Latino, and Caucasian youth. *Journal of the American Academy of Child & Adolescent Psychiatry, 35*, 1086–1094.

Nikodemos, S. (1994). Αγωγή και εκπαίδευση των παιδιών με ειδικές ανάγκες στην Ελλάδα: Γενικές διαπιστώσεις, σύγχρονες τάσεις-προοπτικές [Education of children with special needs in Greece: General findings, contemporary tendencies-expectations]. In M. Kaila, N. Polemikos, & G. Filippou (Eds.), *Ατομα με ειδικές ανάγκες* (Vol. 2, pp. 623–631). Ελληνικά Γράμματα.

Ravid, R. (2005). *Practical statistics for educators* (3rd ed.). University Press of America.

Roberts, C. M. (2004). *The dissertation journey: A practical and comprehensive guide to planning, writing, and defending your dissertation.* SAGE.

Sutton, S. B. (2001). Greece. In M. Ember & C. R. Ember (Eds.), *Countries and their cultures* (Vol. 2, pp. 887–899). Macmillan Reference.

Tsiantis, J. (1993a). Η εκπαίδευση για την ψυχική υγεία του παιδιού [Education for the mental health of the child]. In *Ψυχική υγεία του παιδιού και της οικογένειας* (pp. 229–241) Εκδόσεις Καστανιώτη.

Tsiantis, J. (1993b). Προτάσεις για την παιδοψυχιατρική περίθαλψη στην Ελλάδα [Recommendations for child psychiatric care in Greece]. In *Ψυχική υγεία του παιδιού και της οικογένειας* (pp. 242–271). Εκδόσεις Καστανιώτη.

Tsiantis, J. (1993c). Ψυχοθεραπεία στο γενικό παιδιατρικό νοσοκομείο [Psychotherapy in the general children's hospital]. In *Ψυχική υγεία του παιδιού και της οικογένειας* (pp. 242–271). Εκδόσεις Καστανιώτη.

Vardis, P. (1994). Η ενσωμάτωση των παιδιών με ειδικές αναγκές: Περιεχόμενο και φιλοσοφία ενσωμάτωσης [Integration of children with special needs: Content and philosophy of integration]. In M. Kaila, N. Polemikos, & G. Filippou (Eds.), *Ατομα με ειδικές ανάγκες* (Vol. 2, pp. 740–751). Ελληνικά Γράμματα.

Vlachos, A. (2004). *Οδηγός του ελληνικού εκπαιδευτικού συστήματος* [*Guide of the Greek educational system*]. Βιβλιοσυνεργατική ΑΕΠΕΕ.

Zoniou-Sideri, A. (2000). Η εξέλιξη της ειδικής εκπαίδευσης: Από το ειδικό στο γενικό σχολείο [The evolution of special education: From special to general school]. In A. Zoniou-Sideri (Ed.), *Ατομα με ειδικές ανάγκες και η ενταξή τους* (pp. 22–38). Ελληνικά Γράμματα.

Υπουργείο Εθνικής Παιδείας και Θρησκευμάτων. (2008). Ειδική αγωγή και εκπαίδευση ατόμων με αναπηρία ή με ειδικές εκπαιδευτικές ανάγκες [Special education of individuals with disabilities or special educational needs]. *Εφημερίς της Κυβερνήσεως της Ελληνικής Δημοκρατίας, 199*(1), 3499–3520.

Chapter 11 Speech-Language Pathologists' Barriers to Providing Services to the Deaf and Hard of Hearing Children Ages Two to Nine

Irene García-Benavides

Once parents find out that their children present with a hearing loss, they are surrounded by professionals who focus on this child being out of "normal" parameters. The first professionals with whom they relate speak about concepts as: loss, deficiencies, abnormalities, disability. Parents receive only one side of the views related to hearing loss: the medical vision. Parents start getting in contact with otolaryngologists, audiologists, and speech-language pathologists. The first information received come from these professionals. However, parents are not exposed to a social perspective of deafness from any professionals during the process of finding out their child presents with hearing problems. This is the case for parents who present with normal hearing, which is around 90% of the parents of children with hearing loss.

The level of acceptance toward the use of spoken language (English), sign language (ASL), or a combination of both, seems to be determined by the setting where therapy services are provided. The services at hospitals, home health agencies, and clinics tend to provide services through spoken language as the first choice. Early childhood intervention professionals as well as school professionals seem to be more open to the use of ASL along with spoken language. On the one hand, professionals who work at hospitals, home health agencies, and clinics usually have a medical vision; on the other hand, professionals who work in early intervention, and schools usually have a sociocultural vision when providing services for deaf and hard of hearing children.

The purpose of this qualitative study was to investigate ways in which SLPs approach their practice of providing services to the deaf and hard of hearing children ages two to nine and the barriers they can encounter along the path. This study sought to uncover the knowledge, perceptions, and experiences of SLPs related to the cultural and linguistic processes of the Deaf culture when assessing and treating deaf and hard of hearing children between two and nine years of age in different occupational settings. The primary research question that guided this study was, "What are SLPs' knowledge and experiences related to the culture and linguistic processes of the deaf culture when assessing and treating deaf and hard of hearing children ages two to nine?" Additional research questions:

- What are the linguistic barriers, if any, that SLPs encounter when assessing and treating the language skills of the deaf and hard of hearing children ages two to nine?
- How do SLPs' knowledge and experiences of the culture and linguistic process of the Deaf culture inform Speech and Language therapy practices for the deaf and hard of hearing children ages two to nine?

Theoretical Lens

This study was informed by two theories. First, the sociocultural theory created by Lev Vygotsky (Alkhudiry, 2022). Second, the concept of language deprivation, created by Neil Glickman (Hall et al., 2017). I chose these two frameworks as the focus revolve around the importance of being part of a linguistic community in order to develop language and cognitive skills. The sociocultural theory highlights the importance of a collaborative environment that includes people, objects, and events in order to learn and develop (Javadi & Tahmasbi, 2020). For Vygotsky it was important to determine the ultimate societal goals of education (Linask, 2019). For this purpose, Vygotsky created "The Big Triad," of positive differentiation, creative adaptation, and dynamic development (Skyer, 2020).

Positive differentiation is the need for education to have social goals. Creative adaptation is the need to teach deaf students to use models that are comprehensible along with cultural tools. In this conception, the challenge is for the Deaf educators to reject the concept of deficit by focusing on the many capabilities Deaf children possess. Dynamic development designates the capacity that Deaf children have to develop as any typical-hearing child, but to foster this development, it is necessary to develop the children's mode of knowledge, communication, and language. It is crucial to identify that the brain can develop language through signed or oral modalities. For Vygotsky, being Deaf was not the cause of disability. The social environment was the one that caused disabilities (Skyer, 2020). Vygotsky believed that higher mental functions as attention, memory, formation of concepts, and problem-solving depended highly in language (Ehrich & O'Donovan, 2019; Linask, 2019). A person who is deprived of language experiences the absence of having an own voice. This results in separation from social experiences, which causes exclusion. This idea changed Vygotsky's opinion regarding sign language throughout his professional career.

Additionally, this study was informed by the concept of language deprivation. Hall et al. (2017) defined language deprivation as the result of a "chronic lack of full access to a natural language during the critical period of language acquisition" (p. 762) around five years old. The National Association of the Deaf (NAD) has a position statement regarding the consequences of language deprivation and its effects on early cognitive and language development and education of deaf and hard of hearing children (NAD, 2014). Hall et al. (2017) included the disruption in the area of language development as a factor of social nature that affects the epidemiology of mental illness. NAD (2014) identified language deprivation as a factor that affect the educational and employment development among deaf people lifespan regardless of the good intentions of government, schools, and professionals.

Listening and spoken language specialists, propose refraining any visual cues and exposure to sign language for deaf children, which seems to be a high-risk idea that expose children to not having a strong foundation neither in signed or spoken language (Gulati, 2014; Glickman et al., 2020; Hetch, 2020; Szarkowski, 2018). Language dysfluency designates the stronger language a person possesses as not fluent (Hall et al., 2017). Language deprivation results in a non-fluent primary language. Not knowing the rules and structures of the strong language makes a person dysfluent in his/her own language, which affects all aspects of life (Hall et al., 2017). The lack of native abilities in any language (signed or spoken) is a disadvantage that expose deaf children to "cognitive, socio-emotional, and behavior challenges" (Glickman et al., 2020; Hall et al., 2017).

The most noticeable difference between signed and oral languages is the modality: manual versus spoken (Baker et al., 2016). Hearing parents would teach hearing children sign language in an effort to increase language skills; however, hearing parents would not allow deaf children to use signs in order to learn how to communicate (Hall et al., 2017). Parents are not advised of how language acquisition in oral and sign language follow a common trajectory. Sandler and Lillo-Martin (2006) brought awareness of commonalities between spoken and signed languages by the concept of "separating the code from the mode." Deaf children are denied the possibility of having sign language as a strong language, as well as the possibility to be bilingual by learning the language of the community (Wilkinson & Morford, 2020).

There is an equivalent implicit sequence for acquiring oral and signed language (Hall, 2017) as cognition is the mode to acquire a language (code). However, language acquisition appears to differ around the age of three years (Cupples et al., 2018) when children take the most advantage of language role models available. Given more than 90% of deaf and hard of hearing children are born into a hearing family (Baker et al., 2016), there is a lack of signed language role models, which produces language deprivation demonstrated in late and incompetent first language acquisition (Henner et al., 2019; Sehyr et al., 2018). The number of sign language users is expected to decrease as powerful hearing devices are used in order to switch from signed to oral languages; however, not all recipients of state-of-the-art hearing technology end up mastering an oral language, which has caused language deprivation as a consequence (Hall et al., 2019). For this reason, it is important to develop a strong first language (Sanzo, 2022) in order to be able to acquire spoken language.

Case-Study Research Design

Qualitative case study was chosen as best suitable methodological approach to explore the experiences of SLPs in "natural settings" and as a "bounded system" (Creswell & Poth, 2018). Stake (1995) claimed that case-study research is not a methodology but a choice of what to be studied. Subsequently, my choice was to get an insight into the knowledge and experiences related to the culture and linguistic processes of the Deaf culture when assessing and treating deaf and hard of hearing children ages two to nine. The case as a bounded system for this study represents several parameters, namely, the participants' experiences within the space of their various professional practices and within the timeframe, to date, of their experiences, as well as the issues that constitute the focus of this study. This study represents a single instrumental case study as "having a research question, a puzzlement, a need for general understanding, and feel that may get insight into the question by studying a particular case" (Stake, 1995, as cited in Creswell & Poth, 2018, p. 98).

Participants

The participants for this study included 12 SLPs from five different working settings: early intervention, home health, schools, outpatient clinics, and hospitals. The participants provide services for deaf and hard of hearing children between two and nine years old. Participants have different level of experience mostly (average of 8 years) treating the deaf and hard of hearing children. All participants hold a minimum of a master's degree in communication sciences and disorders. All participants treat deaf and hard of hearing children ages two to nine and provide services through different types of settings. Early intervention professionals provide services for children from birth to three years old. School professionals provide therapy services starting around four years of age. Professionals working on home health, outpatient clinics, and hospitals provide services for deaf and hard of hearing children from birth up to 21 years old. All these professionals work with ages considered in this study.

Data Collection

This study utilized a demographic survey, semi-structured interview, as well as observational and self-reflective notes as sources of data.

Demographic Survey

The online survey obtained basic information regarding demographics as well as awareness of ASL and Deaf culture. The survey was the first instrument to collect data. The survey was made of questions that focus into obtaining the following information: demographics, years of education, bilingual status, types of certifications, and basic information related to deaf and hard of hearing concepts.

Interviews

Interviews typically provide main data for qualitative research (Creswell & Poth, 2018; Saldaña & Omasta, 2018; Taylor, 2005). I used semi-structured interviews as a tool to describe and analyze the experiences of SLPs on their professional path working with deaf and hard of hearing children ages two to nine throughout the different settings where these children receive services. The interviews were conducted virtually through the platform *Zoom*. Interviews were video recorded for authentication of data. Interviews were transcribed verbatim and sent to the participants for verification of accuracy. I analyzed the participants' knowledge and experiences regarding the value of knowledge of ASL and Deaf culture as tools to improve services for this population. The inclusion of the experiences of the participants provided a better picture of issues considered as barriers to the provision of services.

Observational and Self-reflective Notes

Arms Almengor (2018) stated there is a process of "learning to do it" (p. 21) that takes place during the practitioner's experience in order to generate knowledge and theories. Self-reflection creates a more mature attitude among individuals (Park et al., 2022). Reflective journals and reflective writing are tools to be used to increase the ability of weighing the experiences. During this study I used a journal in order to keep records of thoughts and lessons learn from the study. This written information provided a better insight of data analysis.

Data Analysis

Data analysis is the process by which researchers address the issue of representing the data (Creswell & Poth, 2018). Data collection determines the quality of research (Polit, 2017). This skill is crucial to manage and reflecting on data (Saldaña & Omasta, 2018). I started the analysis by processing the data through the transcription of interviews. I identified similar words and groups of words and sentences. I labeled the information using codes (Graneheim & Lundman, 2004). I coded the information using the three analytical approaches: the template analysis, the story analysis, and the metaphor analysis (Cassell & Bishop, 2019). The template analysis is referred to the use of the whole data set to make possible to compare all responses on a given issue. The story analysis highlights the emotional aspects of the phenomenon without asking directly. The metaphor analysis allows different interpretations of the same phenomenon to be identified. It was important for this study to identify themes; however, it is also important to analyze the emotional aspects related to the acceptance or rejection toward the use of ASL and knowing the Deaf culture to provide the best services to the Deaf and hard of hearing population. I set aside the information using data regarding language and cultural barriers as well as lack of awareness of the culture of the Deaf community. Categories and subcategories that made evident what were the language(s) used to assess and treat speech and language needs as well as the existence (or not) of culturally and linguistically informed practices. This information highlighted the importance or lack thereof of ASL and Deaf culture to provide speech and language services.

As a result of data analysis, I identified the following main themes: (a) "The Scope of Practice," (b) "Barriers Regarding Culturally and Linguistically

Informed Practices," and (c) "Awareness of Similarities and Differences in Language Acquisition and Structures in English and ASL." The Scope of Practice theme includes the following subthemes: context of service, assessments used and rationale, and language use and rationale. The Barriers Regarding Culturally and Linguistically Informed Practices theme includes the following subthemes: Language deprivation, ASL proficiency, and lack of knowledge and training related to the deaf and hard of hearing communities. The Awareness of Similarities and Differences in Language Acquisition and Structures in English and ASL theme includes the following subthemes: similarities in language acquisition, language similarities and differences, language similarities and differences and main differences between English and ASL. It should be noted that the language differences include: word to sign correspondence, importance of fingerspelling, iconicity of signs, role of space in ASL, phonology of ASL: handshape, placement, and palm orientation.

The participants of this study provided important information through their knowledge and experience regarding linguistic and cultural informed practices as well as barriers encountered when treating deaf and hard of hearing children ages two to nine. Participants have described the deaf and hard of hearing population under their care by informing of their scope of practice, the processes to evaluate and provide services for deaf and hard of hearing children while taking this population's unique cultural and linguistic characteristics, as well as their family environment. Participants also described coursework during their preparation as students and how this knowledge and experiences have contributed to influence their current professional practice. Participants have also provided information regarding the language(s) used to provide services and how linguistic and cultural barriers have determined the way in which their practice take place at this time.

With regard to the primary research question of this study, the participants expressed their full agreement regarding that the parents seek services from speech-language pathologist, mainly to help their children to produce spoken language. Having spoken language as the ultimate goal for the majority of the parents of deaf and hard of hearing children ages two to nine, SLP's knowledge and experience are important for critical aspects as deciding what language to use in therapy, and how to avoid language deprivation. Most participants highlight the fact that upon hearing loss identification, parents are exclusively presented with the medical perspective of hearing loss. After referrals to otolaryngology and audiology, speech pathologist are the professionals who educate parents regarding communication options and school placement. However, speech pathologists are not educated regarding Deaf culture and/or ASL. Participants report this situation as challenging.

As far as linguistic barriers that SLPs encountered when assessing and treating the language of the deaf and hard of hearing children, the participants of this study indicated that their context of service greatly influence the language in which therapy takes place. The use of ASL for therapy has greatly been reduced to spaces as school, while the use of listening and spoken language is more prestigious and is mainly offered at hospitals or clinics. Moreover, there are clinics that specialize in providing services through listening and spoken language. Parents prefer the use of spoken language over ASL, and even if the progress is limited. Generally, it takes around a year for parents to attempt the use of ASL to increase language and communication skills. Most of the participants of this study were not aware of the existence of assessments that have ASL as the language in which testing tools are standardized in order to assess vocabulary, phonology, morphosyntax, and narrative skills.

Regarding cultural barriers, several of the participants expressed that parents seeking services for their children who are deaf and hard of hearing, are not aware of the existence of a Deaf culture. For these parents, being deaf means only having a diagnosis. What is even more surprising is that a lot of participants of this study have expressed not having been around people who are deaf or hard of hearing prior to treating this population. The participants' knowledge of deaf and hard of hearing people comes only from books that express a medical but not a cultural vision of deafness. During the participants' professional preparation years, SLPs generally do not have a chance to "listen" to Deaf perspective regarding speech and language therapy services.

Finally, there are several components that inform speech and language therapy practices for the deaf and hard of hearing children. The participants of this study singled out several of such components as the scope of practice, the barriers to provide culturally and linguistically informed practices, and awareness of similarities and differences in language acquisition and structures in English, and ASL. Surprisingly, some participants stood out in their responses to expose the point of view of those who received speech and language therapy services during their childhood. This perspective contribute to our professional knowledge and experience and must leave an impression regarding the way speech and language therapy should be viewed and performed.

Discussion of the Findings

The responses and experiences of each participant have been useful to provide context, information, and data regarding the questions of the of the study and understand the reasoning behind their professional practice with deaf and hard of hearing children ages two to nine. The participants have been implementing therapy throughout the years in order to serve this population. In order to better understand these experiences their responses were analyzed under the lens of two theories: the sociocultural theory and the concept of language deprivation. The sociocultural theory recognizes the importance of a linguistic community in order to develop language skills. The concept of language deprivation highlights the fact that a language cannot be acquired without having full access to it and a community where to learn this language from. For this reason, the Deaf community does not consider itself as a handicapped, but as users of another language (Gannon, 2012; Shaw & Delaporte, 2015).

With regard to the speech-language pathologists' knowledge and experiences related to the culture and linguistic processes of the Deaf culture when assessing and treating deaf and hard of hearing children ages two to nine, the participants reported working with all types and levels of hearing loss at five different working setting. Hearing loss included conductive, sensorineural, and mixed types. Degrees of hearing loss fluctuated from mild to profound, as well as unilateral or bilateral. The caseload included children being furnished with hearing aids and/or cochlear implants. These professionals serve children having in mind parents' goals. It should be mentioned that the parent goal for all the participants of the study always includes to make children talk (Glickman & Hall, 2019; Glickman et al., 2020; Hall et al., 2017).

Participants working on early intervention made clear to parents that language exposure is not the same as language access (Hall & De Anda, 2021). For this reason, participants encourage the use of sign language at home and in the community, as a way to learn spoken language (Anderson et al., 2016; Glickman & Hall, 2019; Gulati, 2014). Professionals from home health focused on using listening and spoken language as the main mode of communication, with the close supervision of a listening and spoken language specialist. Therapy services in the home prioritize articulation skills while language skills are targeted at the school environment, as ASL is recognized for educational activities exclusively (Rosen, 2022).

Participants in the hospital setting would strongly support the medical vision of using listening and spoken language to target language development. It should be highlighted that in a recent survey (Ozelie et al., 2022) the use of American Sign Language and interpreters was considered the second most unreasonable accommodation among students in the clinical settings. After all, hospitals have otolaryngologists, audiologists, and speech pathologist "in house" while those who are certified as "Auditory Verbal Therapists" are considered the most knowledgeable professionals to work with deaf and hard of hearing children, regardless of how widely results vary from one child to another (Hecht, 2020; Kelley & McCann, 2021). Once listening and spoken language skills hit plateau, the use of ASL is required. Then, patient is referred out to a speech-language pathologist who is fluent in ASL, even though only 618 SLPs in the nation self-identify as fluent (ASHA, 2021) in ASL.

Culturally and Linguistically Informed Practices

Being culturally informed for SLPs deals with being in contact with the Deaf culture, its language, and its values (Padden & Humphries, 2005). For participants who use ASL in therapy, children are viewed as future members of the Deaf community. It means to pay attention to the experiences Deaf adults have had while they were enrolled in therapy as children. Also being able to use sign language while being around Deaf people while "voice off" is enforced. For participants who are part of the Deaf culture, it is hard to imagine serving Deaf people without being able to communicate with most of the members of the community, which means using ASL (Padden & Humphries, 2005).

For SLPs, being linguistically informed means to self-educate regarding language concepts, and also to be able to educate parents regarding this issue (Murphy, 2018). Self-educating regarding language means to seek opportunities to learn about language development in general as well as general language milestones and language development in ASL. It also means to be aware of how typical and atypical ASL development looks as well as spoken language. SLPs need to know that there are language assessments that have been created for ASL-users having ASL as the language for testing with standardized measures. There are tests that will allow SLPs document children's progress throughout the provision of therapy services.

It is important to inform families about the concepts of language access, language immersion, and effortless language acquisition. Families need to be aware of the dangers of language deprivation, which should be avoided at all costs (Glickman & Hall, 2019; Gullati, 2014). It is necessary to highlight the fact that children can be bilingual. That children can learn to use ASL as well as spoken language (Rowley et al., 2022).

Professional Preparedness

The participants of this study give a different level of importance to the classes taken during their professional preparation years. For professionals working with listening and spoken language, Audiology seems to be the most important class. Along with Audiology, classes such as Acoustics, hearing technology, and those that focus on the audiological management of patients. This makes evident that for participants working on listening and spoken language, the most important aspects of the profession are viewed under medical model perspective, which echoes with what Martin (1997) mentioned in their study.

For ASL-user participants, audiological information (audiometry) appear to be less important than it is for those who focus on listening and spoken language, as clients start therapy after years of language deprivation. The focus for these professionals is on language milestones through the use of the most accessible language: ASL. Therefore, spoken language is not targeted. "Language over speech," seems to be the motto of these participants. This is also related to the fact that ASL classes are part of professional coursework only as an elective class, if offered. Never as a core class, especially in programs with a specific auditory therapy track where some basic classes of ASL are offered, but as electives.

Assessment and Treatment Practices

Most of the participants reported feeling prepared to use tests to assess children's language skills. However, bilingual English-ASL professionals reported not feeling prepared secondary to ASL not being their first language. These participants reported evaluations would be better if provided by an ASL native user, which demonstrates language and cultural awareness. Participants who use English or another spoken language to provide evaluations considered themselves as prepared. A few participants consider themselves capable of providing testing secondary to having an SLP license, but being aware of the many aspects their professional preparation might be missing. This also demonstrates being humble (Moroz et al., 2017) when assessing deaf and hard of hearing children for therapy services.

Tests utilized to assess deaf and hard of hearing children are mostly adapted from tests created for normal-hearing children. Some of the tests were standardized with a sample of deaf and hard of hearing children. Listening and spoken language participants reported not adapting tests created for typical-hearing children when testing the language skills of deaf and hard of hearing children. Listening and spoken language participants would not adapt tests created for normal-hearing children to test the language skills of deaf and hard of hearing children. Very few participants were aware of the existence of evaluations created to assess ASL skills being these tests standardized for the deaf and hard of hearing population throughout different ages as noted by Quinto-Pozos et al. (2017).

Therapy Language

Most participants do not evaluate or provide therapy through ASL. Participants who promote the use of spoken language, might be able to use a few gestures or consider valid the use of these at a very basic level. However, participants who consider themselves as bilingual English-ASL provide therapy through ASL, especially for children who have experienced language deprivation. Spoken language is a goal if children get benefits from this approach. Participants who provide speech and language therapy through the use of spoken language, reported to review children's progress every six months. Once a child does not present with progress through spoken language, then participants start referring children to therapy using sign language or another approach that includes visual cues. This means, the professional should refer children out as this is out of their scope of practice; however, often times participants will continue to provide listening and spoken language upon parent request, even when the child receives little to not benefit, as therapy should revolve around parent goals, which means spoken language (Hecht, 2020).

There is an extended conception that assumes that learning ASL would impede learning spoken language (Baker et al., 2016; Shaw & Delaporte, 2015). This idea assumes that the visual cortex "conquers" the auditory cortex, making impossible to learn spoken language at the same time ASL is learned. This contradicts the idea that the brain should be "wired" with language regardless of its modality as the same areas are used in the brain for language regardless of it being spoken or signed (Banaszkiewicz et al., 2021; Blanco-Elorrieta et al., 2018; Cheng et al., 2020; Newman et al., 2015). Another well extended myth is related to learning ASL can happen at any age. These participants appear to ignore the effects of language deprivation as well as the difficulties faced when presenting a non-fluid first language as indicated by ~~Hill~~ Hall et al. (2019).

It appears some participants are not aware of how similar language acquisition by sight and hearing is (Sandler & Lillo-Martin, 2006). However, there is a condition that should be fulfilled: access to language. Being exposed to listening and spoken language at an early age, and using powerful hearing aids, are not enough to consider listening and spoken language as accessible (Hall & De Anda, 2021). Young children are not able to express if they are having access to all the sounds in the speech range. Not all hearing devices work in an efficient manner or are well calibrated; however, language acquisition through ASL is always effective. And even if not effective, it does not produce any harm, as exclusively auditory language exposure does (Hall, 2017).

Language Commonalities and Differences

Regarding the main differences between ASL and English, it was evident that participants were aware of sign language being its own language with its own rules. An aspect that participants were aware is the fact that English is a linear language, while ASL is a three-dimensional language that can express many concepts at the same time due to its visuo-manual nature (Bradley et al., 2022). Monolingual participants were aware of many, but not all of the aspects presented on the questions of the interview. The lack of correspondence between ASL signs and English words is a well-known concept by all of the participants of the study. The role of fingerspelling is understood by monolingual participants only as a way to loan words from spoken language to ASL, just like any spoken language loans? words from another. However, the role of fingerspelling goes beyond naming (Miller et al., 2021). Some participants are confused regarding fingerspelling as a way to put "in writing" words produced with English grammar. Fingerspelling has been considered as leading to more literacy success as signs that include fingerspelling (Miller et al., 2021) also improve reading and orthographic skills.

Awareness of language commonalities and differences is a first step to understand that therapy can take place in more than one language, in order to provide children with an accessible language (Hall & De Anda, 2021). Access to a language allow kids to understand the world around and to express their thoughts and feelings through their own. The use of the most accessible language for deaf and hard of hearing children is ASL and it should be included as the language in which therapy is provided.

Relevance of the Findings to Theoretical Framework

Throughout the study it was evident that most of the barriers speech-language pathologists face to provide services for deaf and hard of hearing children are due to the lack of culturally and linguistic informed practices, as well as limited awareness of similarities and differences in language acquisitions and structures in English and ASL. One of these barriers include memory as the concept formation that highly depends on language, which is what Vygotsky claims in his studies (Ehrich & O'Donovan, 2019). The hallmark of Vygotsky's theory is the importance of sociocultural contexts in which education takes place and, by extension, language acquisition occurs. This study confirms that children need to have language access through a community of sign language user, as a visual modality is the most accessible and effortless way to acquire a language. It is important for Deaf and hard of hearing children to acquire a strong first language (signed) in order to learn listening and spoken language. In other words, the importance of being part of a linguist community in order to develop language and cognitive skills can be hardly overestimated.

The findings of this study support what Glickman and Hall (2019) called "language deprivation" that negatively impacts the lives of deaf and hard of hearing individuals throughout their lives. While language exposure through hearing is considered the norm, language exposure through visual input is still left outside of the equation for deaf and hard of hearing children (Glickman & Hall, 2019; Glickman et al., 2020). The participants of this study confirmed just that when referring to their professional practice. Regardless of the modality (signed or oral) language acquisition at an early age should be the norm. Speech-language pathologists need to educate themselves and parents regarding the importance of an accessible language in order to develop listening and spoken language.

Conclusions and Implications for Practice

The findings of this study have several implications for the way in which speech and language therapy services are provided for the deaf and hard of hearing children ages two to nine. One of the most important aspects of this study is making evident how the medical vision of the speech-language pathology profession continues to inform speech-language pathology practices (Cripps et al., 2016; Hernández & Hadley, 2020) from assessment to therapy without taking into consideration aspects as language acquisition, commonalities between spoken and signed languages, and the possibility to develop bilingual skills without neglecting the most naturally accessible language. The purpose should be to avoid language deprivation (Gullati, 2014) and to increase communication skills (Hecht, 2020).

Experiences from the deaf and hard of hearing community should also be taken into consideration. The use of ASL has been taken out of the clinical environments and has been only placed on the educational needs (Rosen, 2022), but there are certainly needs regarding disorders in users of sign language (Quinto-Pozos et al., 2017). Speech-language pathologists should be in charge of identifying how typical or non-typical sign language acquisition is taking place (Visser et al., 2017), the order in which sentences take place (Hall et al., 2017), word retrieval regarding categories (Marshall et al., 2018), and/or issues related to literacy (Cammarata-Scalisi et al., 2020; Muncy et al., 2019). Communication is one of the core values of our professional association. All these aspects should be mentioned to parents who seek services for their deaf and hard of hearing children. Therefore, educating parents regarding communication above listening and spoken language turns crucial in order to provide language input for deaf children in order to eliminate language deprivation.

As a speech-language pathologist providing therapy services through ASL, it is my hope that more SLPs will educate themselves and parents regarding the multiple benefits of learning this language. It does not only fulfill the human right of communication, but it also opens doors to have more SLPs who are native users of ASL. This is, I believe, the only manner in which speech-language pathologists can pave the way of ASL to be considered as part of the languages offered for speech and language therapy. Native language users providing services should be the norm in the speech and language therapy field.

By knowing SLPs' struggles as professionals, many barriers can be destroyed in order to provide the best professional services. This study connects with research regarding professional preparedness and is intended to be a contribution to assess strengths and weaknesses in the areas of culturally and linguistically responsive practices. Throughout our professional preparation, speech-language pathologists are conditioned to have a medical vision of hearing loss. I encourage my colleagues to develop a sociocultural vision and to look beyond the diagnosis. When parents seek guidance, let us not be the "permanent grief" individual who perpetuates social, emotional, and cognitive delays. A person with a hearing loss is not a broken person; however, a person without access to one, is. Let us promote the most accessible language available: sign language. Only strong skills in sign language can build strong spoken language skills. Let us not deny the possibility of having strong and meaningful relationships and lives to those who need their language rights to be respected. Let us stop promoting the use of signs among hearing children due to its multiple benefits, while we deny this possibility to those who need it the most. Hearing technology is a great tool that helps our children to find more than one way to communicate. We have the biggest gift of all in our hands: language.

References

Alkhudiry, R. (2022). The contribution of Vygotsky's sociocultural theory in mediating L2 knowledge co-construction. *Theory and Practice in Language Studies*, *12*(10), 2117. https://doi.org/10.17507/tpls.1210.19

Arms Almengor, R. (2018). Reflective practice and mediator learning: A current review. *Conflict Resolution Quarterly*, *36*(1), 21–38.

American-Speech-Language-Hearing Association. (2021). *2021 demographic profile of ASHA members providing multilingual services.* https://www.asha.org/siteassets/surveys/demographic-profile-bilingual-spanish-service-members.pdf

Anderson, M., Wolf Craig, K., Hall, W., & Ziedonis, D. (2016). A pilot study of Deaf trauma survivors' experiences: Early traumas unique to being Deaf in a hearing world. *Journal of Child & Adolescent Trauma*, *9*(4), 353–358. https://doi.org/10.1007/s40653-016-0111-2

Baker, A., Van den Bogaerde, B., Pfau, R., & Shermer, T. (2016). *The linguistics of sign languages: An introduction.* John Benjamins.

Banaszkiewicz, A., Bola, Ł., Matuszewski, J., Szczepanik, M., Kossowski, B., Mostowski, P., Rutkowski, P., Śliwińska, M., Jednoróg, K., Emmorey, K., & Marchewka, A. (2021). The role of superior parietal lobule in lexical processing of sign language: Insights of sign language: Insights from fMRI and TMS. *Cortex*, *135*, 240–254. https://doi.org/10.1016/j.cortex.2020.10.025

Blanco-Elorrieta, E., Kastner, I., & Emmorey, K. (2018). Shared neural correlates for building phrases in signed and spoken language. *Scientific Reports*, *8*(1), 5492. https://doi.org/10.1038/s41598-018-23915-0

Bradley, C., Malaia, E. A., Siskind, J. M., & Wilbur, R. B. (2022). Visual form of ASL verb signs predicts non-signer judgment of transitivity. *PLoS ONE*, *18*(2), 1–25. https://doi.org/10.1371/journal.pone.0262098

Cammarata-Scalisi, F., Willoughby, C. E., Cardenas Tadich, A., Labrador, N., Herrera, A., & Callea, M. (2020). Clinical, etiopathogenic, and therapeutic aspects of KID syndrome. *Dermatologic Therapy*, *33*(4), e13507. https://doi.org/10.1111/dth.13507

Cassell, C., & Bishop, V. (2019). Qualitative data analysis: Exploring themes, metaphors and stories. *European Management Review*, *16*(1), 195–207. https://doi.org/10.1111/emre.12176

Cheng, Q., Silvano, E., & Bedny, M. (2020). Sensitive periods in cortical specialization for language: Insights from studies with Deaf and blind individuals. *Current Opinion in Behavioral Sciences*, *36*, 169–176. https://doi.org/10.1016/j.cobeha.2020.10.011

Creswell, J. W., & Poth, C. (2018). *Qualitative inquiry and research design: Choosing among five approaches* (4th ed.). SAGE.

Cripps, J., Cooper, S., Supalla, S., & Evitts, P. (2016). Meeting the needs of signers in the field of speech and language pathology. *Communication Disorders*, *37*(2), 108–116. http://ezproxy.acu.edu:2059/login.aspx?direct=true&AuthType=sso&db=eric&AN=EJ1084726&site=eds-live&scope=site&custid=s8479690

Cupples, L., Ching, T. Y. C., Leigh, G., Martin, L., Gunnourie, M., Button, L., Marnane, V., Hou, S., Zhang, V., Flynn, C., & Van Buynder, P. (2018). Language development in deaf or hard-of-hearing children with additional disabilities: Type matters! *Journal of Intellectual Disability Research: JIDR*, *62*(6), 532–543. https://doi.org/10.1111/jir.12493

Ehrich, J., & O'Donovan, R. (2019). Morality, language use, and ontogenesis: Vygotsky and Shotter revisited. *Linguistics Journal, 13*(1), 197–207. https://www.researchgate.net/profile/John-Ehrich/publication/335676200_Morality_Language_Use_and_Ontogenesis_Vygotsky_and_Shotter_Revisited/links/5d733cf34585151ee4a3e049/Morality-Language-Use-and-Ontogenesis-Vygotsky-and-Shotter-Revisited.pdf#page=197

Gannon, J. (2012). *Deaf heritage: A narrative history of Deaf America.* Gallaudet University Press.

Glickman, N., & Hall, W. (2019). *Language deprivation and Deaf mental health.* Rutledge.

Glickman, N. S., Crump, C., & Hamerdinger, S. (2020). Language deprivation is a game changer for the clinical specialty of deaf mental health. *Journal of the American Deafness & Rehabilitation Association (JADARA), 54*(1), 54–89. https://nsuworks.nova.edu/jadara/vol54/iss1/4

Graneheim, U. H., & Lundman, B. (2004). Qualitative content analysis in nursing research: Concepts, procedures and measures to achieve trustworthiness. *Nurse Education Today, 24*(2), 105–112. https://doi.org/10.1016/j.nedt.2003.10.001

Gullati, S. (2014). *Language deprivation syndrome.* ASL Lecture Series. https://www.youtube.com/watch?v=8yy_K6VtHJw, Brown University.

Hall, M. L., & De Anda, S. (2021). Measuring "Language Access Profiles" in Deaf and hard-of-hearing children with the DHH Language Exposure Assessment Tool. *Journal of Speech, Language, and Hearing Research, 64*(1), 134–158. https://doi.org/10.1044/2020_JSLHR-20-00439

Hall, M. L., Hall, W. C., & Caselli, N. K. (2019). Deaf children need language, not (just) speech. *First Language, 39*(4), 367–395. https://doi.org/10.1177/0142723719834102

Hall, W. C. (2017). What you don't know can hurt you: The risk of language deprivation by impairing sign language development in deaf children. *Maternal & Child Health Journal, 21*(5), 961–965. https://doi.org/10.1007/s10995-017-2287-y

Hall, W. C., Levin, L. L., & Anderson, M. L. (2017). Language deprivation syndrome: A possible neurodevelopmental disorder with sociocultural origins. *Social Psychiatry and Psychiatric Epidemiology, 52*(6), 761–776. https://doi.org/10.1007/s00127-017-1351-7

Hecht, J. L. (2020). Responsibility in the current epidemic of language deprivation (1990–Present). *Maternal & Child Health Journal, 24*(11), 1319–1322. https://doi.org/10.1007/s10995-020-02989-1

Henner, J., Novogrodsky, R., Caldwell-Harris, C., & Hoffmeister, R. (2019). The development of American Sign Language-based analogical reasoning in signing Deaf children. *Journal of Speech, Language & Hearing Research, 62*(1), 93–105. https://doi.org/10.1044/2018_JSLHR-L-18-0062

Hernandez, P. A., & Hadley, A. J. (2020). Exploring relationships between curriculum and cultural competency in pre-service speech-language pathology students.

Journal of Cultural Diversity, *27*(1), 3–13. https://search.ebscohost.com/login.aspx?direct=true&profile=ehost&scope=site&authtype=crawler&jrnl=2169415X&AN=142291601&h=ahuduJTQt%2F5a%2FHJq7Mf3r8gj9TB52TpPrXu9FnF3Lk%2BowqPQxxsrP4kaU%2F7vZZlwgCuec9KokjWNstffUK3zdA%3D%3D&crl=c

Javadi, Y., & Tahmasbi, M. (2020). Application of sociocultural identity theory to education in EFL textbooks development. *Theory & Practice in Language Studies*, *10*(5), 536–541. https://doi.org/10.17507/tpls.1005.07

Kelley, L. E., & McCann, J. P. (2021). Language intervention isn't just spoken: Assessment and treatment of a deaf signing child with specific language impairment. *Language, Speech & Hearing Services in Schools*, *52*(4), 978–992. https://doi.org/10.1044/2021_LSHSS-21-00038

Linask, L. (2019). Vygotsky's natural history of signs. *Sign Systems Studies*, *47*(1–2), 257–304. https://doi.org/10.12697/sss.2019.47.1-2.10

Marshall, C. R., Jones, A., Fastelli, A., Atkinson, J., Botting, N., & Morgan, G. (2018). Semantic fluency in deaf children who use spoken and signed language in comparison with hearing peers. *International Journal of Language & Communication Disorders*, *53*(1), 157–170. https://doi.org/10.1111/1460-6984.12333

Martin, F. N. (1997). *Introduction to audiology. A review manual.* Allyn and Bacon.

Miller, P., Banado-Aviran, E., & Hetzroni, O. E. (2021). Developing reading skills in prelingually deaf preschool children: Fingerspelling as a strategy to promote orthographic learning. *Journal of Deaf Studies & Deaf Education*, *26*(3), 363–380. https://doi.org/10.1093/deafed/enab004

Moroz, A., Flanagan, S., & Zaretsky, P. (2017). *Medical aspects of disability for the rehabilitation professionals* (5th ed.). Springer Publishing Company.

Muncy, M., Yoho, S., & McClain, M. B. (2019). Confidence of school-based speech-language pathologists in assessing students with hearing loss and other co-occurring disabilities. *Language, Speech, and Hearing Services in Schools*, *50*(2), 224–236. https://doi.org/10.1044/2018_LSHSS-18-0091

Murphy, D., Rena, L., Clare, C., Caulfield, M., & de Paor, G. (2018). Communication as a human right: Citizenship, politics, and the role of the speech-language pathologist. *International Journal of Speech-Language Pathology*, *20*(1), 16–20.

National Association of the Deaf. (2014). https://www.nad.org/about-us/position-statements/position-statement-on-early-cognitive-and-language-development-and-education-of-deaf-and-hard-of-hearing-children/

Newman, A., Supalla, T., Fernandez, N., Newport, E., & Bavalier, D. (2015). Neural systems supporting linguistic structure, linguistic experience, and symbolic communication in sign language and gesture. *Proceedings of the National Academy of Science of the United States of America*, *112*(37), 11684–11689. https://doi.org/10.1073/pnas.1510527112

Ozelie, R., Bock, J., Gervais, S., Schneider, L., & Silhavy, C. (2022). Is It Reasonable? Reasonable and unreasonable Accommodations for occupational therapy students in clinical settings. *Open Journal of Occupational Therapy (OJOT)*, *10*(2), 1–11. https://doi.org/10.15453/2168-6408.1913

Padden, C., & Humphries, T. (2005). *Inside Deaf culture*. Harvard University Press.

Park, K. H., Kam, B. S., Yune, S. J., Lee, S. Y., & Im, S. J. (2022). Changes in self-reflective thinking level in writing and educational needs of medical students: A longitudinal study. *PLoS ONE*, *17*(1), 1–11. https://doi.org/10.1371/journal.pone.0262250

Polit, D. F. (2017). Data collection methods. In J. Fitzpatrick (Ed.), *Encyclopedia of nursing research* (4th ed.). Springer.

Quinto-Pozos, D., Singleton, J. L., & Hauser, P. C. (2017). A case of specific language impairment in a deaf signer of American Sign Language. *The Journal of Deaf Studies and Deaf Education*, *22*(2), 204–218. https://doi.org/10.1093/deafed/enw074

Rosen, R. S. (2022). Foreign language ideology and American Sign Language in US public education. *International Journal of the Sociology of Language*, *2022*(275), 159–185. https://doi.org/10.1515/ijsl-2021-0001

Rowley, K., Snoddon, K., & O'Neill, R. (2022). Supporting families and young deaf children with a bimodal bilingual approach. *International Journal of Birth & Parent Education*, *9*(3), 15–20. https://www.research.ed.ac.uk/en/publications/supporting-families-and-young-deaf-children-with-a-bimodal-biling

Saldaña, J., & Omasta, M. (2018). *Qualitative research. Analyzing life*. Sage.

Sandler, W., & Lillo-Martin, D. (2006). *Sign language and linguistic universals*. Cambridge University Press.

Sanzo, K. (2022). Benefits of visual language: How acquisition of signed language complements spoken language development. *Perspectives of the ASHA Special Interest Groups*, *7*(2), 418–425. https://doi.org/10.1044/2021_PERSP-21-00124

Sehyr, Z. S., Geizen, M., & Emmorey, K. (2018). Comparing semantic fluency in American Sign Language and English. *Journal of Deaf Studies & Deaf Education*, *23*(4), 399–407. https://doi.org/10.1093/deafed/eny013

Shaw, E., & Delaporte, Y. (2015). *A historical and etymological dictionary of American Sign Language: The origin and evolution of more than 500 Signs*. Gallaudet University Press.

Skyer, M. E. (2020). The bright triad and five propositions: Toward a Vygotskian framework for Deaf pedagogy and research. *American Annals of the Deaf*, *164*(5), 577–591. https://doi.org/10.1353/aad.2020.0004

Stake, R. E. (1995). *The art of case study research*. Sage.

Szarkowski, A. (2018). *Language development in children with cochlear implants: Possibilities and challenges*. Taylor and Francis. https://doi.org/10.4324/9781315166728

Taylor, M. C. (2005). Interviewing. In *Qualitative research in health care* (pp. 39–55). McGraw-Hill.

Visser, J. C., Rommelse, N. N., Lappenschaar, M., Servatius-Oosterling, I. J., Greven, C. U., & Buitelaar, J. K. (2017). Variation in the early trajectories of autism symptoms is related to the development of language, cognition, and behavior problems. *Journal of the American Academy of Child & Adolescent Psychiatry*, *56*(8), 659–668. https://doi.org/10.1016/j.jaac.2017.05.022

Wilkinson, E., & Morford, J. P. (2020). How bilingualism contributes to healthy development in deaf children: A public health perspective. *Maternal & Child Health Journal*, *24*(11), 1330–1338. https://doi.org/10.1007/s10995-020-02976-6

Chapter 12 A Paradigm of Critical Discourse Analysis on Neoliberalism: The Case of Haiti as a Neophyte

BAUDELAIRE K. ULYSSE

Mining answers for research questions as well as calibrating one's findings necessitate efficient tools. In this context, tools refer to methods. As such, methods putatively enable the researcher to delve into a subject matter and advance consciously and cautiously along both charted and uncharted paths to cull relevant and sound answers. Charted paths represent extant scholarly works on a particular subject, while uncharted paths represent possibilities of latent theories, perspectives, and new interpretations of established assumptions that lie beneath extant data. However, the search for an efficient method is daunting because there is a multitude of methods available to the researcher.

Critical Discourse Analysis as a Method or Tool for Research

Researchers from a wide array of disciplines have deployed Critical Discourse Analysis (CDA) as a tool in research (McCloskey, 2008), and this trend is even more rampant in educational inquiries (Rogers, 2011). McCloskey (2008) uses discourse analysis as a tool to conduct research in the field of nursing and has found that the structure of this field inheres policies and practices which reflect the components of discourses. By the same token, Rogers (2011) does not simply use discourse analysis in her research, but also teaches discourse analysis. In fact, her work draws upon quantitative data from her own students' understanding as well as effective use of critical discourse analysis. Her data analysis provides insights into the arduous process of students grappling with the tool of critical discourse analysis and effectively using it in their own research. Their deep understanding and effective use of critical discourse analysis yielded multilayered interpretations of how discourse operates within social spheres of human societies. Overall, Rogers' research adds credence to the credibility and validity of discourse analysis as an effective research tool.

Assumptions of Critical Discourse Analysis

Like a theoretical lens, CDA has a few assumptions. It maintains that language is a social phenomenon (Fairclough, 2001). This means that individual human beings, institutions, and social structures have values and meanings that are expressed through language in systematic ways. Thus, according to Fairclough, language has played a vital role in what people do and say, and why and how. This also plays out in the behaviors of multinational corporations, including the goods and services they decide to offer. Further, Fairclough notes that language plays a significant role in providing goods and services offered in the marketplace, particularly the strategic interactions that take place between staff and customers, in printed documents and signs, as well as the messaging and promotion for said products and services. This use of language means that the struggle to impose or resist the new order is in large part a struggle for or against a new language. Hence, any critique of documents such as policies, academic publications, and press releases related to discourse practices becomes imperative before one can successfully delineate as well as assess the discourse of neoliberalism (Fairclough, 2001).

Perhaps more pertinent for the current study is CDA's interest in the nexus between language and power (Fairclough, 2001; Gee, 2005). According to Gee (2005), this relationship between language and power manifests itself pervasively in that "language-in-use is everywhere and always political" (p. 1). In this relationship, language emits and solidifies power, and in turn power reinforces language, which nurtures it to both coexist and self-perpetrate in an extremely dominant way. By the same token, Fairclough (2001) offers helpful insights on the relationship between language and power. He coins the notion of "power behind discourse" and outlines three "aspects" of how power plays out in a discourse—*standard language*, *effect of power*, and *power and access to discourse.*

In all three aspects, discourse is engendered and maintained by the interest of powerholders. In this type of discourse, "the whole social order of discourse is put together and held together as a hidden effect of power" (Fairclough, 2001, p. 46). All three aspects, as discussed by Fairclough, feature explicitly or implicitly a positive correlation of power and domination.

Particularly, the third aspect—*power and access to discourse*—is especially salient because it touches on the issues of inequity and inequality, which are evident in the discourse on neoliberalism and economic globalization.

According to Fairclough (2001), power and access to discourse play right into how the value of *free speech* is implemented in social practice. He argues that the notion of free speech is in fact a myth because there is "a plethora of constraints on access to various sorts of speech and writing" (p. 52). Essentially, these constraints determine what group gets access to cultural capital in each society.

Inequity and inequality represent major concerns in contemporary debates, and the present study maintains that they are inextricably connected to the causality of the power dynamics in the neoliberal discourse. Consequently, the following analysis will focus on delineating and deconstructing these issues, while presenting an alternate vision that is consistent with social justice principles such as freedom, equality, and equity in all democratic contexts.

Gee (2005) credits Fairclough, Wodak, and Meyer, among others, with the use of CDA within the discourse analysis tradition, and he suggests they all share the fundamentals of discourse analysis, albeit they differ in tools of inquiry and linguistic tradition (pp. 116–117). However, all iterations of CDA take a keen interest in language-in-use and its effects on social, political, and economic structures. As such, they examine how language is used on discourses to enact activities and identities (little-d). A combination of the little-d discourse (language-in-use) and non-language "stuff" to enact specific identities and activities yields big-D discourse (p. 7).

Non-language stuff is understood by Gee (2005) as ways of living in the world—acting, feeling, believing, and valuing. Thus, he notes: "All life for all of us is just a patchwork of thoughts, words, objects, events, actions, and interactions in discourses" (p. 7). According to Gee, language has meanings only in and through social practice. People use language when they make things significant, engage in certain activities, build relationships, and argue for or against perspectives.

Also important is that contemporary approaches of discourse analysis assume a *reflexive* component of the relationship between language and context. Accordingly, Gee (2005) posits that "[r]eflexive here means that, at one and the same time, an utterance influences what we take the context to be and context conversely influences what we take the utterance to mean" (Gee, 2005, p. 57). Similarly, Fairclough (1995, 2001, 2008) links Gee's framework of discourse to critical theory. Thus, Fairclough (1995) describes discourse analysis as both analytical and critical. As such, CDA serves as "a resource for people who are struggling against the domination and oppression in its linguistic forms" (p. 1). Central to Fairclough's discussion of CDA are the notions of *text*, *discourse practice*, and *sociocultural practice*. Hence Fairclough expands the boundaries of discourse analysis from linguistic analysis to textual analysis, which includes language, written text, and social institutions. Accordingly, texts for Fairclough could be the content of linguistic texture and structure in written documents where value-driven ideologies are embedded.

Also, texts are viewed as *social spaces* wherein identities of individuals in a particular society are being formed. These individuals, or peoples in general, are being formed precisely in social spaces through certain processes, which Fairclough (1995) alludes to as "cognition and representations of the world and social interaction." Additionally, he argues that "[d]iscourses include representations of how things are and have been, as well as imaginaries—representations of how things might or could or should be" (Fairclough, 2008, p. 207). Thus, these elements, *cognition*, *representation*, and *social interaction* are integral parts of discourses, and they should be factored into any CDA research design. In Gee (2005), these elements would be considered as little-d discourses that contribute to the big-D discourse.

Based on this understanding of discourse as text, Fairclough (1995) argues that the successful analysis of any text or discourse must meticulously and critically analyze one or more of its key elements:

> Such analysis requires attention to textual form, structure and organizations at all levels; phonological, grammatical, and lexical (vocabulary) and higher levels of textual organization in terms of exchange systems (the distribution of speaking turns), structure of argumentation, and generic (activity type) structures. (p. 7)

Fairclough (1995) does not relegate the primary preoccupation of CDA with language. Instead, he views language or linguistic patterns as a broader structure, encompassing written texts and spoken texts (speech or other delivery systems) along with the vital components necessary for proper functioning. Fairclough's schema, which stresses text, discourse practice, and sociocultural practice as key components of discourse, expands the scope of discourse, thus providing a wider range of texts as targets for deeper analysis.

By the same token, Reisigl and Wodak (2009) underscore "text" as an embodiment of power and domination, and thus represent spaces for social struggle. Accordingly, they note:

> [T]exts are often sites of struggle in that they manifest traces of differing ideological fights for domination and hegemony. Thus, we focus on the ways in

> which linguistic forms are used in various expressions and manipulations of power. Power is discursively exerted not only by grammatical forms, but also by a person's control of the social occasions by means of the genre of a text, by the regulation of access to certain public spheres. (p. 89)

In the preceding statement, Reisigl and Wodak espouse and aptly argue for a broader view of text, which is like that of Fairclough (1995). Hence, this broader view of language or text as an embodiment of domination and oppression serves as a suitable framework not only to understand and interpret phenomena associated with global neoliberalism, but also to critique and deconstruct neoliberalism's hegemonic and oppressive agenda.

Research Methodology and Methods

When methodology is discussed as part of a research project, methods become part of the process. As such, methods are used to mine data or data sources in search of evidence and insights are also requisites. This study subsumes the presuppositions of CDA. One of those presuppositions is that discourse uses texts (both spoken and written) to control as well as enact practices (linguistic, social, cultural, institutional, and political) in societies. This enables one group to dominate, control, and or oppress another group (Fairclough, 1995, 2001, 2008; Wodak & Meyer, 2009). Another presupposition is that discourse ironically is "resisted in text and talk in the social and political context" (van Dijk, 1993). Accordingly, in this critical analysis of the discourse of neoliberalism in the global economy context, texts from various sources and disciplines are considered. For instance, the analysis will scrutinize published materials for and against the neoliberal discourse, institutions such as government, schools or educational systems, primarily those in Haiti and the United States, with special attention given to how they support and embody the neoliberal discourse, and materials written about intergovernmental institutions such as the International Monetary Fund (IMF), World Bank (WB), World Trade Organization (WTO), and United Nations Educational, Scientific and Cultural Organization (UNESCO). Additionally, the analysis draws on data from various strata, while concentrating on key aspects such as those proposed by van Dijk (1993): analysis of semantic macrostructure, topics for macrostructure, analysis of local meanings, analysis of subtle structure, analysis of global and local discourse forms, analysis of specific linguistic realization (hyperbolas), and analysis of content. Those aspects are not exhaustive; neither do they lend themselves to a reductive choice of all or none. Rather, they comprise a list of options from which the researcher may select elements to examine based on their topic, research questions, or purposes.

Analyzing the Discourse

To successfully analyze aspects of the neoliberal discourse, this chapter draws from an array of books, journal articles, and respected newspapers that extensively address globalization's history and its current juncture—social, political, educational, and economic—through the prism of neoliberal ideologies. Essentially, the data sources referred to above are delineated, analyzed, compared, contrasted, expounded on, and synthesized to unveil and critique the nature of the discourse or discourses as well as its inherent injustice.

Drawing on Gee's vernacular (2005), particularly his differentiation between big-D discourses and little-d discourses, the analysis of neoliberalism pays close attention to the subtleties and complexities of how power and politics are embedded in "languages" in local settings as embodied in written content. Thus, initiatives such as educational reforms, school textbooks, enactment of trade agreements, and privatization of public assets could be said to represent little-d discourses that take place in local settings while contributing and shaping, both subtly and explicitly, the big-D discourse within the macrocosm of neoliberalism and economic globalization.

Neoliberalism as Discourse: A Politico-Economic Ideology

Neoliberalism, as an ideology, has wielded tremendous influence, both pull and push on human societies across the world (Davies & Bensel, 2007). The influence of neoliberalism is not confined to just one aspect of these societies—its presence is ubiquitous and global. It reaches and impacts many aspects that profoundly affect the material conditions of social, economic, and political structures. One of the consequential shifts in the material conditions of societies engendered by neoliberalism is the transition from a social welfare state to a neoliberal market-driven state, which has served as an apparatus for individual and entrepreneurial interests (Nafstad et al., 2007). Along with this market-based or economic emphasis in neoliberalism, there is a strong push to strengthen nation-states and their law-and-order system (Wacquant, 2010). Neoliberalism may benefit from weak nation-states where lawmakers are easily swayed by personal gains and where capital can be acquired and moved from shore to shore, but it does not fare well in chaos or anarchy where respect for property rights is not enforced. According to Wacquant (2010), law enforcement, the judicial system, and large prison complexes are favored by neoliberalism because these systems "enable political elites to reassert the authority of the state and shore up the deficit of legitimacy officials suffer when they abandon the mission of social and economic protection established during the Fordist-Keynesian era" (p. 198). Other shifts caused by neoliberalism are manifest in social policies enacted in certain societies around the world. For instance, developing countries have embraced privatization as a core market practice. As a result, government-run services, and programs such as telecommunications, electricity, and water plants are now being sold to and run by private enterprises. The most convincing reasoning behind the transfer of these services to private entities is the lack of efficiency and profits. Laden by bureaucracy, corruption, and overhead cost, governments are said to lack the resources and tools to continue offering these services in a sustainable and profitable manner. The solution, according to proponents of neoliberalism, is the private sector where investors are more inclined. Plus, services can be more consistent, and pricing can be driven by supply and demand, and not by necessity of making up shortfalls in governments' budget and coffers. Prime examples of countries that have experimented with these neoliberal or market-based policies are the United Kingdom, Poland, Haiti, Brazil, and Chile. These various shifts engendered by neoliberalism have led many to conclude that the neoliberal agenda has been very effective on a global scale.

Jilberto and Mommen (1993) have correctly noted that "neo-liberalism as political and economic ideology has been one of the most successful elements of the reconstruction of capitalist hegemony over the global system" (p. 3). Similarly, Apple (1999), Hill (1998), and Miraftab (2004) have each painted neoliberalism as a powerful ideological tool that is drastically transforming the fiber of many societies around the world. Miraftab (2004) examines the role neoliberalism plays in the governance of different states around the world, and paints a rather stunning picture of how neoliberalism relates to politics and economies in developing countries:

> Neo-liberal policies and structural adjustment programs have deeply slashed governments' budget for public expenditure and have redefined the state's responsibilities for public services. For example, in developing states in the 1950s–1970s the primary agenda for national economic growth was to provide basic services and infra-structure. But that role has now been shifted to private firms, both local and international, in a market-led strategy for providing basic public services and infrastructure. (p. 240)

While Miraftab's depiction reflects realities as well as actualities in the developing world, neoliberalism's growing influence is by no means confined to that segment. After all, neoliberalism has long achieved a certain pinnacle regarding global dominance, making it undeniably a full-fledged ideological discourse. As Miraftab (2004) points out, neoliberalism has attained such global dominance precisely by strategically creating alliance, albeit coercively at times, with what one might call client governments around the world.

Neoliberalism in Education: Standards, Tests, Accountability, Market, and Profits

If there is doubt about neoliberalism being a discourse or about neoliberalism's global reach, Apple (1999) provides a scathing portrayal of neoliberalism which is sure to dispel such doubt. His work, entitled *Freire, Neoliberalism, and Education*, traces the connection between American conservative ideologies and neoliberalism. This work represents by far one of the most courageous assessments of, and thus a verdict against, neoliberalism in terms of the subtle way in which neoliberalism controls policies related to U.S. economy and education. According to Apple (1999; 2004), one of the major neoliberal hallmarks in education is the No Child Left Behind (NCLB) federal law. The aim of NCLB is to increase "economic productivity" by "improving education," and among its strategies are "increased accountability, high-stakes tests, standards, choice, and centralized regulation of schools" and the reduction of inputs from "teachers and communities" (Lipman, 2008, p. 46). On the surface, the aim of the law appears reasonable, but, as Hursh (2007) notes, "it is not enough to examine a particular policy' stated purpose" (p. 494). In fact, a closer look at NCLB reveals a broader but discursive "...policy texts that are political, cultural, economic as much as they are educational treatises ..." (Olssen et al., 2004, p. 2), which diminish the autonomy and agency of students and teachers. Consequently, schools become like private enterprises with a "single-minded pursuit of profit and showing significantly less regard for the need to limit social costs or for redistribution based on nonmarket criteria" (Tabb, 2002, p. 29). Similarly, the Common Core States Standards (CCSS) initiative, which was enacted nearly a decade after its predecessor, NCLB, promised to usher in a new era in student's preparedness for college and career turned out to be ironically a repackaging of the same neoliberal educational policies, although CCSS gives back some flexibility and agency to teachers and school administrators to augment and implement the curriculum (Applebee, 2013).

Arguably, the most pernicious manifestation of neoliberalism in education is the privatization of school along with its high-stakes tests accountability (Dee et al., 2013). Patterned after market-based principles, it prioritizes the preparation of "workers for jobs in a global economy where capitalism can move jobs wherever it wishes—that is, countries where profits trump working conditions and salaries" (Weiner, 2012, p. 36). Most countries, especially in the third world, where neoliberalism has been implemented have tried to replicate NCLB in their educational systems. Particularly, Haiti's educational system has been molded to reflect similar standards.

Neoliberalism: Economic Policies and Political Interests of the Dominant West

Davies and Bensel (2007) discuss the shift to or the emergence of global neoliberalism. They trace the development of neoliberalism back to the economic policies of Great Britain and the United States. Davies and Bensel also show how neoliberalism started spreading across the world through the concerted effort of neoliberal stakeholders such as France, Great Britain, and the United States. Essentially, they postulate that the spread of neoliberalism has been facilitated by the consent of nation-states' official governments in countries across the world. When these governments grant consent, neoliberalism becomes endowed with unlimited political and economic leverage to influence or undermine existing laws as well as enact new ones which favor the unfettered operation of multinational corporations and other interest groups. This relationship or arrangement between governments of nation-states and global interest groups begets as well as controls the framework within which the neoliberal discourse is promulgated, implemented, and sustained.

Operative within this discourse are various philosophies or notions. These terms, which have surfaced in earlier discussions in no respective order, are *capitalism*, *hegemony*, *neoliberalism*, *colonialism*, and *imperialism*. The assumptions of the study posit that the discourse, which embodies neoliberalism and economic globalization, subsumes most, if not all, of the concepts highlighted above.

Neoliberalism as a Global Expansion of Capitalism

Capitalism is by no means a new phenomenon. It is an economic system or philosophy that has been implemented in many economies around the world, particularly in Western economies such as Great Britain and the United States of America (Frieden, 2006). It is not confined to a restrictive definition, but most economists concur that capitalism refers to and embodies values such as free market and free choice. Because of its putative element of freedom, capitalism is thought by many to be ideal and most compatible with human societies (Bernstein, 2005).

Placing this philosophy in the context of a local economy, it becomes characterized by five distinct features: private property and freedom of choice, self-interest, markets and prices, competition, and limited government intervention (Friedman, 2002; 2007). Thus, the global economy is essentially capitalism driving economies of both the developing and the developed countries into an integrated whole. This entails a "closer integration of the [economies of] countries of the world through the increased flow of goods and services" (Stiglitz, 2003, p. 4).

Neoliberalism as Political and Economic Hegemony

Hegemony, being understood as the dominant discourse (Apple, 2004) or the concurrent enforcement mechanism of a particular ideology by those in control, represents an ideology of domination by others. It is a fascinating phenomenon in that it can be implemented through either coercion (Clayton, 1998) or in a subtle persuasion medium such as spoken languages, educational systems, curricular approaches, and publications. From the vantage point of colonialism and imperialism, the cultures and educational systems of previously colonized countries are steeped in the legacies of their colonizers (Ginsburg & Clayton, 2006), thereby perpetuating and enforcing hegemony.

The type of hegemony discussed and illustrated above reflects a subtle domination, however strategic and intentional. Although this type of hegemony should not be equated with empire, it is often the result of imperial legacies perpetuated through education, cultural, and linguistic devices. However, hegemony also inheres an aggressive dimension that is particularly manifest in economic implementation of neoliberalism and its political ramifications in the global context. Agnew (2005) thinks this kind of hegemony is U.S.-infused and argues that the U.S. usually enlists the help of other countries in propagating and advancing it. Thus, he defines it as "the enrollment of others in the exercise of your power by convincing, cajoling, and coercing them that they should do what you want" (p. 1). According to Agnew, this characterizes the relationship between the U.S. and the rest of the world, particularly in the context of globalization. In fact, he views globalization, without qualification, as a "hegemonic project intimately connected to the geopolitical calculus of U.S. government" (p. 2), thereby dismissing neoliberalism, or "liberalization" as he labels it. The present analysis does not equate globalization with liberalization or neoliberalism because there are various factors contributing to the globalizing process. However, the current engine of economic globalization, or the global economy, is being propelled by neoliberalism as the dominant discourse. Hence, contrary to Agnew's position, the hegemony of neoliberalism in economic globalization cannot be viewed simply through the American prism. In its analysis, this study has assessed that economic globalization stems from a broader coalition among the most powerful and elite economies of the world, including the U.S. Ultimately, this coalition is committed not only to incubate and implement neoliberalism, but also to propagate it in other countries, particularly countries in the developing world.

Ideologies of the Neoliberal Discourse

Having become the preferred economic philosophy in the context of a global economy, capitalism has given rise to a capitalist expansion known as neoliberalism. Neoliberalism represents a hegemonic discourse in the context of globalization (Giroux, 2004; Harvey, 2007), and is manifest particularly in economies, government, and education globally (Giroux, 2004).

Privatization

Megginson (2005) defines privatization as a "deliberate sale by a government of state-owned enterprises (SOEs) or assets to private economic agents" (p. 3). As such, privatization favors private enterprise and private ownership over public or government enterprises. Like deregulation, privatization is another neoliberal ideology that advocates for less publicly run or government-sponsored services. Further, it maintains that private ownership and enterprises ultimately foster entrepreneurship, individual responsibility, competitions on the market, and better services and more competitive pricing for consumers.

Since its introduction, privatization has rapidly become the *darling* of all economic reforms in developed economies and is a major component of neoliberalism as a dominant discourse. Megginson (2005) notes that Chile and Germany experimented with privatization in the 1970s, but he suggests those two countries harvested nominal results from the implementation of privatization. According to Megginson, Great Britain has been particularly singled out as an exemplar that successfully implemented privatization in the early 1980s. Further, other countries such as "France, Austria, Belgium, Canada, Chile, Denmark, Holland, Italy, Jamaica, Japan, Malaysia, Singapore, Spain, Sweden, and the United States all executed significant privatization through public share offerings during the mid-1980s" (p. 17).

As those countries embarked on the journey to implement privatization, there was an aura of heightened optimism that privatization would make their governments more efficient, raise financial capital for their gross domestic product (GDP), and ultimately boost their economies. To date, other countries have launched similar privatization projects. Accordingly, Megginson (2005) estimates that "the cumulative value" of all privatization undertakings "now has surpassed 1.5 trillion dollars" (p. 21). Apparently, there is very much to be had when governments privatize.

Haiti: The Case of a Neoliberal Neophyte

It is no wonder that privatization is being pushed in many developing countries around the world. Haiti is one among many developing countries where privatization as a neoliberal economic reform is currently being implemented. Neoliberals have been courting Haiti on such reforms for a long time. The 1994 return of Aristide, the then-exiled and now former president of Haiti, served as the turning point in this pursuit since Aristide supposedly agreed to a deal that guaranteed his return in exchange for the implementation of neoliberal reforms. However, Aristide had been reluctant to follow through on such reforms because they were not popular among the Haitian masses that rely heavily on public services (Girard, 2005). As it turned out, Aristide's reluctance did not earn him favor with powerful neoliberal interest groups, which arguably became the ground for a second ouster that sent him into exile in Africa.

Since Aristide's second exile, which occurred in 2004, and with the advent of the re-election of Mr. Rene Préval for a second nonconsecutive term as president in 2006, much funding had been disbursed to Haiti through World Bank and International Monetary Fund, purportedly from neoliberal interest groups whose precondition was implementation of the neoliberal agenda (Girard, 2005). Privatization is one focus of this agenda and is typically sold to developing countries as a catalyst for economic development. Harvey (2007) explains how neoliberalism ties privatization to economic advancement:

> Neoliberals are particularly assiduous in seeking the privatization of assets. The absence of clear private property rights—as in many developing countries—is seen as one of the most institutional barriers to economic development and the improvement of human welfare ... Sectors formerly run or regulated by the state must be turned over to the private sphere and be deregulated (free from any state interference). (p. 65)

Economic reforms of this nature pervade many countries, both developed and developing, around the globe. Haiti a country that has been oscillating at the juncture of economic development in the context of neoliberal economic discourse. As a direct result of neoliberal economic reforms in Haiti, a few institutions or services previously run by the Haitian government have been privatized. For instance, Haiti's flourmill and cement factory, which were formerly run by the Haitian government, have been privatized. In 2010, the former Haitian president, Rene Préval, announced that the privatization plan for Téléco, the Haitian national telephone company, was being finalized (Sprague, 2009).

Although the then-president claimed privatization to be in the best interest of the Haitian economy, many Haitians, especially those intimately affected by it, are not particularly thrilled with privatization or other reforms. The fire of neoliberal reforms in Haiti is currently being fanned, and it will likely remain sparked and aflame for a long time because the cash-strapped Haitian government has apparently bought into the neoliberal ideologies, and neoliberals have leveraged that to great effect in exerting influence in the political process in Haiti. Evidence of such influence is seen in the exclusion of the most popular political party in Haiti in the April 2009 senatorial elections. With no constitutional or legal ground, the Haitian national electoral council banned politicians of that party from participating in the elections (Reuters, 2009; Sprague, 2009). Critics of this decision suggested that politicians from this popular party were likely to get elected but unlikely to support the neoliberal agenda. Hence, to clear the way for unfettered and undeterred neoliberal reforms in Haiti, neoliberals purportedly colluded with the election officials to orchestrate a political hacking, resulting into the conundrum in Haiti (Gupta, 2010).

Subsequently, the neoliberal project of liberating the Haitian market promised several milestones, and both local and international businesspeople were invited to learn about how to make money in Haiti (Loewenstein, 2017). Neoliberal initiatives were accelerated after the devastating 2010 earthquake. A key component of these initiatives was the construction of industrial parks to attract foreign manufacturers. Accordingly, Iqbal (2021) notes: "In 2011, the US-controlled Organization of American States (OAS) collaborated with the Haitian elite to install Michael Martelly as the president. Martelly was a neo-colonial stooge, responsible for eviscerating an already weak Haiti through his "Open for Business" policy. The opening of a South Korean manufacturing plant in Caracol, an area in northeast Haiti unaffected by the earthquake, displaced hundreds of Haitian farmers, confiscating arable land" (para. 24). Along with the park, a nearby port was planned as well. The logic of these projects was to attract foreign companies by the prospect of cheap labors, but neither the park nor the port had enough funding to bring them to fruition. While a project of this magnitude may be considered a milestone for the neoliberal project in Haiti, many have seen it as a failure for several reasons. First, the location was formerly farmland where food was grown locally for the people living in that region. Farmers were forced out to make room for the industrial park. The most probably part of this quandary is that farmers were sold on the prospect of getting jobs. Accordingly, Kushner (2019) observes: "While the port stalled, the industrial park underdelivered. When Bill and Hillary Clinton flew to northern Haiti to inaugurate the $300m Caracol park in 2012, the overall project had created just 1,500 of the 65,000 jobs that were promised. In fact, many Haitians may have lost their livelihoods because of Caracol: in the end, 366 families were evicted from their land to make way for the project, according to a report by the NGO ActionAid" (para. 32). Unfortunately, as Loewenstein (2017) points out, these jobs pay low wages, making farmers reliant on the capitalist production instead of producing their own food. Once these farmers get paid, they end up having to use their earning to buy on the marketplace foods that have been imported from the United States and other countries. In the final analysis, the real winners of these transactions are foreign companies that benefit from cheap labors and Western consumers who get to buy lower-priced products manufactured in that context. Meanwhile, Haitian are denied the opportunity to achieve food security and economic development from within (Ramachandran & Walz, 2015).

The evidence on neoliberalism in Haiti shows that privatization or private enterprise rarely delivers on what it purports to do, especially as it pertains to economic development in third-world countries. Giroux (2004) perceptively notes that neoliberalism "pushes for the privatization of all non-commodified public spheres and the upward distribution of wealth. [I]t supports policies that increasingly militarize facets of public space in order to secure the privileges and benefits of the corporate elite and ultra-rich" (p. xxiv). Despite the fact that privatization serves the interests of only a select few, its proponents continue to sell it as a catalyst for widespread economic development in poor countries.

Neoliberalism as "Free" Market

From a policy standpoint, regulations represent rules or interventions by the government intended to contain the market's reach and protect investors from erratic turns (Reback, 2009). Presupposed in the government's regulatory interventions in the market mechanism is a clairvoyance that "the market system may not function ideally in monopolistic or oligopolistic industries" (Baumol & Blinder, 1986, p. 272). For instance, regulation restricts what prices firms and corporations can charge and, in many situations, how products and services are distributed to the markets. Also, regulations may enact and enforce antitrust policies to deter monopolistic business practices (Reback, 2009). These aspects of regulation, among many others, are intended to create competition and fair business habits among firms and to protect consumers and investors who do business transactions on the market (Baumol & Blinder, 1986; Reback, 2009).

In stark contrast to regulation, *de*regulation seeks to minimize government's interventions since government interventions are usually perceived as interference that inhibits the market and that prevents it from naturally stimulating competition in pricing and the production of better products. Further, much like liberalism, this deregulation element of neoliberal ideology holds and professes an unwavering trust in the market, touting the market as sovereign and capable of independently running itself smoothly, equitably, and fairly (Friedman, 2002; Oatley, 2008). Highlighting neoliberalism's influence on economies for the last 20 years and the emphasis on free market, Oatley (2008) notes:

> Neoliberalism is highly skeptical of the state's ability to allocate resources efficiently and places great faith in the market's ability to do so. And in contrast to structuralism's advocacy of protectionism and state intervention is neoliberalism's advocacy of the withdrawal of the state from the economy, the reduction (ideally, elimination) of trade barriers, and reliance on the market to generate industries that produce for the world market. (p. 139)

Further, proponents of neoliberalism argue that deregulation reduces prices on products, improves services, renders the market more competitive and accessible, and makes entry of new businesses feasible and profitable (Baumol & Blinder, 1986). However, it should be noted that these advantages of deregulation do not represent the norms of market's behaviors or across industries. By contrast, opponents of deregulation have argued that regulation initiated by government toward the market fittingly represents the sole, albeit imperfect, restraining force against the excesses of the market (Reback, 2009). In fact, critics have viscerally and adamantly contested neoliberalism's trust in the market, noting that the market lacks the moral or logical autonomy to operate in a socially just fashion (Stiglitz, 2003).

Regarding the issue of moral fiber of the market, Giroux (2004) aptly observes: "Within the discourse of neoliberalism, democracy becomes synonymous with free markets while issues of equality, social justice, and freedom are stripped of any substantive meaning and used to disparage those who suffer systemic deprivation and chronic punishment" (p. xviii). These points made by Giroux adeptly capture some of the issues revolving around the supremacy awarded to the market mechanism.

Philosophical Foundations of Neoliberalism: Freedom and Discontents

Milton Friedman was perhaps the most astute and prominent advocate for the supremacy of the market. In fact, Friedman (1990) co-authored *Free to Choose* with his wife Rose Friedman. Friedman and Friedman (1990) attributed the success of American capitalist economy to the notion of free market, particularly the philosophy that advocates and demands that the market be freed from political influence. Grounded in the arguments originally advanced in Adam Smith's *The Wealth of Nations* (1776), Friedman and Friedman postulated that in almost all cases where the U.S. government has intervened with the goal of protecting the public good and the interests of its citizens, it has managed to produce just the opposite. To corroborate their thesis, they extensively examined services such as education, social institutions, social security, employment, and fiscal matters where the government has frequently yet unsuccessfully intervened.

Having espoused the ideal of free market, they suggested that it is through the "voluntary exchange" among self-interested individuals that an economy develops, grows, and sustains itself. According to them, this voluntary exchange is dictated and facilitated by the pricing structure inherent in the market system and not by some externally commanding force such as the government. As far as the government is concerned, Friedman and Friedman argue that its role must be confined to the protection of its citizens and the administration of justice. This, according to them, will secure the parameters of a free society wherein its people are free from "outside coercion" and free to engage in transactions that are mutually beneficial for all parties involved. Overall, their view can be summed up as such: "Economic freedom is an essential requisite to the political freedom. By enabling people to cooperate with one another without coercion or central direction, it reduces the area over which political power is exercised" (Friedman & Friedman, 1990, pp. 2–3). Hence, Friedman and Friedman effectively linked the *Declaration of Independence* to the economic principle of free market, and they supposed that the parties operating in the market equally enjoy the same freedom.

However, recent conditions and events on the market have challenged the notion of the market as a free mechanism. For instance, the Great Recession between 2007 and 2012 was largely blamed on the malfeasances, speculations, and manipulations by greedy and self-interested players. By the same token, the near failure of several financial institutions was attributed to the lack of deregulation. This is one of the reasons why Harvey (2007) sharply disagrees with the free-market philosophy advanced by Friedman and Friedman.

The crux of Harvey's disagreement is that political freedom does not necessarily translate into freedom for everyone making transactions in the market, and that the neoliberal application at its core undermines both personal and political freedom. Similarly, Chua (2003) argues that the neoliberal ideology destabilizes democracy globally. Giroux (2004) notes that "[n]eoliberalism devitalizes democracy" (p. 69); Stiglitz (2003; 2010) describes how neoliberalism extorts developing countries and brings the global economy to the brink of sinking.

Freedom is assumed for everyone in Milton Friedman's view, and it represents a major premise in his argument for capitalism or its most current form in neoliberalism. However, Friedman has oversold the notion of freedom as understood and practiced in capitalism and neoliberalism, which Harvey demonstrates correctly by portraying the market as an unlevel playing field where equals play fairly. In fact, the evidence shows that the market is a field where unequal people, by virtue or the extent of their power to affect the outcome of transactions, engage in unfair and underhanded play. Ultimately, some players, including nations, get super-rich, while other players lose and remain at the bottom of the totem pole (Frieden, 2006; Stiglitz, 2003; 2010). This process is sanctioned and enjoined by neoliberalism itself, which makes economic freedom virtually impossible to be enjoyed on an equal basis. Therefore, the ethos of freedom in neoliberalism seems more symbolic than material; hence its paradoxical nature is warranted. As such, it is used to create an illusion of democracy and choice to lure weaker players. In fact, the structure, the principles, and the practices of the neoliberal market embed this lack of evenhandedness in transactions, resulting in social inequality, and economic and educational inequities within the hegemonic, oppressive, and exploitative discourse (Giroux, 2004). Further, Stiglitz (2010) suggests that Friedman, along with his followers, is partly responsible for the asphyxiation of freedom and the failure of neoliberalism.

Conclusion

Using the assumptions and tools of CDA, the preceding discussions depict neoliberalism as a discourse, embodying ideologies that parlay political and economic freedom for all but purvey only the interests of the few. Further, they draw on arguments and documents by various scholars to demonstrate how neoliberalism operate, including its implement and reinforcement in political, economic, and social domains. Specifically, they examine how neoliberal ideologies infiltrate, both overtly and covertly, politics, education, and the market through linguistic equivocation, the use of coercion, and consent.

Overall, neoliberalism, despite its promises of political freedom and economic advancement, remains the embodiment of discursive practices and ideologies that predetermine and control, both consciously and subconsciously, the thoughts and behaviors of people from various societies across the globe.

References

Agnew, J. (2005). *Hegemony: The new shape of global power.* Temple University Press.

Apple, M. (1999). Freire, neo-liberalism and education. *Discourse: Studies in the Cultural Politics of Education, 20*(1), 5.

Apple, M. (2004). Creating difference: Neo-liberalism, neo-conservatism and the politics of educational reform. *Educational Policy, 18*(1), 12–44.

Applebee, A. N. (2013). Common Core State Standards: The promise and the peril in a national palimpsest. *The English Journal, 103*(1), 25–33. http://www.jstor.org/stable/24484057

Baumol, W., & Blinder, A. (1986). *Economics: Principles and policy.* Harcourt Brace Jovanovich, Publishers.

Bernstein, A. (2005). *The capitalist manifesto.* University Press of America.

Chua, A. (2003). *World on fire: How exporting free market democracy breeds ethnic hatred and global instability.* Doubleday.

Clayton, T. (1998, November). Beyond mystification: Reconnecting world-system theory for comparative education. *Comparative Education Review, 42*(4), 479.

Davies, B., & Bensel, P. (2007). Neoliberalism and education. *International Journal of Qualitative Studies in Education (QSE), 20*(3), 247–259.

Dee, T. S., Jacob, B., & Schwartz, N. L. (2013). The effects of NCLB on school resources and practices. *Educational Evaluation and Policy Analysis, 35*(2), 252–279. http://www.jstor.org/stable/43773431

Fairclough, N. (1995). *Critical discourse analysis: The critical study of language.* Longman.

Fairclough, N. (2001). *Language and power.* Longman.

Fairclough, N. (2008). *Analyzing discourse: Textual analysis for social research.* Routledge.

Frieden, J. (2006). *Global capitalism: Its fall and rise in the twentieth century.* W. W. Norton.

Friedman, M. (2002). *Capitalism and freedom.* The University of Chicago Press.

Friedman, M. (2007). *Milton Friedman on economics: Selected papers.* The University of Chicago Press.

Friedman, M., & Friedman, R. (1990). *Free to choose: A personal statement.* Harcourt Books.

Gee, J. (2005). *An introduction to discourse analysis: Theory and method.* Routledge.

Ginsburg, M., & Clayton, T. (2006). Imperialism and education. In D. Levinson, P. Cookson, & A. Sadovnik (Eds.), *Education and sociology* (pp. 387–392). Rutledge Falmer.

Girard, P. (2005). *Paradise lost: Haiti's tumultuous journey from pearl of the Caribbean to third world hotspot.* Palgrave Macmillan.

Giroux, H. (2004). *The terror of neoliberalism.* Paradigm Publishers.

Gupta, A. (2010, February). The U.S. in Haiti: Neoliberalism at the barrel of a gun. *The Indypendent.* http://www.indypendent.org/2010/02/18/us-in-haiti/

Harvey, D. (2007). *A brief history of neoliberalism.* Oxford University Press.

Hill, D. (1998). Neo-liberalism and hegemony revisited. *Educational Philosophy & Theory, 30*(1), 69.

Jilberto, A., & Mommen, A. (1993). The political economy of global neo-liberalism. *International Journal of Political Economy, 23*(1), 3–12.

Kushner, J. (2019, October). Haiti and the failed promise of US Aid. *The Guardian.* https://pulitzercenter.org/stories/haiti-and-failed-promise-us-aid

Lipman, P. (2008). Chapter 2: Education policy, race, and neoliberal urbanism. *Counterpoints, 316*, 45–66. http://www.jstor.org/stable/42979838

Loewenstein, A. (2017, September). Haiti: The neoliberal model imposed on the country is failing its citizens. *The Guardian.* https://www.theguardian.com/commentisfree/2014/feb/05/haiti-the-neoliberal-model-imposed-on-the-country-is-failing-its-citizens

McCloskey, R. (2008). A guide to discourse analysis. *Nurse Researcher, 16*(1), 24–43.

Megginson, W. (2005). *The financial economics of privatization.* Oxford University Press.

Miraftab, F. (2004). Making neo-liberal governance: The disempowering work of empowerment. *International Planning Studies, 9*(4), 239–259.

Nafstad, H., Blakar, R. M., Carlquist, E., Phelps, J. M., & Rand-Hendriksen, K. (2007). Ideology and power: The influence of current neo-liberalism in society. *Journal of Community & Applied Social Psychology, 17*(4), 313–327.

Oatley, T. (2008). *International political economy.* Pearson/Longman.

Olssen, M., Codd, J., & O'Neill, A.-M. (2004). *Education policy: Globalization, citizenship, and democracy.* SAGE.

Ramachandran, V., & Walz, J. (2015). Haiti: Where has all the money gone? *Journal of Haitian Studies, 21*(1), 26–65. http://www.jstor.org/stable/24573148

Reback, G. (2009). *Free the market: Why only government can keep the marketplace competitive.* Portfolio.

Reisigl, M., & Wodak, R. (2009). The discourse-historical approach (DHA). In R. Wodak & M. Meyer (Eds.), *Methods of critical discourse analysis* (pp. 87–121). SAGE Publications.

Reuters. (2009, November 26). Haiti bars ex-President's party from elections for parliament. *New York Times.* http://www.nytimes.com/2009/11/26/world/americas/26haiti.html?_r=1

Rogers, R. (2011). Becoming discourse analysts: Constructing meanings and identities. *Critical Inquiry in Language Studies, 8*(1), 72–104.

Smith, A. (1776). *The wealth of nations.* W. Strahan and T. Cadell.

Sprague, J. (2009, April). Haiti: Fanmi Lavalas banned; voter apprehension widespread. *Interpress Service News*.

Stiglitz, J. (2003). *Globalization and its discontents*. W. W. Norton.

Stiglitz, J. (2010). *Free fall: America, free markets, and the sinking of the world economy*. W. W. Norton.

Tabb, W. (2002). *Unequal partners: A primer on globalization*. The New Press.

Van Dijk, T. (1993). Critical discourse analysis. *Discourse & Society*, *4*(2), 352–371.

Wacquant, L. (2010). Crafting the neoliberal state: Workfare, prisonfare, and social insecurity. *Sociological Forum*, *25*(2), 197–220. http://www.jstor.org/stable/40783391

Weiner, L. (2012). Privatizing public education: The neoliberal model. *Race, Poverty & the Environment*, *19*(1), 35–37. http://www.jstor.org/stable/41762537

Wodak, R., & Meyer, M. (2009). Critical discourse analysis: History, agenda, theory, and methodology. In R. Wodak & M. Meyer (Eds.), *Methods of critical discourse analysis* (pp. 1–33). SAGE Publications.

Chapter 13 Narratives of Grit by African American Women: Standing Tall Against Racial Microaggressions While Advancing to Community College Senior Leadership Positions

Toya Michelle Webb

Being the first in my family to graduate from high school led to a never-ending journey to pursue higher education and a higher calling to one day help those who come from backgrounds analogous to mine. I have been faced with numerous life events that seemed unrelenting and impossible to overcome. By the time I turned 21, my second child was born. Married, with two small children, a high school diploma, and a passion for learning, it was my time to go to college. I was nervous. No one in my immediate family had ever taken this step. I was afraid, but I did it anyway. As I walked through the doors of my community college in Upstate New York, only miles from the Fort Drum military base where my husband was stationed, I felt an overwhelming sense of anxiety.

My thoughts almost became paralyzing. But I had come too far and endured too much to cave in to fear. Besides, my two toddlers were counting on me. I knew it would be hard. I also knew it would be worth it. I chose to silence those inner voices and I walked bravely into the admissions office to begin a new journey that would ultimately change the course of my life. Fast forward 20 years later. After earning an associate degree, a bachelor's degree in journalism and sociology, a master's degree in integrated marketing communications and working as a journalist and public relations professional, I found myself back in the community college setting. This time, instead of as a student, I was an employee eager to help improve lives and further the community college mission. As I worked my way into the ivory tower, I was never blinded by my race or gender. Neither was anyone else.

Understanding Microaggressions

Microaggressions is a term from the 1970s that is credited to Chester Pierce (1927–2016), a Black psychiatrist and tenured professor at Harvard Medical School. As an expert on the topic of microaggressions and an author of numerous books and articles, Pierce declared that in today's day and age people of color are more likely to be prone to racism that is subtler than the days of the pre-civil rights era when racism was more blatant and overt (Bridges, 2019). However, Cole (2016) argues that contemporary racism is multifaceted. The same is true of racial microaggressions, defined as brief and everyday slights, insults, indignities, and denigrating messages that are sent to people of color (usually) by well-intentioned White people who are unaware of the hidden messages being communicated (Sue, 2010). "In their totality, racial microaggressions are inescapable and are cumulative expressions of racist views, dysconscious ideologies, and institutionalized practices toward people of color" (Corbin et al., 2018, p. 630). Research has shown that the impact of racial microaggressions is emotional (Holder et al., 2015), physiological, and financial. In fact, Gates (2014) explains that microaggressions in the workplace can diminish and stigmatize employees, contributing to a $450 billion to $550 billion per year loss in U.S. workforce productivity.

Zamani (2003) argues that inequities and injustices in the United States against African Americans as a group have led to the oppression of Black women (p. 3), making their double outsider status even more detrimental. Holder et al. (2015) assert that exposure to the daily assault of racial microaggressions has significant mental health consequences such as anxiety, paranoia, depression, sleep difficulties, lack of confidence, worthlessness, intrusive cognitions, helplessness, and loss of drive (p. 165). Microaggressions have become the norm and even though they can be intentional or unintentional, they communicate hostile, insulting messages that negatively impact people of color, as noted by Davis (2018), Sue et al. (2007), and Wang, Castro, and Cunningham (2014).

The Impact of Microaggressions

Bridges (2019) describes incidents of microaggressions to be verbal (spoken comments) or non-verbal (behavior), interpersonal (individuals who inflict microaggressions on others), or institutional (organization-level arrangements that communicate negative or hostile messages to people of color). To further explicate, Sue et al. (2007) describe three forms of microaggressions:

1. *Microinvalidation.* It is "characterized by communications that exclude, negate, or nullify the psychological thoughts, feelings, or experiential reality of a person of color" (p. 274). This includes telling a Black person that he or she sounds "articulate" or asking a person of Asian descent "where are you really from?" The hidden messages in these examples are the insinuations that Black people do not normally speak well and that Asians are foreigners.
2. *Microassault.* It is an "explicit racial derogation characterized primarily by a verbal or nonverbal attack meant to hurt the intended victim through name-calling, avoidant behavior, or purposeful discriminatory actions" (p. 274). These "old-fashioned" acts of racism may include racial epithets, swastika displays, or refusing to serve Blacks in a restaurant.
3. *Microinsult.* It is characterized by "communications that convey rudeness and insensitivity and demean a person's racial heritage or identity" (p. 274). Bridges (2019) suggests an example of a microinsult is when President Donald J. Trump referred to Mexican immigrants as rapists, drug dealers, and criminals during his 2016 presidential campaign (pp. 214–216).

Additional examples of microaggressions, according to Sue et al. (2007), include "color blindness," the concept of refusing to acknowledge a person's race by stating "I don't see color" or "there is one race, the human race" (p. 282). Edwards (2017) argues:

> By refusing to acknowledge color or privilege, European Americans can reduce guilt while experiencing antagonistic attitudes toward members of racial and ethnic minority groups by blaming them for the continued discussion of race. These challenges, contrary to the expressed beliefs of those who endorse Color-Blind Racial Attitudes (CoBRAs), make resolution of prejudice in our society more difficult. (p. 12)

Moreover, "Second-class citizen" microaggressions transpire when a White person is given preferential treatment as a consumer over a person of color

(Sue et al., 2007, p. 276). The microaggression in this case, according to Sue et al. (2007), is carried out when a Black person is passed over by a taxi driver who instead picks up a White passenger with the assumption that Whites are less dangerous. Another example is when a person of color is mistaken as a service worker or "the help." The underlying message is that Blacks are servants and do not hold high-status positions.

The aforementioned stereotypes, coupled with microaggressions, may add another layer of complexity for the Black woman, thus making it more of a constant struggle for them to succeed in the workplace. While Terry (2013) studied Black women in senior leadership positions in a technical college in North Carolina and confirmed the growing need to further explore the impact of stereotypes, the study did not explore microaggressions (daily slights based on race) against Black women in higher education and the impact thereof. My study sought to understand the repercussions of microaggressions and how Black women successfully navigate these occurrences, in addition to the responsibilities she must handle as a leader. To be successful, it is without question that these women must possess grit.

Statement of the Problem

Even from the days of slavery, a Black woman's full worth has never been fully appreciated (DuMonthier et al., 2017). From the cotton fields to breastfeeding and caring for the children of their White slave masters, the Black woman is no stranger to hard work. Yet, she remains denigrated and disregarded (Burkley. 2010). Even if she tried, she cannot separate her race from her gender. Dualism, the reality of being Black and a woman can feel like a curse (Mosley-Anderson, 2001).

The mass media broadcast of Black women in reality shows can sometimes perpetuate the stereotypes such as the ones that portray Black women as welfare queens, angry, promiscuous, and aggressive (Collins, 2000). The stigma from these stereotypes also carries into the workplace, creating yet another obstacle for Black women to overcome (Corbin et al., 2018; Dickens & Chavez, 2017; Durr &Wingfield, 2011; Jones et al., 2016; Mason, 2016). Stereotypes then become the basis for microaggressions, daily verbal or non-verbal insults based on race, leading to "racial battle fatigue," a term used to describe the stress associated with microaggressions that rear their heads as mental, emotional, and physical strain (Acuff, 2018, p. 175). This can lead to isolation and marginalization of Black women in the workplace. For clarification, the terms African American and Black are used interchangeably throughout this study.

When examining the topic of African American women administrators in higher education, most studies focus on their leadership styles, obstacles to career advancement, their need for mentors, and their experiences with overt racism (Byrd, 2016; Corbin et al., 2018; Hall et al., 2011; Mason, 2016). However, there remains an information gap in the body of research focusing specifically on African American women and their experiences with dealing with microaggressions as senior leaders in community colleges and what motivates them to persist.

Research Purposes and Questions

The purpose of this qualitative study was to explore narratives of grit through the lenses of African American women serving as senior leaders in Illinois community colleges and to share their personal stories of fortitude and perseverance. This study provided a deeper understanding of the challenges that African American women face in positions of leadership at Illinois community colleges and insights into their determination to succeed. The central question guiding this narrative study was: *What are the pathways of African American women to their senior leadership positions in Illinois community colleges?* Additional guiding questions were:

- What are the various contexts of these women's lives that have been shaping their individual identities as African American women and leaders?
- How have their life and work experiences been affected by racial microaggressions?

Theoretical and Methodological Approaches to the Study

One of the dominant research paradigms applied in educational research is the critical paradigm, which suggests that we live in a power-laden society. Lukenchuk (2013) further explains that critical paradigm is grounded in political perspectives on knowledge and research and on neo-Marxist or critical theory perspectives. It is a popular focus among educational researchers and inspires an array of research and scholarly projects focused on feminism, critical race and ethnicity, queer, and disability studies. "The critical paradigm situates its research in social justice issues and seeks to address the political, social, and economic issues, which lead to social oppression, conflict, struggle, and power structures at whatever levels these might occur" (Kivunja & Kuyini, 2017, p. 35). This study drew upon several critical perspectives, including Critical race theory and Black feminist theory, which this study examines in detail.

Creswell (2012) describes qualitative research as an inquiry approach useful for exploring and understanding a central phenomenon. To learn about the phenomenon, the researcher asks participants broad, general questions, collects the detailed views of each participant in the form of words or images, then analyzes the information to create themes. From these data, the researcher interprets the meaning of the information, drawing on personal reflections and past research. This process typically results in a structured report that is flexible and displays the researcher's biases and thoughts (Creswell, 2012, p. 626).

This study employed a qualitative research design by incorporating the following six steps as identified by Creswell (2012): (a) identifying a research process, (b) reviewing the literature, (c) specifying a purpose for research, (d) collecting data, (e) and analyzing and interpreting data. Hesse-Biber and Leavy (2011) define qualitative research as a holistic approach that explicitly integrates epistemology, methodology, and method in order to develop unique approaches to the study of the social world (p. 5).

Hesse-Biber and Leavy (2011) use a metaphor to describe qualitative research as a dance routine, as compared to the linear, step-like characteristic of quantitative research. For example, this qualitative study began with an inductive approach; it started with "specific data out of which more general ideas or theories" later emerged (Hesse-Biber & Leavy, 2011, p. 13). The authors further explain that in qualitative research, questions tend to be exploratory and descriptive in order to: (a) describe social phenomena and their meanings to relevant actors (the *what* questions), and (b) understand and explain social patterns and processes (the *how* questions). The *what* questions in this study focused on individuals (African American women) in social settings (Illinois community colleges), looking for meanings that exist in, emerge from, and are consequential for those settings (Gubrium & Holstein, 1997 as cited in Hesse-Biber & Leavy, 2011, p. 14).

In particular, qualitative researchers attempt to interpret the social meaning people attribute to their experiences, circumstances, and situations. Hesse-Biber and Leavy (2011) further add that, for qualitative researchers, at the heart of their work is the meaning they extract from their data (p. 4). As such, the purpose of this qualitative study was to explore narratives of grit through the lenses of African American women serving as senior leaders in Illinois community colleges and to share their personal stories of oppression and perseverance. This study provided a deeper understanding of the challenges that African American women face in positions of leadership and gained insights into their determination to succeed.

Critical Race Theory

This qualitative study was informed by critical race theory (CRT), an umbrella term for diverse research developed in a multidisciplinary and interdisciplinary context. CRT accepts that racism is insidious and normalized (Hesse-Biber & Leavy, 2011, p. 24). Atwood and López (2014) assert that CRT also counters the traditional methodologies by providing a framework that addresses and ameliorates issues of oppression, poverty, or deprivation of people of color, adding that CRT "challenges dominant stock stories that construct realities in order to legitimize the power of the dominant group" (p. 1144). This study benefited from CRT precisely because it featured African American women whose lives were directly impacted by microaggressions and racism, resulting in marginalization, isolation, invisibility, discrimination, and unfair treatment (Corbin et al., 2018; Graham, 2015; Holder et al., 2015; Howard-Hamilton, 2003; Patitu & Hinton, 2003).

Black Feminist Theory

Black feminist theory was utilized in this study as a theoretical lens that focuses specifically on African American women and their lived experiences. While Black feminist thought can be difficult to encapsulate, Collins (2000) explicates the following:

> Black Feminist Thought must both be tied to Black women's lived experiences and aim to better those experiences in some fashion. When such thought is sufficiently grounded in Black feminist practice, it reflects this dialogical relationship. Black Feminist Thought encompasses general knowledge that helps U.S. Black women survive in, cope with, and resist our differential treatment. (p. 31)

Howard-Hamilton (2003) affirms that using Black feminist thought and critical race as theoretical frameworks offer "promise for understanding the intersecting identities of African American women" and can explain ways in which their needs can be effectively addressed (p. 21). Additionally, there are three key themes that encompass Black feminist thought:

- First, it is shaped and produced by the experiences Black women have encountered in their lives.
- Second, although the stories and experiences of each woman are unique, there are intersections of experiences between and among Black women.
- Third, although commonalities do exist among Black women, the diversity of class, religion, age, and sexual orientation of Black women

as a group are multiple contexts from which their experiences can be revealed and understood. (Howard-Hamilton, 2003, p. 21)

Using CRT and interpretive paradigms, in addition to Black feminist theory, provided a rich foundation for exploring the goals of this study. African American women leaders in Illinois community colleges face a variety of challenges that can be examined in depth and detailed precisely through their lived experiences. Qualitative critical research allows the reader to visualize and better connect to participants' stories through a narrative inquiry and counter-storytelling approach.

While the percentage of Black women holding leadership positions in the Illinois community college system is both dismal and concerning, this study delved deeper into the lived experiences of these women and shared how they navigate the challenges related to their double insider status. Additionally, while some studies describe in broad terms incidents of microaggressions, this study further explored the three forms of microaggressions and dissected the hidden messages and racist ideologies through a storytelling approach. This study explored the challenges, including microaggressions, that these community college leaders face using storytelling and counter-storytelling as a way to delve deeper into their lived experiences and to learn more about their formative years using critical race theory and Black feminist theory as theoretical underpinnings.

Narrative Inquiry Research Design

Wertz et al. (2011) reveal that narrative research aims to explore and conceptualize human experience as it is represented in textual form. Grounded in hermeneutics (interpretive paradigm), phenomenology, ethnography, and literary analysis, narrative research eschews methodological orthodoxy in favor of doing what is necessary to capture the lived experiences of people in terms of their own meaning-making and to theorize about it in insightful ways (p. 225).

Kohler Riessman and Speedy as noted in Clandinin (2006) argue that since the late 1960s "the idea of narrative has penetrated almost every discipline and school," emphasizing that it is "no longer the sole province of literary scholarship, narrative study is now cross-disciplinary, not fitting within the boundaries of any single scholarly field" (p. 45). Clandinin and Connelly (2000), who are experts on narrative inquiry, define the narrative process as a "collaboration between researcher and participants, over time, in a place or series of places, and in social interaction with milieus" (p. 20). The authors further add that the "inquirer enters this matrix in the midst and progresses in the same spirit, concluding the inquiry still in the midst of living and telling, reliving and retelling, the stories of the experiences that made up people's lives, both individual and social" (p. 20). Wertz et al. (2011) explain that a unique aspect of narrative research is that "it endeavors to explore the whole account rather than fragmenting it into discursive units or thematic categories. It is not the parts that are significant in human life, but how the parts are integrated to create a whole—which is meaning" (p. 226).

Narrative, and counter-narrative by extension, was the best suited methodological approach to this study, which sought to understand the lived experiences of African American women from their childhood experiences to the challenges they face as leaders in Illinois community colleges.

Counter-Storytelling

Solórzano and Yosso (2002) define counter-storytelling as a method of telling the stories of those people whose experiences are not often told (e.g., those on the margins of society). Counter-storying is a tool for exposing, analyzing, and challenging the majoritarian stories of racial privilege. Furthermore, counter-stories can shatter complacency, challenge the dominant discourse on race, and further the struggle for racial reform (p. 32).

Much like the stories that come alive in this study, Merriweather Hunn, Guy, and Manglitz (2006) assert that narrative and counter-stories take time to tell, to unpack, and to address, especially when they contain components that make them emotionally liable and invite resistance and denial. Honoring the voices of those who are telling their stories allows the time and respect for experience to be communicated and discussed, thus emphasizing the importance of what is being said (p. 115). Merriweather Hunn et al. (2006) describe three genres of counter-stories that are typically used by CRT scholars. The first is "personal stories"; these include the experiences of persons of color and detail how they have dealt with race discrimination and other unfair treatment. The second is "other people's stories or narratives"; these comprise of stories that other people tell that have a "larger than life" quality. They are usually powerful and relatable to those who have similar experiences or stories to tell. The third genre of counter-stories is "composite stories," which is an accumulation of individual stories (p. 245). This study utilized "personal stories" through narrative inquiry to illustrate the participants' struggles and underscore the need for change.

Ikemoto (1997, as cited in Solorzano & Yosso, 2002) asserts that responding to the majoritarian stories should not be the sole purpose or outcome of counter-stories: "By responding only to the standard story, we let it dominate the discourse" (p. 136), adding that there are numerous stories of people of color whose counter-stories remain unheard and that storytelling and counter-storytelling can help strengthen traditions of social, political, and cultural survival and resistance. Finally, part of the rationale for employing counter-stories is based on the premise maintained by Solorzano and Yosso (2002) that counter-stories serve at least four functions:

1. They can build community among those at the margins of society by putting a human and familiar face to educational theory and practice.
2. They can challenge the perceived wisdom of those at society's center by providing a context to understand and transform established belief systems.
3. They can open new windows into the reality of those at the margins of society by showing possibilities beyond the ones they live and demonstrate that they are not alone in their position.
4. They can teach others that by combining elements from both the story and the current reality, one can construct another world that is richer than either the story or the reality alone. (p. 36)

Moreover, Atwood and López (2014) add:

> Counter-stories highlight what conventional analytic methods, traditional social science theories, and post-positivist research methods often miss: an understanding that the world is not racially neutral but is always already rife with racism ... counter-stories do not aim to provide a truer understanding of truth, but rather, to complicate our understanding of "truth" as such. In fact, as a theoretical and political movement, CRT does not seek permission or approval from the larger research community. (p. 1145)

CRT counter-stories seek to counter the master narrative through the voices of those who have been marginalized and whose lived experiences have been negatively portrayed. As such, narrative inquiry and counter-storytelling were both suitable for this study considering the marginalization and stereotyping of African American women driven by the master narrative has been the dominating discourse since the days of slavery. This study aimed to help change that narrative and reshape how Black women are perceived and treated in today's society and within the confines of academia.

Additionally, this study was born out of a paucity of research that currently exists on the obstacles that Black women encounter as leaders in higher education, especially challenges related to grit and the everyday occurrences of racial microaggressions. While Duckworth et al. (2007) and other researchers such as Arouty (2015), Boatmun (2016), Bogin (2017), Chang (2014), and Patron (2012) have all studied grit, the focus was mainly in relation to student success and was usually conducted through quantitative studies.

Furthermore, a limitation of Kearns's (2015) study on grit in superintendents was that a quantitative instrument could not adequately measure and address "what" contributed to the grittiness demonstrated by participants. With insights gleaned from Kearns's (2015) study, I employed qualitative methods to explore the formative years of participants that allowed me to delve deeper into their stories as well as the "why" in addition to the "what" behind their motivation to persist as leaders in higher education.

Participants

According to Leavy (2014), sampling approaches in qualitative research may be convenient, theoretical, or purposive. Sampling is "the strategic, referred, random, and/or serendipitous selection of participants" (Saldaña, 2011, p. 33). For this study, through purposive sampling based on specific characteristics determined by the goals of the study, I recruited a group of nine homogenous participants out of which all nine consented. Hesse-Biber and Leavy (2011) assert that homogenous groups, members with similar traits or characteristics, "are appropriate when the researcher wants to gain in-depth understanding about how members of a particular group experience or think about a given issue" (p. 179), adding that because qualitative researchers are after meaning, they look at a "process" or the "meanings" participants attribute to their given social situations (p. 4).

During the research phase of this study, I visited the websites of all 48 community colleges in Illinois and discovered that there were only four African American women at the presidential helm; including one who resigned, narrowing the pool of African American women presidents down to only three, thus making the sample size too small to be suitably considered for this study. Additionally, because this study aimed to re-story the lived experiences of African American women who were still advancing to senior leadership positions, college presidents, who had already reached the highest office in academia, did not meet these criteria for this study.

Participants were selected based on the following criteria: Women who (a) identify as Black or African American; (b) work as senior administrators, defined as an associate dean, dean, executive director, chief, or vice president, working in an Illinois community college and still advancing in their careers; and (c) currently reside in close proximity to a large metropolitan city in the Midwest. Nine women agreed to participate in this study.

Sources of Data and Data Collection Strategies

In qualitative research, it is important for the researcher to obtain useful data from an array of sources in order to adequately address the research questions. As such, there were several sources of data that were appropriate for this study: face-to-face interviews, journals and memos, artifacts, and visual materials.

Interviews

Hesse-Biber and Leavy (2011) maintain that an in-depth interview is a commonly used method of data collection in qualitative research because it "relies on individuals as the point of departure for the research process and assumes that individuals have unique and important knowledge about the social world that is ascertainable and can be shared through verbal communication" (p. 94). Kim (2016) further explains that the purpose of interviews in narrative inquiry is to allow stories to be told of those who might have been marginalized or alienated from the mainstream and whose valuable insights and reflections would not otherwise come to light (p. 166). Over 10-weeks, I conducted nine individual face-to-face audio-recorded interviews with Black women leaders from five different community colleges in Illinois.

Documents, Artifacts, and Visual Materials

Qualitative researchers interpret meaning from the data gathered in many forms. This includes documents such as letters, e-mails, journals, files, and other artifacts that participants are willing to share to help tell their story. I used a journal to record my reflections, thoughts, and observations along the way. As noted in Hesse-Biber and Leavy (2011), researchers should describe the research participants in sufficient detail to allow readers to get a clear picture of the salient characteristics. In essence, the descriptive picture drawn of each participant should come alive. Saldaña and Omasta (2018) contend that artifacts have stories of their own, adding that they speak of origins, histories, moments, how they were collected, created, inherited, and/or purchased. "Since artifacts can't speak for themselves, researchers need to infer their history or use them as conversation pieces with participants to learn more about the relationship between objects and humans" (Saldaña & Omasta, 2018, p. 74).

Data Analysis

Individual, face-to-face interviews were the main source of data analysis for this study. Janesick (1998) likens qualitative researchers to choreographers who must find and design a sequence of steps to tell an effective story. This study benefited from building on John Dewey's (1859–1952) theory of experience by utilizing the closely related Deweyan theory outlined by narrative researchers Clandinin and Connelly's (2000) three-dimensional narrative inquiry space—*interaction* (personal and social), *continuity* (past, present, and future) and *situation* (place). Clandinin and Connelly (2000) explain that "interaction" involves a notion that encompasses a four-directions inquiry (Inward, Outward, Backward, and Forward):

- *Inward* (feelings, hopes, aesthetic reactions, and moral dispositions)
- *Outward* (existential conditions such as the environment)
- *Backward* and *Forward* (temporality—past, present, and future) (p. 50).

By employing Clandinin and Connelly's (2000) three-dimensional space approach as well as the three research questions that guided this study, I was able to garner rich data that led to a rigorous coding process.

At the end of this process, the following four major themes emerged: (a) *Challenges with Being Black and a Woman*, (b) *Deconstructing Microaggressions*, (c) *More Than Perseverance: Grit Redefined*, and (d) *Untold Stories: On the Quest to Change.*

Challenges with Being Black and a Woman

Undervalued

For the participants in this study, being undervalued was a common thread in their experiences. This ranged from being thwarted from promotions to being underestimated to not being recognized for the contributions they made to their institutions. Instead of being respected leaders, many of them were treated as if they were of lower rank and authority.

Disregarded

Imagine being in a room full of executives and sharing an idea that will benefit the institution only to be ignored until a White colleague joins the discussion and who later, gets all the credit. This was a typical work day for most of the participants in this study, who often felt that they had no voice, little influence, and were overlooked by their peers.

Defiled by Stereotypes

Stereotypes are still negative forces that impede the success of Black women in the workplace. One of the stereotypes that was cited by all nine participants was the angry Black woman trope. Despite having a noble characteristic of strength, the participants also noted that, if a Black woman is perceived as *too* strong, she may be considered threatening or intimidating. In addition to being perceived as aggressive, other stereotypes described by the participants varied from being viewed as lazy to being labeled a "bitch."

Deconstructing Microaggressions Standing Tall: Conquering Microaggressions

One of the most significant insights that this study contributes to the body of research is the examination of microaggressions and the realization of their pervasiveness in the workplace. While there remains a paucity of research on the topic of microaggressions, specifically in regard to African American women leaders in higher education, solutions on how to address and avert microaggressions in the workplace are also in dearth supply.

While many of the participants in this study agreed that one must maintain a high degree of professionalism when confronted with microaggressions, they all contended that microaggressions in the workplace must not be ignored. From training to confronting the issue head on, each participant offered suggestions on how to respond to microaggressions in the workplace, adding that ignoring them can eat away at productivity and further inflict unjust pain on people of color.

More Than Perseverance: Grit Redefined

In addition to the challenges that participants faced being Black and a woman, along with the pervasiveness of racial microaggressions in the workplace, this study found the concept of grit to be more than just a commitment toward long-term goals. Grit, for the participants in this study, was about how they each interpreted and responded to hardships, believed in their own strength, and sustained an unshakeable faith.

In recent years, researchers have become increasingly interested in the topic of grit; yet, their focus usually pertained to quantitative studies and grit was declared as a trait that only doggedly determined warriors possess. Therefore, as a result of this study, I offer an amended definition of grit. As demonstrated by the participants in this study, grit was shown to be a combination of faith, failure, and fortitude. Despite the general perception of ironclad grit, this study revealed that gritty individuals do grow weary, do get discouraged, and they do fail; however, they do not accept failure as final.

Furthermore, the most common definition of grit is described by Duckworth et al. (2007) as passion and perseverance, or sustained effort over a period of time to reach long-term goals. For the purposes of this study, grit was defined as firmness of mind or spirit, unyielding courage in the face of hardship or danger. From the challenges participants faced to how they overcame them, grit was a dominant theme illustrated throughout this study. It also is another factor that ties to the second research question about the contexts that have been shaping their lives. While many and various factors can be taken into consideration when analyzing the successful careers of the nine participants, including their upbringing, education, character, values, and especially their faith and religion, it was evident that grit was vital to their survival.

Untold Stories: On the Quest to Change

As I ended each interview, I realized that the participants' stories of bravery, success, and courage were not the stories that are typically broadcast in the media. Rarely are there televised stories of Black women, like the participants, who are recognized as educated scholars, system disruptors, and advocates for social justice. These women flourish in places and spaces where they are not welcomed. They persist in the workplace in the midst of intolerable pressure and pain. They stand tall against microaggressions and their stories should not be hidden. They represent the untold and often unseen characteristics of Black women as resilient, beautiful, and survivors, descriptors that if used in the media and in everyday life, could help combat stereotypes and change the narrative.

Summary of the Findings

Essentially, the purpose of this qualitative study was to explore narratives of grit through the lenses of African American women serving as senior leaders in Illinois community colleges and to share their personal stories of fortitude and perseverance. This study was designed to provide a deeper understanding of the challenges that African American women face in positions of leadership in Illinois community colleges and insights into their determination to succeed. Through several cycles of coding and rigorous data analysis, this study used narrative inquiry to re-story the lives of nine participants who discussed their everyday struggles and the realities that have hindered them in the workplace. This study emerged from gaps identified in the body of research and recommendations for future studies made by several researchers and revealed the need for additional studies that focus on the storytelling of Black women working in higher education.

Through narrative inquiry, I aimed to uncover each participant's story, how she developed her sense of identity on the path to leadership, and the obstacles she encountered along the way. As such, this study contributes to lessening an insufficient existing body of literature that denotes a growing interest in exploring those challenges, including the pervasiveness of racial microaggressions, grit, and additional research on Black women in leadership. Moreover, it is important to note that the concept of grit became a major component of this study. Through in-depth data analysis shaped by the participants' stories, this study explored the notion of grit and redefined its characteristics, expanding it from a commonly understood focus on perseverance and endurance to reach long-term goals to a more holistic embodiment that encompasses faith and personal fortitude developed in the formative years.

Overall, data from this study provide convincing evidence demonstrating a harsh reality, confirming that being Black and a woman comes with a double layer of hardship. Each participant in this study detailed various obstacles she encountered due to her race and gender, making it difficult for her to advance or be recognized for her work. Each participant mentioned that being Black and a woman placed her under a microscope that unfairly scrutinized her work and her emotions, leaving her exhausted and oftentimes discouraged. Participants in this study also reported being alienated, denied opportunities for promotion, and being unfairly judged when they showed emotion or expressed an opinion that differed from their White colleagues.

Many participants asserted that their discriminatory and inequitable treatment was related to long-held beliefs and stereotypes about Black women. Throughout this study, the participants shared examples on how they were unfairly treated in comparison to their White colleagues. From being ignored to passed over for opportunities that they were more than qualified for, the data provide convincing evidence demonstrating that Black women are treated differently in a number of ways. For example, when it came to performing on the job, the participants' work was under greater scrutiny and they were expected to carry out their duties with little to no support from their supervisors as compared to their White colleagues. When it came to being considered for promotion, the standard was lowered for their White colleagues who were able to seamlessly advance to higher positions even though they were not the most qualified.

Another insight from this study reveals an inability for Black women to express themselves in meetings, or openly disagree with ideas without being condemned. For example, when my participants countered ideas or expressed themselves in a professional manner, they were perceived as aggressive and even disrespectful, while they noted that White men are seen as powerful when they disagree. These findings portend that if Black women continue to be criticized when they speak up, it will remain nearly impossible for them to successfully challenge inequitable systems and change the status quo. This study also found that even though the nine participants were considered to be leaders at their institutions, at times, the obstacles they faced and a lack of support and resources rendered them powerless.

This study also revealed that the participants in this study, unlike their White colleagues, were often overlooked and not given credit for ideas or noticed for their contributions, even though most of them arrived to work early and stayed late into the night in order to fulfill their duties. An important revelation that surfaced about the motives behind their work ethics, was, despite how they were perceived by their colleagues, my study participants did not work to be praised or to be in the limelight; instead, they worked in higher education because they wanted to make a difference and believed they played a crucial role in transforming the lives of others through the power of education.

The challenges of being Black and a woman are clearly different from a woman of any other race as well as that of a man, including a Black man. However, like most Black women, the participants in this study seemed to project a high level of confidence and a strong sense of self developed early on and fostered by their parents and grandparents. The prevalence of racial microaggressions is another factor among the many challenges that my participants encountered in the workplace. The challenge with microaggressions is that they can be so subtle that the victim may not understand what is happening in that moment. Furthermore, if not addressed, microaggressions can turn into "micro-traumas" and result in "death by a thousand cuts" (Dastagir, 2018, "Death by Cuts," para. 1). Therefore, to combat microaggressions, participants in this study provided suggestions on how to address them when they occur in the workplace. Additionally, the participants called on college presidents and chief human resource officers to lead the charge by offering cultural competence training and taking a stand against all forms of racism, including microaggressions.

The general picture that emerged from data analysis conducted as part of this study reveals that even though the participants concurred that microaggressions should be addressed as soon as they happen, depending on the situation, they were wary that it might be perceived as confrontation and may perpetuate stereotypes of the Angry Black Woman trope. Therefore, the need for institutions to provide education and ongoing professional development is deemed a critical factor in creating an environment conducive to crucial conversations, with the ultimate goal of improving race relations in the workplace. Furthermore, many of the participants stated that institutions must also be willing to see the impact that inaction and silence can have on employees, their greatest resources, in addition to perpetuating a racially hostile work environment.

Additionally, institutions must be culturally responsive, not through lip service or words carefully crafted in their Strategic Plans, but they must be committed to the cause. This will require courageous leaders and fearless change agents. As such, the findings of this study reveal the need for the president of the institution, the president's executive team, and the board of trustees to join forces and leverage this as a means to invest in employees, students, and the overall mission of the institution.

Overall, it appears that institutions struggle with understanding the long-term effects of microaggressions, and uncertainty remains on how to handle these everyday occurrences in the workplace. This lack of knowledge and awareness of the pervasiveness of microaggressions continues to create a conundrum for Black women who desire to stand up for themselves, but must avoid perpetuating stereotypes that can become self-destructive and counter-productive to what they would hope to accomplish.

Additionally, a clear and consistent finding throughout this study was the need to challenge systems that hinder Black women. However, in order for change to occur, there must be fearless change agents leading the cause, and change takes time, years, decades, and even centuries. Many of my study participants would argue that Martin Luther King Jr.'s dream is still a vision yet to be fully realized and that dismantling systems, where racism thrives, is not an easy feat.

"Stronger together" is not just a saying, but a reality from which people from all races can benefit. In fact, the participants in this study contend that nothing will change if people are not willing to challenge systemic and institutional racism, which is primarily responsible for many of the challenges Black women encounter in today's society. Equally important, this study reveals a need for institutions of higher education to take the lead by providing education and ongoing professional development for students and employees.

To put it differently, the participants in this study assert that institutions are well suited to be leaders in this area and must be committed beyond mere words. They portend, that if more people become educated and more light is shed on these pervasive societal issues, positive change would likely infiltrate classrooms, workspaces, and society as a whole in an effort to counter the dominant narrative on how Black women are treated, regarded, and perceived, while simultaneously dismantling stereotypes.

Moreover, when it comes to how Black women are sometimes perceived in relation to their roles and responsibilities, participants in this study recounted times when their qualifications and experience were questioned. This common phenomenon is based on stereotypes that classify Black women as intellectually inferior, even though, according to NCES (2019) and Roberts et al. (2018), Black women are one of the most educated demographics in the United States. The overall composition of my sample population also contradicts this stereotype with eight of the nine participants having earned at least a master's degree, five of them holding terminal degrees, and three of them pursuing their doctorates at the time of this study. Still, it is concerning that with a post-graduate education and years of experience in their respective fields, many of my participants were still undervalued and treated as if they were "unqualified."

Furthermore, it is apparent that stereotypes continue to create an extra invisible barrier for Black women, an impediment that has existed since their childhoods. For instance, during their interviews, participants in this study referenced a coach or another influential figure in their formative years who made them feel inferior during a time when they were still constructing their sense of identity. Their experiences confirm what Thomas et al. (2011) posit, that Black girls tend to experience oppression in their youth and have negative expectations placed on them from a variety of sources, including the media and teachers. By the same token, participants in my study identified the mainstream media, reality TV shows, and the dominant culture as perpetuating negative stereotypes that drive a false narrative.

Finally, in recent years, researchers have become increasingly interested in the topic of grit, yet the focus has mainly centered on quantitative studies related to student success. Researchers have also conceptualized grit as a trait that only doggedly determined warriors possess. However, data from my study show that grit is more than just endurance and the ability to achieve long-term goals.

For the participants in this study, grit was shown to be a combination of faith, failure, and fortitude. Grit is not only the ability to achieve goals, but it encompasses the disposition one possesses when working toward achieving those long-term goals. Specifically, as it relates to the women featured in this study, grit was found to be a four-letter word for faith. Participants referenced

Christ as their cornerstone and faith as their source of hope developed from childhood experiences and shaped through various trials and tribulations.

This study validates previous studies by Byrd (2016), Counts (2012), and Graham (2015) that conclude that Black women's reliance on faith or spirituality is a way to cope and sustain them during times of adversity. Likewise, Stevenson (2012) found that Black women coped with hardships through prayer and support systems. A surprising revelation that emerged from this study recognized that gritty people, as demonstrated by the participants in this study, do indeed fail, but they do not accept failure as final. Participants shared stories of how they bounced back from disappointments and failed opportunities and they credited their faith in Christ, who sustained them. However, faith was only part of their ability to persevere; it was not only their belief in their Savior, but also in themselves that fueled their motivation to persevere.

Noting the scarcity of African American women encompassing less than 5% of administrative positions in the Illinois community college system, Graham (2015) sought to identify the obstacles these women faced and the coping methods they employed to help them persist. Graham's recommendation to increase the sample population was also an impetus for this study; as a result, my study more than doubled the sample size of Graham's study increasing the number of participants from four to nine.

Insights gained from this study can be leveraged by institutions to help retain African American women in positions of leadership as well as to support African American women who aspire to higher levels of leadership. Findings from this study can also be utilized by human resources professionals to dismantle racist hiring practices, reshape institutional policies, address microaggressions, and create administrative procedures that mandate ongoing professional development with a deliberate focus on diversity, equity, and inclusion. Last, this study calls for African American women working in community colleges and those who work alongside African American women in community colleges to step up and serve as mentors and allies in a unified effort to overthrow decades-old racist ideologies and systems.

The findings of this study provide valuable insights into the unique challenges encountered by nine African American women serving as senior leaders in Illinois community colleges. Their narratives of hardship and grit provide first-hand knowledge of the struggles these participants have endured and continue to face. In addition to filling a gap in the body of research, especially as it relates to grit and racial microaggressions, this study provides thorough recommendations and advice on how institutions can improve the work environment in order to attract and retain African American women. I strongly believe that through qualitative analysis that resulted in four major themes and four subthemes, this study provides substantial evidence and in-depth information that can be leveraged to effect change.

Disturbingly, this study confirmed that the duality of race and gender for Black women, along with the pervasiveness of microaggressions and stereotypes still overshadow their success. Yet, the nine women in this study fought back and refused to be silenced; they remained hopeful, resolute, and firm in their faith as they encountered various obstacles and unexpected hurdles along the way.

References

Acuff, J. (2018). Confronting racial battle fatigue and comforting my Blackness as an educator. *Multicultural Perspectives*, *20*(3), 174–181.

Arouty, D. (2015). *Does character matter? The role of grit and resilience in predicting academic success* (Publication No. 3734789) [Doctoral dissertation]. ProQuest Dissertations and Theses Global.

Atwood, E., & López, G. R. (2014). Let's be critically honest: Towards a messier counterstory in critical race theory. *International Journal of Qualitative Studies in Education*, *27*(9), 1134–1154.

Boatmun, T. (2016). *Hope, grit, and academically successful non-traditional students at a regional, rural university: A narrative inquiry* (Publication No. 10038708) [Doctoral dissertation]. ProQuest Dissertations and Theses Global.

Bogin, L. (2017). *A portrait of college success: Grit, theories of intelligence, and cumulative life adversity* (Publication No. 10689593) [Doctoral dissertation]. ProQuest Dissertations and Theses Global.

Bridges, K. M. (2019). *Critical race theory: A primer.* Foundation Press.

Burkley, M. (2010). Are Black women invisible? *Psychology Today.* Retrieved from https://www.psychologytoday.com/us/blog/the-social-thinker/201012/are-black-women-invisible

Byrd, T. (2016). *Experiences of intersectionality: A phenomenological exploration of how black American women leaders respond to stigmatization in the workplace* (Publication No. 10196490) [Doctoral dissertation]. ProQuest Dissertations and Theses Global.

Chang, W. (2014). *Grit and academic performance: Is being grittier better?* (Publication No. 3681407) [Doctoral dissertation]. ProQuest Dissertations and Theses Global.

Clandinin, J. D. (2006, December), Narrative inquiry: A methodology for studying lived experience. *Research Studies in Music Education*, *27*(1), 44–55.

Clandinin, J. D., & Connelly, M. F. (2000). *Narrative inquiry: Experience and story in qualitative research.* Jossey-Bass.

Cole, M. (2016). *Racism: A critical analysis.* Pluto Press.

Collins, P. H. (2000). *Black feminist thought.* Routledge.

Corbin, N. A., Smith, W. A., & Garcia, J. R. (2018). Trapped between justified anger and being the strong Black woman: Black college women coping with racial battle fatigue at historically and predominantly White institutions. *International Journal of Qualitative Studies in Education, 31*(7), 626–643.

Counts, S. A. (2012). *Invisible woman? Narratives of black women leaders in southeastern two-year colleges* (Publication No. 3525892) [Doctoral dissertation]. ProQuest Dissertations and Theses Global.

Creswell, J. W. (2012). *Educational research: Planning, conducting, and evaluating quantitative and qualitative research* (4th ed.). Pearson.

Dastagir, A. E. (2018, February 28). Microaggressions don't just "hurt your feelings." *USA Today*. Retrieved from https://www.usatoday.com/story/news/2018/02/28/what-microaggressions-small-slights-serious-consequences/362754002/

Davis, S. M. (2018): When sistahs support sistahs: A process of supportive communication about racial microaggressions among Black women. *Communication Monographs, 86*(2), 133–157. https://doi.org/10.1080/03637751.2018.1548769

Dickens, D. D., & Chavez, E. L. (2017). Navigating the workplace: The costs and benefits of shifting identities at work among early career U.S. Black women. *Sex Roles, 78*(11–12), 760–774. https://doi-org.libweb.ben.edu/10.1007/s11199-017-0844-x

Duckworth, A. L., Peterson, C., Matthews, M. D., & Kelly, D. R. (2007). Grit: Perseverance and passion for long-term goals. *Journal of Personality and Social Psychology, 92*(6), 1087–1101.

DuMonthier, A., Childers, C., & Milli, J. (2017, June 26). *The status of Black women in the United States*. Institute for Women's Policy Research.

Durr, M., & Wingfield, A. M. (2011). Keep your "N" in check: African American women and the interactive effects of etiquette and emotional labor. *Critical Sociology, 37*(5), 557–571.

Edwards, J. F. (2017, Summer) Color-blind racial attitudes: Microaggressions in the context of racism and White privilege. *Administrative Issues Journal: Connecting Education, Practice, and Research, 7*(1), 5–18.

Gates, J. F. (2014, August 31). *Microaggression: The new workplace bigotry*. HuffPost. https://www.huffpost.com/entry/microaggression-the-new-w_b_5544663

Graham, M. (2015). *African American women administrators at community colleges of Illinois: An investigation of obstacles and persistence* (Publication No. 3739510) [Doctoral dissertation]. ProQuest Dissertations and Theses Global.

Hall, J. C., Everett, J. E., & Hamilton-Mason, J. (2011). Black women talk about workplace stress and how they cope. *Journal of Black Studies, 43*(2), 207–226.

Hesse-Biber, S. N., & Leavy, P. (2011). *The practice of qualitative research* (2nd ed.). SAGE Publications.

Holder, A., Jackson, M. A., & Ponterotto, J. G. (2015). Racial microaggression experiences and coping strategies of Black women in corporate leadership. *Qualitative Psychology, 2*(2), 164–180.

Howard-Hamilton, M. F. (2003). Theoretical frameworks for African American women. *New Directions for Student Services, 2003*(104), 19–27. https://doi-org.libweb.ben.edu/10.1002/ss.104

Illinois Community College Board. (2019). *Illinois community college system facts.* https://www.iccb.org/wp-content/pdfs/reports/ICCS_African_American_Report_2018.pdf

Jones, K. P., Peddie, C. I., Gilrane, V. L., King, E. B., & Gray, A. L. (2016). Not so subtle: A meta-analytic investigation of the correlates of subtle and overt discrimination. *Journal of Management, 42*(6), 1588–1613.

Kearns, J. (2015). *The examination of grit in California superintendents* (Publication No. 3738522) [Doctoral dissertation]. ProQuest Dissertations and Theses Global.

Kim, J. (2016). *Understanding narrative inquiry: The crafting and analysis of stories as research.* SAGE Publications.

Kivunja, C., & Kuyini, A. B. (2017). Understanding and applying research paradigms in educational contexts. *International Journal of Higher Education*, 6(5), 26–41.

Leavy, P. (Ed.). (2014). *Oxford handbook of qualitative research.* Oxford University Press. https://ebookcentral.proquest.com

Lukenchuk, A. (Ed.). (2013). *Paradigms of research for the 21st century: Perspectives and examples from practice.* Peter Lang

Mason, P. A. (2016). *The lived experiences of African American female superintendents* [Doctoral dissertation]. https://etd.ohiolink.edu/!etd.send_file?/accession=ohiou1450790580&disposition=inline

Merriweather Hunn, L. R., Guy, T. C., & Mangliitz, E. (2006, May 18–21). Who can speak for whom?: Using counterstorytelling to challenge racial hegemony. In M. Hagan & E. Goff (Eds.), *The many faces of adult education: Proceedings of the 47th Annual Adult Education Research Conference,* (pp. 244–250). University of Minnesota.

Mosley-Anderson, J. M. (2001). *Their perceptions of how others perceive them: Black women administrators internalize others perceptions of them as leaders* (Publication No. 3023265) [Doctoral dissertation]. ProQuest Dissertations and Theses Global.

National Center for Education Statistics. (2019). *Fast facts: Degrees conferred by race and sex.* U.S. Department of Education. https://nces.ed.gov/fastfacts/display.asp?id=72

Patitu, C. L. & Hinton, K. G. (2003). The experiences of African American women faculty and administrators in higher education: Has anything changed? *New Directions for Student Services, 2003*(104), 79–93.

Patron, I. M. (2012). *Exploring the experiences of successful first-generation community college students in Florida: A qualitative study* (Publication No. 3512970) [Doctoral dissertation]. ProQuest Dissertations and Theses Global.

Roberts, L. M., Mayo, A. J., Ely, R. J., & Thomas, S. A. (2018, MarchApril). Beating the odds. *Harvard Business Review.* Retrieved from https://hbr.org/2018/03/beating-the-odds

Saldaña, J. (2011). *Fundamentals of qualitative research: Understanding qualitative research.* Oxford University Press. https://ebookcentral.proquest.com

Saldaña, J., & Omasta, M. (2018). *Qualitative research: Analyzing life.* SAGE Publication.

Solórzano, D. G., & Yosso, T. J. (2002). Critical race methodology: Counter-storytelling as an analytical framework for education research. *Qualitative Inquiry, 8*(1), 23–44.

Stevenson, T. N. (2012). *Racial battle fatigue, role strain, and African-American faculty at public community colleges* (Publication No. 3530464) [Doctoral dissertation]. ProQuest Dissertations and Theses Global.

Sue, D. W. (2010, October 5). Racial microaggressions in everyday life: Is subtle bias harmless? *Psychology Today.* https://www.psychologytoday.com/us/blog/microaggressions-in-everyday-life/201010/racial-microaggressions-in-everyday-life

Sue, D. W., Capodilupo, C. M., Torino, G. C., Bucceri, J. M., Holder, A. M., Nadal, K. L., & Esquilin, M. (2007, May-June). Racial microaggressions in everyday life: Implications for clinical practice. *American Psychologist, 62*(4), 271–286.

Terry, D. (2013). *At the Intersection of race and gender: A narrative analysis of the career experiences of Black women senior leaders in community and technical college* (Publication No. 3575666) [Doctoral dissertation]. ProQuest Dissertations and Theses Global.

Thomas, A. J., Hacker, J. D., & Hoxha, D. (2011). Gendered racial identity of Black young women. *Sex Roles, 64*(7–8), 530–542.

Wang, K. T., Castro, A. J., & Cunningham, Y. L. (2014). Are perfectionism, individualism, and racial colorblindness associated with less cultural sensitivity? Exploring diversity awareness in White prospective teachers. *Journal of Diversity in Higher Education, 7*, 211–225.

Wertz, F. J., Charmaz, K., McMullen, L. M., Josselson, R., Anderson, R., & McSpadden, E. (2011). *Five ways of doing qualitative analysis: Phenomenological psychology, grounded theory, discourse analysis, narrative research, and intuitive inquiry.* Guilford Press.

Zamani, E. M. (2003). African American women in higher education. *New Directions for Student Services, 2003*(104), 5–18. https://doi-org.libweb.ben.edu/10.1002/ss.103

Chapter 14 Locked Gates and Chain-link Fences: A Generational Phenomenological Story of Disability

SHARON DUNCAN

Roots Planted: A Story

Once upon a not-so-distant time and in a not-so-distant land lived three little girls. Their lives revolved around playing Barbies, games of "ghost beware" at dusk, sewing lessons, riding the bus to Ford City, buying penny candy at the pet shop, and square-scooped sherbet cones at Prince Castle. At times their lives seemed to them idealistic and somewhat fairytale; as they were growing up in a middle-class suburban neighborhood in the 1960s, with stay-at-home moms and dads who arrived home at five for family dinner. The girls were connected by proximity, living in houses separated only by cyclone fences and a grassy alley. They lived so close you could call out, "Yo, Laura," or "Yo, Sharon," or "Yo, Debbie" till someone would answer the door. They shared the same Catholic faith, attended the same parish school, and were all about the same age. They shared dreams and made up fairytale stories while lying on blankets under Sharon's big backyard tree, sipping Kool-Aid from shiny metal tumblers, while munching on sugar wafer cookies. "So what do you want to be when you grow up?" "Where do you think we will live?" "Think we'll still be friends when we're old and married?"

Three girls, three friends for life ... and they lived happily ever after?

In order to understand the present, one has to look into the past. I (Sharon) am the collector of the group. I am compelled to collect the stories, to uncover the lived experiences that were interwoven in the fabric of our lives ... the common threads that bound us together then and continue to link us in the present.

The nine-year-old me runs through the kitchen, pulls open the pantry door and grabs an eight pack of empty Pepsi bottles from the floor. I have a shiny quarter in my pocket just waiting to be spent. With the 16 cents I would get from the bottles, I would be able to get a lot of penny candy. "Mom, I'm going," I yelled. "Where are you going young lady?" my grandmother Mere inquires. "Just up town with Laura and Debbie." "Be careful." "Don't worry Mere." I run by my Aunt Jackie washing dishes at the sink. I grab her apron string pretending to untie it and she slaps my hand. "Oh, Sharon, what a kidder." "See ya!" I run out the screen door and it slams behind me. I hear Mere yelling in the distance, but I'm off ... across the porch ... down the steps ... crisscrossing my fenced backyard, running through the back gate, which is hanging slightly open. I give it an extra shove to open it all the way and I head across the alley to Laura's yard. "Yo, Laura." She comes to the door with a brown bag in her hand holding two empty quart bottles from beer. (She will get five cents each for those.) "Ready? Let's go get Debbie." We travel down the driveway toward Central Avenue to go next door to Debbie's. We approach the fenced-in yard. A locked double gate extending across the driveway stops us in our tracks. Laura takes her free hand and opens the latch while I take my free hand and pull up the pole. In we go. We are sure to lock the gate again or face the wrath of Mrs. E., Debbie's mom. The gate must remain locked at all times. "Yo, Debbie," we call out on her back stoop. "Hi guys! I can go, but I have groceries to buy for my mom at Freshline." She goes back in the house and comes back out with her mom's old brown wallet and a list in one hand, and her little brother Chuckie's small chubby hand tightly clenched in the other. "I gotta bring Chuck; my mom gave me money so we can get sherbet cones from Prince Castle on the way back." We walk down the drive. Laura and I open the gate and Deb pulls Chuck through. We lock it behind us. Looking both ways, we cross Central Avenue. Mere's "be careful" rings in my brain. Laura and I take the lead. "Come on Chuck, walk faster," Deb says. As we make our way from our neighborhood and the safety of the locked gates and cyclone fences into the vast world ... we called: UPTOWN.

> Fenced yards, protecting Chuckie, shopping for groceries, locked gates, teasing Aunt Jackie, being corrected by Mere; the roots of our childhood; the common strings that joined our lives.

As I embarked on my research, I returned to the past: to the relationships, the values, the truths, that connected our experiences. I was compelled to provide a visual to represent the people and the relationships, which represent the roots of this inquiry. I was determined to seek a fluid representation for the connected history. Visually, I was drawn to a root structure and all the little threads that come from and connect to the root. The cyclone fence (like the one that surrounded my backyard and Debbie's whole yard) with its supporting bar and all the angular connections, kept coming to my mind. I visualized the fences and the gates, keeping us in, locking us out, but still allowing us to see out to the other side. The fence provided safety but was imprisoning at the same time. We could lift the lock, pull up the pole, and get out from time to time, but we were compelled to go back into safety.

One can see the correlations with the structure of a chain-link fence and rhizome in the view point of Kurokawa (2001) in an essay covering Deleuzio-Guallaria's architectural theory: "A rhizome is an interlocking web. It is a conjunction of dynamic relations producing bulbs here and there, interweaving with great complexity, reaching outward in its continuing growth" (p. 1031).

Linkages Through Disability Studies

It is critical for a disability study to investigate various ontological and epistemological assumptions underpinning the field and the lived experience of disability. My purpose was to examine the whole of the experience. As a field, disability studies challenge the stereotypes historically associated with disabilities yet does not restrict one to have a singular epistemological understanding of disability (Barnes et al., 2002). Disability studies developed as a field in response to a problem, seeking clarification about the place and meaning of disability in society (Albrecht et al., 2001).

Disability studies embrace an eclectic approach with the ultimate goal of emancipation and self-fulfillment in all areas of life for individuals with disabilities. Disability studies do not emphasize barriers but, instead, they focus on possibilities. Relevant to a disability study is resistance theory that "maintains the social model's focus on the politics of disablement and adds to it recognition of the complexities of resistance" (Gabel, 2005, p. 8). Resistance theory proposes to look at the entire experience of disability. Looking at the totality of the experience is imperative when uncovering meaning, the body and medical support cannot be totally disregarded. Elements of disabled identity are the voice that cannot be heard in a typical way, the brain that works in a particular fashion, or ambulation with a wheelchair.

The rhizome and the fence metaphorically represent the resistance scenario, as they are juxtaposed in "a push me-pull me" connectiveness; the fence with the shutting out but providing protection, and the rhizome, open to all the possibilities that occur in the lived experience of disability. A theory of resistance embraces disability in all its complexity and entirety. My perspective of disability is grounded in disability studies and rooted in resistance theory.

Looking Back, Going Forward--Phenomenologically

Phenomenology allows the researcher to explore the symbolism, the words, and experiences that give meaning to living. Phenomenologists are challenged to describe the lived experience in a manner that portrays person-world intimacy. The *lifeworld* (one of the key notions in phenomenology) includes all the everyday goings-on in life. My lifeworld, as well as my family's and friends' over three generations, and the interconnections to disability were the subject of our story-making. Viewing the lifeworld offers the opportunity to explore the intricacies that hold people and their world together, and view the physical, aesthetic, spatial, and emotional aspects of human life.

This research was a return to my roots, it served as an opportunity to dig into the soil and let it run through my fingers. I delved into the memories, the thoughts, and the lived experiences. Phenomenology served as the "till" for my research. Founded by Edmund Husserl (1859–1938), phenomenology is considered to be one of the most important philosophical movements of the twentieth century (Morse & Richards, 2007). Phenomenology is the study of human experience (Moustakas, 1994; Van Manen, 1990; Seamon, 2000); it serves as a means to give "a rigorous description of human life as it is lived, and reflected upon, in all of its first person concreteness, urgency, and ambiguity" (Pollio et al., 1997, p. 5).

Phenomenological inquiry allowed me to explore endless possibilities of the rhizome and to uncover its multiple meanings. Phenomenological "root strands" of an event are more clearly understood when we bring ourselves "wholly to the transparency of the imaginary, to think about it without the support of any ground, in short, withdraw to the bottom of nothingness. Only then could we know what moments positively make up the being of experience" (Pollio et al., 1997, p. 111).

I sought to "bring into the nearness that which tends to be obscure, that which tends to evade the intelligibility of our natural attitude of everyday life" (Van Manen, 1990, p. 57). It is with a fresh sense of wonder that I immersed myself in research to reveal a story (Merleau-Ponty, 1962). Phenomenology is about revealing, uncovering, exposing, and connecting. The rhizome as an image of thought serves as a model of an open-ended interactive system. There are roots in place, grounded in friendship, family, proximity, history, and disability. The rhizome is fluid and has the ability to grow and change, tiny threads will emerge from the root, linking to other threads, which will grow and flourish over time. Rhizomes are about possibilities, whereas the fence served as a protective boundary, protecting us from the dangers that lurked just outside.

> "Go home Sharon … bye, … we already started" ("but I have all my Barbie Stuff"), "take your Barbies and just go" … (My lip starts to quiver and tears

> come to my eyes), "You're a big crybaby! You act retarded, just like your mongoloid Aunt Jackie and we don't want to play with you!"

Girls from the neighborhood were sitting at the picnic table playing Barbies. I had rushed and gathered my stuff when I saw them out there. The twin girls that lived just on the other side of the fence, right behind my house, yelled at me in unison, adding to the insults in a tag team fashion. I was upset, and I really wanted to play Barbies that day. At first I was mad that they told me to leave, but then my eight-year-old self realized that they called my Aunt Jackie retarded. "No, Jackie's not retarded, Debbie's brother Chuck is retarded, and I heard him called mongoloid, too." Those words described Chuckie, not my Aunt Jackie. Jackie could talk. Jackie took care of me. I ran away, dragging my Barbie cases, and finally I threw them on the ground (I heard the girls laughing at me in the background). I ran faster through the yard and into the house. By now, I was crying loudly in my typical dramatic fashion.

Throwing open the back screen door, I yelled into the house, "M-o-o-o-om, the twins said Jackie is retarded." My grandmother gave me a dirty look (my voice was bellowing through the house). My mom ushered me into the bedroom and told me to "ssh" (now I'm thinking Jackie must have been in hearing distance as the first floor of our house was not large). Between my sobs, my mom tried to speak. She closed the door and said, "I should have told you, but I couldn't." She explained Jackie was "slow." She did not say retarded, she did not say mongoloid. I was told to stop crying and to not say anything to Jackie or in front of my grandmother (Jackie's mother).

Over time, I came to realize both Jackie and Chuck were born with Down syndrome. In the late 1960s, Down syndrome was often called "mongoloid." So Chuck and Aunt Jackie actually were the same, as far as a disability category anyway. They were my roots.

I go back to the past and return home. I was situated in a particular circumstance of disability. I lived in a home where disability and "retardness" (as it was referred to then), was somewhere else, not in our house. Although my Aunt Jackie had a disability due to an intellectual disability, my grandmother refused to call or label her disabled. The norm when my aunt was born in the late 1930s was for children who were declared retarded or mongoloid to be put away. Children like those were sent to institutions. My maternal grandparents, but most especially my grandmother (Mere), defied the norm and made Jackie fit. She taught Jackie to walk, talk, count, read, close her mouth (drooling was not an option) and was determined that she reached those milestones in typical developmental stages.

Although as a child, I never thought of Jackie as different, I always knew Chuckie, my friend Debbie's brother, was "different." He could not read; he needed help with everyday tasks and went to a "special" school. I thought the experience of disability was beyond my fenced yard. It was over there; in Debbie's fenced-in house on the next block. However, as I grew older and more aware of the stares and heard the names, the reality began to hit home. My mom explained to me at ten years old, after my grandmother passed away (at 53 years old), that Jackie and Chuckie both had Down syndrome (much nicer sounding than mongoloid). Laura, Debbie, and I continued to be friends, from high school into young adulthood until today. Our lives were still connected like the links in the fence. Our friendship was a stronghold, and we could always return back to our girlhood memories and the stories of our shared experiences.

> *Friendship, history, labels, families and the impact of disability from the past to the present, and into the future; the links that continue to connect our lives.*

There is a profound story here; a story that crosses generations and stereotypes. This story is "our social construction of what happened" (Ferguson et al., 1992, p. 5). A broad theme of phenomenology is intentionality a "basic structure of human existence that captures the fact that human beings are fundamentally related to the contexts in which they live" (Pollio et al., 1997, p. 7). Home and in-home experiences have been addressed by many phenomenologists. Day (1996) studied "at-homeness," signifying a timeless quality, positive attunement to the present moment, the relatedness to a lived interplay between safety and familiarity. Home offers an attunement into oneself in relationship to others; home relates to healing and personal well-being. Home for us was more than houses on Central or Parkside Avenue. Home was an emotional place where we felt protected and loved. Home is the sense of no matter what occurs around me, I have a place where I am safe emotionally, physically and psychologically. Home is where a person can truly be free, just to be.

Phenomenological incentive to go "back to the things themselves" (Husserl, 1970) prompted me to return again and again, through reflection, to the interviews with family members and with the individuals with disabilities.

Reflections on Perceptions

The eight-year-old me had no thoughtful concept of disability. Rarely were people with disabilities in the public eye in the early 1960s. I never thought of my Aunt Jackie as disabled. The word people used to describe people with intellectual disabilities at the time was "retarded," but even that term was rarely said out loud in my personal experience. Sometimes I noticed Jackie did and said silly or inappropriate things. Yet, for some reason Jackie did not do those "not so adult-like things" around my grandparents or other adults. She seemed to have two distinct personas, the one who acted like an adult and the other who was my own personal silly friend.

I had this internal nagging tension about when to listen to Jackie or not, or why Jackie did things at times that most adults did not do in public. There was also an unspoken rule in my household not to ask about Jackie, especially around my grandmother. Chuckie, my girlfriend's brother with Down syndrome, was never discussed either. Chuck was the only person I knew as a young child with a disability. Jackie, who often said out loud what she was thinking, did talk about Chuck and very sympathetically called him "poor 'tarded Chuck." I share these vignettes about life as I knew it then, because as an adult, I have come to realize that my childhood experiences with Jackie served as a catalyst in forming my own theory about disability. The nagging questions of the little girl, who was to be seen and not heard, are ever present in this adult, as I engage in thoughtful introspection. My view of disability is rooted in my past experiences as a little girl hanging out with Jackie and Chuck. My past cannot be disregarded or set aside but serves as a connective root strand now watered by a disability studies perspective.

Jackie, Chuck, Jonathon, and Jamee made and are making their own histories. Society, cultural factors, family situations, and their particular place in time had much to do with the formation of their personal histories.

Rhizomes and Stories

By virtue of her year of birth in 1991 and her place in this connective rhizome, Jamee has reaped the benefits of the rich soil that has been watered by the experiences of those who have come before her in time. Once upon a time there were three young girls living in the 1960s who were linked by proximity, friendship and disability. These three girls—Laura, Debbie, and Sharon (me)—are connected intricately with Jamee through the offshoots of the rhizomic experiences that have connected our lives through the generations. Jamee is the great-granddaughter of Dorothy, the courageous mother of Jackie who was determined to defy the social constructs of disability imposed on her in the late 1930s.

Stubborn will power and steadfast determination flow through the blood of Dorothy's granddaughter Colleen, the mother of Jamee, as she advocates for choices for her daughter. Colleen (my sister) never knew our grandmother Dorothy (Mere), she was only two years old when she passed away, but when

I look at Colleen, I see my grandmother's sense of control, strong will, and dominance. It is almost as if Colleen had some predisposition to be Dorothy in another time to raise a child with a disability.

Colleen walked up town with Laura, Debbie, Chuck, and I as a young child. Colleen played in Chuck's yard and shared swing time with him. Growing up as Jackie's niece, and sharing personal space with Jackie for more than 20 years, gave Colleen an understanding of living with and loving a person with an intellectual disability. Laura gave birth to a child with a disability (Jonathon) four years previous to Jamee. Laura has been very helpful to Colleen, providing her with the names of orthopedic specialists and programs to support Jamee. Three girls, three families connected through the generations and still growing, continuing the rhizomic connections established between the fences of our youth.

Connections and Revelations

A connective strand that united the families was a fear of the unknown. Typically, when a new baby comes into the world, the family is filled with anticipation and dreams for the future. The birth of a child is a joyful experience. These families had little time to bask in the happiness of a new life. Instead they embarked on emotional quests searching for answers. Initially, the parents sought answers so they could understand their role as parents. They wanted to find the means to assist their children. All of the families in this research went through emotional struggles with the professionals. The parents in this story were all subjected to "category bound activities" (Sacks, 1972).

Parents of children with disabilities are looked at in a particular manner. The parents were told by medical professionals they could not handle their child, or nothing was wrong in Jamee's case. The professionals put the parents in categories. Colleen, Dorothy, and Mrs. E. (Chuck's mom) were dismissed as young mothers. Laura was thought of as being too assertive. Social constructs of which the families had no control caused additional anxiety to these families who were already under much pressure. Upon realizing that the professionals did not have all the answers, after time, the parents discovered that they had the answers all along. All of the parents found the strength from within themselves to do whatever was necessary for their children.

Externally the families went about their lives, yet within the spatiality of their homes their experiences were complex. Without any training, my grandmother took on the roles of therapist and teacher. She discovered that neckties and belts were useful in supporting Jackie as she learned to walk, and match sticks could be used as manipulatives as Jackie learned to count. Chuck's parents discovered that elastic bands could be used to stretch Chuck's limbs. Jonathon, born with agenesis of the corpus callosum, was sent home from the hospital to die. Laura and her husband Steve decided their son was going to live and found programs to support his growth. Colleen and Bob kept bringing Jamee to doctors to treat her medical difficulties and sought help from anyone and everyone. All the parents took action, but fear remained under the surface.

Fears

Fear connected the families, but it was manifested differently in their lived experiences. Historically, parents or siblings of children with disabilities often wondered what they did to deserve this fate, or if they did something wrong for this to occur in their family. My grandmother is representative of this as she was trying to place the blame on someone for Jackie's "condition." Much of this blame had to do with the time in history. People did not understand the medical reasons for Down syndrome. I cannot fathom the deep anxiety a mother would feel upon realizing their beloved child was viewed by society as subhuman, a burden, or a product of sinfulness (Castles, 2004). Parents who gave birth to children with obvious disabilities in this era were often fearful of people trying to come and put their child in an institution. Due to this particular time in history, as a member of the silent generation (Strauss & Howe, 1992), my grandmother did not discuss her feelings regarding Jackie's disability. She repressed her fears and had emotional breakdowns.

With the progress of medical science over the decades and having a clearer understanding of the etiology of their children's disabilities, the other parents did not have the same type of fears as my grandmother. Yet fear was a connective element experienced by all the families in this research. Chuck's parents are not preparing financially or psychologically for Chuck's future. Laura still checks on Jonathon when he sleeps too long. Colleen worries if caregivers in Jamee's future will care for her medical needs and provide her with choices. Jenna, Jamee's sister, cried as she discussed her worries about Jamee's physical fragility. Jonathon fears being alone and is purposely working on overcoming his shyness. The fear was ever present, but it was accompanied by resilience and resistance.

Resistance

The rhizomic strand of resistance was evident as the stories were told. This was demonstrated by my grandparents refusing to call Jackie anything but Jackie and demanding that she attend the local Catholic school with her sister.

Chuck's parents (Mr. and Mrs. E.) moved to the suburbs to find a school for Chuck, and continued to fight the school district for funding because their son was happy at his private school. Chuck resisted societal expectations when he is the "man in charge" on his work crew. Laura confronted the doctor when he did not think baby Jonathon should have prostheses because of his fragile state. She continued to resist the expectations of doctors and other professionals throughout his childhood. Demonstrating resistance, Jonathon enrolled in anatomy and physiology classes against the advice of his counselors and received *A*s in the classes. Colleen demonstrates resistance by living in the moment; she does not dwell on the past, but moves forward, providing Jamee with choices in her daily life. Jamee, through making choices and navigating her environment with the support of her communication device and power wheelchair, is resisting the social constructs assigned to individuals with significant intellectual and physical disabilities. The families in this story had unique perspectives and situations, yet self-fulfillment for their own child was a personal goal in each circumstance.

Mother to Mother

A common strand, linking story to story, generation to generation, is the inner strength of the mothers. The mothers are resilient and strong, taking on doctors, teachers, and anyone who denied their children opportunities. These women played the dominant role while the husbands played supportive roles (Herbert & Carpenter, 1994). The women were grounded in actualization and hope; negativity was not an option. Each of the women was fenced-in by the constraints of the times in which they lived. Historicality served as a fence for which they had no control.

Historicality

Jackie was born in the era of when disability was regarded as sinful, deviant, or a societal burden (Kevles, 1995). In the 1930s, institutionalization was recommended for most people with disabilities. My grandparents did not give in to the societal expectations of the time. As Jackie's parents, they negotiated their lived experience through rebelling. By putting their daughter "out there" in the local catholic school, the community, family gatherings and social situations, they were quietly, but forcefully, rebelling. Particularly revealing was the fact that my grandmother put Jackie out into the world full of pride, but internally she was fighting her own emotional difficulties. The literature (Blancher & Baker, 2007) does indicate that many parents with children with disabilities have internal and emotional struggles. Unfortunately, my grandparents' personal and emotional struggles support the studies that indicate that parents could exhibit depression or emotional shock.

The 1930s and 1940s was a difficult era to live openly with a child of disabilities and my grandparents were victims of the societal fences of their times. The fact that Jackie lived in this time, yet portrayed a level of self-confidence and did not see herself as disabled, had much to do with the fences they collectively built to protect their daughter.

Chuck was born in the time of parent involvement (Schwartzenberg, 2005). Down syndrome now had a biological explanation, so once he was diagnosed his parents at least had a name and a reason for his particular disability. While the Mr. and Mrs. E. did not define Chuck by a label, they needed to have a diagnosis to understand why Chuck was not developing like his sister Debbie. While medical science had come far, there were still many misconceptions about Down syndrome. At the time of Chuck's birth, Down syndrome was still being referred to as "mongoloid" (Trent, 1994). The Es were told Chuck would not live long and were also told to think about placing their son in an institution. The Es resisted the advice offered to them and began to make plans for their son. They sought a new life in the suburbs because they had heard there were schools nearby "for children like Chuck." Chuck had a special school to attend, and during his school years, laws were written to mandate education for children with disabilities. They, like many parents in the 1960s, joined with other parents to support their child with a disability.

White, middle-class parent advocacy groups were able to help society make the shift from disability being thought of as undesirable, sinful, or lower class (Trent, 1994). The Es were representative of their particular time in history, their son was not hidden away and they were creating programs for his support. As a grass root organization, Chuck's school was representative of the time (Kliewer, 1998; Winzer, 1993). My grandparents could be considered cutting edge in their accessing an inclusive education for Jackie in the 1940s, the Es' situation is representative of the historicality of disability in the mid-1960s.

Jonathon and Jamee went to school in the era of inclusion (Friend, 2008). They were the products of school systems in the infancy stages of such practices. The school districts in both Jonathon's and Jamee's early educational experiences were working through the kinks in their own school settings. Their education was full of fences and rhizomic possibilities, isolation and inclusion involved in an intricate dance with everyone trying to learn the new steps. Initially, both families desired an inclusive school experience for their children. Jamee's parents, while philosophically embracing inclusion for all people with disabilities, had to act in the best interests of their daughter and transfer Jamee to a more secluded school setting. For two years Jamee's parents worked with the school district to bring about changes in the inclusion program. During this time Jamee was actually regressing. The community school was experiencing constant personnel and philosophical changes and lacked the training and understanding to support students with significant disabilities. Colleen and Bob could no longer risk their daughter's personal growth in order to bring about change in the school. There are circumstances when parents have to make difficult decisions to support their child that may not necessarily reflect their philosophical stance.

Another example of a philosophical conundrum was when Jonathon entered high school and Laura and Steve felt it was in his best interests to be in a more secluded freshman program. Laura had fought for the least restrictive learning environment for Jonathon throughout his elementary years and yet supported his placement in the freshman learning center program. Jonathon himself faces a struggle with his own personal philosophy as he accesses support in college. Jonathon told me he does not embrace the label of "disabled," yet he must have a disability label to navigate in the university setting. He also recalled that his high school counselor seemed angry when he insisted on enrolling in a higher level physiology and anatomy class. Mercer (1973) describes this construct and states, "People with disabilities are rewarded for behavior that conforms to the social expectations associated with the disability role and are punished for behavior that departs from the expectations" (p. 73). Jonathon had his own personal expectations, which did not coincide with the counselors desire to keep Jonathon within a particular construction.

Jonathon and Jamee did benefit, however, from a society that had grown in awareness both philosophically and technologically. They both had the benefit of technology to assist them in accessing their education, which was not available for Jackie and Chuck. Their parents also reaped the benefits derived from a historical era that was beginning to be more open about disability. Laws had been implemented to not only educate but also to include children with disabilities in school. Parents of children with disabilities in contemporary times have the ability to engage in mediation and voice their concerns. Laura and Colleen were not products of the silent generation, and as such they were able to voice their concerns in a more open forum than my grandmother and Mrs. E.

Exposure

A theme that represents the stories of the families and the corporality and temporality of their situations is: "They were there." They put themselves and their children out in the community to face whatever life had to offer. Simultaneously, the parents were there to protect their children from whatever society put in their way. They exposed them to opportunity, but put up fences whenever necessary. To these families, life was and is something to partake and opportunities are not only for the strong, but for everyone. Laura and Colleen stressed over and over, "It is what it is." In fact, all of the parents used those words to describe their lives of raising their children. The rhizomic strand that served as a connection in the shared stories is acceptance. The parents sought answers for the purpose of helping their children, and they focused on the possibilities, not the disabilities. Laura said she "wasn't going to have a pity party." Colleen said she never said, "Why me?" Mr. and Mrs. E. told people, "Don't feel sorry for us, Chuck is a gift, not a burden."

Roots

The neighborhood of our youth served as the soil for our rooted experience. Representing the existentials of spatiality and relationality, it served as the place where the families became connected. Disability was not thought of as something abnormal, it was life. It was our life. The neighborhood was surrounded by busy streets; danger right outside Laura's and Debbie's front doors, but there was the grassy alley that protected us, separated us, and connected us. We could cross the alley and be together. As children, we had an idealistic view of life. We knew if we yelled loud enough, someone's mother would come and save us, we knew our Dads would come home at the same time for dinner every night, and most important we knew we had each other. In our lived space, Jackie would entertain us, we would take our siblings uptown or to the park; life was simple. The "fence" was difficult to break through. In many ways the fence kept us naive and unaware of the big world outside. Children were seen and not heard. We did not question why Jackie could not drive, or why Chuck and Debbie always had to play in their yard. We were so blinded by simplicity that we did not even realize that Chuck and Jackie looked alike, until someone pointed that out to us in a cruel way. We held Chuck's hand both figuratively and literally and walked him home.

It's Just Life

Perhaps because as children we were steeped in this particular lived experience, Laura and Colleen, upon giving birth to children with disabilities, understood the experience as life. They went about the business of mothering their children. It was not different for them, it was life. Colleen tagged along with Laura, Debbie, and I when she was a toddler. The strands of the rhizome connected Colleen back to Laura as an adult. Jamee continues to receive physical therapy from the therapists recommended by Laura more than 15 years ago. The rhizomic threads still continue to connect the families generationally, mother to mother.

Gardening

I am the gardener, keeping the roots fed, watering the soil, making sure the root strands stay strong. I could never surmise that I truly understand their lived experiences, but I know my life is intricately linked to theirs; passing on information, being there to listen, or just being present. We are linked because we were there. We share our beginnings; we know where we came from, surrounded by strong women, caring men, and air filled with the aroma of protection.

Jackie, Chuck, Jonathon, and Jamee have taken all of us linked to their lives, places we never thought we would go. They have forced us to look outside ourselves, to be empathetic involved people. While others may see disability as wrong, it is normal for us.

Jackie's Life

Compared to the majority of the individuals born with disabilities in the late 1930s, Jackie led an accomplished life. Most important, Jackie did not think she was disabled, just "short." Disability to Jackie was "poor 'tarded" Chuck across the alley, or the people in wheelchairs at her club—it definitely was not her. Disability was not her identity. Shakespeare and Watson (2002) remind me that "to assume that disability will always be the key to [their] identity is to recapitulate the error made by those from the medical model perspective who define people by their impairment" (p. 22). Disability did not define Jackie.

Jonathon's Perceptions

Jonathon refuses to call himself disabled. Yet he is well aware of his blindness, his brain agenesis, along with a myriad of medical issues. He is supposed to have an intellectual disability, but he has a different type of intelligence and he has determined how to negotiate school and life using his intelligence.

Rapley (2004) suggests that it is not necessary to theorize or retheorize intellectual disability: "Maybe we should just refuse to do so" (p. 206). Jonathon is an example of just such refusal. He has constructed a fence blocking out disability. The fence has served him well, leading to possibility as he now exemplifies a college graduate with a medical research degree.

Chuck's World

Chuck is not able to voice his feeling about disability. Based on immersing myself in the world of Chuck, he appears content with his life. He has activities he enjoys, work which has given him a level of self-assurance, his girlfriend Lee, and parents who are very dedicated to his well-being. Chuck does not appear to mind living in a protective environment. His needs are simple and watching his TV programs and being a part of a day program brings him a certain level of comfort and joy.

Happy Jamee

Jamee is a happy young woman. Her difficulties with mobility and communication do not appear to affect her spirit. She has never known life as anything different. Jamee has definite interests and is able to express them in her individual manner. Utilizing an augmented communication device for her school work, she can access her education on her level. Routine is clearly important to Jamee and her family recognizes and honors this need. Within her structured world there are choices. Her quick smile and pleasant personality denotes a young woman who is content. Her contagious laughter resonates with pure joy.

Connected Individuals

Through watering the rhizome with independence and fertilizing it with love, these individuals identified themselves as Jackie, Chuck, Jonathon, and Jamee, not as intellectually disabled, retarded, or a person with Down syndrome. To be called "retarded is to have one's moral worth and human value called into question" (Bogdan & Taylor, 1982, p. 14). Jackie was referred to as Jackie, Chuck is just Chuck, Jonathon is "what he is," and Jamee is Jamee. They are one of us.

Uncovering Meaning

The purpose of this research was to uncover the meaning of the lived experiences of four individuals with intellectual disabilities and their families over three generations. While this journey took me to places I never imagined, I believe I uncovered the meaning of their lived experiences by sharing their stories. Van Manen (1990) asks, "Can phenomenology, if we concern ourselves deeply with it, do something with us?" (p. 47). This process was revealing for me and yes it did something to me. I am not the same person I was when this root was planted. I have evolved and find myself in a new place.

In this new place I am further convinced that a theory of disability must be malleable. There must be a meeting at the fence. Individuals with disabilities must bring the dominant culture into their "yards" and the gates to the world must be universally designed so everyone can have access. The gate keepers must be the individuals with disabilities themselves, not members of the dominating social institutions. For change to evolve there must be negotiation. Resistance theory allows Jonathon, for instance, to push against the stereotype, yet to negotiate a system of support. I especially found Jonathon's idea about disability refreshing—and truthful. He has his own theory about disability. He said, "When you call someone 'blah, blah, blah' then you expect them to act 'blah, blah, blah' and you think they need 'blah, blah, blah.' " He refuses to be defined. Jonathon has never read a book about disability theory or models of disability, yet in those words, he is describing the medical model of disability that ascribes certain attributes to people with disabilities. He is also rejecting such notions. Jonathon has come to this philosophical viewpoint through his lived experience. His voice is a voice of resistance. A theory of disability based on resistance can bring society into to Jonathon's way of knowing and understanding.

The stories must be written, lives must intersect; able and disabled can meet at the fence and open the gates. Rich stories written within a phenomenological perspective can allow people who have not been heard to have a voice. Stories can bring about social reform and understanding.

Three childhood friends, four families, four individuals with disabilities connected by proximity, understanding, and love. Together, we wrote a story.

Once upon a time lived three little girls, their lives were connected by friends, family, and disability.

References

Albrecht, G., Seelman, K., & Bury, M. (2001). Introduction. *Handbook for disability studies.* (pp. 1–10). SAGE.

Barnes, C., Oliver, M., & Barton, L. (2002). *Disability studies today.* Polity.

Blancher, J., & Baker, B. (2007). Positive impact on intellectual disability on families. *American Journal of Mental Retardation, 106*, 173–188.

Bogdan, R., & Taylor, S. (1982). *Inside out: The social meaning of mental retardation.* University of Toronto Press.

Castles, K. (2004). Nice average Americans. In S. Noll & J. Trent (Eds.), *Mental retardation in America* (pp. 351–370). New York University Press.

Day, M. (1996). *Home in the postmodern world: An existential phenomenological study* [Paper presentation]. International Human Science Research Conference, Halifax, VA, United States.

Ferguson, P., Ferguson, D., & Taylor, S. (1992). *Interpreting disability: A qualitative reader.* Teachers College Press.

Friend, M. (2008). *Special education, contemporary perspectives for school professionals.* Pearson.

Gabel, S. (2005). *Disability studies in education: Readings in theory and method.* Peter Lang.

Herbert, E., & Carpenter, B. (1994). The secondary partners: Professional perspectives and a father's reflections. *Children and Society, 8*(1), 31–41.

Husserl, E. (1970). *The crisis of European sciences and transcendental phenomenology.* Northwestern University Press.

Kevles, D. (1995). *In the name of eugenics: Genetics and the uses of human heredity.* Harvard University Press.

Kliewer, C. (1998). *Schooling children with Down syndrome.* Teachers College Press.

Kurokowa, K. (2001). Towards a rhizome world or chaosmas. In G. Gensoko, G. Deleuze, & F. Guattari (Eds.), *Critical assessments of leading philosophers* (pp. 1027–1034). Routledge.

Mercer, J. (1973). *Labeling the mentally retarded.* University of California Press.

Merleau-Ponty, M. (1962). *Phenomenology of perception.* Routledge & Kegan Paul.

Morse, J., & Richards, L. (2007). *Users guide to qualatative methods* (2nd ed.). SAGE.

Moustakas, C. (1994). *Phenomenological research methods.* SAGE.

Pollio, H., Henley, T., & Thompson, C. (1997). *The phenomenology of everyday life.* Cambridge University Press.

Rapley, M. (2004). *The social construction of intellectual disability.* Cambridge University Press.

Sacks, H. (1972). On analyzing the stories of children. In J. Gumper & D. Hynes (Eds.), *Directions in sociolinguistics: The ethnography of communication* (pp. 329–345). Holt, Rinehart & Winston.

Schwartzenberg, S. (2005). *Becoming citizens: Family life and the politics of disability.* University of Washington Press.

Seamon, D. (2000). A way of seeing people and place: Phenomenology in environment behavior research. In S. Wapner, J. Kemick, T. Yamamoto, & H. Minami (Eds.), *Theoretical perspectives in environment-behavior research* (pp. 157–178). Plenum.

Shakespeare, T., & Watson, N. (2002). The social model of disability: An outdated ideology? *Research in Social Science and Disability, 2*, 9–28.

Strauss, W., & Howe, N. (1992). *Generations: The story of America's future 1584–2069.* Morrow.

Trent, J. (1994). *Inventing the feeble mind: A history of mental retardation in the United States.* University of California Press.

Van Manen, M. (1990). *Researching lived experience.* State University of New York Press.

Winzer, M. (1993). *The history of special education from isolation to integration.* Gallaudet University Press.

Postscript

Antonina Lukenchuk

Once upon a Time, the Message of Love Was Born

> What is truth is real.
> What is not truth is not real.
> It's an illusion, but it looks real.
> Love is real.
> It's the supreme expression of life.
>
> —*A Toltec Wisdom Book* (Ruiz, 2004, p. xiv)

Before the curtain falls on work of this book, I would like to reflect on aspects of it which I deem are particularly meaningful in terms of its conception and advancement. Rather selfishly, I must admit, I have received absolute satisfaction from being able to engage in this work. Coincidentally, throughout the process of composing this manuscript, *my ego* had a chance to be transformed into *a sense of self with a new level of understanding*. The process has enabled me to dialogue with myself, to come to terms with my intellectual discontents and emotional frailties, and to evoke *my redemptive self* (McAdams, 2012). I have traveled a full *re*-search circle only to realize all over again that at the end of this journey, my *inquisitive self* has emerged with a renewed *sense of wonder*.

Wonder is natural to human beings and it sparks a desire within to pursue unimaginable projects. We may never know many details of how our ancestors went about their lives, but the vestiges of their existence reflect different stories of heroes, warriors, craftsmen, magicians, and builders. The coded messages of our ancestral tales tell us that ancient people also contemplated existential questions: *Where do we come from? What are we? Where are we going?* They were, in brief, philosophers and their pursuit of knowledge had been essentially through the exchange of ideas (Kenny, 1997).

The beginnings of philosophy, which are as ancient as humankind, can be rightfully considered the beginnings of research. Like philosophy, research begins in wonder and attempts to answer multitudes of questions and to solve myriads of problems pertaining to the human realm and its near and far surroundings. Like philosophers, researchers have at their disposal many and varied intellectual and methodological tools to employ in their quest to know. Extraordinary opportunities are open, especially for twenty-first-century researchers who can choose from among many and alternative paradigms of knowledge to pursue projects focusing on specific issues and amplifying our understanding of them contingent upon conceptual and methodological boundaries. Competing paradigms of knowledge do not necessarily imply privileging some of them over others. Instead, existing paradigms compete for the best available explanation or understanding, taking into account new vistas in the future that can challenge them.

Epistemological pluralism is the fact of the day even though some may not agree with or accept it. Contemporary researchers and scholars seek new ways of understanding themselves and their realities within and beyond the boundaries of their geographical locations. Modern marvels of communication and travel afford them the possibility of crossing the borders of the world's continents and countries much faster and to go farther than their predecessors could in the remote past. It is no surprise that the exchange of ideas and learning experiences among different people transpires at an unprecedented rate in this day and age. The accounts of most Westerners' journeys to other parts of the world are no longer accounts of conquest, colonization, enslavement, or prejudice. In the twenty-first century, most Westerners undertake pilgrimages to learn from the global world and, as a consequence, have an opportunity to rethink their personal identities, stories, and histories.

Imagine a white American woman, a professional psychologist, venturing on a spiritual quest around Mount Kailash, one of the three sacred mountains in Tibet. Mount Kailash is a spiritual center to the religions of Hinduism, Buddhism, Bön (a syncretic religion in Tibet), and Jainism. The sacred ritual of prostrations around Mt. Kailash is said to have been attempted by only a few representatives of these religions, and certainly not by many foreigners. What drew Tracy Allyson to this sacred pilgrimage was the spiritual passion which she considers integral to her practice as a professional psychologist. Without any special training or preparation, except for her prior travel to and knowledge of Tibet's cultural and spiritual traditions, Allyson performed prostrations around Mt. Kailash at an elevation of 14,500 feet, with the highest point of the path located at an altitude of 18, 500 feet. "I did not know," writes Allyson (2008), "if my body would hold up. There was nothing to encourage myself, nothing to gauge progress, and really, this is as it should have been. There is no progress, no goal. There is the experience and there is surrender to the invitation to attempt this" (p. 91).

Circumambulating Mt. Kailash is called *khora*. It took Allyson 28 days to finish the prostrations:

> Doing khora was an invitation that came to me in prayer. I felt that my role was to show up and do the best I could each moment. Khora is surrender in the not-knowing. The Void filled me. It wrapped itself around me. It was inside and outside of me. It was infinite, it was everything. I let the Void hold me because I just did not know; I could not assess or control my experience; I could only show up or not show up. There is an enormous freedom when we let go of the illusion of knowing. After all, life is enacting itself along some pattern, some dance, but that dance is not for me or you. It is for itself, it is dancing itself. (Allyson, 2008, p. 91)

To Allyson, doing khora turned into the most difficult and most meaningful experience of her life. She returned "home" "more mature, more open, less knowing, more conscious, more loving, more humble, and more confident" (Allyson, 2008, p. 91).

The twenty-first-century paradigms of knowledge offer educational researchers endless possibilities to advance rigorous inquiry that can illuminate economic, social, political, psychological, or spiritual dimensions of the human realm and their power to transform the lives of individuals and communities. For many people who hold spiritual beliefs dear to their hearts and minds and who practice various forms of spirituality, an engagement in social and political arenas constitutes an integral part of their day-to-day existence. Many of them consider the various aspects of their lives as manifestations of the whole, or wholeness of the experience. Spirituality can be conceived as life force, wholeness, or interconnectedness (Tisdell, 2000). Spirituality and social justice efforts can be integrated into empowering ways of life and doing research. Researchers may find themselves inspired by "new insights from different paradigms and [...] spiritual traditions" (Tisdell, 2000, p. 84).

Russell (2009) shares his experience of participating, with a group of Hispanic Roman Catholics, in an annual, hundred-mile pilgrimage to a shrine of healing dirt in New Mexico. To him, this journey becomes a discourse on social compassion. Driven by the desire to know, this "middle-aged, Anglo professor from Brooklyn" with a "recalcitrant agnostic spirit" trod the path that challenged his "niche in academe" and offered him a "model of compassion to sustain social concern" (p. 583). Prior to taking this journey, Russell researched, spoke, and wrote about pilgrimage. Yet he admits that it was *walking* the pilgrimage that had shifted the conception of it from description to performance, from telling to showing: "Walking is integral, a connecting thread of movement as coherent as a thread of thought. In pilgrimage, walking becomes a medium for understanding spiritual participation in the world" (Russell, 2009, p. 584).

The *performance* of pilgrimage is a "way of knowing," a way of learning to walk—learning through singing, healing, sacrifice, mistakes, humility, vulnerability, and learning step by step. It is also learning to return.

> My lessons in pilgrimage began with unlearning. I had been ignorant of my cultural resistance to the rich symbolism and embodied practice of Roman Catholicism. My old, familiar *habitus* was shaped by a Protestant, middle-class aesthetic more comfortable with a priest in a white lab coat than a black cassock. Religious sacrifice seemed superstitious to me [. . .]. My Anglo culture's ignorance and my middle class discretion about the messiness of [these] issues seemed Victorian in its avoidance of physical and emotional contact. The pilgrim community of compassion was a startling alternative to the stoic despair of my secular world. (Russell, 2009, p. 591)

Russell's return "home" illuminates the most significant lesson that he has learned throughout the journey and along the path: that the practices of pilgrimage "teach compassion for others"; that the routes themselves represent "the moral and ethical strength of [the] experience"; and that "the paradigm of walking to a holy place is a paradigm of access to power, [which is] compassion, the only healing power we truly possess" (Russell, 2009, pp. 600–601).

The possibilities of choosing among many alternative paradigms entail responsibilities of educational researchers to master their craft beyond the technical knowledge of *how* and to develop creative approaches to research and the innovative ways of its representation. Our capacity to wonder enables us to choose the paradigms that resonate with our artistic sensibilities and the *new ways to see* (Leavy, 2009; Stanczak, 2007). Visual research methods, such as photography, film, digital images, and website designs, represent shifting relationships between the production of a written text and new digital possibilities (Stanczak, 2007). Arts are known for being "emotionally and politically evocative, captivating, aesthetically powerful, and moving" (Leavy, 2009, p. 12). The practice of arts-based research is "one about fusion, affinity, resonance, and above all *holistic approaches to research*" (Leavy, 2009, p. 253). Image conveys meaning. Visual and arts-based research practices are about "composing, weaving, and orchestrating—creating tapestries of meanings" (Leavy, 2009, 254):

Finally, my heart understands it: I hear a song,
I see a flower,
***Behold, they will not wither!* (Unknown Aztec philosopher-poet)**

Truly, we live in a remarkable time when the sky becomes the only limit to pursuing inquiries of our own liking. Scientific, spiritual, socioeconomic, political, pragmatic, or arts-based paradigms of research as multiple and alternative ways of knowing call forth our imaginative powers *to know*, *to understand*, *to test*, *to emancipate*, *to deconstruct*, or *to reveal* the truth.

Reflecting on this journey granted me the opportunity to reenact the story of my personal quest for knowledge. I was accompanied on this journey by a few dedicated pilgrims with whom I had the privilege to share the path. Many roads lead to the truth and each of us chooses our own road. What can bind us together in the long run is *the paradigm of walking*—an act of communion that evokes the redemptive and healing power of compassion. We learn to love as we walk together.

***

Love cannot be contained within our speaking
or listening; Love is an ocean whose depth cannot
be plumbed.
Would you try to count the drops of the sea?
Before that Ocean, the seven seas are nothing.
Love cannot be found in erudition and science,
books and pages. Whatever is discussed by people—that is not
the way of lovers.
Whatever you have said or heard is the shell:
The kernel of Love is a mystery that cannot be divulged.

—Rumi

References

Allyson, T. (2008). One woman's journey around Mount Kalish. *Quest, 96*(3), 87–91.

McAdams, D. P. (2012). Exploring psychological themes through life-narrative accounts. In J. A. Holstein & J. F. Gubrium (Eds.), *Varieties of narrative analysis* (pp. 15–32). SAGE Publications.

Kenny, A. (Ed.). (1997). *The Oxford illustrated history of Western philosophy.* Oxford University Press.

Leavy, P. (2009). *Method meets art: Arts-based research practice.* Guilford Press.

Ruiz, M. (2004). *A Toltec wisdom book: The voice of knowledge.* Amber-Allen Publishing.

Russell, L. (2009). Learning to walk. *International Review of Qualitative Research, 1*(4), 583–602.

Stanczak, G. C. (Ed.). (2007). *Visual research methods: Image, society, and representation.* SAGE Publications.

Tisdell, E. J. (2000). Spirituality and emancipatory adult education in women adult educators for social change. *Adult Education Quarterly, 50*(4), 308–335.

Notes on Contributors

Editor

ANTONINA LUKENCHUK is Professor of Educational Foundations and Research at the School of Advanced Professional Programs, National College of Education, National Louis University, Chicago, IL, where she teaches graduate courses in educational foundations and research. She holds advanced degrees in English and General Linguistics from Chernivtsi University, Ukraine. She also holds a doctorate degree in Adult Education from Northern Illinois University, IL. Antonina's scholarly interests are in philosophy of education, epistemology, higher education, and international education. Some of Antonina's recent publications include: Against all odds: Reflections on violence and civility through personal narratives of Ukrainian students (2021) *Journal of Ethnographic & Qualitative Research*, *15*(4), 284–299; *Outliving Your Dissertation: A Guide for Students and Faculty* (Peter Lang, 2017).

Contributors

EIRINI ADAMOPOULOU holds a doctorate in Educational Psychology/Human Learning and Development from National Louis University. She is currently the project coordinator of the RaRE Project at the National Centre for Social Research (EKKE), Greece. She has worked as a school psychologist at public schools in US and Greece, as well as in non-formal education programs for the psychosocial support of refugee and immigrant families and children. She has taught educational and school psychology courses in the National and Kapodistrian University of Athens, Aristotle University of Thessaloniki and University of Crete, Greece. She has written articles and contributions in scientific journals and books and has participated in international workshops and conferences. Her main teaching and research interests are the promotion of well-being and resilience in educational settings, development of multi-level prevention and intervention programs in the school community and building trauma-informed schools.

CHERYL DEROO holds a doctorate degree in Education with a Major in Curriculum, Advocacy, and Policy from National Louis University, Chicago, IL. She is currently an Independent Consultant and Principal Mentor for the Illinois Principals Association. She holds a strong belief in the value of Action-Based Civic Education as a means for children to grow into problem-solving, critical thinking, independent, and active citizens. Her research and scholarly interest are in developing educators, both administrative and classrooms teachers, to hear the voice of their students, families, and communities to create a future where today's children are an integral part of a more equitable nation.

SHARON DUNCAN holds a doctorate degree in Disability and Equity Studies at National Louis University, Chicago, IL. Sharon's research interests include literacy for students with significant intellectual disabilities, models of disability, neurodiversity and family stories. She has worked in Puerto Plata in the Dominican Republic providing training for special educators and caregivers. Sharon is passionate about advocating and supporting individuals with disabilities as the founder and director of the Abide in Me charitable organization, which provides assistance to individuals with disabilities for leading engaged lives. Sharon volunteers as an advocate and as a former Professor of Special Education in the Graduate School of Education at Purdue Calumet University in Hammond, IN, she continues to support her students and teachers. Dr. Duncan is the author of *Roots and Fences: A Generational Story of Friends, Family, and Disability.*

IRENE GARCÍA-BENAVIDES holds a doctorate degree in Educational Leadership from Abilene Christian University, TX. She is currently a Senior Bilingual Speech-Language Pathologist at Texas Children's Hospital. Irene advocates for the use of American Sign Language for the provision of Speech-Language Pathology services. Irene is also passionate about languages and the many commonalities among them. Her research interests include, but are not limited to, investigations of the barriers that speech-language pathologists face in order to provide services for the deaf and hard of hearing children.

amy kendryna holds a doctoral degree in Curriculum, Advocacy, and Policy from National Louis University, Chicago, IL. She is currently a semi-retired elementary school principal who serves, on an as needed basis, as a school administrator for the Elgin U-46 School District. She also works for the Illinois Principals Association as a mentor to first year school administrators across Illinois. Amy is passionate about equity in public education and her dissertation includes the views of classroom teachers about students with Adverse Childhood Experiences (ACEs).

EILEEN M. KOLICH holds a doctorate in curriculum and instruction from the Pennsylvania State University. She is emerita Professor of Education in the College of Education and Health Sciences at Benedictine University in Lisle, IL. Eileen co-founded the doctoral program in Higher Education and Organizational Change (HEOC). She taught a number of HEOC courses, including qualitative research methods, and supervised doctoral dissertations. Her research interests focus on the scholarship of teaching and learning as it relates to instructor collaboration in the development of curriculum for qualitative research courses in HEOC.

REGINA SCHURMAN holds her doctorate in Higher Education and Organizational Change from Benedictine University, Lisle, IL. She is currently the Director of Pre-Health Professions at Benedictine University. Regina's passion lies in the area of preparing her students to be well-prepared applicants for professional school. Previously she was the Administrative Program Director of the Master of Science in Clinical Exercise Physiology program. Her doctoral research was focused on developing a model of the factors that make practitioners successful in the field of clinical exercise physiology. Many of these factors overlap with the preparation of pre-health students and are being used to counsel students as they prepare for admission to professional programs.

THERA TILMON holds a doctorate degree in Education, curriculum, and Advocacy from National Louis University, Chicago, IL. She is currently the Assistant Professor of Early Childhood and Elementary Literacy at National Louis University. As an instructor, Dr. Tilmon focuses on preparing prospective teachers for the challenging entry into the teaching profession. Her qualitative study centers on the narrative stories of Black female elementary teachers and the strategies these teachers use to navigate Whiteness in our society and schools. Her dissertation incorporates inspiring storytelling with sound scholarly research.

BAUDELAIRE K. ULYSSE holds a Doctorate in Curriculum and Social Inquiry from National Louis University, Chicago, IL. Additionally, he is finishing his Master of Science in artificial intelligence/machine learning. He has taught various master and doctoral courses at National Louis University, including action research, curriculum theory, and social justice perspectives on class, gender, and race. Currently, he teaches moral philosophies at Elgin Community College, IL, where he has also served on various committees and led impactful, advocacy-driven institutional initiatives. He has published numerous works on moral philosophies (Eastern and Western), environmental ethics, business ethics, research ethics, racial identities and politics, gender and sexual ethics, school reform and policies, qualitative research methodologies, and artificial intelligence/facial recognition. *Racialized Consciousness: Mapping the Genealogy of Racial Identity and Manifestations in Socio-Political Discourses* (2018), and *In Search of Moral Equilibrium and Wisdom: Assessing and Applying Ancient, Medieval, and Modern Moral Philosophies to Controversial Issues* (2021) are his two most recent books. *The Curvature of Feminist Activism in the #MeToo Movement* is forthcoming (under review by Peter Lang). Also, he founded a consulting, marketing, and training firm, OrganoSys Corp., that provides, among others, support for startups and dissertation services for doctoral students.

TOYA WEBB holds a doctorate in Higher Education and Organizational Change from Benedictine University, Lisle, IL. She is currently the Chief of Staff and Vice President of Strategy at Waubonsee Community College, Sugar Grove, IL. Previously she served in various leadership capacities, ultimately advancing to the role of Chief Marketing, Communications, and Government Relations Officer at Elgin Community College, IL, where she is currently an adjunct faculty member. As a certified professional life coach and the CEO of Dr. Webb Inspires LLC, Toya is a sought-after speaker and a staunch advocate of Diversity, Equity, Inclusion and Belonging. A dynamic trailblazer and visionary leader, her career has been marked by her ability to successfully lead organizations through strategic and innovative change management initiatives. Toya is also a passionate narrative researcher whose in-depth qualitative study centered on the experiences of Black women leaders in higher education and the harmful impact of racial microaggressions. Her dissertation incorporates profound storytelling with sound scholarly research.

MATTHEW WOOLSEY holds a doctorate in Higher Education and Organizational Change from Benedictine University, Lisle, IL. He is the recipient of the Edward R. Murrow Award for Excellence in Broadcasting from Washington State University. Dr. Woolsey's expertise spans communication, leadership, team development (including cross-cultural teams), and strategic visioning for human capital in domestic and international markets. His expertise and learning programs have received recognition by the Association of Professional Communication Consultants, Consulting.Com Magazine, and Experience.com. His research interests include Asian Indian leaders in America's higher education institutions with future projects targeting leadership competencies specific to this community of practice. Dr. Woolsey is a certified professional coach (ICF credentialed) and an executive leadership consultant and trainer.

JOANNE YONAN holds a doctorate in Education with a major in Curriculum, Advocacy and Policy from National Louis University, Chicago, Illinois. She has an in-depth background in Life Sciences with degrees from Purdue, Cornell, and the University of Arkansas. Currently, she is working with Dual enrollment students at Chicago City Colleges in science instruction, mentoring first-generation college students to successfully bridge from their high school diploma to their first year of college. Joanne Yonan is dedicated to altruism, and she is a part-time farmer and master gardener who consistently works in native restoration to reduce future flooding and produces organic vegetables and fruits for those in need.

COUNTERPOINTS

Studies in Criticality

Series Editor
Shirley R. Steinberg

Counterpoints publishes the most compelling and imaginative books being written in Education and Cultural Studies today. Grounded on the theoretical advances in critical theory, feminism, and postcolonialism in the last two decades of the twentieth century, Counterpoints engages the meaning of these innovations in various forms of educational expression. Committed to the proposition that theoretical literature should be accessible to a variety of audiences, the series insists that its authors avoid esoteric and jargonistic languages that transform educational scholarship into an elite discourse for the initiated. Scholarly work matters only to the degree it affects consciousness and practice at multiple sites. The editorial policy of *Counterpoints* is based on these principles and the ability of scholars to break new ground, to open new conversations, to go where educators have never gone before.

For additional information about this series or for the submission of manuscripts, please contact:

Shirley R. Steinberg, Series Editor
msgramsci@gmail.com

To order other books in this series, please contact our Customer Service Department:

peterlang@presswarehouse.com (within the U.S.)
orders@peterlang.com (outside the U.S.)

Or browse online by series:

www.peterlang.com

Made in the USA
Monee, IL
08 April 2025

15389239R00208